CENSORSHIP IN THE T~) IRELANDS
1922–3(

Censorship
in the
Two Irelands
1922–39

PETER MARTIN
University College, Dublin

IRISH ACADEMIC PRESS
DUBLIN • PORTLAND, OR

First published in 2006 by
IRISH ACADEMIC PRESS
44 Northumberland Road, Dublin 4, Ireland

and in the United States of America by
IRISH ACADEMIC PRESS
c/o ISBS, Suite 300
920 NE 58th Avenue
Portland, Oregon 97213-3786

Website: www.iap.ie

© Peter Martin 2006

British Library Cataloguing in Publication Data

ISBN 0-7165-3338-3
ISBN 0-7165-2829-0

Library of Congress Cataloging-in-Publication Data

Printed by
MPG Books Ltd, Bodmin, Cornwall

For Marie

Contents

Abbreviations

BBC	British Broadcasting Corporation
BBC WAC	BBC Written Archives Centre
BBFC	British Board of Film Censors
CASPA	Civil Authority (Special Powers) Acts
CEL	Committee on Evil Literature
CID	Criminal Investigation Department
CPB	Censorship of Publications Board
CTSI	Catholic Truth Society of Ireland
CYMS	Catholic Young Men's Society
DFIN	Department of Finance files
DMP	Dublin Metropolitan Police
DORA	Defence of the Realm Act
DORR	Defence of the Realm Regulation
DJUS	Department of Justice files
DT	Department of the Taoiseach files
FFA	Fianna Fáil Archives, UCDA, Belfield
IAL	Irish Academy of Letters
ICD	*Irish Catholic Directory*
IHS	*Irish Historical Studies*
IJA	Irish Jesuit Archives, Dublin
ILHSA	Irish Labour History Society Museum and Archive, Dublin
INTO	Irish National Teachers' Association
IRA	Irish Republican Army
NAI	National Archives of Ireland, Dublin
IVA	Irish Vigilance Association
KRSGBI	Kinematograph Renters' Society of Great Britain and Ireland
LOL	Loyal Orange Lodge
MPPDA	Motion Picture Producers and Developers of America

NAA	National Archives of Australia, Canberra
NAGB	British National Archives, formerly Public Record Office, Kew
NCCL	National Council for Civil Liberties
NIHC	Northern Ireland House of Commons
NIMHA	Northern Ireland Ministry of Home Affairs
NIS	Northern Ireland Senate
NLI	National Library of Ireland, Dublin
NUI	National University of Ireland
PRONI	Public Record Office of Northern Ireland, Belfast
RIC	Royal Irish Constabulary
RNBSA	Retail Newsagents', Booksellers' and Stationers' Association
ROIA	Restoration of Order in Ireland Act
ROIR	Restoration of Order in Ireland Regulation
RUC	Royal Ulster Constabulary
TCD	Trinity College, Dublin
TLS	*Times Literary Supplement*
UCCC	United Council of Christian Churches
UCD	University College Dublin
UCDA	University College Dublin Archives
UDC	Urban District Council
YIA	Young Ireland Association

Tables

Acknowledgements

Throughout the time that I have been preparing and writing this book, I have found myself dependent on the advice and help of others. Some of that help was professional, some was personal, but all of it was essential.

This work originated as a Ph.D. and my supervisor Professor David Fitzpatrick of Trinity College, Dublin has been of enormous importance from the very beginning. His criticisms of my work, arguments and style have been rigorous, sometimes ruthless, usually correct and always helpful. This work has been substantially improved by his advice and especially by his ingenuity in finding new ways to analyse old or sparse data. I want to thank him for his trust in me and his support.

The staff of the Department of Modern History in Trinity College, Dublin made me very welcome firstly as a student and then as a colleague. In particular I would like to thank Professor Eunan O'Halpin and Professor Aidan Clarke for their advice. I would also like to acknowledge the support and advice of my fellow postgraduates in the department. Much of the process of turning this work from a Ph.D. to a book took place at St Patrick's College, Drumcondra. I would like to thank the History Department there, especially Doctor Jimmy Kelly and Dr Diarmaid Ferriter for their help and support. Dr Deirdre McMahon of Mary Immaculate College, Limerick and Professor Mary Daly of UCD also offered invaluable and constructive criticism.

My research was greatly helped by the courtesy and efficiency of the staff in many archives and libraries. In particular, the National Library of Ireland, the Public Record Office of Northern Ireland, Trinity College Library (particularly the staff in Early Printed Books), the National Archives of Great Britain, the UCD Archives, the Dublin and Armagh Diocesan Archives and the BBC Written Archives Centre.

Finally I wish to thank my family who have supported me whole-heartedly throughout this project: my mother and father, Marie and Frank Martin, as well as Joseph, Anne, Anna Louise and Niall. They provided a place of sanity in the most difficult times. I would also like to thank John and Rose Coleman for their support and friendship.

The original thesis on which this book is based was prepared with the assistance of a Government of Ireland Postgraduate Scholarship from the Irish Research Council for the Humanities and Social Sciences. I am grateful to them and hope that this enlightened policy of state funding for research in the arts will continue. The book itself was produced with the aid of a post-doctoral fellowship from the Humanities Institute of Ireland.

Most of all I must thank my colleague, advisor and wife, Dr Marie Coleman who made every effort both professionally and personally to see to it that I finished this book while still of sound mind and body. Her advice and careful proofreading have been important and her love and support have been indispensable.

Foreword

The diligence, detailed research and expository skills of young Irish historians in recent years have forced a reassessment of many long-held assumptions about the nature of Irish society in the 1920s and 1930s. This book makes an important contribution to this on-going process, and Peter Martin deserves great credit for subjecting the issue of censorship, in all its manifold forms, to a fresh scrutiny. This erudite and mature book reflects a commitment to the highest standards of archival research; it is balanced, fair and insightful, a considerable achievement given the emotiveness of the theme under review; a theme that has an enduring relevance in the context of defining public morality.

It was quickly apparent that free speech in the new free state in the 1920s would rest on shaky foundations, but the censorship question incorporated many other issues and it was by no means an isolated free state phenomenon. Much of the strength of this book derives from the authors determination to analyse both northern and southern Ireland, and to place developments in both jurisdictions in an international context, something lacking in other accounts of twentieth century Ireland. Censorship in Ireland may have been highly centralised and severe, but it was not unique- Australia had one of the strictest censorship systems in the world in the 1920s.

The idea that the political chaos of the early twentieth century had resulted in a moral crisis was shared on both sides of the border, as Martin's perusal of a great variety of archival sources makes clear. Sex, or 'the morals of the poultry yard', to use the memorable description of the Irish film censor, James Montgomery, was not the only concern; the censorship process was also about the interaction between church, state and the power (often exaggerated and resented) of social reform movements and lobby groups. Active state intervention was much less pronounced in the north, but even with the excessive centralisation of the censorship process in the free state, much doubt, confusion and resentment existed about how to define indecency, given that many accepted, as articulated by Seán Lemass, that there was nothing intrinsically wrong with sexual passion.

Both jurisdictions were perhaps more comfortable with the issue of political censorship, strict security laws, and a distaste for left-wing movements, which, the author observes, was out of all proportion to their actual presence on the island. But in other areas it was more complicated- despite the stereotype of Catholic hidebound reaction and triumphalism, there was admiration from some Protestant quarters in the North for the free state's more active and systematic film censorship, and there was widespread frustration within the free state's censorship of publications board which frequently felt unappreciated and misunderstood. There were many undercurrents of unofficial complaints and bullying; in this context the wry comment of James Montgomery in 1934 that "there are at least one million censors in Ireland, I am only the official censor", is illuminating, and highlights the significance of the archival material the author has unearthed in order to skilfully sift through the many layers of the censorship question. This important book will re-open debate on the whole process of and nature of censorship, north and south, during two crucial decades in the development of modern Ireland.

Diarmaid Ferriter
January 2006

Introduction

Communication is an important part of what makes humans feel that they are separate from other animals. It is perhaps for this reason that we find the idea of controlling expression an uncomfortable one. This book is an attempt to investigate how expression was controlled in the two Irelands, north and south, between 1922 and 1939. The first challenge is to define the subject itself. The *Oxford English Dictionary* is, for once, unhelpful: it defines a censor firstly as an office in ancient Rome, then as an official put in charge of the control of the production of plays and films. Finally it produces something useful: 'one who exercises official or officious supervision over morals or conduct' or an official who examines publications before publication. These leave obvious gaps: what about censorship by non-governmental groups such as the British Board of Film Censors, or censorship after publication which is the *modus operandi* of both the Irish Censorship of Publications Board and the judiciary in the UK? A better definition is given by Harold Laswell: 'Censorship is the process of restricting the public expression of ideas, opinions, conceptions and impulses which have or are believed to have the capacity to undermine the governing authority or the social or moral code which that authority considers itself bound to protect.' Paul O'Higgins offers something even broader: 'the process whereby restrictions are imposed upon the collection, dissemination and exchange of information, opinions and ideas'.[1]

These provide us with a starting point. Now we can look next at what kinds of censorship are possible. To do this, let us consider the idea of the right to free expression. What kinds of expression are protected by the right? This is known as its *coverage*. We can then consider what the limitations are on what is covered. This is called the *protection* offered by the right. Combining the two we can analyse the extent to which expression is given a privileged place in society, what is called the *principle of freedom of expression*. To take a simple example, it is illegal to damage a stage show by taking a hammer and wrecking its sets, but theatre critics are entitled to criticize it, even if their words cause it to close after the opening night at great financial loss to the promoters. Such rights have limits however, and it is illegal to cause a clear and present danger to the audience by shouting 'Fire!' in a crowded theatre. The matter becomes more complicated when we consider how far a citizen is entitled to go in criticizing the state. It seems essential in a democracy that we should be allowed to challenge the policies of the government, but can we call for the state to be annexed by a neighbour or question its right to exist? In the period under examination such problems were integral to politics not just in Northern Ireland but also in Czechoslovakia, Austria and other states with large ethnic minorities who wished to rejoin their motherlands.

Now let us look at how systems of censorship can work. Sometimes material is censored before it is disseminated, this is known as *prior censorship*. *Repressive censorship* describes regulation after dissemination. For example, Irish film censorship is a prior censorship because it requires all films to be examined before they can be screened publicly but Irish censorship of publications is a repressive censorship as the Censorship of Publications Board only examines books that are already on sale. Censorship can be carried out by different agencies: the state, private bodies acting with state approval or authority, or independent groups. Again, Irish film censorship is an example of censorship by a state agency, while British film censorship is carried out by the BBFC which is a state approved body. When a group of campaigners force a shop to withdraw offensive magazines, however, they are acting independently of the state but are still censors.

There are a huge variety of practices that can be considered as censorship. This work will focus on censorship on moral grounds and on grounds of national security. Other restrictions on freedom of expression such as the law of defamation did not change substantially during this period. Self-censorship poses a particular problem. To examine the enormous number of decisions taken by writers, editors and political leaders and to ascertain why exactly they removed certain parts of their work would require detailed studies of each individual and I have only attempted to give a flavour of the moral climate in which they worked.

SOURCES AND HISTORIOGRAPHY

Despite considerable public interest in the subject there is not a great deal of secondary material available on Irish censorship, and even less relating to Northern Ireland. Michael Adams's *Censorship: The Irish Experience* has been very influential in this field. It remains the standard text and both Terence Brown's *Ireland: A Social and Cultural History, 1922–1985* and J.H. Whyte's *Church and State in Modern Ireland, 1923–79* draw heavily on it. Adams's book was written in the late 1960s when it seemed obvious to everyone that the censorship was an anachronism. Although it is a classic work of contemporary history it reflects that view somewhat. So does Kieran Woodman's *Media Control in Ireland, 1923–1983* which takes it for granted that those arguing in favour of censorship were wrong. What is striking to a researcher with access to recently released collections is how accurate Michael Adams was despite his reliance on published material and documents made available to him privately. While this book was in the process of completion, Kevin Rockett published his definitive *Irish Film Censorship* which offers an in-depth study of the subject in southern Ireland from 1916 to the modern day.[2]

I propose to incorporate the history of censorship in the wider history of social reform movements and state security in Ireland in this period. Maurice Curtis, Susannah Riordan and Margaret O'Callaghan[3] are among those who have reassessed the role of Roman Catholic groups in Irish social history. They have done so by assessing these groups according to their own aims and the contemporary context. In a similar fashion, Eunan O'Halpin, Laura K. Donohue and Colm Campbell[4] have assessed the issue of state security in Northern Ireland and the south from a point of view based on contemporary sources rather than modern politics.

Much of the debate over censorship took place in a variety of religious and other journals, papers and pamphlets. I must beg the reader's indulgence for dealing with these at length although in some cases the arguments involved were not of a high quality. My purpose is to paint an accurate portrait of the arguments from all sides of the censorship question and from a wide variety of sources. These publications can be divided into several types. There were some such as *Irish Ecclesiastical Record* or *Ireland To-Day* with small circulations but which were nonetheless read by people of influence and which were responsible for providing the intellectual foundations for the debate. There was also a range of popular publications, Catholic Truth Society magazines, the *Sacred Heart Messenger* and the *Irish Rosary* that were widely read. Though they often lacked the intellectual rigour of their more elite counterparts, they were frequently the point of contact with the debate for ordinary people. The value of publications from the radical fringe such as the *Catholic Bulletin* is disputed. They were not representative of opinion within mainstream Roman Catholic or government circles.[5]

It is not the purpose of this work to decide the issue of whether censorship is or is not justifiable. It is for the reader to assess the relevance, if any, of the debates of seventy years ago to the present day. It is both instructive and disturbing to compare those debates to modern concerns over internet pornography and child abuse. Then as now concerns over public morality and the safety of children were genuine. However, misinformation, vigilantism and panic damaged those efforts and may do the same today. Likewise, in the light of 11 September 2001 and the subsequent 'War on Terror', it is important to look back at how governments have treated freedom of speech when faced with a crisis of national security. In the past they have proven reluctant to relax controls and give up special powers even when the threat has subsided.

Some readers who have backgrounds in literary or film studies might be surprised that I do not discuss the works banned in more detail or offer my own readings. This is a product of our respective disciplines for I have no special qualifications for literary or cinematic analysis and, as a historian, my objective is to keep as closely to contemporary accounts as possible. In this book I am deliberately trying to stick to what was said about the material banned at the time, regardless of its subsequent reputation. The objective of this work is to offer as balanced an account as is possible and in particular to examine the arguments for and against censorship in their contemporary contexts. It is also an attempt to look at the subject in a broad way, including security, film and publications. The period 1922 to 1939 was the state-building phase of both territories when they took on their legal and social characteristics. They did not start with a blank slate and before treating the period as a whole it is important to survey briefly the important legacies of censorship in Ireland under British rule.

CENSORSHIP BEFORE 1922

Obscenity and the law

Obscene libel was a misdemeanour under British common law and had been defined since 1727 and was tried before a magistrate. In the nineteenth century private campaigners against obscene literature brought 159 prosecutions between 1802 and 1857. In the latter year the Obscene Publications Act allowed magistrates to order the destruction of obscene publications or publishers to be prosecuted. It was an attempt to codify anti-obscenity law and fight what was seen as a rising tide of vice and immorality.[6] In 1868 the prosecution of the publisher of a series of anti-Catholic pamphlets raised the question of whether a crime of publishing obscene material existed where there was no intent to corrupt. On appeal to the Queen's Bench, the case was heard by Chief Justice Cockburn. He decided that the intent of the publisher was not relevant and defined obscenity as, 'whether the tendency of the matter charged as obscenity is to deprave and corrupt those whose minds are open to such immoral influences, and into whose hands a publication of this sort may fall'.[7] His judgment was to define the issue throughout this period. It meant that questions of the intent of the author or the publisher or the artistic merit of a work became irrelevant. All that mattered was the effect of the work on a hypothetical person whose mind was open to immoral influences. This view was confirmed in 1877 with the trial of Charles Bradlaugh and Annie Besant who were found guilty of selling a pamphlet on sex education despite the jury's decision that they had no corrupt motives in doing so.[8]

Moral campaigners were concerned at the rise of novelists such as

Henry James, Thomas Hardy, George Moore and Oscar Wilde. At this time big circulating libraries which purchased expensive three-volume sets of books in bulk had a financial stranglehold over publishers. These libraries could effectively blacklist a writer by refusing to stock his work. George Moore fell foul of Mudie's and W. H. Smith's libraries when they refused to buy *A Modern Lover*, *A Mummer's Wife* or *Esther Waters*. Hardy had trouble getting a publisher for *Tess of the D'Urbervilles*. Most of all, the moral campaigners sought to prevent the public reading the works of Emile Zola. When Henry Vizetelly published cheap, one-volume editions of the French author's works he was prosecuted and eventually sentenced to three months in prison. The last important obscenity trial of the nineteenth century was that of Havelock Ellis whose book on homosexuality, *Sexual Inversions*, was tried in part because the police wanted an excuse to prosecute the publisher.[9]

In the period leading up to the Great War, these legal precedents remained in place in Ireland and were supported by a large amount of other legislation: the Dublin Police Act 1842, the Town Improvement (Ireland) Act 1854, the Customs Consolidation Act 1876, the Indecent Advertisements Act 1889 and the Post Office Act 1908.[10] These equipped the authorities with the power to seize obscene material in the post, at the ports, in public advertisements or on the newsstands and to bring prosecutions. What they did not offer was any way to circumvent the courts and ban controversial material outright.

Obscenity in Ireland

It is not altogether clear why Irish moral reformers became so interested in obscenity in 1911. It was not as if the Catholic Church had ever been less than condemnatory on the subject, although the papal encyclical *Pascendi Gregis* (1907) which condemned 'pernicious books' may have reminded them of their duty. By 1911 Irish Catholicism was in a confident mood. The university question had been effectively resolved and the influence of the Nationalist party had grown as a result of the budget crisis of 1909. Despite these encouraging developments, the Irish hierarchy was also perturbed by the Liberal government's views on education and by the influence of British culture in Ireland. In 1909, the Catholic Truth Society's annual conference discussed the press, and Bishop O'Dwyer of Limerick issued a pastoral condemning English books and newspapers. In October 1911, the inaugural lecture of the Catholic Truth Society of Ireland was devoted to the condemnation of 'evil literature'.[11] The campaign against obscenity was to find its greatest support in O'Dwyer's seat of Limerick. Male Catholic life in the city was dominated by the Confraternity of the Holy Family which numbered some 6,000 men. The power of the confraternity had been notoriously demonstrated in 1904 when its director, Fr.

Creagh, had orchestrated an anti-Semitic boycott. For its members, the confraternity offered a combination of spiritual guidance, civic duty and a social club. In October 1911, the Redemptorist order which ran the confraternity enlisted its members in a campaign against 'evil literature' dedicated to stopping English Sunday papers and other types of immoral reading matter. A vigilance committee was set up and twenty-two of the city's newsagents were convinced or coerced into pledging not to stock objectionable publications. The newsboys were similarly organised.[12]

A vigilance committee had already existed in Dublin but had been mostly concerned with campaigning against proselytism. It began to take an interest in objectionable literature around 1907, and in November 1911 that became its main focus.[13] A meeting in North Great George's Street under the auspices of the Catholic Young Men's Society re-established the campaign. They pressured the Dublin papers not to follow the example of their British counterparts. Sodalities and spiritual directors were recruited to support the cause.[14] The movement spread through Waterford, Cork, Belfast, Donegal and Cavan.[15] Campaigns against 'evil literature' became part of Irish expression of Catholic Action. Some Protestant leaders, such as Bishop O'Hara of Cashel, supported the movements[16] and Lord Aberdeen, the Lord Lieutenant, offered his blessing also.[17]

The campaigners worked by lobbying local authorities, holding public protests and by vigilantism. All of these strategies were supported, publicly or implicitly, by the hierarchy. For example, the Bishop of Galway's 1916 Lenten pastoral called on Roman Catholics to shun the sellers of 'evil literature'. In Dublin in 1913 the vigilance committee claimed credit for the returning of two tons of English newspapers, many in unopened bundles.[18] Later, W.B. Joyce, who was an activist in Limerick before the revolution, claimed that the vigilance committee had persuaded all the newsagents to sign undertakings not to stock immoral papers and books. His group was allied with the labour organizations and the Gaelic League and they patrolled the streets, picketed offending shops and stoned the agents of English publishers.[19] It seems that such activity was more influential than the judicial system as it was directed against popular newspapers that would not have been considered obscene by a court.

The censorship of films

Britain had two parallel systems of film censorship. The 1909 Cinematographic Act allowed local authorities to license cinemas in order to protect public safety. Local authorities added special conditions in licences regulating the attendance of children at cinemas and the types of films that could be shown. As complaints about films began to increase, the film trade decided that self censorship was their best protection against further controls and set up the British Board of Film

Censors (BBFC) in 1912. In 1915 a series of councils called for a central, state, film censorship to make the systems uniform. The film trade offered to reform the BBFC and this was combined with model conditions for cinema licences issued by the Home Office to local authorities.[20]

These events had echoes in Ireland. In 1911, the Archbishop of Dublin and the Bishop of Ossory publicly praised the decision of the London County Council to ban footage of the Johnson–Jeffries fight and demanded that it not be shown in Ireland. Despite support for their position from various municipal officials, it was shown during the horse show. Although their protests merely condemned the brutality of boxing, the fight was especially controversial because it featured a black man fighting a white one.[21] In 1913 Dublin Municipal Council added a condition to its cinema licences regulating the attendance of children at films. In 1915 the Irish Vigilance Association (IVA) asked the council to appoint film censors and add conditions to the cinema licences preventing the showing of immoral films.[22] The council declined initially but decided to do so in 1916 after discussions with the IVA.[23] Two cinema inspectors were appointed but over time more were required.[24] These inspectors watched films in the cinemas to ensure that they were keeping to the terms of the licences.

In Galway in 1915 Roman Catholic leaders demanded that the attendance of children at cinemas be regulated. The urban council and the cinema managers both agreed to this but the council decided not to issue licences with moral conditions.[25] In 1917 the Lord Lieutenant circulated the model conditions drawn up by the Home Office which asked councils to put conditions in licences preventing films 'that will offend against morality and public taste' from being shown. They were encouraged to accept the verdicts of the BBFC.[26] The same year Dublin Municipal Council appointed two nominees of the IVA as cinema inspectors.[27]

In Belfast, the corporation's Police Committee waited until 1920 before considering a system of film censorship. When they did so it was 'in view of the effect which some films may have on children and young people'. The reason for the delay was that the Belfast cinemas had been showing only films passed by the BBFC. The committee decided to place new conditions on the licence to require that if a cinema wished to show a film not passed by the BBFC it had to submit a synopsis to the committee and allow its representative to view the film in advance. The committee also reserved the right to prohibit any film.[28] There were only a few occasions before 1922 when these powers were used.[29]

Censorship during the First World War

The Defence of the Realm Act 1914 (DORA) included an offence of 'communicating with the enemy or obtaining information for that purpose'. This was expanded in the Defence of the Realm (No. 2) Act of August

1914 to include 'reports likely to cause disaffection or alarm'.[30] From 15 August 1914, these regulations applied to the press.[31] These regulations were strictly enforced in Ireland. In 1915, a Belfast man was sentenced to six months in prison for sending a letter to his sister in Germany. His offence was to give it to a man to post in America instead of using the local post.[32] In Dublin, several people were arrested for making speeches against recruiting and another man was fined for writing 'God Bless Germany' on a wall.[33] Although the numbers of seditious leaflets reported in Ireland by the Royal Irish Constabulary (RIC) increased from five in 1912–13 to sixteen in 1914 this was not objectively a very large number.[34]

The Sinn Féin paper *Scissors and Paste* was kept under close scrutiny, as it criticized the war, and it was seized in Cork on 2 January 1915. As it published extracts from other papers there were questions about whether it offended against the DORA.[35] In February, the paper was suppressed.[36] Not every paper was treated so harshly. *The Worker* was seized in 1915 in Glasgow but although 4,000 copies were sent from Belfast to Dublin, the military felt that it was not necessary to act against it.[37] The *Leinster Leader* escaped suppression between 1914 and 1916 despite its constant opposition to recruiting.[38] The *Dublin Evening Telegraph* was asked to give the name of an anonymous correspondent in 1915 but no action was taken when it refused.[39] The *Enniscorthy Echo* was warned about its anti-recruitment position in 1914[40] and post intended for its manager, editor and staff was detained.[41] This was only done because a seditious pamphlet was produced at the paper's offices.[42]

Postal censorship involved examining mail both to remove offensive or seditious material and also for intelligence purposes. This means that only that part of postal 'censorship' involving the actual suppression of communications need concern us here. According to Novick, postal censorship in Ireland was used mostly against political targets. Warrants were issued by the Lord Lieutenant or the Lord Justice of Ireland at the request of high ranking members of Dublin Castle, the Post Office or the Irish Command's military intelligence section. The latter was the source of most requests. The majority of this work was aimed at intelligence-gathering so actual prevention of the communications would have been counterproductive. To prevent its targets becoming too suspicious, censorship was applied to a particular person for only a month at a time. The enormous numbers of letters posted in Ireland in this period made a general censorship of the mail impossible. There were 192 million letters posted in 1914–15 while the censorship consisted of one officer with five assistants. The RIC stopped sixty-four packets of correspondence between November 1915 and March 1916 but were aware that this was only a small contribution to the fight against seditious literature.[43]

The 1916 Rising led to the appointment of Lord Decies as official press censor.[44] Despite Maume's description of him as 'notoriously dimwitted and inefficient', Decies's reports showed that he was well aware of the conditions of the country and the limitations of his office.[45] His role was initially to regulate news about the war. Reports of the Battle of the Somme were initially heavily censored. Readers of the *Belfast Telegraph* were told that after ninety minutes of bombardment, troops had confronted heavily fortified German positions that were protected by machine guns. They 'had marched towards the front singing songs and with merry hearts – clearly the soul of Tommy'. On 5 July the paper printed a leader which warned that casualties had been large but no figures were printed. Only over the succeeding days did lists appear.[46]

The Home Office also dispatched warrants for the examination of post, parcels and telegrams to Decies.[47] Interestingly not all citizens objected to this. The Irish Post Office Clerk's Association requested that correspondence between Ireland and America be censored in Dublin instead of Liverpool thus requiring the hiring of one hundred girls at £1 per week.[48] Censorship of post between Ireland and Canada was also re-introduced in the hope of intercepting material destined for the USA.[49] Post to and from Irish prisoners was also censored. Convicts were allowed to write and receive one letter every three months while internees were able to write weekly and could receive any number of letters. Inmates' letters were also examined by their own 'postmasters' before submission to British censors. Similar provisions were applied to the prisoners arrested in regard to the alleged German plot.[50]

Censorship and the War of Independence

After 1916 the censorship system had to deal with the rise of advanced nationalism as well as the war. Decies treated the former primarily as a threat to British security and the war effort. As his role was somewhat similar to that of the southern censor, Piaras Béaslaí, in the Civil War, it is worth examining in some detail.

Decies understood that advanced nationalists were able to gain great propaganda value from the stories of Irish prisoners. He complained that 'there are many articles now being published giving absolutely untrue statements as regards the conditions of Frongoch prisoners' and warned the press 'to be careful what they published'.[51] Such warnings were little use in dealing with papers like the *Cork Free Press* under the editorship of the republican propagandist Frank Gallagher, which was suppressed when it accused the British authorities of lying about the situation.[52] From August 1917 on, Decies made it his priority to deal with 'statements which are a frank defiance of all government and authority in Ireland'. He suppressed the *Kilkenny People* which greatly increased the readiness of other editors to co-operate. His job was made difficult by the skill with which propagandists like Arthur Griffith skirted the line between criticism of the government and sedition. He also had to censor news coming from the Irish Convention in an attempt to keep that assembly free from political pressure. Despite behaving leniently at the start of the year, by the end of 1917 Decies believed that the censorship should be applied strictly and wanted the government to apply the Defence of the Realm Regulations (DORRs) in full.[53] As Sinn Féin orators continued their campaigning most papers were willing to submit their reports in advance but some did not and these were often the subject of action under the DORRs. Decies warned in April 1918 that if censorship were relaxed, an anti-war campaign was very likely. That month he made examples of the two papers which 'had an effect of the most salutary nature on the whole Irish press'. Decies warned that the press was united in its opposition to conscription. The Chief Secretary ordered him to censor all appeals to force, incitements to strike and, where appropriate, passive resistance.[54]

By mid 1918, Decies detected a diminution in the amount of seditious oratory in the country. Letters from the interned leaders to the press were sent to him before publication and he allowed only the harmless ones – this made their publication unattractive to editors. Decies censored all Sinn Féin reports very strictly which led to complaints from the press. The effect was to deter them from printing anti-recruiting articles or speeches. In the last month of the conflict, Decies had censored all reports of the torpedoing of the *Leinster* between 10.30 a.m. and late in the day on the orders of the Admiralty. The *Evening Herald* printed the story at 7.30 p.m. and was suppressed for it. In particular Decies was careful 'to prevent the publication of the fact that a large number of soldiers were on board the "Leinster", and so far no mention of it has appeared in any Irish paper'. By contrast, censorship during the 1918 general election campaign was quite relaxed and only incitements to violence and attacks on the military were forbidden. After the result Decies offered his resignation, citing the strain of the job and the fact that he believed the censorship should be withdrawn.[55] He stayed in office until May 1919.[56] During this time the censorship was gradually relaxed.[57]

The wartime censorship was far more effective in regard to well established newspapers than against the short lived productions of advanced nationalist propaganda. It was designed as a system of prior scrutiny but was unsuccessful in preventing men like Arthur Griffith and Herbert Pim from producing newspapers.[58] All it did was make their jobs more challenging. It was arguably more effective in dealing with local and national papers whose editors were known and which had fixed premises and machinery.

British censorship during the period 1920–21 was based on the Restoration of Order in Ireland Act 1920 and its attendant regulations. The act made all extant DORRs into Restoration of Order in Ireland Regulations (ROIRs). These allowed the authorities to arrest people for possession of seditious material, suppress newspapers, ban public meetings, remove flags and otherwise act to suppress expressions of what they considered sedition. Essentially this marked a return to military censorship from the civilian authority administered by Decies and his successors. This was a logical response to the problems he had experienced in dealing with advanced nationalist propaganda. However, it had the negative effect of diminishing the government's moral authority as its enforcement was frequently arbitrary and severe.

The government's censorship was directed against separatist propaganda and displays as well as regular newspapers. Inquests were prohibited in many counties to prevent embarrassing verdicts and outbursts.[59] Responding to the limited effectiveness of postal censorship during the Great War, the War Office suggested the introduction of a passport system for everyone travelling to and from Ireland. This was intended to prevent persons carrying uncensored mail through the ports but was rejected as the Home Office considered it 'absolutely absurd and unworkable'.[60] Censorship of telegrams was introduced in September 1919 and was intended 'to guard against acts of sedition', and to prevent republicans from getting financial or other aid from the UK or abroad.[61]

The British administration's policy on censorship was weakened by the competing aims of its publicity and military sections. In August 1920, the press were warned against publishing 'incitement to murder or disaffection' or 'spreading false reports'. Despite this the newspapers were not prevented from expressing political opinions hostile to the Crown forces.[62] As Charles Townshend has pointed out, the army, as represented by Brigadier General Brind who was responsible for censorship, had little interest in the freedom of the press as an abstract principle. They wanted to ensure that only a positive view of the government and Crown forces was published. This approach was opposed by Basil Clarke, a former war correspondent who was placed in charge of propaganda.[63] Clarke advocated a system of 'propaganda by news' as opposed to one in which stories were repressed and denied.[64] He believed that the censors should liaise with the propagandists: the latter were to correct errors in the press and advise the censors on the degree to which newspapers should be considered culpable for breaches of the rules.[65]

Even large, national papers were censored. In December 1919, the *Freeman's Journal* suffered formal suppression for attacking the government. It challenged the decision in court but lost its case.[66] The paper was allowed to resume publication in January 1920.[67] In December 1920 its editor and proprietor were convicted by a court martial for an article about the shooting of policemen in Tullow, Co. Carlow.[68] The British press reacted strongly against this decision and the British government ordered their release.[69]

Newspapers also faced the prospect of violent repression by both sides. In December 1919, IRA men smashed machinery in the *Irish Independent*'s offices in Abbey Street, Dublin.[70] In September 1920, the *Galway Express* suffered similar treatment at the hands of the Black and Tans who dismantled and removed printing machinery.[71] Within the martial law areas, in the later stages of the conflict, the press was kept under 'firm control' according to General Strickland.[72] The *Irish Bulletin*, the main propaganda paper of the revolutionaries, was temporarily closed down in March 1921 when Crown forces took the equipment from its base in Molesworth Street. Although the rebels promptly repaired to Exchequer Street and continued to publish, the British were able to use the seized equipment to produce counterfeit copies of the paper.[73]

THE BRITISH LEGACY

The above discussion of censorship under the Union shows that both the Irish regions inherited several legal and philosophical principles from Britain. The first was a tradition of legislative and judicial action against immoral publications dating back to the nineteenth century. The Cockburn judgment of 1868 had set a standard by which obscenity could be judged and, although it had grave deficiencies, it defined the terms of the debate about moral censorship in the emerging states. The situation in regard to film was less clear cut. The British film censorship was a chaotic one based on a compromise between local authorities, the film industry and the central government. This made it very flexible, but those who wanted clear, strict definitions of what was to be permitted saw this as a weakness.

In the realm of state security, the new governments had two British models on which to draw: *ad hoc* repression by security forces and the courts, or prior censorship by a state official. The former model worked best against an enemy such as the IRA, that was capable of producing propaganda rapidly and changing its titles, printers and methods of distribution quickly. The prior censorship was quite effective in dealing with established newspapers which could be prosecuted or shut down. It had the advantage of being less arbitrary than *ad hoc* repression and allowing extensive consultation with friendly or neutral papers. As we shall see, the Northern Irish government opted for the *ad hoc* system, while the pro-treaty southern government initially tried prior censorship before using a repressive system once the Civil War proper was coming to an end.

The period from 1911 to 1922 offered the new governments plenty of examples of how to put together a censorship policy. The demands of the major religions were clear: immoral literature and cinema were to be controlled. Irish nationalists combined this with their objections to British and American culture. The British had left not one but two policies for dealing with sedition. The government could set up a prior censorship or suppress offenders one by one. What no one had thought to leave the new states was a strong belief in freedom of expression. The British government had always been willing to limit the right in Ireland to defeat its enemies, the revolutionaries had learned at first hand the power of propaganda and were determined not to have their own weapons turned against them, and the Churches had consistently seen censorship as a lesser evil than immorality. As a result, free speech in the new Irelands would rest on shaky foundations.

NOTES

1. *Oxford English Dictionary*, Vol.II, p.1029. Harold Laswell, 'Censorship', in E.R.A. Seligman (ed.), *Encyclopaedia of the social sciences* (New York: Macmillan, 1930), Vol.3, p.290. Paul O'Higgins, *Censorship in Britain* (London: Thomas Nelson & Sons, 1972), p.11.
2. Michael Adams, *Censorship: the Irish Experience* (Dublin: Scepter, 1968). Terence Brown, *Ireland: a social and cultural history, 1922–1985* (London: Fontana Press, 1985). J.H. Whyte, *Church and state in modern Ireland 1923–79* (2nd edition (Dublin: Gill & Macmillan, 1980). Kieran Woodman, *Media control in Ireland, 1923–1983* (Illinois: S. Illinois University Press, 1985); Kevin Rockett, *Irish film censorship: a cultural journey from silent cinema to Internet pornography* (Dublin: Four Courts Press, 2004).
3. Maurice Curtis, 'Catholic action as an organised campaign in Ireland, 1921–1947' Ph.D. thesis, UCD 2000); Susannah Riordan, 'The unpopular front: Catholic revival and Irish cultural identity, 1932–48', in Mike Cronin and John M. Regan (eds) *Ireland: the politics of independence, 1922–49* (London: Macmillan, 2000), pp.98–120; Margaret O'Callaghan, 'Language, nationality and cultural identity in the Irish Free State, 1922–7: the *Irish Statesman* and the *Catholic Bulletin* reappraised', *Irish Historical Studies*, Vol.XXIV, No.94 (Nov. 1984), pp.226–45.
4. Eunan O'Halpin, *Defending Ireland: the Irish state and its enemies since 1922* (Oxford: Oxford University Press, 1999); Laura K. Donohue, *Counter-terrorist law and emergency powers in the United Kingdom, 1922–2000* (Dublin: Irish Academic Press, 2001); Colm Campbell, *Emergency law in Ireland, 1918–1925* (Oxford: Clarendon Press, 1994).
5. For more on these publications see O'Callaghan, 'Language, nationality and cultural identity'.
6. Norman St John Stevas, *Obscenity and the law* (London: Secker & Warburg, 1956), pp.66–9.
7. R. v Hicklin (1868) LR3 QB360 at p.371.
8. St John Stevas, *Obscenity and the law*, pp.70–4.
9. Ibid, pp.75–84.
10. Adams, *Censorship*, p.14.
11. *Irish Catholic Directory 1912*, p.532.
12. Ibid., p.526.
13. Curtis, 'Catholic action', pp.46–9, 53–8.
14. *Irish Catholic Directory (ICD) 1912*, p.532.
15. Ibid., pp.536–7.
16. Alan Megahey, *The Irish Protestant churches in the twentieth century* (London: Macmillan, 2000), p.124.
17. *ICD 1913*, p.527.
18. *Galway Observer*, 11 March 1916, 5 July 1913.
19. Joyce, evidence to the Committee on Evil Literature, 21 April 1926, NAI, Department of Justice JUS7/2/12.
20. 'Development of the Film Censorship', 1922, NAGB, Home Office HO45/22906.
21. *ICD 1911*, p.480.
22. Dublin Municipal Council, Minutes, 6 Oct. 1913, 9 Aug. 1915.
23. Ibid., 9 Oct. 1916; Report of the Public Health Committee, 15 Aug. 1916; Dublin Corporation Reports 1916, Vol.2, No.153.
24. Report of the Public Health Committee, 14 Aug. 1917, Dublin Corporation Reports 1917, Vol.3, No.173. For a detailed discussion of Dublin film censorship see Rockett, *Irish Film Censorship*, pp.51–7.
25. *Galway Observer* 10 April 1915.
26. Ibid., 3 March 1917.
27. James P. O'Connor, 'Censorship of Films 1894–1970' (Ph.D. thesis, UCD, 1996), p.382.
28. Minutes of Police Committee, 1 July 1920, 19 Aug. 1920, PRONI, LA7/10AB/1/17.
29. Ibid., 26 Nov. 1920, 30 Nov. 1920, 16 Dec. 1920.
30. Campbell, *Emergency Law in Ireland*, pp.10–12.
31. Virginia Glandon, *Arthur Griffith and the advanced nationalist press in Ireland, 1900–1922* (New York: P. Lang, 1985), p.147.

32. *Down Recorder*, 5 June 1915.
33. Ibid., 19 June 1915.
34. 'List of seditious leaflets and notices circulated in Ireland from 1905 to the present', Nov. 1914, NAGB, Colonial Office CO/904/161/3.
35. Treasury Solicitor's opinion, 15 Feb. 1915, NAGB, Colonial Office CO/904/160/2.
36. DORA order, 27 Feb. 1915, ibid.
37. GOC (General Officer Commanding) to Under Secretary for Ireland, 25 Jan. 1915, ibid., CO/904/161/7.
38. NAGB, CO/904/160/3.
39. Ibid., CO/904/160/3.
40. W. McConnell, District Inspector General to County Inspector, Wexford, 2 Dec. 1914, ibid., CO/904/160/4.
41. Post Master General, warrant, 12 Jan. 1915, ibid.
42. Mathew Nathan to Secretary, GPO, Dublin, 15 Jan. 1915, ibid.
43. Ben Novick, 'Postal Censorship in Ireland, 1914–16', *Irish Historical Studies*, Vol.XXXI, No.123, (May 1999), pp.344–51.
44. Glandon, *Arthur Griffith*, pp.159.
45. Patrick Maume, *The long gestation: Irish nationalist life, 1891–1918* (Dublin: Gill & Macmillan, 1999), p. 187. Maume bases his assessment on the verdict of Frank Gallagher in *Four glorious years* (Dublin: Irish Press, 1953). Given Gallagher's own political position it was in his interests to contrast the failures of British propaganda and censorship with his own successes.
46. Malcom Brodie, *The Tele: a history of the Belfast Telegraph* (Belfast: Blackstaff Press, 1995), pp.33–4.
47. Warrants issued, 25 April 1916, NAGB, HO45/199665.
48. *Down Recorder*, 22 Jan. 1916.
49. Mark Graham, *British censorship of civil mails during World War I, 1914–19* (Bristol: Stuart Rossiter Trust Fund, 2000), p.99.
50. Ibid., pp.133–4.
51. Decies to Under Secretary, 19 Nov. 1916, NAGB, CO/904/160/3.
52. Ibid., 24 Nov. 1916.
53. Reports of the censor, Aug.–Nov. 1917, NAGB, CO/904/166.
54. Ibid., March–April 1918.
55. Ibid., July–Dec. 1918, CO/904/167.
56. *Galway Observer*, 3 May 1919.
57. Reports of the censor, Jan.–March 1919, NAGB, CO/904/167.
58. Ben Novick, *Conceiving revolution: Irish nationalist propaganda during the First World War* (Dublin: Four Courts Press, 2001), p.36.
59. Campbell, *Emergency law*, p.27.
60. W.M.P., minute, 27 Feb. 1920, NAGB, HO45/19665.
61. Col. Arthur Browne, 'Orders for emergency censorship of telegrams to and from Ireland', [Sept. 1919], ibid.
62. Michael Hopkinson (ed.), *The last days of Dublin Castle: the Mark Sturgis diaries* (Dublin: Irish Academic Press, 1999), p.44 (23 Sept. 1920).
63. Charles Townshend, *The British campaign in Ireland, 1919–1921: the development of political and military policies* (Oxford: Oxford University Press, 1975), p.116.
64. Clarke to Assistant Under Secretary, 10 March 1921, NAGB, CO/904/840–843.
65. 'Notes on the above chart' [Aug. 1921], CO/904/579.
66. *Down Recorder*, 20–23 Dec. 1919.
67. *Galway Observer*, 31 Jan. 1920.
68. Ibid., 27 Nov. 1920.
69. Townshend, *The British campaign in Ireland*, p. 159.
70. *Down Recorder*, 27 Dec. 1919; *Galway Observer*, 27 Dec. 1919.
71. *Galway Observer*, 11 Sep. 1920, 25 Sept. 1920.
72. Townshend, *The British campaign in Ireland*, p.176.
73. Glandon, *Arthur Griffith*, p.185.

CHAPTER ONE

Chaos 1922–24

In 1922 the question facing the leaders of the new Irish states was not what kind of societies they would build, but whether their states would survive at all. In the south, the split in the Dáil over the Treaty was followed by that of the IRA. Over the next few months the country drifted towards civil war and the pro-Treaty side began to face the prospect of turning the power of the state upon their erstwhile comrades. The situation in the north was, if anything, even worse. There the conflict between the Crown forces and the IRA was intermingled with vicious sectarian rioting, intimidation and murder. Three hundred murders were officially recorded in Northern Ireland in 1922; the violence peaked in May when 80 people were killed. Over 550 murders were committed in the province between 1920 and 1922; including some 80 of the Crown forces, 300 Catholics and 170 Protestants.[1] The majority of the violence took place in Belfast. Northern nationalists, seeing themselves as a people in exile, had no interest in supporting the government, and Unionists had no desire to offer them concessions. The largely Protestant RUC was supplemented by the wholly Unionist Special Constabularies which alienated Catholic opinion even further.

In these contexts censorship had two functions. One was to inhibit the enemies of the state by preventing them from spreading their message to the public. This was meant both to inhibit their military actions and aid the governments' propaganda campaigns. Censorship also offered a convenient means of criminalizing activists as it was easier to prove that they possessed illegal documents than that they were members of illegal organizations.

Civil War censorship in the south

The southern authorities began to censor newspapers in July 1922. The responsibility for this fell to the National Army's Publicity Director, Piaras Béaslaí, a 41-year ally of Michael Collins. Béaslaí had edited the Irish Volunteer paper, *An tÓglach* during the War of Independence, as well as the Gaelic League newspaper,[2] but he was now expected to assemble a censorship process quickly and with few guidelines. The system used depended on the co-operation of the newspapers themselves and on the help of Eason & Son Ltd 22, Charles Eason met with a government official and was told to stop selling English papers.[3] This proved to be a temporary step but, from then on, Béaslaí would work closely with the newsagent. Throughout July and August, the company dispatched papers to the censor's office as they were landed at port and sent the list of titles to Béaslaí.[4] He trusted Eason enough to allow him to handle the *Financial Times, Financial News* and *Financier* 'without submitting every copy'.[5] Eason also undertook to send lists of magazines to Béaslaí and to submit any issues containing Irish articles for censorship.[6] Eason seems to have co-operated fully with the censor and their good relationship helped the wholesaler to keep his clients happy by speeding up the issuing of permits.[7] Béaslaí's office recognized the help it was getting. When several uncensored copies of British magazines went on sale through a rival newsagent, the assistant censor commented that 'Eason who have dealt fairly with us are penalised by whatever newsagent is ignoring the rules'.[8] Eason also refused to distribute the *Voice of Labour* until the firm received assurances that it was submitted to the censor every week before publication.[9]

Béaslaí was primarily concerned with military and political censorship. His authority covered 'any matter bearing on the fighting, the military and political situations' only. His office checked proofs of the Dublin morning and evening papers, all the British and foreign reporters' wires and all photographs and films of military operations. Other subordinate censors dealt with their local newspapers. The office acted as a liaison with the press, providing them with copies of all general headquarters' official bulletins. It also authorized private firms to use ciphers and controlled the censorship of private wires and post.[10] Postal censorship focused mostly on letters to the press but covered a large amount of correspondence; in the first two weeks of August 1922, for example, 416 letters were referred to Béaslaí.[11] The censor's office suggested sending copies of wires to the Intelligence Department[12] but it seems that that office had its own arrangements with the Post Office.[13] Although it seemed clear on paper, the censorship was, in practice, a ramshackle operation. Béaslaí was constantly short of personnel, money and time and functioned with a confused chain of command.

The politician to whom Béaslaí reported was Desmond FitzGerald, the Minister for Publicity. Although a veteran of 1916, he was now firmly a part of the civilian wing of the new state. As such he paid a great deal of attention to the propaganda role of censorship. His instructions to the press showed that he intended to deny the trappings of legitimacy to the Republican side. FitzGerald went into great detail over the terminology to be used in describing the conflict. The pro-Treaty forces were to be called the 'Irish Army', 'National Army' or simply 'the troops' while the Republicans were to be described as 'bands', bodies' or 'armed men' and were to be designated 'irregulars'. The new government was to be called the 'Irish government' not the 'Provisional government' while the Republicans were never to be called the 'Executive forces'. The ranks of Republican officers were not to be printed. Neither were stories about the treatment of Republican prisoners to be printed. Any news or correspondence about peace was to be censored. Despite these strictures, FitzGerald's instructions echoed Béaslaí's conciliatory tone towards the press: censors were not to rewrite reports in their own words, for example.[14] Despite at least one private complaint against a paper on moral grounds, there is no evidence that censorship in this period was motivated by anything other than military or propaganda considerations.[15] Indeed, in the case of the *Morning Post*, Béaslaí passed what he considered a 'consistently scurrilous and blackguardly' paper as it was 'in no way detrimental to our military or political interests'.[16] Béaslaí felt that his job was not taken seriously by the military authorities and in July 1922, after only a few weeks in office, he threatened to resign as his staff had not been paid and he had had to reimburse them from his own resources and by borrowing money from Desmond FitzGerald.[17] His departure was avoided, but as a military man reporting to a civilian his position was unusual.[18] This incident showed the confusion surrounding the censor's office. It was unclear whether his position was civilian or military, what the extent of his powers were or how his office should be organized.

Such confusion annoyed the press considerably. The secretary of the Dublin and Provincial Retail Newsagents', Booksellers' and Stationers' Association, wrote to Béaslaí to complain about the seizure of English Sunday papers. He demanded that censorship be applied to only 'the smallest number of papers' and that his members receive timely notice of prohibitions.[19] Sean Lester of the Department of Publicity also complained against the banning of the *Daily Herald*, commenting that it had been a 'staunch and courageous friend' of Ireland in the War of Independence and he found it 'extraordinary' that the *Daily Mail, Daily Sketch*, and *Daily Mirror* were permitted.[20] Béaslaí found such complaints exasperating; he did not consider the ban to be a punishment but saw it as necessary because the paper had published Republican bulletins. He complained that 'it is useless to expect me to carry on my job as censor if English papers are allowed to circulate matters in Ireland which the Irish papers are prevented from publishing'.[21] He complained that his critics failed to appreciate 'the unpleasant and thankless task I have to perform'.[22]

Film was taken seriously by the pro-Treaty government. On 12 July, Michael Collins wrote to Béaslaí to ask about his plans for film censorship. Béaslaí had already ordered picture houses not to display 'pictures or titles of pictures' unless his department had passed them.[23] By 16 July this order was amended so that only 'war films' would be censored.[24] These were defined as 'all topical films and posters dealing with or bearing on the fighting or military operations in Ireland at the present time'.[25] In response to requests from cameramen and filmmakers, the southern government set up a film censorship office in London in July 1922.[26]

Despite the detail of the censor's instructions, there were several errors and abuses of the system. Béaslaí complained of letters being opened without his authorization.[27] Later, he had to explain that the postal censors were 'a little too zealous' when English journalists complained at the mangling of their copy.[28] A more serious abuse of power occurred in Waterford where the acting military censor dictated to the editor of the *Waterford News* how to lay out his paper on the day of the funeral of a pro-Treaty officer. Even the headline, 'Hero laid to rest', was specified.[29] Béaslaí was furious, describing the orders as 'indefensible' and contrary to his own instructions.[30]

His own decisions could be eccentric. In August, for example, he banned a government advertisement seeking a supplier of coffins for fear that it 'would be quoted by the Irregulars as showing that we expected a long and bloody slaughter'.[31] The death of Michael Collins prompted the censorship to go beyond political and military matters. FitzGerald complained that the *Sunday Independent* leader on the subject was too short and insufficiently condemnatory of the Republicans.[32] Béaslaí also wrote to three newspapers condemning a biography of Collins by Hayden Talbot.[33] When the *World's Pictorial News* ran a story entitled 'the secret history of Michael Collins', he banned the paper as it had given 'much pain and annoyance' to Collins' friends and relatives and had placed the late general 'in a ridiculous light'.[34] Around the same time, Béaslaí ordered the press not to print full accounts of the inquest of Patrick Mannion, a Republican shot dead by the Free State forces. Béaslaí believed that the government had not presented its case well at the inquest and wanted to buy it time to give its side of the story in the Dáil.[35] Instead he handed the Republican side a propaganda opportunity. Dorothy MacArdle and Count Plunkett wrote to the *Irish Independent*, alleging that the inquest evidence had been suppressed.[36]

From early on, the pro-Treaty side considered the abolition of censorship. Even in July, as it was just being established, FitzGerald and Collins had agreed that their objective was to relax censorship 'almost to vanishing point'.[37] Collins argued that the public 'discounts, to an undue extent, censored news, and in any case we have the situation so well in hand ... that the newspapers themselves may be trusted to do what is right'.[38] As the conflict moved from conventional warfare to guerrilla actions by the Republicans, steps were taken to wind down the machinery of censorship. By the first week of October, Béaslaí had heard that his office was to be abolished. Though he was furious that he had not been consulted,[39] he readily complied with the order issued on 12 October 1922 to begin closing down the censorship system.[40] Over the next two weeks, newspapers were told only to send Béaslaí proofs if they were doubtful about their stories.[41] The censorship of letters and telegraphs was discontinued from 18 October.[42]

The pro-Treaty side was not alone in its desire to control the media. In January 1922, machinery was damaged at the offices of the *Clonmel Nationalist* when it refused to publish an anti-Treaty manifesto.[43] When its rival, the *Clonmel Chronicle*, protested, Republicans seized the town's supply of the *Chronicle* and threatened further action against the *Nationalist* when it resumed production.[44] In April 1922, a consignment of newspapers was thrown into the river Foyle before being fished out by pro-Treaty forces.[45] A consignment of Belfast morning papers was seized at Dundalk and burned the same week.[46] That month several thousand copies of the pro-Treaty *Sligo Champion* were destroyed and, some weeks later, its offices were damaged.[47] In March 1922 the *Freeman's Journal* published a report of a speech by Tom Barry. In retaliation armed men smashed its printing machinery in Dublin.[48] The editor of the *Freeman's Journal* was later warned not to refer to the anti-Treaty IRA as 'irregulars' or to print their ranks in parentheses. A fine of one pound would be levied for each offence with the threat of more severe action for persistent abuses.[49] Similar letters were sent to the *Irish Independent* and *Irish Times*. The latter paper did use the word 'republican', while the *Independent* stopped using 'irregular' much to the disgust of the Free State authorities.[50] By November the Republicans were winning the battle for terminology and FitzGerald was warned that 'the newspapers generally are now obeying the orders they received recently from Ernie O'Malley'.[51] He warned his colleagues that although the *Freeman's Journal* was holding out, it would come under pressure if the others were allowed to 'placate the irregulars'.[52] Within a few months, however, the papers had reverted to Free State language, possibly because of a diminished Republican threat to them.

As the Republicans became more desperate they threatened cinemas and newspapers. On 14 March 1923, the anti-Treaty Minister of Home Affairs, P.J. Ruttledge, proclaimed a time of national mourning for recently executed Republicans, during which all amusements were to be suspended. The Free State government responded by ordering events to go ahead – which most did.[53] In late March, Kevin O'Higgins met cinema owners and ordered them to open or be taken over by the state.[54] The cinemas did stay open despite two bombing attempts. In both cases the bombs were petrol bombs and were probably designed to aggravate the Free State forces and terrorize the cinema owners rather than to destroy the properties.[55] When the proprietors protested in April that they were losing money during Holy Week, O'Higgins only offered to consider an application for complete closure by any cinema if it was for a specific period of time.[56] Clearly the authorities wanted to avert any bad publicity. In April, the Republicans issued over one hundred orders to businesses not to advertise in those newspapers opposing them. The Free State refused to offer any protection to the advertisers as it was believed that the anti-Treaty camp was trying to tie up government forces.[57] These actions were not meant solely as censorship since their aim was not only to restrict expression, but also to distract the Free State's forces and terrorize the civilian population.

Emergency law and freedom of expression in Northern Ireland

In the northern government's battle for survival, censorship acted both as a way of controlling public opinion and as an easy way to criminalize those who opposed the state. The key legislative weapon in the government's armoury was the Civil Authorities (Special Powers) Act 1922. The man who wielded it, Richard Dawson Bates, had been rewarded for his party loyalty and vigorous opposition to the third Home Rule Bill with the Home Affairs ministry.[58] Despite lacking either great charisma or ability he was to remain there until 1943, a visible sign that the spirit of Orangeism was present at the Cabinet table. His enemies spread rumours that he slept with a revolver and a copy of the Special Powers Act under his pillow.[59] That act (hereafter referred to as the CASPA) itself was a draconian work, based on the Restoration of Order in Ireland Act 1920 and the wartime Defence of the Realm Acts. The military recommended that it be stronger than its predecessor as 'it was not contemplated [during the War of Independence] that forces of the crown would meet with the armed resistance which they are now liable to meet'.[60] Its first article set the tone, giving the minister power 'to take all such steps and issue all such orders as may be necessary for preserving the peace and maintaining order'. It banned incitement or solicitation to violate a regulation. It was also a crime not to inform the civil authorities of a person who had committed, or was about to commit, such a deed. The most remarkable features of the act were articles 2.4 and 2.6, derived from wartime legislation. Under these provisions it was a crime to do anything contrary to the preservation of the peace, even if it was not specifically outlawed, and if a person claimed that he was acting legally, the burden of proof was on him. Several provisions of the act directly affected freedom of expression. The Minister of Home Affairs could prohibit meetings, processions, assemblies as well as the wearing of uniforms or badges. Collecting, publishing or communicating details on the police force was forbidden. The unauthorized use of codes and ciphers was also banned. Article 24 made it illegal to promote the objects of an unlawful organization; furthermore if any person possessed documents relating to such a group it was up to him to prove he was not a member. Under article 25, the police were given special protection: no one could spread false reports about them, or make statements, films or stage productions which would interfere with them or discourage recruiting.[61]

The most important censorship provision was article 26, under which the minister could ban any newspaper for a specified period. As the act was renewed every year such prohibitions had to be renewed or allowed to lapse every twelve months. The Civil Authority acted by making regulations which were not subject to parliamentary debate: the first thirty-six such regulations formed a schedule to the CASPA, thus making it impossible to challenge them in court as *ultra vires* of the act.[62] Some sixteen regulations affected freedom of expression and fifteen of these were derived from the wartime Defence of the Realm Regulations (DORRs).[63] The derivation of the CASPA tells a great deal about how the regime viewed its censorship powers. In reality, the CASPA was a war powers act used in an internal conflict by government not authorized to declare war. The republicans were seen not merely as enemies of the state, but as invaders. Newspapers or individuals who did not support the authorities were to be treated as if they had given comfort to the enemy in the Great War. These facts were recognized in a memorandum for the British Home Secretary. He was advised that there was a risk that the CASPA would make the troops 'the agents and servants of the local instead of the Imperial government'. This, it was feared, would become a problem if the northern government was ever replaced by one 'less easy to co-operate with', in other words a coalition of Nationalists and Labour.[64]

The Civil Authority (Special Powers) Bill sailed through the parliamentary process with minimal scrutiny, aided by the fact that the Nationalist members had not taken their seats. Dawson Bates's Parliamentary Secretary, Megaw, emphasized the new state's weakness compared to the IRA which 'has at its command a yellow press, which for the production of foul and slanderous lies would be hard to equal. That press daily vomits its calumnies against our Ulster people, against our parliament, and against our government.' The argument that censorship was necessary to exclude hostile, alien influences would recur in both territories. Megaw reinforced the idea that the IRA were an alien threat by claiming that there had been no IRA organization in the six counties prior to the truce.[65] Thus the IRA became the invasion force of a foreign power. Although the speech demonstrated that censorship was intended to be part of the government's fight against the IRA from the start, article 25, limiting reporting on the police, was introduced as a late amendment at committee stage. The timing of this change was queried, but there was no vote and the amendment passed without further comment.[66] The Senate managed no debate of substance on the freedom of expression provisions.[67]

As Campbell has pointed out, the northern government had no power to impose martial law and the British government would have had problems doing so as long as the ROIA remained in place.[68] This was clear to the press, and many Unionists did not trust London to look after their security. The *Belfast Newsletter* had opposed martial law because it feared the Imperial government would 'kow-tow to the Provisional government in Dublin'. It supported emergency powers as they allowed the northern government to take its own action.[69] The nationalist *Irish News*, on the other hand, saw the CASPA as a danger to nationalists. It made it clear that it trusted neither the government nor the police to enforce the law fairly.[70] It particularly resented the censorship provisions of the act, commenting: 'if every man who has "spread false reports or made false statements" in printed publications was put in jail, how many of those who adopted the Belfast Coercion Act [CASPA] would be at liberty?' Instead, the paper feared that Roman Catholics would be returned 'to the era of the penal code'.[71] When the bill was finally passed, the paper summed up its case that 'during the period of the Great War the press was not free; but the restrictions were accepted as necessary evils and, for the most part, rigidly adhered to, while those entrusted with the work of censorship were persons whose impartiality could not be questioned or doubted', but this was not true of a Unionist government and of Dawson Bates in particular.[72] This view was, more politely, endorsed by Bishop MacRory, who questioned how the powers could be necessary in the light of the newly signed Craig–Collins pact and called for them to be applied with 'strictly impartial justice'.[73]

One of the earliest forums of expression affected by the government was that of local government. During March and April 1922, some seventeen local bodies – Poor Law Unions, Rural District Councils and Urban District Councils – were dissolved with appointed commissioners replacing the elected officials. The purpose of the dissolutions was not so much related to what was being said or done by the bodies as their refusals to give allegiance to the northern government, but it had the effect of limiting local debate.[74]

Despite its new powers the Cabinet hesitated before attempting to censor press reports. Unlike their southern counterparts they never introduced a prior censorship of the press. When troops complained that the Belfast press were being 'one sided' and were publishing names of military witnesses, the government only authorized Dawson Bates to act 'unofficially'.[75] The administration also delayed in seeking to have the IRA proclaimed. At the root of this tardiness, Craig explained to Londonderry, was a desire to avoid martial law if at all possible.[76] By 16 May 1922, it was still resisting the military advice that republican organizations be banned.[77] Four days later, it decided that the situation was too serious to allow further delay and Lord Londonderry was dispatched to 'get the matter carried through' with the Lord Lieutenant.[78]

On 23 May 1922, a few weeks after the CASPA became law, five newspapers were seized from the headquarters of the Sinn Féin club. A worried Charles Eason contacted A.P. Magill, the Assistant Secretary at the Ministry of Home Affairs to ask if he should continue to sell these titles in the north.[79] The police were considering proscribing the papers but Eason was told to carry on selling them in the meantime.[80] The northern government also asked the British to help it censor post to, from and within the region.[81] The problem was that, as the Republicans could communicate freely with the south, complete censorship of the mail was impossible. Furthermore, local post offices were unreliable which made even an internal censorship of the post difficult. The northern administration asked for a travelling censorship with the power to make surprise inspections. The objective of this plan was not to gather intelligence but to force Republicans to use other, more easily watched, means of communication.[82]

In fact the censorship actions of the government under the CASPA can be grouped into two categories. In some cases, publications were banned from circulation for various periods of time. In others, documents were branded as 'seditious' to expedite the arrest, detention or harassment of suspected republicans. The minister could ban almost any newspaper or periodical for up to twelve months at which time the CASPA needed to be renewed. Having banned a newspaper, the minister had to apply to the Lords Justices of Northern Ireland and to the Governor to have copies of the paper sent by post detained.[83] The threat of a ban was often enough to ensure compliance. In mid April 1922, for example, Dawson Bates considered issuing an order to prohibit the publication of the names of witnesses but did not have to do so as the major newspapers, including the nationalist *Irish News*, gave voluntary undertakings to 'exercise great discretion'. The RIC officer who was asked to get similar commitments from the local press was told to warn them that the CASPA could be used if they did not co-operate.[84]

In June, the *Irish News* accused the 'specials' of torture and arson during a raid in Derry. Although even the Ministry admitted privately that the arson claim was true, it pressed for a prosecution and ordered a raid on the newspaper's offices. Aware of the risk of embarrassment, the official responsible warned that 'it is very important that the prosecution should not fail' due to carelessness. Despite this the case was dropped by the Attorney General.[85] Similarly when an article appeared in the *Irish Independent* entitled 'War on Belfast Catholics' and allegedly written by Mr Anderson, the special correspondent in Belfast for the *Manchester Guardian*, the ministry's immediate reaction was that 'proceedings should be taken against him'. When it learned that he had fled to England after receiving a threatening letter, and that the article had really been written by nationalist historian Alice Stopford Green, it was decided not to proceed.[86] The implication was that the government was more concerned with the possibility of there being an unfriendly correspondent in place than with the article itself.

The *Newry Telegraph* was prosecuted for printing a priest's accusation that the police were guilty of a local murder. The editor was fined £20.[87] In August the *Freeman's Journal* and the *Dublin Evening Telegraph* were banned for attacking Lord Justice Andrews; the latter ban required the seizure of 24,255 papers.[88] An official statement was issued to the press rebutting the allegations against the Lord Justice in detail.[89] When the *Irish Catholic* criticized the Belfast assizes under the headline 'Orange Travesty of Justice', the Ministry of Home Affairs decided to act despite the risk of 'a calumnious outburst in doing so'. Although the ministry officials would have preferred a prosecution, the minister banned the paper for a month on the advice of the Attorney General. Within the government the decision was justified on the grounds that t the article was a 'violent attack on the northern Judiciary'. The Prime Minister duly gave his full approval.[90] After the ban had elapsed, the government press officer complained that the *Irish Catholic* had reported the murders of Catholics but the ministry decided that there was 'nothing much in this' and declined to take action.[91] Likewise, when the nationalist *Ulster Herald* published letters from internees, it was left alone.[92] This suggests that there was a difference between a paper criticizing the government or reporting embarrassing news and one attacking the institutions of the state or the police.

Explicitly republican publications were more closely scrutinized. The republican newspaper *Poblacht na hÉireann* was banned from 7 April 1922. In that case, one Civil Servant complained that 'this publication is never lawful. It is in its name and nature seditious to the utmost limit. No temporary remedy or punishment is suitable. It should be seized as seditious literature whenever and wherever found without any time limit.'[93] *Éire,* which replaced *Poblacht* in February 1923 was not banned until it defended guerrilla warfare in its second issue. However, when the ban was reviewed, the reason given for renewing it was that 'the paper advocates a Republic for all Ireland, and has no other raison d'être'. The limits of the government's power were highlighted by the fact that, as the paper was published in Manchester, they had no powers to prevent it entering Northern Ireland.[94] The police had to rely on intercepting banned papers after they were received. In one case, they captured 140 copies of *Éire* addressed to a lady in Belfast but were unable to do more than warn her as she had never technically received them.[95] The strongly republican paper *Sinn Féin* was similarly left unscathed, despite the urgings of the RUC that it be banned, as it had a tiny northern circulation and 'does not comment on the northern administration'. Crucially, it was 'not very violent'.[96] When the two papers merged in 1924 a confused

District Inspector of the RUC reported that Cathal Brugha, the Irish republican leader who had been killed some time earlier, was the new editor, to which the assistant secretary retorted that if so 'it must be hot stuff'.[97] The existing ban on *Éire* then applied to the combined paper.

Nationalist and republican papers seem to have fared worse than those of other political hues. The Larkenite *Irish Worker* was not banned as it lacked 'any advocacy of immediate violence'.[98] It is clear that while strict limits existed as to what could be said or reported, it was possible for a newspaper to function even if it was not approved of by the minister. It was not always necessary for the minister to use the CASPA, however. Following complaints from the *Armagh Guardian* that its loyalty in refusing Sinn Féin advertisements had not been rewarded with the receipt of government business, the parliamentary secretary ordered that 'no bargains can be made with respect to advertisements but the attention of those in charge of selecting newspapers for advertisements should be called to those which issue disloyal or illegal paragraphs whether in the shape of advertisements or news'.[99] The government had little to fear from the major Unionist papers as it had a special relationship with them. Thomas Moles, editor of the *Belfast Telegraph*, was a Unionist MP in both the UK and Northern Irish parliaments throughout the decade, as was his counterpart at the *Northern Whig*, Robert John Lynn, while William Anderson, editor of the *Newsletter* was close to the Unionist leadership.[100] They did criticize the government on various issues but they were all unfailing supporters of its security policy.

Under the CASPA, a variety of written material could be banned or branded 'seditious'. This might appear to have been a form of censorship. However, an examination of some of the case histories makes it clear that the objective of such cases was more complicated. As well as seeking to censor the distribution of republican literature, the authorities found it much easier to charge a suspect with possession of seditious literature than to prove sedition. In the case of Thomas Bennett, for example, who was arrested in June 1922 for possession of documents relating to Cumann na mBan and Sinn Féin, his defence that he had no knowledge of the documents was invalid under the CASPA and he was fined.[101] The case of Michael McGleenan is also relevant. Found in possession of several seditious documents, he was not prosecuted because they all dated from the period 1919–20. Clearly what was at stake was not whether he possessed republican material but whether he himself was still politically active. The material was still confiscated, which shows that censorship was at least part of the authorities' aim.[102] The clearest example of the use of the seditious documents regulations to obtain an easy conviction occurred in spring 1923. Vincent McCabe was arrested by the RUC who believed that he was the quartermaster for the IRA. He was prosecuted, however, for possessing IRA accounts, training manuals and orders along with a two-year-old copy of the *Leader*. Despite his protests that he was no longer politically involved, McCabe was convicted and bound over.[103]

The sort of material banned says a great deal about the objectives of those responsible for security. While Bennett was prosecuted for having Sinn Féin pamphlets and a summons to a Cumann na mBan meeting, McGleenan had a copy of the 1916 proclamation and various songs and poems. In a more straightforward case of censorship in 1923, Dawson Bates issued a forfeiture order for the sheet music collections, 'Ireland's Songs of Freedom', 'The Irish Lament' and the 'Barricade Song Sheet'.[104] In another case, a man was prosecuted for possessing anti-Treaty propaganda,[105] while in August 1922, police raided the shop of Patrick Dempsey and seized a large quantity of material including newspapers, song books, ballads, flags, buttons and brooches, books and pictures of the 1916 leaders. Although even the official at the ministry admitted that 'I am unable to point to any item which could be made the subject of a prosecution', Dempsey was held for four weeks on a detention order and five books and twenty other items were confiscated permanently.[106]

The regime did become somewhat more lenient after the early crisis of 1922–23 had passed. In 1924, a woman found selling banned newspapers was not prosecuted because 'it is doubtful whether a court would impose a serious penalty'[107] and a man was not prosecuted because he had only possessed a single copy of the proscribed publication *Éire*.[108] In both cases, the publications were confiscated. In 1925, Joseph McGurk, was found in possession of material directly relating to the IRA so he was prosecuted and, having refused to recognize the court, was jailed for three months.[109] The implication is that the seditious literature clauses of the act were used more to expedite the conviction of suspected insurgents than as a method of repressive censorship of the nationalist population.

The government also concerned itself with more private expressions of sedition. In response to a parliamentary question in October 1922, Dawson Bates confirmed that letters had been censored 'for some time back ... to assist them [the northern government] in dealing with the exceptional situation'. The questioner, Mr Thompson Donald, pointed out that 'grave anxiety has been caused to Loyalists through their letters having been censored' and he demanded that the government 'be more careful in censoring the letters of loyal subjects'. The minister asked that any complaints be brought to his attention.[110] The system was fully functioning in 1923 when several pamphlets were intercepted at Enniskillen.[111] Even in the comparative calm of 1925, Dawson Bates insisted that 'correspondence for delivery to or emanating from persons in Northern Ireland suspected of engaging in seditious activity is liable to censorship ... the time has not yet arrived when this valuable precaution can be safely abandoned'. The work was carried out by two officials of the Ministry of Home Affairs under the supervision of a Post Office official.[112] As Northern Ireland did not control the Post Office, this could only have been done with the consent of the UK authorities. It also affected the Irish Free State. After a letter from Dublin to Donegal was opened in 1922, the two governments agreed that mail from one part of the Free State to another would not be censored while passing through Northern Ireland and that the southern post office would not detain mail for the north which did not originate in the twenty-six counties.[113] They later agreed that northern censors on the train from Belfast to Dublin would be allowed to take parcels off the train at Portadown so that any northern mail they contained could be censored before being sent on.[114]

A serious incident during the elections of 1923 raises questions as to whether the CASPA was used for purely political purposes. In a circular extolling the virtues of a Unionist candidate critical of Craig, several allegations were made accusing the Prime Minister of betraying the Union by meeting southern leaders and favouring Catholics in public appointments. Walter Magill, Principal Secretary at the Ministry of Home Affairs, drafted a note to the RUC in which he originally described the pamphlet as 'most objectionable and libellous', which it probably was, but he amended the letter to describe the circular as 'a seditious and criminal libel' for which the authors 'should be made amenable'. The change might seem merely rhetorical but by introducing the phrase 'seditious' he had opened up the possibility of the Special Powers Act being used in a political dispute. This is confirmed by his account of a discussion with the Chief Crown Solicitor who told him that to arrest the distributor would be 'a stretch' of the CASPA but 'he could however be "questioned" [his quotation marks] which might prove equally efficacious'.[115] A request was sent to the Postmaster in Belfast for permission to inspect the register of those who had delivered election literature for postage. He replied that this required a warrant from either the Governor of Northern Ireland or the Home Secretary in London.[116] Meanwhile the distributor of the documents had proved to be a boy of 16 who had simply handed out a handful after finding them on the street.[117] When the Ministry of Home Affairs attempted to get a warrant to examine the postal records it was rebuffed by the Imperial Secretary's Department: 'I am now told by them [the Home Office] that procedure by warrant in this case does not seem appropriate, and I am afraid that I cannot properly send on the warrant to the Governor.'[118] The whole embarrassing incident demonstrated both the dangers inherent in an act as broad as the CASPA and the tight limits to the sovereignty of the northern administration.

A crucial part of the government's security strategy was the imposition of curfews. While not primarily intended as a form of censorship they obviously had that effect by limiting the ability of the public to congregate. All curfews operated under the same basic rules: people in the area affected had to remain 'in their usual places of abode', visitors were required to stay in registered lodgings or to notify police of their whereabouts; inmates and employees in schools, hospitals and charitable institutions were allowed to remain at work and persons could be conveyed to hospital. The early focus for the curfew orders was Belfast, particularly areas such as Ardoyne and Marrowbone that had experienced significant disorder. Other contested urban areas were also affected. From April 1923, the curfew was extended to the six counties.[119] Police enforced the curfew and the evidence suggests that they took this duty seriously. In July 1922, for example, a patrol in Enniskillen shot a man who ran away when caught out after hours.[120] The law required, however, that the accused be actually caught in violation of the curfew, merely proving that he was not at his place of residence was not enough.[121] More compliant offenders were simply fined five to ten shillings by the courts, a leniency lamented by some Unionist papers.[122]

The curfew proved controversial, especially in quieter areas and this led to requests from Lurgan and Portrush urban councils to have it relaxed by half an hour to facilitate theatregoers and others.[123] The Council of Ulster Tourist Associations also asked for it to be relaxed for the Easter holidays in 1924.[124] Such calls went unheeded. The rules were unpopular with the nationalist community as evidenced by the controversy over midnight mass in Armagh Cathedral in 1924. Cardinal Logue applied to have the curfew relaxed to allow a midnight mass for Christmas on the grounds that 'there is absolutely no disturbance in this area'. The application was nonetheless refused on the orders of a 'higher authority' according to Logue who threatened to proceed regardless, if necessary by keeping the congregation in the cathedral until the curfew ended at 5 a.m. This threat was condemned as 'monstrous' by the Unionist press and Logue eventually backed down rather than risk defying the government directly.[125]

When in 1925 the government decided that things had settled down enough to allow them to abolish the curfew, some in the Unionist community were disappointed. Many felt that the timing was wrong as the Boundary Commission was soon due to report, while others extolled its beneficial impact on the community: men came home to their wives at a reasonable hour, the causes of temperance and health were aided and 'the greatest good of the greatest number' was promoted.[126] It was no coincidence that such sentiments were heard in the border areas, especially Fermanagh where the County and Urban Councils both demanded its return; the chairman of the latter demanded, with scant regard for constitutional or diplomatic niceties, that it be re-imposed for five miles either side of the border.[127] Dawson Bates was forced to defend his policy, pointing out that improving male behaviour, stopping street noise and keeping youths out of mischief were not the reasons for which the curfew had been imposed and the security situation no longer demanded its retention.[128]

The government did take action to control the large public meetings that were an important part of contemporary political life. This issue is somewhat problematic. All states have to police assemblies and prevent riots. On the other hand, it is a restriction of freedom of expression to prohibit an assembly because of its political or cultural associations. The problem in Northern Ireland was that the official reason given for prohibiting a march was almost always that it represented a threat to public order. In many cases this was the case: in 1922, for example, the Minister of Home Affairs introduced regulations restricting bands and processions in Belfast that did not have authorization from the police or the city commissioner. This regulation was issued for fear that such displays on routes where they were considered provocative would worsen the already bad situation in the city.[129] A similar concern led to the banning of a carnival in the city in 1923 as it was planned to hold it 'on the border between the two parties'.[130] Somewhat more doubtful were cases such as the ban on a concert in St Patrick's Hall, Portadown in January 1923. The ban was issued as the local RUC believed that money, raised ostensibly for a football team would be used for more sinister purposes.[131] Underlying this was a view that, although nationalist and republican parties were not banned, 'Sinn Féiners' should not be allowed to hold public meetings: this attitude led to the state preventing the opening of a hall in Lisnaskea in June 1923, even though the official cause was that the event would tend 'to disturb the peace and impose extra duty on the local police force.'[132]

The institutional opposition to expressions of nationalism can be seen in the debate with the Ministry of Home Affairs over whether to ban a performance of a play in Portaferry in November 1923. It was described as 'of a seditious character' and the artists were 'stated to have Sinn Féin tendencies'. The District Inspector of the RUC favoured a ban but the County Inspector demurred, arguing that 'its suppression would tend to stimulate seditious feeling in Portaferry which lately have been dormant'. His pragmatism won out over departmental paranoia and the play was performed; in fact the players had edited the play and the local RUC could find no fault with the performance which attracted several local Protestants.[133] The incident illustrated a view within the Ministry of Home Affairs which went far beyond a justifiable desire to hinder subversive activities and instead tended to see anything with a nationalist or republican tint as seditious.

This mentality also affected the attitude of the security forces to the display of flags and emblems. During the 1922 elections, the RUC in Derry, Tyrone and Fermanagh were ordered that 'as it is *possible* that a display of Sinn Féin flags during the election may lead to a breach of the peace, they should not be permitted [my emphasis]'.[134] This later drew the opinion in the Ministry of Home Affairs that, while it was 'a matter of policy' to seize flags, 'the legal right to order their removal where a breach of the peace is not apprehended seems doubtful'.[135] The RUC took a provision intended to prevent a real and present danger of a breach of the peace and extended it into a policy to cover all occasions where Sinn Féin flags were displayed. In practice the rules could be applied pragmatically. In 1924, the RUC had to police the arrival from Dublin of the remains of Joseph McKelvey, a senior Republican IRA man who had briefly been Chief of Staff of the anti-Treaty wing of the organization and had participated in the occupation of the Four Courts in Dublin. He had been executed by the Free State authorities in reprisal for the shooting of Sean Hales. Fearing that the coffin would be paraded through the streets wrapped in a flag, the authorities decided to have the flag removed while the coffin was in public but not to object if the flag covered it in the cemetery. This procedure was followed and few protests ensued but, the RUC reported, 'it could be observed from the demeanour of the crowd that determination was still there, and were it not for fear of the consequences would be as rampant as ever, to enforce their disloyal tendencies'.[136]

The victory of the state

The year 1923 was to prove a turning point for both governments. In the south, Republican resistance ebbed steadily until the death of Liam Lynch in April 1923 paved the way for an end to the military campaign in May. In the north, violence declined to about a third of its 1922 level.[137] The administrations had each won a victory over their opponents through brutal repression and the price was to be lasting division and resentment within both jurisdictions. They now faced the challenge of governing.

In both parts of Ireland there was a sense that the political chaos of the previous decade was reflected in a moral crisis. According to Rev. M.H. MacInerny, the editor of the *Irish Rosary*, 'the turmoil of the last four years [1918–22] has crippled the [vigilance] association's activities with the result that the banned [sic] Sunday papers now circulate almost as freely as ever'.[138] The *Irish Catholic* described the state of the country in 1924 as 'a pathological crisis' as the nation was 'convalescing from the fever and prostration of two wars'.[139] The vigilance committees seem to have lost some of their zeal: Eason received less correspondence from them,[140] and important members like Richard Devane SJ began to concentrate on seeking legal reform. During this period, the British Home Secretary, Sir William Joynson-Hicks, was similarly concerned with indecent literature and he presided over an increase in the number of prosecutions for the importation of indecent books.[141]

The northern press was also active in the matter. An article in the nationalist *Derry People* in 1922 that was reprinted from the *Catholic Truth Annual* put forward arguments that would soon become familiar. The author condemned 'a class [of literature] emanating from no well-known author of established literary repute, and which in style or the manner of treatment of the subject can hardly be called classic'. By this he meant the 'abominably written' modern novel. Books, he asserted, should not contain 'moral or immoral conundrums', 'mysteries of psychology', 'bigamy, divorce nor hereditary disease'. All of these themes were prominent in the books that flooded bookstalls and libraries. He informed his readers that 95 per cent of books borrowed from libraries were novels and that these were not the classics, by which he meant Dickens, Trollope or Scott, but '*risqué* and frequently prurient' books. He claimed that the borrowers were mostly women.[142]

In January 1922, *Our Boys*, a magazine published by the Christian Brothers, began a campaign for clean literature. It published resolutions signed by forty-two newsagents, all in the Free State, pledging not to stock 'literature calculated to lower the Catholic mind of the young'. By February, the newsagents' representative had expressed a willingness to set up a committee of their members, the vigilance associations and the board of film censors (presumably local authority censors).[143] In March the congregation assembled at St Patrick's Cathedral in Armagh to receive the papal benediction from Cardinal Logue heard a sermon by Fr Joseph from Dublin on the perils of obscene literature.[144] The Roman Catholic Bishops' Lenten pastorals of 1924 served as a call to arms on the subject of public morality. Although they reserved their strongest barbs for the evil of immodest dancing, the hierarchy also condemned 'unclean' literature in no uncertain terms. The Bishop of Clogher alleged that thirty tons of newspapers reporting 'the scandals of the world' were 'dumped on our shores' every week. He connected this sort of journalism to the 'pleasure-mad, self-gratifying, materialistic mode of life' of the modern age epitomized by the lifestyles surrounding the theatre, cinema, billiard club and jazz music. Cardinal Logue, in Armagh, condemned the decline in modesty he had observed among women, while Archbishop Byrne of Dublin advocated a revival of a strong, Catholic public spirit to combat these evils.[145] The Archbishop of Tuam, addressing a Catholic Truth Society conference later that year, called for the exclusion from Ireland of 'corrupting books'.[146] Not every locality experienced as much pressure. Two sermons by different priests in Kilkenny both pointed out that the demand for Sunday papers and novels in the town was unusually low.[147]

Protestant churchmen also raised the issue. Rev. W.A. James from Belfast preached against Sunday papers which 'catered for low moral taste, and as far as he could see, contained mainly accounts of murder trials and divorce actions'.[148] The *Irish Churchman*, commenting on a recent murder case, recorded 'our protest against the disgusting and demoralising manner in which these facts were dangled in the public eye, especially in the columns of English newspapers'. The paper later carried an article attacking such papers for their irreverent attitude to Christianity.[149] The Presbyterian *Witness* commented sadly that 'there seems to be a growing habit of buying and reading the Sunday newspapers'. At the Belfast synod the Rev. J.W. Gibbs complained that 'the Sunday newspaper was not only on sale but regularly bought and read by their people'. He mentioned the issue again the next year.[150]

Events abroad had some effect on the debate. In 1923, the Second International Convention on Obscene Publications was signed in Geneva. This agreement failed to define obscenity due to a dispute between Britain and France over jurisdiction and also left open the question of whether publications advocating birth control were obscene. It did form an agreement, at least in principle, that countries would act to end the trade in obscene publications and prosecute those involved.[151] The British government consulted Northern Ireland about applying the convention to the province. The Home Office advised the northern cabinet that 'all parts of the British Empire should co-operate in bringing this disgraceful trade to an end'.[152] Northern Ireland agreed and British ratification ensued. This brought the UK, New Zealand, South Africa and India into the convention.[153]

In the UK, Sunday papers came under increasing criticism for their lurid reporting of divorce cases. In 1922, the Home Secretary promised action to curtail such publications. The *Irish News* welcomed this as 'not too soon' and hoped the Irish Free State would also act. It made its feelings about its less savoury fellow newspapers clear and advocated extending censorship to 'other matters' as 'the decent public do not want the wretched stuff which attracts the coppers of the mob'.[154] The Unionist *Down Reporter* agreed with such sentiments, especially after the reporting of the notorious *Russell* v. *Russell* divorce case of 1921 in which a man had sued for divorce claiming that the birth of a child to his wife proved her infidelity as they had never consummated their marriage. It claimed that in every other country it was impossible to print anything other than the results of a divorce case and that the excesses of the British popular press were 'unparalleled possibly in any country in the world'.[155] It is interesting that there were no calls for exclusively Northern Irish legislation. The northern government had no control over what was published in Britain and the lack of agitation for censorship of this sort in the region suggests that newspapers published there were not among the offenders. This is confirmed by reading Northern Irish newspapers for the period. A letter to the *Down Recorder* in 1923 congratulated them on 'not following the bad example of their British contemporaries'. The paper's editorial argued that 'the Sunday newspapers are such sinners … that it is little wonder that a ban has been put upon them in various parts of Ireland'.[156]

Film censorship in the south

Moral campaigners were also deeply concerned about cinema. As we have seen, film censorship in Ireland was carried out by local councils. By 1922 there were between twelve and twenty municipal censors in Dublin at any time, nominated by the Vigilance Association, Priests' Social Guild and Dr Gregg, the Church of Ireland Archbishop. The system cost £350 a year to run which was raised by tripling the cost of cinema licences to £10 10s. This made the film exhibitors unhappy; they argued that the Cinematograph Act 1909 allowed a fee of only £1. Had they been proved correct, the council would have needed legislative sanction to continue its censorship.[157] The system was not running smoothly anyway and the council passed a motion in May 1922 calling for its replacement by 'a Board of Film Censors for all Ireland'. In November 1922, a deputation from the IVA, Priests' Social Guild and the Church of Ireland addressed the council and criticized the censors.[158]

Many other local authorities had systems of censorship, although the standards and rules varied greatly. For example, the licence issued by Tipperary South Riding was considered reasonable both by the cinema owners and the Department of Home Affairs. It forbade any film 'likely to be injurious to morality or to encourage or incite to crime or to lead to disorder or to be offensive to public feeling, or which contains any offensive representations of living persons'. It also required that publicly accessible areas of the cinema be well lit, and that films passed by the licensing authority be shown in the form approved by the censor. The regulations also extended to posters. The licence issued by Clonmel Borough in 1921 was considered too restrictive. It forbade cinema opening on Sundays, Christmas, the last three days of Holy Week and outside the hours of noon and 11 p.m. A synopsis of every film to be exhibited had to be given to the committee of censors three days before the performance and one month's notice of forthcoming bookings was required. Children under 14 were banned from all shows after 7 p.m. The cinema owners resented such regulations as they treated them differently from dance halls or theatres.[159]

Representatives of the Roman Catholic Church also expressed their unhappiness with the state of the cinemas. Galway priests condemned the 'virtually lawless passions', divorce stories and the 'reckless gaiety of Bohemian life' displayed on the screen and called for a municipal censorship.[160] The Bishop of Galway, Thomas O'Dea, took up the issue in his 1922 Lenten pastoral. He feared that if young people 'feed their eyes and their minds on sexual indulgence whether at the cinema, or in books, or papers or in sex companionship, they will eventually become degraded, and brutalized and corrupted'.[161]

In March 1923, Kevin O'Higgins, the Minister for Home Affairs met a deputation representing the IVA, the Priests' Social Guild and the Roman Catholic, Protestant, Episcopalian and Presbyterian Churches. They sought a national film censorship to replace those of the local authorities, which, they alleged, had broken down. They also wanted government licensing of the cinemas and a special levy on them to finance the new system. They argued that these measures were made necessary by the youth of Irish cinema audiences and the effect of undesirable films upon them:

> It is obvious that the mental and moral outlook of those who frequent such picture houses must be largely formed by what they see in them ... It is evidently undesirable that our people should be accustomed to see and applaud scenes of murder, robbery, violence of every kind, offensive suggestiveness [and] sexual immorality.

The deputation had no faith in self-censorship by the film trade. They believed that greed would overcome even a well-intentioned cinema owner.[162]

The Free State Department of Home Affairs consulted local authorities in spring 1923 about the idea of a national film censorship. Twenty-four expressed their approval, several in strong terms. Youghal UDC described the proposal as 'most essential in the interests of public morals',[163] the Mullingar Town Commissioners considered it 'very advisable',[164] Cork City Council described it as 'a proper step',[165] while Bray UDC, having consulted the local Vigilance Committee, not surprisingly called it 'a crying necessity for some years past'.[166] Kilkenny Corporation decided to 'take no action in the matter'.[167] This may have been due to the influence of Senator Peter de Loughry, Mayor of Kilkenny, who was opposed to film censorship and chaired that meeting of the Corporation.[168] Wexford Corporation opposed the plan. It preferred its own system whereby five censors attended films for free 'as they may find it convenient' to ensure that nothing immoral was shown. 'Considering the state of the national exchequer', they felt it was 'inappropriate' to create a national censorship.[169] In fact the plan envisaged involved charging a fee for censoring films, thus making it self-financing.

Kevin O'Higgins introduced the Censorship of Films Bill in the Dáil on 3 May 1923. He referred specifically to the 'thoroughly representative deputation' that had visited him and to the call from the Dublin Municipal Council for a national censorship a year earlier. He also emphasized the fact that the system would be financially self-supporting.[170] A week later, as he introduced the bill at its second stage, he again mentioned public dissatisfaction with the local censors and outlined his proposals for reform. There would be a prior, state-run censorship by a single official censor. If the film renter disagreed with the censor's decision he could appeal to an Appeals Board. The bill ruled out appeals to the board from the public and O'Higgins suggested that if members of the public disagreed with the censor they should go to their TDs. The minister presented the bill as enjoying widespread support, although he admitted that the film renters were uneasy about paying for the process.[171] With 150 cinemas in Ireland, and 31 in Dublin alone, attended by some 20,000 people every day, he argued, it was unsurprising that local control had failed. O'Higgins envisaged that the censor would act according to 'the average outlook of decent, respectable people' which would reflect the 'improvement in the social standard' since the eighteenth century.[172]

Thomas Johnson, leader of the Labour Party and, in the absence of de Valera and his followers, of the opposition, decided not to fight the bill but he did express some doubts about the scheme. Based on his own experiences of 'trying to make certain films unpopular' he questioned the efficacy of 'this kind of censorship'. He pointed out that nearly all films shown in Ireland were already censored by the BBFC and he was concerned that the clause in the bill banning films 'contrary to good morals or social order' might be applied to productions about property relations.[173]

William Magennis, TD for the National University of Ireland and Professor of Metaphysics at UCD, gave one of the few speeches to explore the thinking behind film censorship. Unusually, despite being a staunch moral conservative, he started from the basis that cinema was an art form. An educated community would have no need of censors, he claimed, but 'we are not an ideal community'. Instead, 'works of art are "occasions of sin for some people"' and a standard of art 'applicable with regard to the individual spectator is not applicable to the whole crowded audience, particularly mixed audiences that witness in the same city Dante's *Inferno* and Charlie Chaplin'. The censor could not afford to act with 'liberality and breadth of mind' or 'appreciation of the photographer's art' when dealing with the 'general audience' threatened by the 'veiled presentation of vice'. Few people could read 'the worst French novels' but many could go to the cinema. Only education immunized a man to such threats. Magennis clearly saw censorship in class terms; the 'general audience' was to be protected from things that should only be seen by the educated – which in 1923 meant the privileged.[174]

The bill moved to the committee stage where Johnson attempted to alter the definition of an objectionable film from 'contrary to good morals or social order' to 'contrary to public morality'. He was trying to ensure that left-wing films would not be banned. The term 'public morality' was taken from the Free State constitution and carried no odour of politics. Although O'Higgins claimed that the original words were 'very innocent' he accepted the amendment.[175] Johnson also suggested that the Appeals Board should overturn the censor's ban unless it unanimously voted to uphold it, thus establishing that 'the "prisoner" should have the benefit of the doubt'. O'Higgins rejected this idea strenuously. He feared that it would make the whole system unworkable, especially if the censor and a clear majority of the Appeals Board wished to ban a film. He did agree to increase the size of the board to nine.[176] Johnson still advocated that in case of a tied vote, the film be permitted on the grounds of '"in all things doubtful, liberty."' O'Higgins refused but assured him that 'there will be no war on new ideas but rather on old and unsavoury ideas'.[177]

The measure passed the Seanad quickly. De Loughry stated that the industry welcomed it although he did not. He also extracted a promise from Ernest Blythe, who was taking the bill in O'Higgins's absence, that fees would be reduced for those films previously passed by the Dublin censors.[178] Blythe rejected a proposal to exclude members of the film business from the Appeals Board but promised that the minister would never appoint such people anyway. He also refused to exclude children under sixteen from cinemas, although this had been demanded by pro-censorship campaigners.[179] This suggests that the government saw the bill as a middle way between the demands of the pro-censorship activists and the film trade.

The press responded favourably to the new law. The *Cork Weekly Examiner* welcomed 'real and effective control of Irish cinemas by Irish authority'. The *Irish Catholic*, which was a vigorous critic of the film industry, praised the government's fight against the 'moral plague' of bad films. The paper did consider that cinema had great potential for education and pointed to the USA, France, Germany and the dominions as examples of countries where the state had taken action to control films. The *Irish Times* considered the proposals 'shrewd and sensible'. It accepted the logic of having a single censor who would be swift and decisive and also agreed that restricting access to the appeals process to the film renters would prevent frivolous complaints. Above all it advised the prospective censor to be moderate, hoping that if he had 'good taste and a vigilant eye and is free from fads, he will not be a bad censor'. It particularly hoped that the censor would tackle films whose 'long-drawn-out ineptness, vulgarity and triviality' was a greater danger to the man on the street than more obviously immoral material.[180] The *Church of Ireland Gazette* made no mention of the new law. This may suggest that there was no great controversy about film censorship on the southern Protestant side.

Twenty-seven people applied for the post of film censor, four of whom were women. Of the candidates, five had experience as municipal censors, five were connected to the cinema business, three were artists, three had political backgrounds on the pro-Treaty side, three mentioned connections to Roman Catholic lay organizations and three had experience as journalists. Five had no special qualifications. More applicants emphasized their interest in films than stressed their moral qualifications. The authorities decided to exclude both members of the film trade and those who had campaigned for the establishment of the censorship. It was probably on this basis that the application of Frank O'Reilly, secretary of the Catholic Truth Society of Ireland (CTSI), was rejected despite his claim to have had the support of the Catholic hierarchy.[181]

James Montgomery, a man with no obvious qualifications, was selected. Fifty-three years old and educated by the Christian Brothers in Westland Row, Montgomery had worked in the Alliance and Dublin Consumers' Gas Company until he was forced out by ill health.[182] At the time of his appointment he was a member of the Standing Committee of Cumann na nGaedheal.[183] He was a friend of Oliver St John Gogarty, and his neighbour, Léon Ó Broin, described how they would exchange 'witty impromptus which may have been prepared with some care'.[184] Writing on Montgomery's behalf, Ernest Blythe's wife asked O'Higgins to give him the job on account of his young family and loyal service to the pro-Treaty party. She also pointed out that he was 'a man of very considerable culture'. Montgomery later revealed that he had given a private paper around this time arguing that the main threat facing Irish culture was not Anglicization but 'Los Angelesicization' and that he had also contributed anonymous articles on the subject to the *Irish Statesman*.[185] It is very likely that these views would have been known to his allies in the government. The decision meant that the standards for film censorship would be decided by a man lacking a background in either the vigilance campaigns of the past or the realities of the film trade.

Free State film censorship in action

James Montgomery faced immediate opposition from the film exhibitors who disputed the fees they were asked to pay. Renters and exhibitors agreed not to show officially censored films, and *The Hunchback of Notre Dame* was boycotted because it had been submitted. The Attorney General recommended prosecutions but the police found that witnesses did not wish to come forward as the trade hoped for an out of court settlement. The threat of police action was effective and the boycott ended.[186] The dispute caused the IVA and the Priest's Social Guild to publicly support the censor. The *Irish Catholic* condemned the 'control of Jewish and cosmopolitan financiers' over the film business and asserted that 'the official censorship is as necessary as are sanitary laws'.[187]

The first few years of the censorship established the procedures under which different types of film would be regulated. The Department of Justice agreed that trade shows would not be subject to censorship as they were not open to the public.[188] Pathé Ltd made representations about its newsreel *Pathé Gazette*. As it was the only topical news film depicting Irish events and was not very profitable, the company asked that it be exempt from censorship fees. This view was supported by W.T. Cosgrave and the Department of Publicity. The Secretary of the Department of Home Affairs, Henry O'Friel, also agreed that 'news films should not be censored'.[189] The legislation did not allow for a full exemption so a reduced rate, half that for a normal film, was charged for newsreels and the censor agreed to make only the minimum changes necessary.[190]

The special rates for news films inspired the distributors of weekly serials to seek similar treatment. As the films were only delivered on Saturdays before being shown on Mondays, the trade hoped for concessions. They found the Department of Home Affairs unsympathetic and were told to get their deliveries in earlier. Montgomery insisted that 'all episodes in a serial should be censored. There are many complaints of the unhealthy sensationalism of these pictures, and I propose adopting a very exacting attitude when dealing with future imports.'[191]

Film Censorship in Northern Ireland

While Northern Ireland was not free of voices condemning the cinemas, they were neither as well organized nor as powerful as those in the south. An article in the *Irish Churchman* expressed the common view that film 'vitiates the character in the young, and destroys all hope and opportunity for the development of the better qualities of the mind'.[192] The *Northern Whig* carried a report of a speech at the Educational Association conference in which it was argued that 'it is a defect of the cinema that utterly false aspects of life may be presented, familiarizing spectators with garish travesties of truth without any call upon the mind or the attention'.[193] Non-subscribing Presbyterians were particularly incensed that a church in Newtownards had not only been sold but had been turned into a cinema.[194]

Northern local authorities were reluctant to take on any responsibilities that might force them to raise the rates.[195] This tendency discouraged them from engaging in censorship. There was a film censorship in Belfast, carried out by the Police Committee of Belfast Corporation, and cinemas were closed on Sundays in some towns such as Omagh.[196] Belfast also had special children's cinemas where films were censored by a committee of women.[197] In July 1923 the Home Office in London sent a circular to the British local authorities with the aim of producing 'substantial uniformity' of local cinema licence regulations.[198] The Home Office also suggested changes in the model conditions it had first recommended in 1917. Now it recommended that no film be permitted without the consent of the local authority unless it had received a 'U' certificate from the BBFC.[199]

The circular was not binding in Northern Ireland and the Ministry of

Home Affairs officials there were not sure initially what censorship powers the northern government possessed.[200] They considered two approaches: local authorities could follow the Home Office's model conditions, or the government would have to set up a film censorship for the region. Despite the 'obvious advantages' of a centralized censorship, it was felt that 'so vital a difference in practice between Great Britain and Northern Ireland would dislocate the trade and would give rise to much opposition both from the trade and the local authorities'.[201] The police had no responsibility for the moral character of films but also felt that:

> there does not appear to be any necessity for a more stringent censorship of cinematograph films … None of the films shown can be said to be of a dubious moral type, and generally they are not of a character which would tend to encourage crime … The precautions taken [in Britain] … to ensure that film pictures shown in Great Britain are clean, is [sic] sufficient protection for Ulster.[202]

The Ministry decided to issue a circular to the licensing authorities. It emphasized that the minister 'doesn't want to interfere in any way' with the rights of local bodies but recommended that they adopt the model conditions suggested by the Home Office.[203] The secretary of the department, Sam Watt, believed that 'it would be much better, if anything is to be done, to have a central censorship than to entrust such decisions to local bodies whose decisions may vary'. He warned that this should 'wait until some form of central censorship is established in ENGLAND' [his capitals].[204]

Although there were many in Northern Ireland who objected to cinema or to specific films, they were not as well organized or as effective as their counterparts in the south in the 1920s. The Churches were all-Ireland institutions and Roman Catholic teaching on the subject applied as much in Belfast as in Dublin. That Church did not have a relationship with the northern government that would have allowed it to press for censorship, however. The Protestant Churches, as in the south, were not opposed to censorship but it was a lower priority than their campaigns on temperance and education. Opposition to cinema came from isolated individuals and groups and there is no evidence that it was supported by the loyal institutions with any strength.

The first objective of each of the new governments was to fight those that threatened their rule and their states. To them censorship was at first merely a weapon in that war, not an end unto itself. Censorship in this context had two purposes. It was a form of propaganda, allowing the state to control the way in which both sides in the conflict were described and how much its opponents could say to the public. It also had a more subtle use in the procuring of convictions; it was far easier to prove that an accused person had possession of an illegal publication than that he or she was a member of an illegal organization. As the situation stabilized and violence diminished, demands began to come from outside the government for a campaign of moral reform. The two governments responded differently to this challenge because of their different circumstances. Northern Ireland had not been set up to be a proactive state but rather to defend against Catholic domination. There was little appetite among its ministers for grand schemes of any sort, especially ones that would have put it out of sync with the rest of the UK. The south had been established on the premise that an independent Ireland could do better than a British province, and censorship was to become part of the exercise of that independence. As the Free State became calmer and more peaceful, there was an opportunity to put that ideal into practice.

NOTES

1. David Fitzpatrick, *The two Irelands, 1912–1939* (Oxford: Oxford University Press, 1998), p. 119.
2. Marie Coleman, 'Biographical note on Piaras Béaslaí (1881–1965)', *National Library of Ireland Collection List No.44: Piaras Béaslaí Papers*, p.ii.
3. L. M. Cullen, *Eason & Son: a history* (Dublin: Eason & Son Ltd, 1989), p.214.
4. Eason & Son Ltd to Béaslaí, 14 July 1922 and after, National Library of Ireland (NLI), Piaras Béaslaí Papers, Ms. 33915 (14).
5. Charles Eason to Béaslaí, 12 July 1922, ibid.
6. Cullen, *Eason & Son*, p. 216.
7. Eason to Béaslaí, 12 July 1922, NLI, Béaslaí Papers, Ms. 33915 (14).
8. P. Hoey to Béaslaí, 26 July 1922, ibid., Ms. 33915 (16).
9. Cathal O'Shannon to Eason & Son Ltd, 26 July 1922, Cathal O'Shannon papers, Irish Labour History Society Museum and Archive, COS/51.
10. 'Memorandum on the work of the censor's department', [no date], NLI, Béaslaí Papers, Ms. 33915 (8).
11. Béaslaí to Superintendent, Sorting Office, GPO, ibid., Ms. 33915 (6).
12. Commandant General, Army Publicity Director to Mr Butler [censor's office], 15 Aug. 1922, ibid.
13. Acting Military Secretary to Commander-in-Chief to the Director of Intelligence, 2 Aug. 1922, University College Dublin Archives (UCDA), Mulcahy Papers, P7/B/4/83.
14. 'Military censorship, general instructions' [no date], Desmond FitzGerald Papers, UCDA, P80/282(12/2).
15. Norris Goddard to Béaslaí, 22 July 1922, NLI, Béaslaí Papers, Ms. 33915 (12).
16. Béaslaí to Postmaster General, 28 Oct. 1922, ibid., Ms. 33915 (8).
17. Béasaí to Adjutant General, 22 July 1922, ibid., Ms. 33915 (10).
18. Gearoid O'Sullivan to Béaslaí, 26 July 1922, ibid.
19. J.J. Hart to Béaslaí, 13 July 1922, ibid., Ms. 33915 (11).
20. Lester to Béaslaí, 14 July 1922, ibid., Ms. 33915 (13).
21. Béaslaí to Adjutant General, 19 July 1922, ibid., Ms. 33915 (5).
22. Béaslaí to Mr Murphy, 9 Aug. 1922, ibid., Ms. 33915 (6).
23. Béaslaí to Collins, 13 July 1922, ibid., Ms. 33915 (5).
24. Superintendent J.J. Purcell to Chief Commissioner Dublin Metropolitan Police [hereafter DMP], 16 July 1922, National Archives of Ireland [NAI], Department of Justice [DJUS], H/84/7.
25. Béaslaí to exhibitors, 17 July 1922, NLI, Béaslaí Papers, Ms. 33915 (5).
26. Béaslaí, 'Memorandum No. 3' [n.d.], ibid., Ms. 33915 (10).
27. Béaslaí to Superintendent Sorting Office, GPO, 21 July 1922, ibid.
28. Béaslaí to Minister of Defence, 27 July 1922, ibid., Ms. 33915 (10).

29. C.S. Quinlan [Acting Military Censor] to Editor *Waterford News*, 18 Aug. 1922, UCDA, FitzGerald papers, P80/282 (11/4).
30. Béaslaí to Desmond FitzGerald, 6 Sept. 1922, ibid., P80/282(12/1).
31. Béaslaí to Officer in Charge of Contracts at Portobello Barracks, 15 Aug. 1922, NLI, Béaslaí papers, Ms. 33915 (6).
32. 'Memo re: Dublin Press', 29 Aug. 1922, UCDA, FitzGerald papers, P80/295(35).
33. Béaslaí to *Daily Express, Irish Independent, Freeman's Journal*, 5 Sept. 1922, NLI, Béaslaí Papers, Ms. 33915 (7).
34. Béaslaí to Editor *World's Pictorial News*, 13 Sept. 1922, ibid.
35. Béaslaí, 'Memorandum on the inquest of Patrick Mannion [26] Sept. 1922', UCDA, FitzGerald Papers, P80/285(14).
36. *Irish Independent*, 19 and 20 Sept. 1922, ibid., P80/285(10).
37. FitzGerald to Collins, 25 July 1922, ibid., P80/283(1).
38. Collins to FitzGerald, 26 July 1922, ibid., P80/283(2).
39. Béaslaí to Commander-in-Chief, 4 July 1922, NLI, Béaslaí Papers, Ms. 33915 (8).
40. Commander-in-Chief to Béaslaí, 12 Oct. 1922, ibid.
41. Béaslaí, letter to newspaper editors, 13 Oct. 1922, ibid., Ms. 33915(8).
42. Béaslaí to Postmaster General, 28 Oct. 1922,. ibid.
43. *Northern Whig*, 20 Jan. 1922.
44. Ibid., 26 Jan. 1922.
45. Ibid., 8 April 1922.
46. Malcom Brodie, *The Tele: a history of the Belfast Telegraph* (Belfast: Blackstaff Press, 1995), p.42.
47. *Northern Whig*, 22 April 1922.
48. John Horgan, *Irish Media: a critical history since 1922* (London: R the Editor *Freeman's Journal*, 28 Oct. 1922, UCDA, FitzGerald Papers, P80/281(13).
49. Assistant Adjutant General for GHQ IRA [Ernie O'Malley] to the editor, *Freeman's Journal*, 28 October 1922, UCDA, FitzGerald Papers, P80/281 (13).
50. L.O'S [Assistant Adjutant General] to Cmdt General Ó Murthuille, 30 Oct. 1922, Béaslaí Papers, Ms. 33915(10).
51. Press Room, 'Memo', 6 Nov. 1922, UCDA FitzGerald Papers, P80/295(44).
52. FitzGerald, 'Memo re: Dublin Press', ibid., P80/295(45).
53. Station Report, Mountjoy, 20 March 1923, NAI, DJUS, H84/13.
54. P.J. Munden to Minister for Home Affairs, 3 April 1923, ibid.
55. DMP Station Report, 23 March 1923 and 29 March 1923, ibid.
56. Kevin O'Higgins to P.J. Munden, 5 April 1923, ibid.
57. Director General's Office CID to Henry O'Friel, 13 April 1923, ibid., H180/11.
58. S.J. Connolly (ed.), *The Oxford Companion to Irish History* (Oxford: Oxford University Press, 1998), p. 40.
59. James Kelly, 'Memories of the *Irish News* 1929', in Eamon Phoenix (ed.), *A century of Northern Life: the* Irish News *and 100 years of Ulster History, 1890s–1990s* (Belfast: Ulster Historical Foundation, 1995), p.41.
60. Maj. Gen. Cameron to Secretary to the Cabinet, 20 March 1922, PRONI, Northern Ireland Cabinet Files CAB/9B/83/1.
61. Civil Authorities (Special Powers) Act 1922.
62. Colm Campbell, *Emergency law in Ireland, 1918–1925* (Oxford: Claredon Press, 1994), p.333.
63. Ibid., pp. 383–405.
64. 'Restoration of Order in Ireland Act 1920': memorandum by Army Council No. 2, 16 Oct. 1923, British National Archives (NAGB), Home Office HO/45/19,666.
65. Northern Ireland House of Commons (NIHC) debates, Vol.II, 21 March 1922, 89.
66. Ibid., Vol.II, 23 March 1922, 185–6.
67. Northern Ireland Senate (NIS) debates, Vol.II, 6 April 1922.
68. Ibid., pp.325.
69. *Belfast Newsletter*, 15 March 1922.
70. *Irish News*, 22 March 1922.
71. Ibid., 24 March 1922.
72. Ibid., 6 April 1922.
73. Ibid., 1 April 1922.

74. *Belfast Gazette*, March–April 1922.
75. *Irish News*, 19 April 1922, PRONI, CAB/4/40.
76. Craig to Londonderry, 23 May 1922, ibid., CAB/4/44/10.
77. Cabinet Conclusions, 16 May 1922, ibid., CAB/4/42.
78. Ibid., 20 May 1922, ibid., CAB/4/43.
79. A.P. Magill, 'Memo', 30 May 1922, Northern Ireland Ministry Home Affairs Files (NIMHA), PRONI, H/5/544.
80. A. Solly Flood to Secretary, 1 June 1922, NIMHA, ibid.
81. E.M. Archdale to Winston Churchill, 24 May 1922, NAGB, HO45/19665.
82. C.R., 'Censorship in Northern Ireland', 14 June 1922, ibid.
83. NIMHA, PRONI, HA/5/558.
84. H. T[opping] to Lt Col Maylor, 18 April 1922; S. W[att] to Divisional Commander RIC, 24 April 1922, ibid., HA/32/1/31.
85. H. Topping to Attorney General, 16 July 1922; H. Topping, Minute, 21 Aug. 1922, ibid., HA/5/994.
86. R.P. Pim, note 23 June 1922; Haldane, Minute, 1 July 1922, ibid., HA32/1/192.
87. A. Henry for District Inspector, report, 13 Sept. 1922, ibid., HA/5/979.
88. District Inspector's report, RIC, Newry, 7 Aug.1922, ibid., HA/51/16.
89. *Down Recorder*, 19 Aug. 1922.
90. *Irish Catholic*, 12 Aug. 1922; Minute [no author name], 16 Aug. 1922; Watt to Blackmore, 21 Aug. 1922; Blackmore to Watt, 1 Sept. 1922, NIMHA, HA/5/260.
91. A.P. Magill, note on letter from D.G.W. Cowell to the Secretary to the Ministry of Home Affairs, 26 Sept. 1922, ibid.
92. S. Watt, Minute, 26 Jan. 1923, ibid., HA/5/307.
93. Campbell, *Emergency Law in Ireland*, p. 282; J.R. Moorhead, Minute, 7 Aug. 1922, NIMHA, PRONI, HA/5/643.
94. J.W.E. Poynting to the Secretary, 7 Feb., 4 April 1923, 26 May 1923, ibid, HA/5/307.
95. J.W.E. Poynting to Chief Crown Solicitor, 19 May 1923, ibid., HA/5/366.
96. Inspector General RUC to the Secretary, Ministry of Home Affairs, 20 Aug. 1923; J.W. E. Poynting, Minute, 21 March 1924, ibid., HA/5/549.
97. District Inspector RUC to the Secretary, Ministry of Home Affairs, 22 Dec. 1924; A.P. Magill note, 29 Dec. 1924, ibid., HA/5/549.
98. J.W.E. Poynting note to letter, District Inspector RUC to Secretary, Ministry of Home Affairs, 18 July 1923, ibid., HA/5/1287.
99. D. Trimble [editor *Armagh Guardian*] to Dawson Bates, 19 Sept. 1923; R.D. Megaw, Minute, 22 Sept. 1923, ibid., HA/5/1311.
100. Denis Kennedy, *The widening gulf: Northern attitudes to the independent Irish state, 1919–49* (Belfast: Blackstaff Press, 1988), pp.14–17.
101. HC RUC Armagh report, 28 June 1922, 7 July 1922, 19 July 1922, NIMHA, PRONI, HA/5/1478.
102. RUC report to District Inspector Armagh, 29 Aug. 1922; J.W.E. Poynting to Inspector General RUC, 19 Sept. 1922, ibid., HA/5/1481.
103. District Inspector's report RUC, 13 April 1923; J.W.E. Poynting, minute, 2 May 1923, ibid., HA/5/344.
104. Order 13 June 1923, ibid., HA/5/369
105. *Ulster Gazette*, 1 July 1922.
106. Minutes J.W.E. Poynting, 25 Aug., 5 Sept. 1922; Order under Civil Authorities (Special Powers) Act 1922, 12 Dec. 1922, NIMHA, PRONI, , HA/5/1014.
107. J.W.E. Poynting to Attorney General, 8 Aug. 1924, ibid., HA/5/478.
108. J.W.E. Poynting to Attorney General, 7 Aug. 1924, ibid., HA/5/477.
109. *Belfast Newsletter*, 22 Sept. 1925, ibid., HA/5/510.
110. NIHC debates, Vol.II, 27 Oct. 1922, 1136.
111. Gilfillan (District Inspector for Inspector General RUC) to Minister of Home Affairs, 4 April 1923, NIMHA, PRONI, HA/5/334.
112. NIHC debates, Vol.VI, 28 April 1925, 223.
113. Devonshire to Healy, 11 Dec. 1922; J.J. Walsh to Cosgrave, 13 Dec. 1922 NAI, DJUS, H197/10.
114. L. Simon [GPO London] to the Secretary, GPO Dublin, 1 June 1923, ibid.
115. W.A. Magill to Inspector General RUC, 6 Dec. 1923; W.A. Magill, Minute, 11 Dec. [1923], NIMHA, PRONI, HA/32/1/409.

116. S. Watt to Postmaster, Belfast, 11 Dec. 1923; T.M. MacDowell to Minister of Home Affairs, 12 Dec. 1923, ibid.
117. Commissioner RUC to Minister Home Affairs, 13 Dec. 1923, ibid.
118. Tallent to W.B. Spender, 29 Dec. 1923, ibid.
119. *Belfast Gazette*, 28 April to 19 May 1922.
120. *Fermanagh Times*, 13 July 1922.
121. *Witness*, 21 March 1924.
122. *Fermanagh Times*, 3 Aug. 1922.
123. *Ulster Gazette*, 11 Nov. 1922.
124. *Witness*, 21 March 1924.
125. *Irish Catholic Directory* 1924, p. 545; *Tyrone Constitution*, 5 Jan. 1923.
126. *Fermanagh Times*, 1 Jan. 1925.
127. Ibid., 8 Jan. 1925; *Derry People*, 17 Jan. 1925.
128. *Ulster Gazette*, 24 Jan. 1925.
129. Divisional Commander to Secretary, Ministry of Home Affairs, 26 April 1922, NIMHA, PRONI, HA/5/945.
130. H. Topping, Minute, 23 March 1923, ibid., HA/5/1261.
131. Capt. H. Andrew (RUC Portadown) to County Inspector Armagh, 24 Jan. 1923, ibid., HA/5/1173.
132. *Down Recorder*, 23 June 1923.
133. W.A. Magill, Minute, 23 Nov. 1923; J. McReady, County Inspector to District Inspector McDaid, 20 Nov. 1923; Report of Sgt P. Byrne, 24 Nov. 1923, NIMHA, PRONI, HA/5/135.
134. R.T. Hamilton (County Inspector) for Inspector General, RUC to County Inspectors for Derry, Tyrone and Fermanagh, 14 Nov. 1922, ibid., HA/5/1383.
135. J.W.E. Poynting, Minute, 31 March 1925, ibid.
136. A.P. Magill to Inspector General, RUC, 29 Oct. 1924; E. Gilfillan (District Inspector) for Inspector General to the Secretary, Ministry of Home Affairs, 1 Nov. 1924, ibid., HA/5/1383.
137. Fitzpatrick, *The two Irelands*, p.119.
138. M.H. MacInerny, 'Catholic lending libraries', *Irish Ecclesiastical Record*, 5th series, Vol.19 (Jan.–June 1922), p.562.
139. *Irish Catholic*, 23 February 1924.
140. Cullen, *Eason & Son*, p.62.
141. Alan Travis, *Bound and gagged: a secret history of obscenity in Britain* (London: Profile, 2000), p.87.
142. *Derry People*, 14 Oct. 1922.
143. Cullen, *Eason and Son*, pp.261–2.
144. *Irish Catholic Directory* 1923, p.555.
145. *Irish Catholic*, 8 and 15 March 1924.
146. *Irish Catholic*, 11 Oct. 1924.
147. *Kilkenny People*, 12 and 29 March 1924.
148. *Church of Ireland Gazette*, 2 March 1923.
149. *Irish Churchman*, 18 Jan., 1 March 1923.
150. *Witness*, 27 April 1923, 28 March 1924.
151. Norman St John Stevas, *Obscenity and the law* (London: Secker & Warburg, 1956), pp.96–7.
152. John Anderson (Home Office, London) to the Imperial Secretary to the Governor of Northern Ireland, 6 Nov. 1923, PRONI, Cabinet Secretariat, CAB/9B/102/1.
153. R.H. Campbell (Foreign Office) to the Secretary General of the League of Nations, 9 Dec. 1925, ibid.
154. *Irish News*, 20 July 1922.
155. *Down Recorder*, 29 July 1922; for more on the effect of the Russell case see Gail Savage, 'Erotic stories and public decency: newspaper reporting of divorce proceedings in England', *Historical Journal*, Vol.41, No.2 (1998), pp.511–28.
156. *Down Recorder*, 24 March 1923.
157. Dublin Municipal Council, Report of the Public Health Committee 1922, No.317, 21 Nov. 1922.
158. Minutes of Dublin Municipal Council, 1 May 1922, 6 Nov. 1922 and 27 Nov. 1922.
159. Charles M.A. O'Farrell to Theatre and Cinema Association, 6 Dec. 1923, NAI, DJUS H231/26.

160. *Cork Examiner*, 27 Jan. 1922.
161. *Galway Observer*, 4 March 1922.
162. 'Statement by Deputation to Minister for Home Affairs on the Licensing of Films and Picture Houses in Ireland' [no date], NAI, Department of the Taoiseach [DT], S3026.
163. M.A. Walsh to Minister, 16 March 1923, NAI, DJUS, H84/12.
164. A.B. Carroll to Minister, 21 March 1923, ibid.
165. William Hegarty to Minister, 28 March 1923, ibid.
166. John McCaull to Minister, 15 March 1923, ibid.
167. E. O'Connell to Minister, 23 March 1923, ibid.
168. *Kilkenny People*, 10 March 1923.
169. A. Browne to Minister, 3 April 1923, ibid.
170. Dáil Debates, Vol.III, 3 May 1923, 586–7.
171. Ibid., 10 May 1923, 751–2.
172. Ibid., 763–4.
173. Ibid., 752–3.
174. Ibid., 752–60.
175. Ibid., 17 March 1923, 998–9.
176. Ibid., 1003–10.
177. Ibid., 28 May 1923, 1178.
178. Seanad Debates, Vol.I, 6 June 1923, 1141.
179. Ibid., 7 June 1923, 1143–7.
180. *Cork Weekly Examiner*, 19 May 1923; *Irish Catholic*, 26 Jan. 1924; *Irish Times*, 4 May 1923.
181. 'List of Applicants: Censor of Films', [Aug. 1923]; Secretary, note on letter from Aubrey Clancy to Minister for Home Affairs, 13 March 1923; Frank O'Reilly to Minister for Home Affairs, 24 April 1923, NAI, DJUS H84/9.
182. Royal Irish Academy, *Dictionary of Irish Biography* (Cambridge University Press, forthcoming).
183. John M. Regan, *The Irish counter-revolution, 1921–1936* (Dublin: Gill & Macmillan, 1999), p.231.
184. Leon Ó Broin, *Just like yesterday* (Dublin: Gill & Macmillan, 1986), p. 80.
185. E. Bean de Blaghad to Kevin O'Higgins, 31 Aug. 1923, NAI, DJUS, H84/9; James Montgomery, 'The menace of Hollywood', *Studies* Vol.31 (Dec. 1942), pp.420–8.
186. Attorney General to Chief State Solicitor, 3 June 1924; CID report, 6 Sept. 1923; Minute to Secretary 29 Nov. 1924, ibid., H231/13.
187. *Irish Catholic*, 7 March 1925.
188. O'Friel to Revenue Commissioners, 22 Feb. 1924, DJUS, H84/30.
189. Pathé Ltd to Ministry for Home Affairs, 14 Nov. 1923; President's Office to O'Higgins, 15 Dec. 1923; Note by O'Friel, 14 Nov. 1923, ibid., H231/5.
190. O'Friel to Seán Lester, 11 Dec. 1923, ibid.
191. O'Friel, notes of meeting with representatives of Gaumont, Universal and Pathé, [March 1924]; Montgomery to O'Friel, 27 March 1924, ibid., H231/6.
192. *Irish Churchman*, 1 Feb. 1923.
193. *Northern Whig*, 2 Jan. 1923.
194. *Down Recorder*, 24 June 1922.
195. Patrick Buckland, *The factory of grievances: devolved government in Northern Ireland, 1921–39* (Dublin: Gill & Macmillan, 1979), p.4.
196. *Tyrone Constitution*, 9 March 1923.
197. *Church of Ireland Gazette*, 18 May 1923.
198. L.B. Freestone, 'The Censorship of Cinematograph Films', 6 July 1923, PRONI, NIMHA, HA/8/639.
199. Freestone to A. Glen [Imperial Secretary's Department], 10 July 1923, ibid.
200. A.P. Magill, note on letter, A. Glen to A.P. Magill, 11 July 1923, ibid.
201. W.A. Magill to Secretary NIMHA, 16 Aug. 1923, ibid.
202. C. Davis [for Inspector General RUC] to Secretary NIMHA, 18 Sept. 1923, ibid.
203. Draft Circular, 10 Oct. 1923, ibid.
204. S. Watt, Minute, 18 March 1924, ibid.

CHAPTER TWO

Discipline 1924–29

Film censorship in the south in the 1920s

From 31 March 1924, cinema owners showing uncensored films became liable to prosecution, although the police had to catch them in the act. To facilitate this, the censor's certificate had to be shown before each screening. Even so, there was nothing to prevent someone from possessing an unlicensed film so long as they did not show it.[1] Montgomery faced the labour of viewing and judging four or five films a day. Sitting in a tiny screening room watching silent films, he took copious notes. These serve as valuable, and often witty, insights into his thoughts. Understandably he became frustrated when presented with films that were, to him, obviously unacceptable, commenting in 1925, for example, after rejecting *Locked Doors*, 'I can't understand why a film of this nature was imported. You would think that by this time it would be recognized that such an immoral picture could not by any chance receive a certificate.'[2] He was opposed to the creation of special title cards for films to be shown in Ireland as the film might be subsequently re-imported in its original form.[3] The Censorship of Films (Amendment) Act 1925 made film advertisements as well as posters, handbills and cards promoting a film subject to censorship. It was passed without controversy thus completing the range of powers needed by the censor but increasing his workload even further.

Montgomery's own report of the number of drama films he cut or rejected is given in Table 2.1 and demonstrates the extent of the task imposed on him: an average of over 1,200 drama films a year, or twenty-four a week. As a result his decisions seem to have been made quickly

TABLE 2.1:
DRAMA FILMS CENSORED 1923–29[4]

Year	Total	Cut	%	Rejected	%	Passed	% Passed
1923/4*	1307	166	12.7	104	7.9	1037	79.1
1925	1205	172	14.3	115	9.5	918	76.2
1926	1327	166	12.5	121	9.1	1040	78.4
1927	1211	219	18.1	145	11.9	847	69.9
1928	1121	224	20.4	134	11.7	763	68.1
1929	1284	290	15.8	127	9.8	867	67.5

*November 1923 – December 1924.

TABLE 2.2:
REASONS FOR REJECTION AND RESULTS OF APPEALS[5]

Reason	1923/4	1925	1926	1927	1928	1929
Immorality	57	66	69	70	71	102
Infidelity/Divorce	27	40	32	34	41	22
Crime	12	14	6	7	9	12
Religious	2	3	2	3	2	1
Nudity	3	7	16	14	23	27
Offensive to a						
Foreign Country	1	1	6	6	5	1
Other/unclear	3	0	8	29	15	3
Appeals made	20	18	19	39	46	28
Decisions reversed	3	3	1	4	4	3
Reversed with cuts	1	5	7	16	20	9

and were based on rigid criteria. It seems unlikely that he spent long hours agonizing except in the most difficult cases. Based on his figures for 1928, drama films accounted for 64 per cent of films censored, but 98 per cent of films cut and 92 per cent of films rejected were of this type. The remainder was made up of 'interest' or educational films.[6]

The reasons for his decisions to reject and the decisions of the Appeals Board are given in Table 2.2. These figures show that there was an increase in the proportion of drama films rejected or cut from 1927 on. This was accompanied by an increase in the numbers of appeals made and the number of censor's decisions reversed with cuts. This suggests that Montgomery was becoming stricter but that this development did not have the full support of the Appeals Board.

Montgomery's most common complaint was 'immorality', or as he sometimes called it 'the morals of the poultry yard'.[7] He ruled that 'sexational [sic] pictures ... should not be imported for general exhibition'.[8] The prohibition extended to sensational titles and he declared that 'if it were the story of Cinderella, I would not pass it with the title of "The Pagan Princess"'.[9] The increase in the number of these rejections may have been caused by the popularity of films aimed at young audiences and starring young, attractive actresses like Clara Bow, Colleen Moore and Constance Talmadge as free-spirited 'flappers'. In 1928, Montgomery noted 'numerous complaints are made about American co-ed films. The caddish boys and brazen girls are not regarded as desirable models for our young people.'[10] He also complained about the love scenes in such films which had provoked numerous complaints: 'we have had enough of faces 10 ft long with mouths 3 ft wide engaged in "close up" kisses!'[11] The women in these pictures were the opposite of his ideal of female morality; he complained of the characters in the Marion Davies film *Varsity Girl*, 'if American girls are like these it may account for the number of American men who came to Europe cheerfully to "win the war" ... I can't stop it for vulgarity, wish I could'.[12]

Clara Bow, at the time one of the most popular film stars in America, was a particular object of Montgomery's ire. Commenting on *Hula* he summed up both the essence of her appeal and of his objection:

> Miss Clara Bow's great asset is said to be 'It' which is the euphemism for 'Sex Appeal' adopted by that edifying novelist Elinor Glyn. This film was evidently designed to get 100 per cent of 'It' and 'It' has succeeded so well that I reject 'It' with pleasure.[13]

One of the censor's most common complaints was nudity or semi-nudity. Increasingly a reason for rejection from 1926 on, nudity was also often a part of the broader allegation of immorality. His instructions for cuts to *Garden of Eden* show the strictness of Montgomery's views on the issue: 'eliminate *all* glimpses of the semi-nudity of the heroine whether unhealthily suggested through diaphanous drapery or actually revealed in scant stage clothing or in underclothing' [his emphasis].[14] He was also adamant that 'there will be no navel displays on the screens of Ireland'.[15] The use of scantily dressed dancers was similarly disapproved of and led to the rejection of several films.[16] It should be noted, however, that similar regulations governed the display of nude and semi-nude figures in the UK: it was in his application of these standards, rather than the standards themselves, that Montgomery was stricter than his British counterparts.

Montgomery used a curious definition of his power to prohibit blasphemous films. In one case he rejected a film which 'asks for the acceptance of the doctrine of reincarnation and of humanity being the helpless toys of an ironic fate. Consider these anti-Christian ideas on the screens of the Saorstát and their effects on the minds of many.'[17] He rejected *The Man in the Iron Mask* because he judged that 'the anti-Catholic aspect is offensive'. He also ordered cuts in Erich von Stroheim's magnificently eccentric *The Wedding March* as scenes of conversation and the depiction of the elevation during the mass 'display the cynical disregard of Hollywood for the sincere feelings of Catholics'.[18] In another case he decided that 'the story of a priest who has broken his vows is not a desirable subject for exhibition in Ireland'.[19] Montgomery found himself in a quandary over Cecil B. de Mille's controversial epic *King of Kings*. Since 1925, in common with the British Board of Film Censors, he had not allowed films 'in which Christ is materialized' but, perhaps aware that the film had been praised by several religious sources, he suggested an appeal. The Appeals Board allowed the film with cuts.[20] In all these cases, he interpreted blasphemy exclusively according to a Roman Catholic, or at least a Christian, sensibility.

Divorce offended both Montgomery's religious and moral standards and he set out to purge it completely from the films. His approach combined strict Roman Catholicism with a bizarre misunderstanding of Irish law. Arguing that divorce was 'subversive of public morality' under the terms of the censorship of films act, he claimed the right to cut or ban films to remove it from the screens. In 1928, for example, he proclaimed that 'the [divorced] "heroine" is a bigamist according to the moral and civil codes of the Saorstát' and demanded that the renter 'get rid of the husband by sickness or accident'. Although he had misrepresented Free State law, he later defended his view:

> It is not absurd to say that the heroine in the film is a bigamist. There was no mention of an annulment in the story as presented to me – divorce was definite ... so far as Saorstát Éireann is concerned it has ceased to take its civil code from Westminster, and I'm sure it won't take its moral code from Wardour Street.[21]

The emergence of gangster films concerned Montgomery greatly. In 1928 he explained, 'I have constantly in my mind when dealing with underworld films the memory of a crowd of children from the neighbouring slums attending the Picture House in Pearse Street'.[22] He was worried that children would imitate the crimes that they saw on the screen and this problem was exacerbated by his refusal to issue certificates for adults alone. This was a revealing admission. Montgomery saw the cinema as a medium for children and, in many ways, treated all its audience – adult and child alike – as if they were too immature to make their own decisions about what was going on. This tendency was self-fulfilling as Montgomery's cuts removed much of the subtlety of the films, making them less attractive to those who might have appreciated cinema as an art form.

His rigid moral vision both reduced the complexity of films and cut through Hollywood's obfuscations. When a female character struggled with a man before submitting to his advances, Montgomery saw not romance but rape – a view with which the modern audience might agree. These 'sex struggles' were regularly cut. While his reactions to divorce and crime on screen were those of a rigid conservative, it was also a sign that he was unwilling to accept the approach to such subjects favoured by the Hollywood studios in which the remarriage of a divorcee or the death or capture of a gangster was sufficient to atone for their 'sins'.

In the troubled international climate of the 1920s, how foreign countries were portrayed in films was a sensitive matter. Both Germany and France tried hard to control the images of their nations presented on the world's screens. In 1924, the German Consul General wrote to the Minister for External Affairs to complain that *The Four Horsemen of the Apocalypse*, which he alleged was anti-German, was shown in Ireland. He was told that there was no provision in the 1923 Act allowing the censor to ban such a film. Montgomery was very sympathetic to the German view. In another case he noted, 'I conscientiously believe that such pictures are a menace to peace and I feel that the admission of

Germany to the League of Nations should not be made to coincide with the exhibition of this and similar films'. Nor was his sympathy confined to Germany. He rejected *Beau Geste* in 1926 because it insulted the French Foreign Legion, although it was passed on appeal.[23] In rejecting such films Montgomery was acting beyond his powers in the hope that the Appeals Board would not oppose him.

In March 1927, Kevin O'Higgins reacted to the protests from France and Germany by proposing new legislation 'so as to make it mandatory on the Film Censor to reject any film which in his opinion is calculated to be offensive to the people of a friendly nation'. The Department of External Affairs was consulted and agreed although it wanted the right to send a report to the Appeals Board in such cases. The proposed law would have amended the grounds for banning a film to include 'tending to promote racial hatred, rivalry or ill-feeling or be calculated to give offence to people of a friendly state'. The minister would also have the right to refer films passed by the censor to the Appeals Board if he received complaints about them on such grounds; these reviews would be free of charge and would be attended by a representative of the Minister for External Affairs. After O'Higgins was assassinated on 10 July 1927, the bill was given a low priority, probably because the government need-ed to pass a large body of emergency legislation quickly and it lacked an influential patron. In 1928 it was postponed for twelve months and, as the new minister, James Fitzgerald-Kenney, showed little enthusiasm for the measure, it soon died.[24] The BBFC and several other foreign censors already had such provisions in their codes. The Irish censorship was comparatively lax in this regard because of the rigorously non-political terms of the 1923 Act.

Montgomery's middle class, Roman Catholic tastes were reflected in his opinions on comedy. He disliked 'the trousers off stunt' deeming it to be 'vulgarity without fun'.[25] This disapproval extended to other aspects of slapstick from 'the sanitation of a baby' to the comedic use of skele-tons.[26] Although he personally disliked 'stage Irish' performances he had no choice but to pass them reluctantly.[27] Montgomery believed that stricter standards had to be applied to film than to plays or books. This was because the latter appealed 'to a more sophisticated class than the average cinema patron'. Rejecting *Carmen* he wrote, 'one must dismiss memories of opera, novel and drama and remember that this is a work of the screen with a dangerous appeal to unsophisticated minds by its flattery of the passions'. The Appeals Board disagreed and passed it with cuts. These comments reveal a great deal about Montgomery, whose pre-ferred social *milieu* was among writers and actors. His circle were 'sophisticated' in contrast to the 'unsophisticated', passionate minds of the lower classes. His own love of wit, so evident in his scathing reports on the films he viewed, was clearly offended by the vulgar comedy designed to please cinema audiences; comedy that owed its origins to popular theatre and music hall.

When a film met his own artistic standards, Montgomery found himself torn between love of art and morality. He would later express his admiration for the work of Eisenstein, Pudovkin and John Ford. Admiring *The Divine Woman* (1928), which starred Greta Garbo as a woman who deserts her lover for a life on the stage, he admitted that although he considered it 'almost vandalism to alter an artistic film' he had tried to save this one through cuts but had been unable to do so and rejected it. Likewise he rejected F.W. Murnau's *Faust* (1927), although it was 'one of the finest films I have seen', as 'I am unable to cut it without injury to its artistic side'. The distributors appealed whereupon it was passed with cuts.[28] It is indeed one of the finest films of the silent era but it is not hard to see why its displays of nudity, deviltry and magic made it unacceptable to the censor. One can only imagine the mutilations wrought on it by the distributors as it was cleaned up for the Irish public.

Film and public opinion

The establishment of the film censorship did not silence the debate on film in the Irish Free State or the efforts of private groups and local authorities to control it. In January 1924, Monaghan County Council considered attaching moral conditions to its cinema licences. This showed that, only a year after its passage, the councillors had no idea what the Censorship of Films Act contained. The act did not prevent local authorities from restricting the opening hours of cinemas and this was used in Waterford to close them on Sundays. The proponent of the motion made it clear that he did not believe the censor could cope with the 'backwash of English picture houses and music halls' shown in the town. The motion was passed by twenty-three votes to two and had the support of the local Roman Catholic clergy.[29] Dublin Corporation also used this procedure to restrict the hours in which unaccompanied children could attend the cinemas.[30]

Vigilante action against films occasionally occurred. In 1929, a group of students staged a demonstration against *Smiling Irish Eyes*. The group, which included Cearbhall Ó Dálaigh, Cyril Cusack and Liam O'Leary, objected to its stage-Irish characters.[31] Violent republicans also took action against films they disliked. In 1925, the Masterpiece Theatre in Dublin was raided and its copy of the war film *Ypres* was taken. After the cinema procured a new copy, the front of the building was blown up with a land mine that shattered nearby windows. Charles Eason commented to his cousin that the incident 'shows that the unruly elements are not yet under control'.[32] Later that year, in Galway, a copy of *Zeebrugge* was seized by masked men who burned it, describing it as a 'British propaganda film'.[33] Two years later, a cinema in Dundalk was raided and *Mons* was seized and burned.[34]

Criticism of the cinema was especially impassioned within Roman Catholic circles. In 1923, soon after the passage of the Censorship of Films Act, the Catholic Young Men's Society (CYMS) protested to the Department of Home Affairs against 'the introduction of indecent pictures' into Ireland. Fr J.S. Sheehy, the Dean of All Hallows College in Dublin, at an IVA meeting that December, complained that 'the "living picture" is like a drug', even the best films had 'highly erotic scenes' and the worst were 'positively indecent and immoral'. However, it was the 'border-line [films] … for which the renters of pictures would make a great fight, and try to stampede the censor into letting them through' that posed the greatest threat. This critique was echoed by the *Irish Catholic* in 1924 which claimed that 'unwholesome' films were the most profitable and therefore the renters could not be trusted.[35]

There were some correspondents who argued that, rather than condemning films constantly, the Catholic Church needed to act to improve them but this challenge was not taken up. Bishops tended to offer only broad condemnations. Three statements on film: a sermon by Bishop O'Doherty of Galway in April 1924, another by Bishop Keane of Limerick that November, and the statement on the subject by the Maynooth synod of October 1927[36] all show a consistent approach. All three pointed out that cinema had great potential for good. They expressed suspicion of the film industry and the fear that profitable films would not be wholesome. The synod statement also suggested that crime films could incite young boys 'to do deeds of theft and violence'. Similar sentiments were expressed by other bishops throughout the period. The Church of Ireland was less vocal with its opinions but a letter from Bishop Grierson of Down to his clergy in 1929 suggested that he believed films had improved in quality. The *Church of Ireland Gazette* agreed but argued that 'with regard to the portrayal of sinful passions by the cinematograph, the Irish Free State, with its admirable film censorship, must be reckoned as ahead of Northern Ireland'.[37]

There were some expressions of dissatisfaction with the censor, mostly from those who felt he was not strict enough. One letter writer to the *Irish Catholic* claimed that his local cinema had to cut further the films supplied to it. W.B. Joyce, principal of Marlborough Street Training College, lamented that 'from all I can see I cannot believe that films are censored'.[38] Despite such sentiments, the IVA publicly supported Montgomery. In 1925 it offered 'special congratulations' for his 'splendid work' and protested 'against any attempts to intimidate the censor or dictate to him or his colleagues, the manner in which they should carry out the duties imposed on them by the Oireachtas'. There were also many who were satisfied with the situation. In 1926 the *Galway Observer* doubted 'that the moving pictures influence boys to become bandits'. It argued that although films often portrayed a false picture of life and promoted materialism they were potentially positive and useful.[39]

Film censorship in Northern Ireland

Despite intermittent calls for stricter film censorship in Northern Ireland the government did as little as possible about the issue. Although the Ministry of Home Affairs considered regulating pawnbrokers and servants' registries, it had no intention of censoring films, mainly because 'the cost of establishing a censorship for Northern Ireland would be heavy'.[40] Although the Belfast Women's Advisory Council, the Belfast and District Christian Citizenship Council and the Armagh branch of the Mothers' Union all sought stronger censorship regulations, preferably along British and Irish lines, the government preferred to rely on the BBFC to scrutinize films.[41] As the censorship regimes in England and Dublin were radically different it seems that these groups lacked a clear idea of what sort of censorship they wanted.

In 1927, the British government introduced a new Cinematograph Films Bill requiring that 5 per cent of films shown in British cinemas be British. This was a response to the aggressive marketing of American films which was increased after Congress set up the Motion Picture Department within the Department of Commerce at the request of the film industry. The dominance of US films in the British market created both a commercial and moral debate as American films seemed to many to be advertisements for a materialistic and foreign way of life. The northern government was initially enthusiastic about the new bill and asked for it to be applied to the region. It then discovered that 14 per cent of films shown in Belfast were already British but that if a quota were imposed, costs would increase and the cinemas would reduce the number they showed to the minimum. It then decided to draft its own measure as it feared that 'amendments to adapt the Imperial measure to Northern Ireland conditions would be likely to embarrass the Imperial government'.[42]

Film censorship remained in the hands of the local authorities and they implemented it with varying rigour or, in most cases, not at all, preferring to rely on the BBFC.[43] Several controversial films in this period illustrated the policies adopted both by these bodies and the government. The most important market for films was Belfast which had 31 licensed cinemas in 1922. The Police Committee of Belfast Corporation examined any films not passed by the BBFC. In some cases the procedure was quite casual: for example, *White Slave Traffic* was permitted after a favourable report from the executive officer of the committee.[44] The fact that Belfast could act in this way showed the relative unimportance of Northern

Ireland to the UK film censorship system. When the London authorities disagreed with the BBFC over *Married Love*, a compromise was reached in which the BBFC passed a cut version to prevent the system from collapsing. No such arrangements were required for a small provincial city like Belfast. There was also a degree of self-censorship by the distributors and cinemas; for example, the manager of the Midland Picture House rejected several titles sent to him by film companies on the ground that they were 'unsuitable for our audience'.[45]

In 1928, *Dawn*, a war film focusing on the life and death of Edith Cavell, was rejected by the BBFC because it was deemed to be offensive to Germany. It was also believed that the UK government did not want the film to be shown. This provoked some disquiet and questions in the British House of Commons. The film was shown in Enniskillen and the Belfast Police Committee allowed it without a screening on the grounds that the London County Council and several other British authorities had passed it.[46] This suggests that the Corporation was more responsive to local practice in Britain than a desire to please the Imperial government. As in the south, *King of Kings* excited some controversy in Northern Ireland. The BBFC had always forbidden portrayals of Christ so the film's producers avoided the board and submitted it instead to individual local authorities. Letters of protest followed both in Britain and Northern Ireland. One correspondent condemned the film as an 'attempt to exploit the personality and life of our Blessed Lord for the purposes of making money'. In Armagh the film was delayed for nearly a year but was shown. The cinema owners emphasized the fact that it was a 'reverent' treatment of its subject. The film was shown initially to 'a considerable number of clergymen of all denominations' who were, the cinema owners claimed, 'loud in their praises'. Belfast Corporation Police Committee also passed the film after viewing it. Lurgan, however, prohibited the film on the ground that 'it would open a very wide door if they allowed pictures to be shown which were not passed by the British Censor'.[47]

It should be no surprise that Northern Ireland's cinemas came under considerable pressure to close their doors on the Sabbath. Despite the support of religious groups, local authorities often had little power to enforce such a policy. In 1924, the Armagh city council considered banning Sunday opening but was told that they would have to amend the cinema licences to do so. Instead a resolution was passed calling on cinemas to close on the Sabbath. Its chief advocate explained that 'it would be painful to see a queue lined up at the picture house when people are coming out of church'. The motion was proposed to put pressure on a single cinema that was breaking an unwritten rule. When the cinema ignored the resolution the council decided to single it out for an inspection by the City Surveyor to see if it met the appropriate health and safety requirements.

The cinema passed this test and the councillors reluctantly accepted this.[48] In Belfast, the Police Committee had sole discretion as to whether to grant permission for shows on a Sunday. In practice this was done only for religious shows usually organized by clergymen. In Enniskillen there was even controversy over a showing of *The Ten Commandments* in the Town Hall, for charity, on a Sunday.[49]

Overall, however, Northern Ireland seems to have experienced fewer concerns over film than its southern neighbour. *Gift of Life* was shown in Belfast although it had only been approved in London for adult viewing. In Armagh, *Foolish Wives* was shown, despite its 'puritan critics'. *The Kelly Gang* was also shown, whereas in the south it was initially rejected as 'the showing of this picture would be dangerous', though it was passed on appeal.[50] Even Clara Bow's films were shown without comment. At the same time the City Cinema in Armagh liked to advertise the fact that it catered 'for the needs of picture-goers who desire "clean stuff"'.[51]

The UK government occasionally acted against left-wing films through the expedient of issuing warrants for their seizure. New Scotland Yard sent these to the RUC to allow them to seize the films in Northern Ireland. Many of the films banned through this method were undoubtedly communist but were also among Russian cinema's greatest achievements: for example, *The Mother*, *Battleship Potemkin* and *Ten Days that Shook the World*. In practice 'seditious' films were treated differently to documents. Whereas the latter were frequently used as a means of getting convictions, the aim of the police where communist films were concerned was to seize them: in 1929, for example, the Minister for Home Affairs refrained from banning a meeting at which a copy of *Battleship Potemkin* was to be shown so that the RUC could capture it.[52]

The international context

Censorship of films was a worldwide phenomenon and an integral part of the production process. Films were scrutinized by the studios during pre-production or distribution. They were then censored before entering Britain by the BBFC. In 1926, the BBFC codified its rules and these bore several similarities to those applied by Montgomery. The British censors opposed nudity, semi-nudity, shadow nudity and leering at underclothes. Abortion, rape, brothels and venereal disease were not allowed. Religiously sensitive material included the materialized Christ, irreverence and mockery of services. 'Themes which are likely to wound the just susceptibilities of our allies' were to be avoided. Infidelity and collusive divorce was discouraged. A range of sexually suggestive scenes and characters ranging from habitually immoral women to passionate and unrestrained embraces drew the censors' ire. Imitable crimes and sympathy for criminals were forbidden. Cruelty to children and animals was, along with realistic torture scenes, firmly banned. What differentiated the BBFC from the Irish film censor were the facts that the rules were applied more flexibly by the former and that it issued 'A' or adult-only certificates which Montgomery refused to do.[53]

In the United States, the Motion Picture Producers and Distributors of America (MPPDA), under the presidency of former Postmaster General Will Hays, produced a loose set of rules called 'the formula' in 1924 to deflect criticism of their product. This was refined in 1927 into the first production code, familiarly known as the 'Don'ts and Be Carefuls'. The eleven 'Don'ts' were not to 'appear in motion pictures irrespective of the manner in which they are treated'. They were: profanity, licentiousness or suggestive nudity – 'in fact or in silhouette', illegal drugs, sexual perversion, white slavery, miscegenation, venereal disease, actual childbirth, children's sex organs, ridicule of the clergy, and wilful offence to any nation, race or creed. The 'Be Carefuls' were subjects where 'special care' was required. These included: international relations, a wide variety of crimes, marriage, seduction, religion, and 'excessive or lustful kissing'. These measures were not yet strictly enforced and were promoted more to forestall criticism of the films than to reform them.

Other countries had their own systems. In the Netherlands and Scandinavia, violence was considered more serious than sex. South African and Australian censors were considered more prudish than their British counterparts. In Australia, although the individual states had the legal right to censor films, they delegated this power to a Commonwealth film censorship from 1917 on. The system was reformed after a Royal Commission in 1928.[54] Like the Irish, Australian censors found the fact that they were in a small, peripheral market for films made their decisions stricter than their American and British equivalents. In France film censorship was, from 1928, directly connected to issues of trade and national interest, and all Soviet films were banned.[55] In 1927, the Roman Catholic Church in France, responding to the urgings of Pope Pius XI, set up the *Comité Catholique du Cinema* to publish notes on new films for local clergy.[56] Film censorship was, therefore, a pressing issue at this time. Ireland was like other peripheral countries in its unwillingness to accept the verdict of American or British censors and its determination to adopt its own, stricter standards.

The campaign for a censorship of publications

Film censorship in the Irish Free State was established at a time when relations between the state and the Roman Catholic Church were evolving. For many, controlling films was only part of a process of moral regeneration that would transform Ireland into an ideal Catholic nation. These activists were not controlled by the hierarchy; they included many laypeople and priests who were quite capable of campaigning on their own initiative. The bishops were swift to see that such campaigns could attract support and endorsed them enthusiastically. What differentiated these activists from the pre-independence IVA was their belief that the state should act to regulate obscenity.

The libraries were among the first institutions to come under pressure. Since 1913, these had been run by the Carnegie Trust. Books were kept at repositories in county towns and distributed periodically to local centres.[57] The Irish Advisory Committee to the trust became controversial in July 1924 when its president, Lennox Robinson, published a short story, 'The Madonna of Slieve Dun', in Liam O'Flaherty's short-lived paper *Tomorrow*. The Talbot Press had already refused the story, which concerned single motherhood, and rumours began that the Free State government would intervene and ban the paper. The Carnegie committee split bitterly and both the Roman Catholic and the Church of Ireland representatives resigned in protest. In December the Carnegie Trust intervened by suspending the committee and dismissing Robinson.[58]

After the scandal the Galway circulating libraries decided to send their catalogues to the Catholic Archbishop of Tuam for vetting. Several books were withdrawn including 'treaties [sic] on philosophy and religion that were definitely anti-Christian works', and novels that fell into one of five categories:

> (1) Complete frankness in works dealing with sex matters; (2) insidious or categorical denunciations of marriage or glorification of the unmarried mother and the mistress; (3) the glorification of physical passion; (4) contempt of the proprieties or conventions; (5) the details and the stressing of morbidity.[59]

In the Kilkenny county rural libraries, even before the scandal, the works of Bernard Shaw had been banned. The *Kilkenny People* considered it ridiculous that 'the most brilliant living writer for the stage in any country in the world' had been blacklisted. It argued that if Irish people were only allowed to read things they agreed with 'our brains will soon be reduced to pulp'. Many libraries also withdrew the novels of Liam O'Flaherty and Thomas Hardy from their shelves at this time.[60]

In acting in this way, the county committees most likely felt they were carrying out their duties 'to see that the books provided are in every way suitable'.[61] Local authorities were required to strike a rate to maintain the libraries and by 1929 there were fifteen county library schemes in the Irish Free State and five in Northern Ireland, making the libraries vulnerable to local pressure. In the north the Public Libraries Bill was debated in 1924 and passed into law with little controversy. The only questions regarding book selection were posed by Dehra Chichester, MP for Londonderry County. She pointed out that literature 'can do an inestimable amount of harm unless it is properly supervised and selected'. She particularly questioned the provision of books on Irish history, which she called 'a debatable subject' and not one written from 'an Imperial standpoint'. Senator James Leslie also advised that 'we do not want to banish classics from our libraries but we do want to exercise some discrimination' against 'trashy' or 'pernicious' books.[62] Book selection worked in one of two ways. In some cases, such as Belfast and Lurgan, the librarian was solely responsible for selecting books and the library committee confined itself to matters of finance. In others, such as Antrim and Fermanagh, a library selection committee decided what books would be bought. Antrim adopted a quota system whereby adult fiction was limited to 35 per cent of books purchased and juvenile fiction to a further 30 per cent. In Fermanagh, the Book Selection Committee encouraged members of the library to report books they considered unsuitable. Three members of the selection committee judged such books. If two of them voted to withdraw the book, it was removed from the shelves and kept by the librarian to be given out if specially requested. If all three decided the book should be removed, it was withdrawn altogether.[63] Libraries in the Irish Free State seem to have followed similar procedures.

The body which, more than any other, was to cause the state to establish a censorship was the Catholic Truth Society of Ireland (CTSI). Founded in 1899 as an Irish counterpart to the English Catholic Truth Society it originally stuck to publishing pamphlets on various aspects of Roman Catholic doctrine. By 1918 its good intentions had outrun its funds, and the Society faced ruin. That it survived was due to the ability of its organizing secretary, Frank O'Reilly, an ex Civil Servant who raised the Society's prices and moved it into the business of selling religious goods and producing a wider range of publications. By 1925, the reorganized CTSI had given new vitality to the campaign for moral reform. O'Reilly, and the organizing secretary Hugh Allen, who was a journalist at the *Evening Herald*, were energetic, committed and ruthless. The Society both increased its traditional activity of publishing and selling religious pamphlets and became a powerful campaigning and lobbying force. Indeed the two roles reinforced one another as the Society used its network of local sellers, and its power as a publisher to promote its moral agenda. The Roman Catholic hierarchy supported the organization, and preachers from the religious orders praised it in special sermons in parishes across the country.[64] Bishop O'Donnell of Armagh endorsed the Society in his Lenten pastoral of 1925. It organized a campaign in Derry in December where priests gave sermons condemning 'the corruption of countless minds' by 'evil literature' and the 'suggestive filth flung upon the screen of the cinema'.[65] The Society increased its membership and activity greatly over the next few years. In Tralee, for example, the number of publications it distributed grew from 9,628 in 1926 to 62,698 by 1929.[66]

In May 1925, the CTSI set up a special sub-committee to examine the issue of 'evil literature'. This body included William Magennis, Michael Tierney, Professor of Greek at UCD, and Rev. M.H. MacInerny, the chairman of the IVA and the editor of the *Irish Rosary*. They recommended that the Society put forward 'reasonable and effective demands' supported by public opinion. Several members of this committee were members of the Knights of St Columbanus which also had a strong presence within the other vigilance organizations. Many councils of the Knights had their own vigilantes who watched the ports and lobbied for quotas to be placed on imported newspapers and for more customs inspectors to be hired.[67]

The Irish Vigilance Association also re-organized in January 1925, announcing a 'New Forward Movement'. One of its leaders, Rev. J.S. Sheedy, outlined its programme, warning against the 'recrudescence towards paganism as part of the aftermath of the Great War'. The new campaign would recruit the young to lobby for a ban on unfit 'periodicals, novels and newspapers', and the enforcement of 'certain guiding principles' in the theatre. He accepted that voluntary action alone was not going to solve the problem – a significant change in the tactics of the vigilance organizations. Instead he called on the government to find a definition of 'indecency', that would make the law effective. By the autumn of 1925, the *Irish Catholic* was praising the efforts of the Dublin based Good Literature Guilds, affiliated to the IVA, which promoted Catholic newspapers. The *Derry People* also praised the campaigners for 'the cause of good literature'. It echoed the reformers' claim that 'day by day many tons of filth are deposited on the shores of Ireland [and] brought into the most out of the way rural districts'. It argued that while such publications might initially be read out of curiosity, it would soon become habit-forming until 'readers are the slaves to the degraded appetite that can only be satiated with the records of the most repulsive crime that English criminals are addicted to'.[68]

In August 1924, a newsagent in Tuam reported to the Gardaí that he feared that vigilantes would destroy papers sold by him. In common with many others, the seller was an agent for a newspaper, and could not refuse to sell the papers although he had been forced to sign an undertaking to do so. In 1925 Eason's agent in the town reported that 'all 2d novels are stopped here'. The local vigilance association, spurred on by the support of the Catholic Archbishop, had recruited the help of other local organizations including the Society of Saint Vincent de Paul, the Sacred Heart Sodality, the Pioneers and the local Sinn Féin club. The same year, the commander at the Curragh banned several papers sold by the Eason shop at the camp. Charles Eason had been warned that the Catholic Truth Society was behind agitation against publications sold in his shops.[69]

In 1925 Kevin O'Higgins, the Minister for Justice, met representatives of the Priests' Social Guild and the Irish Vigilance Association. Although the teetotal O'Higgins was no liberal, he avoided committing the government to their agenda arguing that the country could not afford the measures they wanted and that a whole new department might be required. In January 1926, the Secretary of the Department of Justice wrote to the High Commissioner in Britain, James McNeill, in exasperation. His minister was 'being subjected to considerable pressure' to control indecent literature and contraceptives. In his opinion the latter issue, was 'bristling with difficulties' as the main Christian Churches held 'radically different views' on the subject. He feared that if the state banned advertisements for, or literature about, birth control, it would find itself under intense pressure to ban the 'contraceptive articles themselves'. He accurately foresaw that 'many clergy would expect us to do this and I do not see that it is our business'. He believed that the state had no right to dictate to people on such a delicate matter. He concluded that 'the subject is not very savoury but as the pressure on the minister to do something is great, the whole question has to be considered'. McNeill firmly advised him to avoid legislation, arguing that the government could 'use the Customs Acts most effectively' and threaten the newsagents that 'if need be you will examine every book in every consignment'; those dissatisfied with the results of this policy would have to take their complaints to court where 'a public outcry on their behalf is unlikely'.[70] This exchange gives us an insight into the power of religious groups to pressure a minister. It also shows that Protestant objections to censorship were grounded less in a concern for art than a fear that it would lead to a ban on the discussion of contraception and, eventually, to the prohibition of contraceptives themselves. McNeill's proposal to use the customs laws was clearly modelled on the British example where a wide range of books were banned in the 1920s by this method. It is also interesting how little enthusiasm for censorship there seemed to be within the ministry. O'Friel saw it as an encroachment by the state into people's private lives to which his natural conservatism made him averse. It was also an extraordinarily complicated legislative problem to solve and no Civil Servant welcomes such difficulties.

McNeill underestimated the ferocity of the campaigners. Brother Craven, the editor of *Our Boys*, sent the Minister for Justice large petitions collected around Cork by boys from the local Christian Brothers schools and warned that if this government did not act he would seek help from de Valera. By 1926, this threat had some force as the newly formed Fianna Fáil was more appealing to official Catholicism than Sinn Féin had been. The CTSI was also demanding extreme measures and confidentially circulated a draft bill to license booksellers in the same manner as pubs. District Justices would be able to refuse licences to applicants

who had not 'taken all reasonable precautions to guard against the distribution of immoral or dangerous literature', a register of prohibited
publications would be prepared by the Department of Justice and, in the
event of a publication being banned, all the output from the printer or
publisher would also be prohibited.[71] This proposal was probably circulated for tactical purposes: to define the terms of the debate and to maintain the pressure for reform. The CTSI's own committee on the subject
had not managed to develop a suitable definition of obscenity or to agree
on an easy remedy. The government's decision, in early 1926, to set up
a Committee on Evil Literature to examine the whole question was,
therefore, understandable since it offered the mirage of action without
doing anything real. While the committee sat, newspapers were seized
and destroyed in Kanturk, Cobh, Killiney and Cork by vigilantes. In the
latter case, those accused of the damage were defended by local clergymen and at a monster meeting in Grand Parade, a letter of support from
the local bishop was read and was endorsed by the Minister for Posts and
Telegraphs, J.J. Walsh.[72]

The arguments for censorship

When discussing censorship, the danger of anachronism is always present. Woodman has dismissed the case put forward by pro-censorship
campaigners as 'a motley crew of arguments'.[73] It must be asked how then
these supposed intellectual pigmies not only won the debate in the 1920s
but preserved their victory for at least another thirty years. To explain
this phenomenon it is necessary to look afresh at what those who wanted stricter laws were saying.

The campaign against immoral publications concentrated first of all
on imported newspapers, especially the Sunday press. These were an easy
target: they were populist, somewhat vulgar and many carried advertisements for suppliers of birth control products. MacInerny described them
as 'not fit reading for Catholic people' as their appeal was based on 'stories of crimes and sexual infamy served up hot and strong' to make them
attractive. He also pointed out that 'most of them were brutally anti-Irish
during the whole period of the Troubles'. The foreign press found its
most determined opponent in the person of Fr Richard Devane SJ. The
son of a Limerick merchant, he had been a curate in a working-class
parish and garrison chaplain in his home town for several years before
joining the Jesuits in 1918. He was, by 1925, director of a retreat house
for working men and was 49 years old. He was energetic, committed and
intelligent,: capable of formulating detailed and logical arguments supported by huge quantities of factual material.[74] His views were well
respected among moral campaigners and greatly influenced the thinking
of the CTSI.

Devane argued that 'our new-won powers to legislate according to Irish ideals and Catholic standards'[75] should be used to break what he called 'the stranglehold of an alien press' which offered 'overpowering competition' to the Irish newspapers.[76] Despite the fact that the Irish press had 'upheld morality in the face of many inducements from cross channel purveyors of filth',[77] he claimed that the British press sold so well that 'no other civilised nation is dependent on outside journalism to the extent we are'. This sort of intellectual protectionism could be used to counter even legal difficulties: Devane complained to Fr Dempsey of the Committee on Evil Literature that 'the legal mind is still dominated by English tradition and practice'.[78] Devane campaigned for Irish newspapers to be protected by both stronger obscenity laws and a tariff on foreign competitors. This had the attraction of linking a moral issue to a fashionable economic cause and connecting the campaign for clean literature to the 'Irish-Ireland' ideals held by many at the time. Devane intended the tariff to apply only to 'popular' publications: literary, scientific, artistic and trade journals would be exempt.[79]

Devane's view was supported by MacInerny but Michael Tierney, then a Cumann na nGaedheal TD for the NUI and no longer a part of the pro-censorship campaign, had his doubts. He claimed that many attacks on foreign papers were 'hypocrisy so long as they let our own equally objectionable press go free'. His answer was to ban all reporting of foreign crimes. Senator P.J. Hooper, the former editor of the *Freeman's Journal*, also expressed misgivings about simplistic solutions. He argued that the problem was one of public taste, which not even censorship would improve, and a lack of enterprise among Irish publishers. Most proponents of censorship denied this. The Catholic Writers' Guild told the Committee on Evil Literature that all bad newspapers were imported and, while it exempted some such as the *Sunday Times* or *Observer*, it alleged that the foreign press was guilty both of making feature stories out of the reporting of sexual crimes and – even worse in its view – carrying advertisements for birth control products.[80]

While advocating intellectual protectionism, those in favour of censorship also presented their proposals as part of an international trend. MacInerny had held New Zealand up as an example of a state which had legislated to keep out 'noxious' papers. The Catholic Truth Society of Ireland, in its evidence to the Committee on Evil Literature, spoke in glowing terms of the restrictions on birth control literature and products in France, the USA, Canada, New Zealand and the Australian states of Tasmania and Victoria. The Committee held its own investigations into the subject and examined extracts from the Australian Trade and Customs Orders and parliamentary debates, the Canadian Postal Guide, the 'black list' of publications banned in Canada, the South African Union Customs Management Act, and the League of Nations

International Convention for the Suppression of the Circulation of and Traffic in Obscene Publications (1923). This demonstrates that, while Irish-Ireland concerns were a part of the censorship debate, the policy was not drafted in isolation nor were its architects oblivious to international practices. The CTSI's source for most of this material was Richard Devane. In a curious twist he had received it from the British Association for Moral and Social Hygiene who had got it from the British Home Office.[81]

The most contentious item on the reformer's agenda was birth control. As we have seen, the government was afraid of alienating the Protestant community and interfering in people's private lives if it were forced to act. On the other hand, advertisements for contraceptives and articles supporting birth control were, as far as the pro-censorship lobby was concerned, among the most objectionable features of the foreign press. In 1925 Devane claimed that there had been a massive growth in birth control literature since the war, and the CTSI supported this contention and supplied the Committee on Evil Literature with a long list of offending publications ranging from books by Marie Stopes, Isobel Hutton and Oster Mann, through advertisements in newspapers and magazines and including articles in the press on the subject which backed the views of the birth control advocates. The Society endorsed the views of the Rev. Vincent McNabb OP that birth control was 'mutual marital masturbation'.[82] Other anecdotal evidence was given, including the allegation, from the Catholic Headmasters' Association, of 'a Jew who had a lot of Marie Stokes's [sic] books and went through the country selling them'. W.B. Joyce, a former activist with the Vigilance Association asserted that 'some of the Sunday papers were good journals ... we objected to certain advertisements'.[83] The government was put in a difficult position later in the year when the Archbishop of Dublin complained that he had received, unsolicited, circulars advertising a 'very objectionable type of publication [probably birth control literature]'. A mortified J.J. Walsh promised that 'every possible step has been taken' and that the state's defences against such intrusions would be tightened.[84] It is unclear how much of what was sold in Ireland was really objectionable, even by contemporary standards. The advocates of censorship certainly exaggerated the situation and many contemporary politicians and commentators seem to have known this. The campaigners did succeed in convincing many people that a problem existed even if it was not as bad as they suggested. There were no voices at the Committee on Evil Literature to deny that there was any need to act.

The campaigners were clear enough about what they wanted banned: indecent publications, reports of divorce cases and sexual crimes, exploitative reports of other crimes and advertisements for, or articles endorsing, birth control. They had more difficulty, however, finding a definition of obscenity or indecency. This had been a problem with obscenity law for decades, based mainly on the fact that most definitions of the words in question were vague at best. The campaigners believed that the Cockburn test had been so strictly interpreted as to become ineffective. Devane claimed that 'English social and moral ideals and teachings', had undermined the judgment. Nonetheless, he admitted to the Committee on Evil Literature that 'if we make it [the definition] too comprehensive I think it will involve us in continual prosecution'. He felt that this reinforced the case for a censorship board, which could develop a blacklist without going through the courts. He firmly adhered to the view that standards should be set based on what one would put 'into the hands of a girl of sixteen years of age'. His preferred formulation was 'anything calculated to influence the passions or to suggest or invite to sexual immorality or in any other way to corrupt or deprave'. This was supported by other organizations, particularly the Catholic Headmasters' Association. By contrast, the Catholic Writers' Guild opposed the idea of a strict definition, preferring a system of minimum standards. These would have outlawed material on birth control or venereal disease, and that 'offensive to moral sense or decency'. The Christian Brothers recommended that the definition be broad and suggested 'insulting to modesty'. The Marian Sodalities agreed that the terms 'indecent' and 'obscene' were unhelpful and argued that it was also pointless to try to prove that harm had been caused as 'a sanitary engineer in condemning a drain does not need to show that it has made a particular person sick'.[85]

The CTSI proceeded carefully in this matter. It first defined decency as 'the sense of honest shame caused by the apprehension of something likely to outrage propriety, modesty or honour'. Indecency was therefore more serious in regard to children who were not yet protected by a fully developed sense of decency. Furthermore, obscenity was culturally conditioned, the CTSI argued. It could be defined only as material 'offending the cherished traditions of their [the committee's] and our Irish ancestors'. At a rhetorical stroke, modernism, internationalism and the foreign media were vanquished. The first part of this definition of indecency was the same as that used by M. Hennequin, the French delegate, at the League of Nations conference on obscenity in 1923.[86] Common to all the arguments of the pro-censorship lobby was the belief that formulating a legal form for these aspirations was a job for lawyers. The Irish Vigilance Association did not even offer a suggested definition.

The question of whether to give special treatment to works of artistic value was one of the most difficult that the committee faced. The Catholic Truth Society stated, promisingly enough, that 'different people have quite honestly widely different views as regards certain types of books', but concluded, 'standards of public opinion and good taste are not as high as they might be'. Given that the same organization had previously declared that 'we don't mind if eminent poets call us fanatics. Eminent poets are not our pastors', their apparent moderation seems to have been more tactical than sincere. Devane had also pronounced on the issue. Noting that Canada had banned the works of Guy de Maupassant he declared that

> a similar drastic treatment of some of our own plaster-of-Paris realist poseurs would do the Anglo-Irish literary revival a world of good. Indecency is indecency even though the cunning hand of some degenerate artist pretends to hide its nakedness under the transparencies of a seductive style.[87]

Fr Thomas F. Ryan SJ for the Marian Sodalities gave as examples of works that deserved censorship *The Tent* by Liam O'Flaherty, and *Ulysses* and 'books relating to psycho-analysis for other than scientific purposes'. W.B. Joyce believed that 'Shakespeare could well be served by Bowdler' but was more afraid of the modern authors who wrote too much and too favourably about sex. There were, he believed, three types of dangerous book: those concerned with birth control, 'authors like Balzac and Rabelais', and 'an alluring class of current fiction bursting with dangers'. He included James Joyce in the third category and the chairman interjected to add Elinor Glyn.[88]

The Committee on Evil Literature was subjected to organized campaigning by the pro-censorship side. During its hearings, witnesses frequently endorsed the CTSI's published proposals. CTSI groups around the country were herded into submitting resolutions, as did a wide range of clubs, associations and local authorities; most enclosed a form text supplied by the Society itself. The Society tried to co-ordinate its evidence with that of the Catholic bishops and initially refused to give any testimony until it was sure the hierarchy was not going to. Frank O'Reilly went as far as to ask whether the committee had the power to compel witnesses to attend and asked if evidence would be given under oath; having been assured that no such powers existed he agreed to testify. Although reluctant to be subject to scrutiny, the Society understood that it would appear as if its campaign had not been serious if it did not give evidence. It also feared that the committee would be influenced by the government to endorse the existing law.[89] To prevent this the CTSI raised public support with advertisements in the Munster press outlining other countries' restrictions on the reporting of divorce and attacking existing Irish laws as an inadequate remnant from English rule.[90]

Devane, although not in good health, met the Knights of St Columbanus and the Catholic Writers' Guild and worked hard 'to organise evidence, and get witnesses'. The Bishop of Galway, in declining to give evidence recommended that the committee interview Devane as he had shown the Bishop 'some horrible things'. The Jesuit's importance was emphasized by the committee itself when it sent two of his articles to Garda Deputy Commissioner Eamon Coogan for him to consider before giving evidence. When the committee came to interview Devane the chairman told him that it was 'largely in agreement' with him on birth control.[91] Devane provided the intellectual credibility to complement the brute force of the CTSI's publicity. In all the campaigners must be credited with an impressive and sophisticated campaign. They took ideas from elite, intellectual journals and used them to drum up support from a sufficiently wide public to worry politicians. They also took care to mobilize a wide range of witnesses in support of their views. As a result, the committee, which could have been a burial ground for the issue, became an engine to advance the reformers' agenda. The decision of the Roman Catholic bishops not to testify also helped to avoid tainting the issue with sectarian conflict, although there was no doubt that they wanted the censorship laws to be strengthened.

The pro-censorship cause had almost a free hand in regard to the Committee on Evil Literature. Many of those who would most vehemently oppose the censorship of publications bill were conspicuous by their absence from the debate in 1926. While writers and artists were not specifically invited to give evidence, there is no sign that they sought to do so, nor did they write or campaign at this time. Under these circumstances the book trade had to make a case for itself. It was represented by the Retail Newsagents', Booksellers' and Stationers' Association (RNBSA) and the Catholic Writers' Guild. Other groups who may have had misgivings, such as the, largely Protestant, Schoolmasters' Association and the Dublin YMCA declined to give evidence. Like writers, the Protestant Churches failed to offer their views to the committee.

The RNBSA expressed the view that 'the extent of the evil is exaggerated by the vigilance people'. They still accepted that objectionable literature was a problem and 'rejoiced' that action was to be taken. To protect themselves from blame for the problem they wanted a censorship board representing the trade as well as government, religious bodies and the public. The Catholic Writers' Guild also denied that objectionable novels were a serious problem as 'Irish people are not, I think, a reading public'. It did, however, accept that birth control literature was a danger as were bad English newspapers. The guild was opposed, however, to the establishment of a state censor, which would be 'cumbersome and costly'. It preferred to trust a system of jury trial under new obscenity laws. It highlighted the risk that censorship would 'encourage this new tendency to autocratic control'.[92] Committee member William Thrift, who was TD for Dublin University and Professor of Natural and Experimental Philosophy at TCD, suggested that education was the way forward and that 'cultured people pass by these vulgar publications'. The *Irish Times* had declared its hand early in the debate with the assertion that 'censorship would feed the national vice of self-complacency [sic]'. It also condemned the culture which had led to the campaign against evil literature and which included those who had protested at the character of a streetwalker in the Abbey's production of *The Plough and the Stars*, commenting that if children wanted to see prostitutes 'they can rub shoulders with the real thing every night of the week in the central streets ... it is only when a prophet like Mr. O'Casey traces the malady to its source ... that the name of decency is invoked'.[93]

Charles Eason also expressed doubts about censorship. He asserted that of over one hundred papers banned in Canada, none were on sale in his shops and the authorities could suppress them 'without any additional legislation'. Eason had thought deeply about the problem of censorship and although he opposed a state censor he did dislike birth control literature and believed that only a revival of religion would discourage people from buying bad books and papers. He refused, however, to use his position as a large wholesaler to force papers to conform to his opinions. He advocated voluntary self-censorship by libraries, publishers, newsagents and the press, combined with a system of restricting the sale of some materials, such as birth control literature, to those who had placed orders for them. He also believed in abolishing the term 'obscene', for 'whatever is obscene is indecent', and clarifying the definition of 'indecent' in line with the Cockburn judgment. Only in extreme cases – reports of divorce cases and sex crimes, for example – would a ban be necessary.[94] The Dublin Christian Citizenship Council, a Protestant organization, preferred positive measures to improve public opinion to prohibition. It advocated banning the sale of birth control literature to anyone under 21, restricting the advertising of such literature and products, and banning the reporting of divorce cases.[95] These were really quite conservative views and seemed moderate only when compared to those of the CTSI and its allies. All accepted that bad literature was to be discouraged and most believed in some form of legal prohibition. They were representative of commercial, professional or minority groups and were more concerned with protecting their own businesses or religious interests than making an ideological stand.

At this time, the censorship debate centred mainly on newspapers and advertisements; books were hardly mentioned by either its advocates or opponents. Two of the witnesses most closely involved in education had, while strongly favouring censorship, been unable to provide evidence that bad books were hurting the young. M. Quinlan SJ of the Catholic Headmasters' Association admitted that he had only come across one case of boys possessing bad books, while W.B. Joyce, of the Dublin branch of the Irish National Teachers' Organisation, revealed that 'I have not had as a teacher one case of reading matter I could object to in the hands of schoolboys'. Liam O'Flaherty was convinced that the campaign for censorship was 'mostly all directed against Yeats, Lennox Robinson,

Joyce and myself, under the pretence of being directed against Sunday newspapers. 'That's what I like', he commented, 'I must write a story about sodomy in Irish seminaries as a fitting reply.'[96] In this he combined a certain amount of intuition with paranoia. The campaigners had always fought against Sunday newspapers and cheap books rather than novels, but they saw no reason why artistic merit should give writers a special licence to create works of which they disapproved.

The Gardaí, the Post Office and the Customs were interviewed by the committee. The Garda Crime Branch declared that 'the existing acts are inadequate'. It wanted measures to make it easier to get search warrants as well as detailed definitions of obscenity and indecency. The Gardaí also favoured a censorship board and a ban on the reporting of divorce and murder cases. It also asserted that a 'considerable traffic in indecent prints, postcards etc. through the post existed'.[97]

The Post Office revealed that its officials already withheld contraceptives sent from abroad as obscene articles. Birth control literature could only be stopped, however, if it contained obscene words or pictures. Prior to 1908, it had been possible to prosecute the sender of contraceptives but the British courts would no longer uphold such cases. In this area at least, it seemed, distinctively Irish standards were already being applied. In fact, if any obscene matter from Britain or Northern Ireland was intercepted it was returned to the British Post Office and it was up to them to take action. The Irish Post Office lacked exact guidelines on obscenity and indecency, recommending the use of 'ordinary common sense and the generally accepted meaning of those terms in Ireland'. It admitted that postmasters were 'inclined to be over-scrupulous' in such matters. An officer would refer a suspicious article to his superior, who would stop it and send it up the chain of command to the local postmaster who would then send it to Dublin for a final decision. Under the 1903 Post Warrant No. 10777, no indecent or obscene prints, paintings, photos, lithographs, engravings, books, cards or other articles could be sent by post, nor could materials with indecent or obscene covers.[98]

The Customs authorities had a similar system but submitted suspicious items to the Revenue Commissioners if they were dutiable or sought government direction if they were not. Lacking any kind of blacklist, however, the customs officers rarely searched for obscene material, as they feared the customs would be held liable for wrongful detentions. They dismissed as unworkable the idea of a tariff on foreign publications.[99]

The report of the Committee on Evil Literature

In December 1926 the CEL recommended that the legal definitions of 'indecent' and 'obscene' be widened, that the reporting of judicial proceedings be regulated, that it be made easier for the police to get warrants to search for indecent publications and that the maximum penalties for violations of the Indecent Advertisements Act 1889 be increased. The two most important recommendations of the committee were the setting up of a censorship committee and the banning of publications advocating contraception. The committee accepted that, in the case of objectionable newspapers, 'no new definition of the terms "indecent" and "obscene" would enable the authorities to check what is an undoubted evil'. This led it to favour the creation of a board of censors who could use their judgement to ban publications harmful to 'public morality rather than applying a legalistic approach'. The proposed board which would have between nine and twelve members, representing religious, educational and artistic interests, would scrutinize publications and recommend to the Minister for Justice those which should be prohibited. It reported that books were not as important as newspapers for its purposes but that witnesses had been divided on how to deal with them. It rejected the idea that only material suitable for a child should be allowed but condemned a decline in standards among modern writers. It believed that it would be easy for a censorship board to 'recognise books written with a corrupt intent' and recommended that those with 'a purely literary aim' should escape censure. Pornography should be banned. The committee unanimously recommended a ban on literature advocating contraception, the effects of which it described as 'vicious in the extreme'.[100]

The report received a broad welcome. The *Irish Independent* saw its recommendations as 'very moderate', which was not necessarily a compliment, but believed that the report proved that the present law was inadequate and that the state had a duty to intervene. The *Evening Herald* also welcomed its 'quite reasonable' conclusions and recommended that the 'great menace to public morality' of evil literature be dealt with as a matter 'of great urgency'. Even the *Irish Times*, always suspicious of censorship, found 'no positive fault with the report' but believed that 'if old fashioned manliness were revived among our people there would be no need for a censorship other than public opinion'. The *Irish Catholic* welcomed the report and called on the customs and postal authorities to tighten their scrutiny until its implementation. *An Phoblacht* supported the report, hoping censorship would 'check the flow of filth from Britain into Ireland'.[101]

Within a few months, the reformers were getting impatient. The Irish Vigilance Association warned that legislation on the issue seemed 'hung up' and Brother Craven, editor of *Our Boys*, called on the IVA membership to write articles for the newspapers demanding change. The Roman Catholic bishops' Lenten pastorals for 1927 and 1928 strongly condemned 'evil literature' and demanded legislation. The *Irish Catholic* began to raise the idea of censoring the theatre. Vigilante action resumed in May 1927 when a group calling itself the 'Angelic Warfare Association' held up a train at Dundalk and burned its cargo of Sunday newspapers. Kevin O'Higgins warned that 'we have got to work away from that tradition of direct action'.[102] He had met a deputation from the Roman Catholic bishops early in 1927 and had promised legislation. His successor, James Fitzgerald-Kenney, reiterated that promise in January 1928 when lobbied by the Bishop of Galway. In the June 1927 election the CTSI sought commitments of support for legislation from all candidates for the Dáil. Of the 114 who replied, 112 promised their support. One of these was Kevin O'Higgins who pledged that the legislation was being prepared and would be introduced if he were again made Minister for Justice. P.S. Doyle, a Cumann na nGaedheal TD and member of the CTSI kept O'Reilly informed on what the government was doing. He reported that the government did not believe the issue could be tackled in one bill, leading the Society to renew its lobbying. Fianna Fáil decided to support the Committee on Evil Literature's report in April 1928, and in May, Cosgrave promised a bill within months.[103] This did not prevent further direct action, including the burning of thousands of papers in Sligo in 1928 while the censorship bill was being debated in Dublin.[104] The government's eventual decision to introduce legislation that it clearly did not want was a tribute to the organization, skill and sheer bloody-mindedness of the moral reformers.

State security and freedom of expression in the Irish Free State

While the issue of obscene publications was being debated in the south, the two Irish states began to consolidate the mass of security legislation and practices that had seen them through the crisis years of 1922–23. The Free State government used a variety of emergency legislation for most of its first six years in office. While this legislation contained few explicit references to controlling freedom of expression, it did have some effects in this area. All the Public Safety Acts were based on the 1923 Public Safety (Emergency Powers) Act. The central provisions of this act concerned imprisonment without trial and the establishment of special Appeals Councils but it also banned the wearing of state uniforms by unauthorized persons, coercion and incitement to overthrow the state. Under the Treasonable Offences Act 1925, further offences of inciting the Civil Service, military or police to mutiny, desert or neglect their duties were introduced. More importantly, the act permitted a justice of the District Court to issue a search warrant allowing the Gardaí to search for 'treasonable documents' which were any material relating directly or indirectly to the commission of a treasonable act. This provision led to controversy on several occasions when the Gardaí used the act to seize post. In 1925, the Department of Justice decided that a garda had acted within the law in seizing a letter as he had waited until the minute the postman delivered it before using a normal search warrant on the addressee's premises. By contrast in 1926, a garda ordered a Tralee post office to hand over six letters intended for the IRA. The Minister for Justice had to send a special warrant authorizing such seizures. After a similar occurrence in Bandon the Garda Commissioner was forced to issue special instructions reminding his men that they could not behave in this way.[105]

Another method for controlling potentially treasonable documents was through the Customs who would hold the offending person and material until the Gardaí arrived.[106] Article 10 of the 1927 Public Safety Act gave the Minister for Justice the right to apply to a judge of the High Court for the power to ban a periodical which had published seditious libel or otherwise encouraged its readers to offend against the act within the previous month. The government also denied advertisements to 'anti-state' newspapers after 1924 but only two papers, the *Waterford News* and the *Kerry News*, lost advertising as a result as they were the only opposition papers that had previously received it.[107]

Public meetings and assemblies received a varied response from the state. In 1923 John A. Costello, then a solicitor in the Attorney General's office, drew up a memorandum on the law of free assembly. In it he pointed out that there was no such specific right under British law. Interference with a lawful assembly was only illegal in so much as it was a violation of the rights of the individuals involved. There were no special places where free assembly was protected. An unlawful assembly was normally defined as a group which intended to commit a crime or which gave a firm and courageous person reason to believe a breach of the peace was likely. Having a lawful object did not of itself make a gathering lawful. While a lawful meeting could not be prohibited just because of the action of a few wrongdoers, the authorities could prevent even a peaceful assembly to prevent a breach of the peace.[108] These basic principles applied in both Irish jurisdictions.

Republican gatherings were frequently banned in the south as well as in Northern Ireland; for example, a demonstration at Newbridge detention centre in November 1923 was prohibited for fear that it would cause the prisoners to 'mutiny and riot'. The government also seemed uncomfortable with large crowds; the Gardaí were directed to prevent demonstrations, whether favourable or otherwise, from crowding Cosgrave and his ministers as they left the Pro-Cathedral after funerals.[109]

Despite the conditions in the country at the time of their formation, the Gardaí evolved a general policy of tolerance towards public assemblies. In advance of the 1923 elections, the Commissioner, Eoin O'Duffy, issued instructions that a garda at a meeting should help the speaker to be heard. He should intervene only if an attempt was underway to disrupt the meeting and should act in a 'good humoured and pacificatory way'.[110] Such skills were useful when coping with near riots such as those which disfigured the 1923 Irish Labour Party and Trade Union Congress. Johnsonites, Larkinites and striking dockers all converged on the Mansion House, the latter two determined to prevent the former from meeting. Despite allegations of violence on the part of the authorities towards the dockers, the meeting went ahead eventually.[111] The state was less sympathetic to republican demonstrations. An alleged 'Monster Meeting' arranged for Kildare Street to campaign for protectionism was banned in 1924 on the ground that it would obstruct the traffic. Over one hundred gardaí were deployed to control a crowd of about 300, and the organizer, an elderly man later described as 'considerably demented' was arrested.[112] There were also frequent allegations from Fianna Fáil of harassment by the CID.

Northern Ireland and the politics of normality

Writing in May 1925, District Inspector Gilfillan, on behalf of the Inspector General of the RUC, gave the Ministry of Home Affairs an optimistic view of affairs: 'the IRA as an organised force cannot be said now to exist in Northern Ireland'. The reason for his candour was that he was briefing the Prime Minister before the latter gave an interview to United Publishers News. He also claimed that 'the Civil Authorities Act, although still in force, is comparatively seldom invoked ... for all practical purposes the government of Northern Ireland is now carried on under ordinary law'.[113] While it was true that a person committing a crime could expect to be dealt with under normal law, the CASPA was still very much in use and had become a normal part of the working of government. This was recognized in part of the briefing which warned that the border question posed a danger and that 'leniency to the rebellious elements' under the Imperial Government had led to outbursts of crime in the past. It was not a mistake the northern government intended to make.

Nonetheless, the emergency of 1922–23 was certainly over. Most local bodies had been reconstituted in 1924 and the curfew had ended. There was still a question about whether expressions of nationalist and left-wing opinions were to be treated in the same way as Unionist views. To the nationalist community, the prosecution of the *Irish News* for spreading false reports was a worrying sign. The paper had reported that a bomb had been planted at a Roman Catholic house. Finding that the report was not accurate, the Resident Magistrate determined that it was 'calculated to stir up a feeling prejudicial to the maintenance of law and order' and fined the paper and its editor £10 each plus costs. He declared that while the law only applied to false reports that were prejudicial to the maintenance of order, it was not necessary to prove that the editor or publishers had known that they were false. The only concession because of their ignorance was the smallness of the fine.[114] The authorities were more lenient towards the Unionist *Belfast Telegraph* in 1926 when its headline 'Republican Uprising – Attacks in Six Counties' turned out to refer to Cork, Tipperary, Waterford, Meath and Kilkenny. Although feeling that the report 'might have led to panic and possibly disturbances in Northern Ireland' the Minister decided to talk privately to representatives of the paper.[115]

Many republican newspapers were still banned and the ban on *An Phoblacht* was re-imposed regularly. There was more debate within the Ministry of Home Affairs about several other publications. *Irish Freedom* was banned in 1926 because 'its contents may possibly not do much harm but the paper is out to decry everything that the ordinary loyalist respects'. Likewise in regard to *The Nation*, one Civil Servant felt that 'there is really very little in this. I would be inclined to give them a little more rope', but the paper was banned in March 1929. By 1930, the RUC felt that its tone had moderated but that as 'the official organ of the Fianna Fáil party, it would print seditious material if allowed to circulate in Northern Ireland'. The Ministry of Home Affairs agreed that 'it is, of course, anti-English and anti-Imperial' and continued the ban. When *The Nation* was replaced with the *Irish Press* in 1931, the Ministry decided not to ban it as its content was deemed acceptable.[116]

The northern government saw communism as a threat to the state and acted accordingly. A problem arose with regard to censoring left-wing newspapers as they were generally published in Britain. In 1927, for example, the *Communist International* came to the attention of the RUC, and the Ministry of Home Affairs would have liked to ban it as, despite its low circulation and relatively high price, it was believed to be influential among the communist leadership. As the paper was published in Britain, the northern government felt that it had to be a specific threat to the peace and security of the province before they could ask the British government for help in suppressing it. Another paper, *Worker's Life*, was banned as it had a circulation of over one hundred and was considered a threat. The difference in security cultures between Northern Ireland and the rest of the UK was expressed by a minute commenting that 'it [*Worker's Life*] is seditious in almost every line and it seems extraordinary that it should be allowed to be printed and circulated in Great Britain'.[117]

Managing the public utterances of the police when they were predominantly Unionist in membership was a challenge for the administration. The most significant case was that of District Inspector John Nixon who was dismissed in 1924 for making a political speech. The real question in this case, however, is why it took so long for Nixon to be dismissed. Already hated by nationalists for his alleged role in the murders of the McMahon family, he became a thorn in the government's side when he was passed over for promotion to County Inspector in 1922. He was allowed to build a strong base of support among loyalists in East Belfast which included founding his own Orange Lodge within the local RUC. As a result of his disappointment, he circulated a letter in which he savagely criticized superiors, accusing them of a 'conspiracy against Ulster' for promoting four men from the twenty-six counties ahead of him as well as making several allegations about the running of the Belfast RUC. Several loyal institutions passed resolutions on his behalf on that occasion and the government's military adviser, Solly-Flood, advised Craig to brief their leaders before dismissing Nixon. Craig refused to do so and complained of 'undue delay' in dealing with the troublesome officer. A year later, Nixon was still in place and, at an Orange Lodge meeting, he criticized another RUC officer as untrustworthy and hinted that he would break the police code rather than deal with him. Craig again told the Ministry to act quickly, but by October Nixon had been awarded the MBE.[118]

In January 1924, the Inspector General issued a circular reminding his men that although they enjoyed greater leniency in political matters than had the RIC – they could vote and were only barred from those secret societies which were disloyal – it was still 'improper for any member of the force to abuse their privileges by expressing manifestly political or sectarian opinions'. Rather, he ordered, RUC men should not even speak at discussions where such opinions were likely to be uttered. Perhaps overestimating the security of his position, Nixon made a speech on 29 January 1924 in Clifton Orange Hall in which he promised that Unionists in the cities would come to the aid of their fellows on the border if needed. The government felt it had no choice but to act and the Inspector General proceeded against Nixon by Court of Inquiry. The attempt was a failure 'owing to the intimidation of witnesses'. The various loyal institutions responded with a furious defence of Nixon, and resolutions poured in from Orange Lodges, Black Chapters and other organizations. The presence of many identical wordings suggests there was some central organization involved. Some of these contained direct threats to unseat ministers at the next election. In May, District Inspector Nixon was dismissed and the government weathered the storm.[119] He went on to become an independent Unionist MP and continued his criticisms of Craig's governments.

In 1925, Sir Basil Brooke told a Unionist Party meeting at Bessborough that any loyalist who did not vote was 'a Lundy who intended to open the gates and let the enemy in'. Such sentiments might well have been deemed normal in local Unionist politics had it not been for the fact that Brooke was a Special Constable – indeed he was one of the founders of the force in Fermanagh – and one Civil Servant commented, 'I don't see how, after the Nixon episode, we can pass over this'. Brooke was asked to account for himself but took the rebuke with little grace commenting that the Special Constabulary was made up of 'people with country interests ... [who joined] as a patriotic duty', and explaining his political interests as arising out of the fact that 'I, myself, will pay very considerable rates and taxes'. He did, however, accede to the demand that he refrain from politics while he remained a 'special'.[120] After a slow start the government had imposed its authority but the cost in terms of its own image and that of the RUC had been high.

Another challenge awaited the government in responding to the plans of Archbishop Daniel Mannix of Melbourne to visit Northern Ireland during his Irish tour in 1925. The Ministry of Home Affairs judged that 'Mannix is an ardent protagonist for complete Irish freedom and wields a strong influence over Irish circles in Australia', and it was decided to prepare an exclusion order to prohibit him from Northern Ireland. As was usual, the order was phrased so as to allow him into one district of the province, in this case part of Ballymena. This strategy had been devised to prevent any claim that Northern Ireland was exceeding its constitutional powers by preventing free movement from one part of the UK to another. The order was kept secret and copies issued to the local RUC stations with orders not to serve it 'unless an agreed code word is wired to [the] counties'. Publicly, Dawson Bates warned that Mannix would be banned from entering Northern Ireland as his speeches 'are calculated to revive dissension and ill feeling'. When Mannix cancelled his visit, the order was recalled but not revoked and was kept at hand, to be reissued if necessary.[121]

There was no consensus between the communities on the issue of what flags should be flown. The 1925 election proved a testing ground on the matter. At Derrytrasna in Armagh, the parish priest refused to open the local school as a polling station until two Union Jacks were removed from it. They were placed elsewhere instead. The RUC sergeant responsible explained that he lacked the men to stop republicans causing trouble over the issue and the Ministry of Home Affairs supported him.[122] It is interesting to compare the attitudes of the Ministry of Home Affairs to the display of the red flag with their approach to the tricolour. In the former case, the Ministry decided that it did not 'have the power to order its removal except where it may be likely to lead to a breach of the peace'. Although the red flag was a recognized emblem of revolution, 'nowadays its display in connection with the advanced labour movement has become a commonplace event'. The Ministry opposed the flying of the tricolour as it was 'the recognized flag of an illegal association' but recognized that it was also the flag of the Irish Free State. The Chief Crown Solicitor warned that it was doubtful that the state possessed the power to remove a flag unless it was likely to cause a breach of the peace. The County Inspector of the RUC in Co. Down had noted that 'Sinn Fein colours were removed from cars during the last election and I would have no hesitation in doing so again'. The Ministry instructed that 'unless the police have reason to believe that the display of such a flag will not lead to a breach of the peace it will be well to prevent it'.[123] Unionist opinion supported this attitude. Derry Urban Council, for example, forbad any flags but the Union Jack and the Derry Arms on civic buildings. When the tricolour was flown from a private residence as the Governor passed, a question was asked in parliament and Dawson Bates condemned 'this outrage' to the derision of nationalist members. In response to a nationalist question in 1928 he explained that it was not an offence to wear a tricolour but that if illegal organizations adopted it or if its display was 'likely to be prejudicial to the maintenance of peace' then such display was prohibited 'even where the colour of the emblems so adopted and displayed happen to coincide with those of a neighbouring state'.[124] The red flag was presumed innocent until proven guilty of inciting disorder, while the tricolour was almost always removed in the same circumstances.

Posters and emblems were also controversial. An example of what could be considered seditious was a poster put up by a republican candidate for the Newry South Poor Law Ward in 1927. Robert Kelly's poster complained against the oath 'of allegiance to a foreign power', calling it 'a brand of slavery' which 'would lead to the stabilisation of the unnatural partition of Ireland'. For this he was sentenced to two months without hard labour.[125] During Easter Sunday 1928, eight people wearing republican emblems to a demonstration in Belfast were asked by the police to remove them and arrested when they refused. On the orders of the Attorney General, they were released within a week. When these events were debated in the House of Commons, the Under-Secretary for Home Affairs explained that 'the display in Belfast on Easter Sunday of any emblem indicating Republican sympathies was calculated gravely to imperil the peace of the city'.[126] The absence of prosecutions even under the relatively easy terms of the CASPA cast doubt on these claims. By 1929, even Labour posters were the objects of the Ministry's hostility. The Ministry of Home Affairs ordered the removal of two posters: one of these quoted James Connolly and was deemed 'calculated to encourage disloyalty', while the other quoted Patrick Pearse but was 'merely socialistic'.[127]

The labour movement suffered considerable disruption of its meetings and public speeches during the decade. A meeting in Sandy Row, Belfast held by Harry Midgley, was broken up by a mob during the 1924 general election, for example. In 1926, several thousand organized demonstrators with drums disrupted an Irish Labour Party meeting in Belfast and followed it around as the organizers tried to move it to a safe place. The RUC attitude was unsympathetic, dismissing the incident as 'useful propaganda which will be welcomed by the Labour Party' but also recommending that such meetings not be interfered with. The trouble had originated in a dispute between Labour and a group of Christian volunteers over the use of a meeting place. When the organizers of this disruption attacked a Labour meeting the next week, police held the sides apart – the 2,000 or so demonstrators outnumbering the 750 Labour supporters. The Labour

Party leaders planned another meeting for the next week but it was prohibited on the advice of the Belfast City Commissioner. A meeting the next summer was cancelled, leading District Inspector Gilfillan to comment that 'this will remove a possible source of serious trouble'.[128] This illustrated the central problem with the Ministry of Home Affair's approach: it was focused solely on the problem of preventing a breach of the peace without regard for the rights of those involved.

The state was suspicious of the labour movement, fearful of the prospect of socialist revolution. In one case, a man was prosecuted for a speech advocating violent revolution and attacking the government, Craig and the royal family. The authorities were concerned that he was trying to provoke them but felt they had to act. He completed a six-month sentence then held a meeting in Shankill calling for revolution. Faced with six months' hard labour he paid bail and undertook to keep the peace for a year. A Nationalist MP compared this man's treatment unfavourably with the lack of action over a speech by the Grand Master of the Co. Antrim Grand Orange Lodge in which he allegedly promised that there would be no united Ireland while one Orange man remained with one rifle. The government treated the question with derision.[129] Regardless of whether the allegation was justified, the question summed up a widely-held view that Unionist causes were given more leeway and protection, both from prosecution and intimidation than left-wing or nationalist movements. As we will see, this view would be reinforced by events in the 1930s.

The later years of the 1920s saw the consolidation of the two states. In each case there was a marked reluctance to establish a strong right of free speech. Instead, political expression was carefully scrutinized and while opposition to the governments was permitted, anything smacking of sedition was punished harshly. It is significant that Northern Ireland made little effort to censor films or publications except when security was an issue. This seems to have been due to a desire to keep as closely to UK practice as possible rather than any liberal ideology. It was also in keeping with the northern government's general policy of keeping state intervention in society to the minimum. There was little sign that Protestants were innately more liberal on issues of free speech than were Roman Catholics. There was, however, a difference in priorities between religious campaigners in the north and the south. Whereas the former focused on temperance and Bible study in schools, the latter were more concerned with sexual morality and obscenity. This concern was given expression in the censorship of publications which was to become one of the most infamous symbols of Catholic Ireland.

NOTES

1. O'Friel to Montgomery, 20 March 1924; Montgomery to O'Friel, 30 Oct. 1924; S.A. Roche to Montgomery, 16 Sept. 1927, NAI, DJUS, H231/11.
2. Register of films rejected, 7 Sept. 1925, NAI, DJUS, FCO4 98/29/1.
3. Ibid., 11 Nov. 1925, FCO4 98/29/2.
4. Montgomery to O'Friel, 23 Sept. 1930, ibid., H231/34.
5. Register of Films Rejected, ibid., FCO4 98/29/1–2.
6. Ibid., 9 Oct. 1929.
7. Ibid., 24 Nov. 1923, FCO4 98/29/1.
8. Ibid., 23 Aug. 1924.
9. Ibid., 19 March 1925.
10. Reserve Book, 19 December 1928, NAI, DJUS, FCO3 98/28/2.
11. Ibid., 9 and 12 May 1928, FCO3 98/28/1.
12. Record of Films Censored, 20 Jan. 1928, ibid, FCO2 98/27/1.
13. Ibid., 27 July 1928.
14. Reserve Book, 15 March 1928,NAI, DJUS, FCO3 98/28/1.
15. Ibid., 2 March 1928.
16. Ibid., 20 Dec. 1928, FCO3 98/28/2; Register of Films Censored, 16 Nov. 1928, FCO2 98/27/1.
17. Films Rejected, 19 July 1927, FCO4 98/29/2.
18. [*Man in the Iron Mask*] ibid., 21 Jan. 1925, FCO4 98/29/1; [*Wedding March*] Reserve Book, 30 Sept. 1929, FCO3 98/28/3.
19. Record of Films Censored, 22 May 1928, FCO2 98/27/2.
20. Ibid., 13 Dec. 1928, FCO2 98/27/3; Films Rejected, 13 Dec. 1928, FCO4 98/28/2.
21. Reserve Book, 3 Aug. 1928, FCO3 98/28/1; ibid., no date [Aug. 1928]. Divorce had not been prohibited in the Irish Free State. The standing orders of the Dáil had merely been amended to prevent private divorce bills being brought forward. It was thus impossible to get an Irish divorce but not illegal to be divorced. See David Fitzpatrick, 'Divorce and separation in modern Irish history', *Past and Present*, no.114 (Feb. 1987), pp.172–96.
22. Films Rejected, 1 Nov. 1928, FCO4 98/29/2.
23. G. von Dehn to Minister for External Affairs, 18 July 1924, NAI, DJUS, H231/14.; O'Friel to von Dehn, 22 July 1924, ibid.; Montgomery, Films Rejected, 18 Oct. 1926, FCO4 98/29/2; [*Beau Geste*] ibid., 6 Dec. 1926.
24. Minute, 10 March 1927; Secretary Department External Affairs to Secretary Department of Justice, 22 March 1927; Draft bill, 'The Censorship of Films (Amendment) Bill 1928'; John A. Costello to O'Friel, 30 Dec. 1927; O'Friel to Fitzgerald-Kenney, 29 May 1929, NAI, DJUS, H266/53.
25. Reserve Book, 25 April 1928, NAI, DJUS, FCO3 98/28/1.
26. Ibid., 1 June 1928; 18 June 1928.
27. Record of Films Censored, 23 Oct. 1928.
28. James Montgomery, 'The menace of Hollywood', Studies, Vol.31 (Dec. 1942) p.428; Films Rejected, 21 June 1926, [*Carmen*] ibid., 5 July 1927, FCO4 98/29/2; [*Divine Woman*] Record of Films Censored, 23 May 1928, FCO2 98/27/2; [*Faust*] Films Rejected, 1 April 1927, FCO4 98/29/2.
29. Secretary, Monaghan County Council to Minister for Home Affairs, 22 Jan. 1924, NAI, DJUS, H84/27; *Irish Catholic*, 22 Jan. 1927.
30. Dáil debates, Vol.XXXII, 27 Nov. 1929, 1439–41.
31. Louise Burns-Bisogno, *Censoring Irish nationalism: the British, Irish and American suppression of republican images in film and television, 1909–95* (North Carolina: McFarland & Co., 1997), pp.51–2.
32. *Galway Observer*, 16 Nov., 21 Nov. 1925; L.M. Cullen, *Eason & Son* (Dublin: Eason & Son Ltd, 1989), p.218.
33. *Fermanagh Times*, 3 Dec. 1925.
34. *Down Recorder*, 4 June 1927.
35. Honorary Secretary to Minister for Home Affairs, 21 Nov. 1923, NAI, DJUS, H84/24; *Irish Catholic Directory* 1925, pp.547–8; *Irish Catholic*, 26 Jan. 1924
36. *Irish Catholic*, 19 April, 15 Nov. 1924, 8 Oct. 1927.
37. *Church of Ireland Gazette*, 22 March 1929.
38. *Irish Catholic*, 18 Aug. 1928; Evidence of W.B. Joyce to Committee on Evil Literature, 21 April 1926, NAI, JUS 7/2/12.
39. *Irish Catholic Directory* 1926, p.563; *Galway Observer*, 16 Oct. 1926.

40. W.A. Magill to Town Clerk, Belfast Corporation, 13 March 1925; R. Pim, Minute, 5 March 1925, PRONI, Northern Ireland Ministry of Home Affairs NIMHA, HA/8/639.
41. Belfast Corporation Police Committee, Minutes, 5 Nov. 1925, PRONI, LA/7/10AB/1/18; *Irish Churchman*, 4 March 1925; Armagh Mothers' Union, Resolution, no date [1929], PRONI, NIMHA, HA/8/639.
42. Ruth Vasey, 'The worldwide spread of cinema', in Geoffrey Nowell-Smith (ed.), *The Oxford history of world cinema* (Oxford: Oxford University Press, 1996), p.57; NI Cabinet Conclusions, 25 April 1927, PRONI, Midland Cinema, Belfast, records CAB/4/192 and 19 April 1928, CAB/4/208.
43. A. Robinson to T.M. Wilson, Lisburn UDC, 23 July 1929, NIMHA, HA/8/639.
44. Belfast Corporation Police Committee, Minutes, 29 Dec. 1921, LA/7/10AB/1/17; [*White Slave Traffic*] ibid., 4 Oct. 1928, LA/7/10AB/1/19.
45. James C. Robertson, *The British Board of Film Censors: Film censorship in Britain, 1896–1950* (London: Croan Helm, 1985), p.32; J.H. Craig to First National Pictures Ltd., 23 Nov. 1925, PRONI, D3413/3.
46. *Down Recorder*, 25 Feb. 1928; *Fermanagh Times*, 1 March, 13 Sept. 1928; Belfast Police Committee, Minutes, 17 May 1928, PRONI, LA/7/10AB/1/19.
47. Tom Dewe Mathews, *Censored* (London: Chatto & Windus, 1994), p.67; *Down Recorder*, 27 Aug., 24 Dec. 1927; *Ulster Gazette*, 7 April 1928, 16, 23 February 1929; Belfast Corporation Police Committee, Minutes, 20 Dec. 1928; *Down Recorder*, 6 April 1929.
48. *Ulster Gazette*, 6 Dec. 1924, 10 Jan., 7 Feb. 1925.
49. Belfast Corporation Police Committee, Minutes, 24 Sept. 1925, 28 Jan. 1926, PRONI, LA/7/10AB/1/18; *Fermanagh Times*, 5 Nov. 1925.
50. [*Gift of Life*] Belfast Corporation Police Committee, 20 October 1927, PRONI, LA7/10AB/1/19; [*Foolish Wives*] *Ulster Gazette*, 3 Jan. 1925; [*Kelly Gang*] Register of Films Censored, 1 Oct. 1924, NAI, DJUS, FCO4/98/29/.
51. *Ulster Gazette*, 15 Sept. 1928, 1 Nov. 1924.
52. M. Connor [New Scotland Yard] to Inspector General RUC, 2 May 1927, PRONI, NIMHA, HA/32/1/518; W.A. Magill note, 16 Dec. 1929, ibid., HA/32/1/569.
53. Robertson, *The British Board of Film Censors*, pp.180–2.
54. Ira Bertrand, *Film censorship in Australia* (Queensland: University of Queensland Press, 1978), pp.45, 69.
55. Richard Maltby, 'Censorship and self-regulation' in Nowell-Smith, *Oxford history of world cinema*, pp. 236–41.
56. Colin Crisp, *The classic French cinema, 1930–1960* (Indiana: Indiana University Press, 1993), p.255.
57. Library Association of Ireland, *Report of the Executive Board 1928/29*, (Wexford, 1929), pp.8–10.
58. Lennox Robinson (ed.), *Lady Gregory's Journals, 1916–1930* (London: Putnam, 1946), pp.276–81.
59. *Galway Observer*, 6 Dec. 1928.
60. *Kilkenny People*, 12 July 1924; Cathal O'Shanon, 'The fight over censorship in the Irish Free State', *Evening Times*, 24 Feb. 1928, Irish Labour History Society Museum and Archives [ILSHA], Cathal O'Shannon papers, COS/51.
61. Library Association of Ireland, *Report of the Executive Board 1928/29*, p.10.
62. Chichester, NIHC debates, Vol.VI, 6 May 1924, 725–6; Leslie, Northern Ireland Senate debates [NIS], Vol.III, 20 March 1924, 41.
63. Minutes of Co. Antrim Book Selection Committee, 7 March 1925, PRONI, LA/1/3AG/40; *Fermanagh Times*, 9 July 1925; Minutes of Belfast Library, Museum and Arts Committee, 30 Dec. 1927, PRONI, LA/7/14/AA/2.
64. P.J. Corish, 'The first fifty years', in *The Catholic Truth Society of Ireland: the first fifty years* (Dublin: CTSI, 1950), pp.12–17; *Derry People*, 17 Jan. 1925.
65. *Irish Catholic Directory 1926*, p. 559; *Derry People*, 12 Dec. 1925.
66. *Up and Doing*, Vol.1, No.1, May 1935, p.20.
67. Maurice Curtis, 'Catholic action as an organized campaign in Ireland, 1921–1947', (Ph.D. thesis, University College Dublin, 2000), pp.178–9; Evelyn Bolster, *The Knights of Saint Columbanus* (Dublin: Gill & Macmillan, 1979), p.50.
68. *Irish Catholic*, 24 Jan., 5 Sept. 1925; *Derry People*, 7 March 1925.
69. H. Ruddy [Tuam Superintendent's Office] to Chief Superintendent, 22 Aug. 1924, NAI, DJUS, H180/16; Cullen, *Eason & Son*, p.263; *Irish Catholic*, 15 Aug. 1925.
70. M.H. MacInerny, 'Comments on the foregoing article', *Studies*, XVI (Dec. 1927), p.555;

O'Friel to McNeill, 21 Jan. 1926; McNeill to O'Friel, 13 March 1926, NAI, DJUS, JUS7/1/4.

71. Craven to Minister for Justice, 10 Dec. 1926, ibid., JUS7/1/5; 'Outline of suggested legislation for the suppression of immoral and indecent literature in the Irish Free State', UCDA, Tierney papers, LA30/333(19).
72. Cullen, *Eason & son*, pp.264–7.
73. Kieran Woodman, *Media control in Ireland, 1923–1983* (Illinois: S. Illinois University Press, 1985), p.43.
74. M.H. MacInerny, 'Catholic lending Libraries', *Irish Ecclesiastical Record*, 5th series, XIX (Jan.–June 1922) p.561; Obituary, *Irish Province News*, Vol.VI, No.1, Jan. 1950, p.82, IJA, Devane papers, J44/1.
75. R.S. Devane, 'Indecent literature – some legal remedies', *Irish Ecclesiastical Record*, 5th series, (Jan.–June 1925), p.182.
76. R.S. Devane, 'Suggested tariff on imported newspapers and magazines', *Studies*, XVI (Dec. 1927), p.545.
77. Devane, 'Indecent literature', p.194.
78. R.S. Devane, 'The gravity and extent of the evil of certain English press publications'; Devane to Dempsey, 21 April 1926, NAI, DJUS, JUS7/2/9.
79. Devane, 'Suggested tariff', p. 551.
80. M.H. MacInerny, Michael Tierney and PJ. Hooper, 'Comments on the foregoing article', *Studies*, XVI (Dec. 1927), pp.554–60; Evidence of P. de Búrca, Catholic Writers' Guild, to Committee on Evil Literature [hereafter CEL], 28 April 1926, NAI, DJUS, JUS7/2/5.
81. MacInerny, 'Catholic lending libraries', p.563; 'Evidence of the Catholic Truth Society to the Committee on Evil literature' [1926], Michael Tierney papers, UCDA, LA 30/333(3); Dept of Justice to CEL, 12 Feb. 1926, NAI, DJUS, JUS/7/1/2; NAGB, Home Office HO45/20912.
82. Devane, 'Indecent literature', p.194; 'Evidence of the Catholic Truth Society of Ireland', UCDA, LA 30/333 (3), pp. 6 and 11.
83. Evidence of Rev. M. Quinlan SJ to CEL, 21 April 1926, NAI, DJUS, JUS7/2/3; Evidence of W.B. Joyce to CEL, 21 April 1926, ibid., JUS7/2/12.
84. Fr O'Donnell, Secretary to Dr Byrne to Minister for Posts & Telegraphs, 6 Nov. 1926, DDA, Byrne papers, Posts & Telegraphs file; Walsh to O'Donnell, 8 Nov. 1926, ibid.
85. Devane, 'Indecent literature', pp.189–90; Evidence of R.S. Devane to CEL, 24 June 1926, NAI, DJUS, JUS7/2/9; Evidence of Rev. M. Quinlan SJ (Catholic Headmasters' Association) to CEL, 21 April 1926, ibid., JUS7/2/3; Evidence of P. de Búrca to CEL, op. cit; Evidence of Br Craven to CEL, [March 1926], ibid., JUS7/2/7; Evidence of Rev. Thomas F. Ryan SJ (Marian Sodalities) to CEL, 28 June 1926, ibid, JUS7/2/15.
86. Evidence of the Catholic Truth Society to CEL, UCDA, Tierney papers, LA30/333/(3); League of Nations documents on microfilm, c.734.M.299.1923.IV, Records of the international conference for the suppression of the circulation of and traffic in obscene publications (Geneva, 1923).
87. 'Evidence of the Catholic Truth Society of Ireland', p.42; *Irish Catholic*, 4 April 1926; Devane, 'Indecent literature' p.197.
88. Evidence of Fr Thomas F. Ryan SJ to CEL, 28 June 1926, NAI, DJUS, JUS7/2/15; Evidence of W.B. Joyce to CEL 21 April 1926, op. cit..
89. Various submissions, NAI, DJUS, JUS7/1/5, Frank O'Reilly to the secretary of the CEL, 24 Feb. 1926; note of telephone conversation, 29 April 1926, NAI, DJUS, JUS7/2/4; Curtis, 'Catholic action', pp.182–4.
90. *Munster News*, 13 March 1926; *Limerick & Clare Advocate*, 13 March 1926.
91. Devane to Fr Dempsey 21 April 1926, NAI, DJUS, JUS7/2/9; Bishop of Galway to CEL, 15 March 1926, ibid., JUS7/2/20; Secretary CEL to Coogan, 27 May 1926, ibid., JUS7/2/11; Evidence of Rev. R.S. Devane SJ to CEL, op. cit.
92. Evidence of D. Bridgman [RNBSA] to CEL, 26 May 1926, ibid., JUS7/2/13; Evidence of P. de Búrca to CEL, 28 April 1926, ibid., JUS7/2/5.
93. Evidence of W.B. Joyce to CEL, 21 April 1926; NAI, DJUS, JUS7/2/12; *Irish Times*, 13 Feb. 1926.
94. *Irish Times*, 18 Oct. 1926; Evidence of Charles Eason to CEL, 26 May 1926, NAI, DJUS, JUS7/1/2.
95. Evidence of Dublin Christian Citizenship Council to CEL, ibid.
96. Evidence of M. Quinlan SJ to CEL, 21 April 1926, ibid., JUS7/2/3; Evidence of W.B. Joyce to CEL, 21 April 1926, ibid., JUS7/2/12; O'Flaherty to Edward Garnett, 11 Oct. 1927, in A.A. Kelly (ed.), *The letters of Liam O'Flaherty* (Dublin: Wolfhound, 1996), p.197.
97. Statement by Garda Crime Branch, 17 May 1926, DJUS, JUS7/2/11.

98. Evidence of Dept Posts and Telegraphs to CEL, 10 May 1926, ibid., JUS7/2/17.
99. Evidence of Mr J. Redmond, Superintending Inspector of Customs and Excise to CEL, 9 June 1926, ibid., JUS7/1/2.
100. *Report of the Committee on Evil Literature* (Dublin, 1926).
101. *Irish Independent*, 1 Feb. 1927; *Evening Herald*, 1 Feb. 1927; *Irish Times*, 1 Feb. 1927; *Irish Catholic*, 5 Feb. 1927; *An Phoblacht*, 11 Feb. 1927, quoted in Peter Hegarty, *Peadar O'Donnell* (Dublin: Mercier Press, 1999), p. 184.
102. *Irish Catholic*, 2 April, 5, 7 and 28 May 1927, 25 Feb. 1928.
103. *Galway Observer*, 12 May 1928; Curtis, 'Catholic action', pp.187–8; Fianna Fáil Parliamentary Party Minutes, 17 April 1928, UCDA, Fianna Fáil Archives [FFA], P176/443; *Irish Catholic*, 19 May 1928.
104. Cullen, *Eason & Son*, p.268; *Irish Times*, 15 Sept. 1928.
105. O'Friel to Secretary, Dept. Posts and Telegraphs, 6 Oct. 1925 and 9 Nov. 1926; O'Friel to Garda Commissioner, 10 Jan. 1927, NAI, DJUS, H235/269.
106. O'Friel to Revenue Commissioners, 16 Sept. 1927, ibid., H308/36.
107. A.D. Codling to Secretary of the Department of the President, 21 May 1932; S.A. Roche to Secretary of the Department of Finance, 14 June 1932, NAI, DFIN, S3/11/34.
108. Costello, 'The right of public meeting' [1923], ibid., JUS/8/438.
109. Sean Hughes [Military Governor Newbridge Barracks] to Supt. Civic Guard, 3 Nov.1923, ibid., H75/23; O'Friel to Chief Commissioner DMP, 22 Nov. 1923, ibid., H75/25.
110. O'Duffy, 'Circular to all officers', 16 Aug. 1923, ibid., H236/14.
111. Report of Inspector P. Colohan, DMP, 6 Aug. 1923, ibid., H75/19; O'Friel to T. Nagle TD, 7 Aug. 1923, ibid., H156/39.
112. Public Notice, 22 Jan. 1924; Report of Sgt. R. Buttimer DMP, 25 Jan. 1924, ibid., H75/26.
113. E. Gilfillan to Secretary, Ministry of Home Affairs, 11 May 1925; 'Note on the state of Northern Ireland when the Government was set up and on the present condition', PRONI, NIMHA, HA/32/1/456.
114. *Irish News*, 24 Dec. 1924, *Fermanagh Times*, 1 Jan. 1925.
115. E.W. Shewell, Minute, 20 Nov. 1926, PRONI, Ministry of Home Affairs, HA/5/1443.
116. E.W. Shewell, Minute, 1 Feb. 1927, ibid., HA/5/588; W.A. Magill, 6 March 1929; E.W. Shewell, Minute, 24 Feb. 1930; Gilfillan to Secretary, Ministry of Home Affairs, 22 Sept. 1931, ibid., HA/5/1468.
117. E.W. Shewell, Minute [*Communist International*] 18 Feb. 1927, ibid., HA/32/1/515; [*Worker's Life*], 3 March 1927, ibid., HA/5/558.
118. General Letter by J. Nixon, 11 July 1922; Craig to Megaw, 6 Sept. 1922; Megaw to Craig, 6 Sept. 1923; R. Armstrong to Craig, 4 Oct. 1923, PRONI, Cabinet Office, CAB/9B/18/1.
119. C.G. Wickham, Circular to RUC members, 17 Jan. 1924, ibid., NIMHA, HA/32/1/455; Charges against Nixon, CAB/9B/18/1; Cabinet conclusions, 15 Dec. 1924, PRONI, CAB/4/100; John Camlin to John M. Andrews, no date [March 1924], CAB/9B/18/1; *Down Recorder*, 17 May 1924.
120. *Northern Whig*, 28 Oct. 1925; Note by A.P. Magill, 1 April 1925; Basil Brooke to Inspector General, 16 April 1925, ibid., NIMHA, HA/32/1/455.
121. E.W. Shewell, Note, 1 Oct. 1925; *Newsletter*, 5 Oct. 1925; E.W. Shewell to Inspector General RUC, 20 Nov. 1925, ibid., HA/32/1/463.
122. *Belfast Newsletter*, 4 April 1925, ibid., HA/5/1384; Sergeant R.J. Wilson, Report, 4 April 1925; W.A. Magill, Minute, 20 April 1925, ibid.
123. E.W. Shewell, Minute, 9 April 1925, ibid., HA/5/1385; Shewell, Minute, 23 April 1925; County Inspector, Note, 20 April 1925; D.L.C. (for Assistant Secretary) to Inspector General RUC, 27 April 1925, HA/5/1383.
124. *Derry People*, 20 June 1925; NIHC debates, Vol.VI, 10 Nov. 1925, 1783; Ibid., Vol.IX, 1 May 1928, 1161.
125. *Down Recorder*, 28 May 1927.
126. NIHC debates, Vol. IX, 24 April 1928, 954–5; unsigned note, NIMHA, PRONI, HA/5/2606.
127. E.W. Shewell to Inspector General RUC, 7 Feb. 1929, ibid., HA/5/572.
128. Graham S. Walker, *The politics of frustration: Harry Midgley and the failure of Labour in Northern Ireland* (Manchester: Manchester University Press, 1985), pp.34–6; Gilfillan (DI for Inspector General) to Secretary, Ministry of Home Affairs, 8 Sept. 1926; R.R. Spears (DI) to Inspector General RUC, 13 Sept. 1926; E.W. Shewell, Minute [no date]; Gilfillan to Secretary, MHA, 17 June 1927, PRONI, NIMHA, HA/32/1/508.
129. Ibid., HA/5/1299; NIHC debates, Vol.VIII, 24 May 1927, 1907.

CHAPTER THREE

Evil Literature

The Censorship of Publications Bill

James Fitzgerald-Kenney had the misfortune to succeed a hero. Replacing Kevin O'Higgins would never have been an easy task, but to do so after the latter's murder was harder still. It is no wonder, therefore, that it took him some time to draft a censorship bill; he had more important things to do. A 51-year-old barrister who represented Mayo South, Fitzgerald-Kenney had neither O'Higgins's fierce personality or intellect. He was ill equipped to adjudicate between the competing claims of artistic freedom and public morals that had bedevilled every attempt to censor literature throughout human history.

The bill that emerged in August 1928 was very different from the report of the Committee on Evil Literature. The Censorship of Publications Board was to have only five members, the definition of indecency was very broad and included works which offended against 'public morality' and, most controversially, the bill allowed the Minister to give private groups the power to submit material to the censorship board. Such 'recognised associations' were to be the only mechanism whereby the public would be able to complain about a publication. The first expressions of disquiet came from the largely middle-class, Protestant readers of the *Irish Times*. Opinion in the paper's letter columns was almost uniformly negative. Many of these commentators questioned whether a Catholic board could censor for the Protestant population given that the latter Churches believed in allowing people to take an independent line, especially on birth control. Fears were also raised about how 'future administrations' might amend the bill to make it less acceptable.[1] The *Church of Ireland Gazette* was initially aloof, describing the bill as applying to 'the Roman Catholic population' as Protestants did not buy evil literature. Very quickly, however, it became worried that 'a censorship, once established, will tend to extend and tighten, rather than relax, its grip'.[2]

William F. Trench, Professor of English at TCD, emerged as one of the few Protestant defenders of the bill, despite his desire to amend it in the Dáil. He argued that what was proposed was very different to wartime censorship under which the press had been told in advance what they could write. Instead, as with film, the press and writers could write whatever they liked and the censors would prohibit only 'specified class-es of matter'. This, he argued, followed practice in other dominions and was acceptable in principle.[3] Many of his co-religionists were uncon-vinced. A Church of Ireland deputation saw the Minister for Justice on 15 October 1928. One of its members, Bolton Waller, who had been an independent candidate in the 1927 election, reported that Fitzgerald-Kenney was 'polite and patient but extremely obdurate'. The Minister was 'unyielding' over the recognized associations and the use of the term 'public morality' in the bill. He explained that he wanted to ban anything 'attacking the institution of marriage'. The deputation was left with the impression that 'there may be prohibition on the strength of a single pas-sage in a book'. On the question of contraception 'the minister was still more stiff' and opposed anything which 'even incidentally advocated it'. When asked if this included the works of George Bernard Shaw or Dean Inge he replied that 'he was not afraid of big names … if they were as I alleged they would have to go'. Waller told Michael Tierney that 'a large number of Protestants do, absolutely genuinely and sincerely regard this as an intolerant and unfair bill', although he did not think that was the government's intention. 'I want to avoid sectarian controversy of the old type but this bill makes it very difficult', he complained.[4] Archbishop Gregg of Dublin implicitly criticized the proposal during a sermon in Belfast: he compared it to a failed attempt by Belfast Corporation to cen-sor the racing results in newspapers many years earlier.[5] Many Protes-tants had already been alienated by the administration's position on divorce and they feared that the state's early promises to treat them fair-ly were being forgotten. The proposed role of the recognized associations suggested to them that censorship would be run by Roman Catholic activists. At the same time, they had no desire to provoke a conflict with the majority denomination that they had no hope of winning. They seem to have been more concerned to reform than to defeat the measure, and there is no sign that Protestants were any more tolerant of obscenity than Catholics.

Fr Richard Devane defended the bill against charges of sectarianism. He pointed out that several members of the Committee on Evil Literature had been Protestant and that such Protestant states as Canada, the United States and Germany all had some form of literary censorship. The CTSI was less accommodating. Its committee of management told Michael Tierney that 'it is necessary that all Catholic forces should be united in the endeavour to prevent any weakening of the Catholic posi-tion in connection with the Censorship Bill'. It opposed a suggestion that clergy be excluded from the censorship board on the ground that no min-ister of religion should suffer discrimination.[6] The fact remained that the prospect of Catholic priests deciding what Protestants could read was a disquieting one for the minority. The bill was also strongly supported by the Roman Catholic Archbishop of Cashel and the Bishops of Kildare and Waterford. The last of these, Dr Hackett, condemned 'the secret influence employed to mutilate the principles of the Evil Literature Bill', and argued that 'there can be no compromise with these [people] who, under the plea of safeguarding liberty would minimise the provisions of this bill'.[7]

At this late stage, writers and artists finally began to take the threat of censorship seriously. Desmond FitzGerald, the Minister for External Affairs, had many friends in these circles and was subjected to their anger and scorn. Francis Hackett – no relation to the Bishop of Waterford – wrote to him that 'Ireland = Paraguay. We are, on this side of affairs, probably the most ludicrous nation outside the Negro state of Liberia'. Ezra Pound was relentless, 'what the HELL does this mean ... Can't you keep condoms and classics in separate parts of your law books?!!!' Pound also questioned whether such legislation would help the cause of a united Ireland.[8] While such complaints were doubtless socially embarrassing for FitzGerald, they were politically irrelevant; the support of the hierarchy for the bill was always going to trump the opposition of the writers.

The most important and effective defender of the writers' cause was George Russell (Æ), the editor of the *Irish Statesman*. He was politically well informed and his intellectually rigorous attacks on the bill remain the best critiques of censorship policy in the period. Echoing the view of many of the bill's opponents Russell condemned the grounds for censorship as vague. He questioned what 'public morality' was to include: would it mean banning socialist, agnostic or rationalist works? He was especially perturbed by the idea of recognized associations, commenting that 'uniting their intellectual obscurity into a recognized association will not create a collective wisdom'. Unusually for a commentator on the issue he tried to deal with the philosophy behind the bill, denying that 'people could be made moral by an act of parliament'. He also questioned whether it was a good idea to censor even intelligent discussion of contraception when it was being debated internationally. As Nicholas Allen has pointed out, Russell was not in favour of unlimited freedom of speech but wanted it regulated by the criminal law rather than a censor. He was particularly opposed to the idea of recognized associations which he labelled 'illiterates'.[9]

George Bernard Shaw weighed in behind Russell and defended the need to discuss birth control, if only to prevent quacks from exploiting the ignorant. Unfortunately he went on to deal with the issue via uncharacteristically poor satire. Predicting that the Catholic Church would have to make statues of the Virgin ugly lest they excite sexual passion was clever but unconvincing, while condemning the pro-censorship lobby as 'a handful of morbid Catholics, mad with heresyphobia, unnaturally combining with a handful of Calvinists mad with sexophobia' may well have been accurate but was never going to win over TDs or ordinary voters.[10]

Yeats produced two articles on the bill. The first was simultaneously too high minded for the ordinary public and too eccentric for educated Catholics. Putting forward the proposition that it had been Catholic Thomism that had allowed the revival of sensual art from Giotto to Titian, he claimed that banning material 'calculated to excite sexual passion' was against Catholic teaching. He conceded there was 'such a thing as immoral paintings and immoral literature' but denied that a legal definition was possible. Instead he preferred that censorship be left to 'men learned in art and letters' or 'average, educated men'. That Yeats was serious about this is clear from his suggestion to Ernest Blythe that the state establish an academy of literature to adjudicate on the artistic merit of books. Scientific books could be sent to the Royal Irish Academy. Blythe demurred, arguing that the proposal was too controversial.[11] It was rumoured in 1926 that the Royal Irish Academy had planned an Irish *Académie des Belles Lettres* but had been unable to resolve the difficulty of whether to include controversial writers like Joyce, Robinson and O'Flaherty.[12]

Yeats's second article was a more effective critique of the bill. He compared the 'men and women of intellect' who opposed the bill with its supporters: 'ecclesiastics who shy at the modern world as horses in my youth shied at a motor car.' He warned that the CTSI was likely to be among the recognized associations and that the censorship of material relating to birth control would threaten even respectable journals. Yeats felt that censorship would give the government 'control over our very thought'. He admitted that no one intended this to occur 'but in legislation intention is nothing, and the letter of the law is everything'. Had there been a censorship of the stage, he commented, the Abbey would never have existed. Yeats saw the issue as one defining the relationship between Church and state. If the government wanted to pass legislation that was desired by the Church, it had to show that the good of the state demanded it, he argued. 'Those who belong to the Church of Ireland or to no church should compel the fullest discussion', he believed, especially on the issue of birth control. He had been told by a government official that those supporting censorship 'cannot understand why the good of the nine-tenths that never opens a book should not prevail over that of the tenth that does'.[13] Taken together these articles showed both Yeats's passionate support for freedom of artistic expression, and his inability to fight the populist arguments of the pro-censorship advocates. He did not discuss the potential effects of censorship on ordinary people but on artists and intellectuals. His defence of free speech was limited to that which was of aesthetic or intellectual value.

Desmond FitzGerald was privately contemptuous of Yeats, telling Pound that 'Uncle William and the *Irish Times* notwithstanding, the [censorship] committee will be enlightened' and would not 'prevent any single person from reading anything that you or I think it desirable should be read'.[14] Artists may have been outraged and they could muster a strong case, but they could not woo the same public and politicians to whom the pro-censorship campaigners had sold the trinity of intellectual protectionism, international practice and opposition to birth control. They did have some powerful supporters; Andrew Jameson wrote to Yeats to thank him for his articles. He blamed the situation on 'the pathetic condition of ignorance they [the Roman Catholic bishops] have kept their flocks in and their loss of control over the young. No bill of this kind will remedy these things.'[15] Frank Gallagher, the republican journalist and writer who would later edit the *Irish Press*, was enraged by the criticisms of the bill. He told a correspondent that the bill's opponents 'hold Ireland up to ridicule. Æ has a scandalous attack in the London *Nation*. It makes me squirm to have been praised by him.'[16]

The debate moved on to the Dáil and here the government found that it could not rely on its own TDs to support the bill. Michael Tierney and Sir James Craig, Professor of Medicine and independent TD for Dublin University, called for books to be excluded from the bill's remit. Tierney warned that they ran the risk of producing 'a list of prohibited books ... which will make a laughing stock of this country'. He condemned the Canadian blacklist, so beloved of the reformers, pointing out that there were many good books on it. Hugh Law, a Cumann na nGaedheal TD for Donegal, was of the same mind, arguing that books were harder than newspapers for the censors to judge. He put forward four test cases: *Boule de Suif* by de Maupassant, *Les Trois Filles* by Dupont, and two works by Shaw, *Mrs Warren's Profession* and *An Intelligent Woman's Guide to Socialism and Capitalism*. All were adult, three dealt with prostitution and venereal disease while one was about birth control. Law had no confidence that such works would be protected under the bill.[17] Most importantly Patrick Hogan, Minister for Agriculture and a friend and ally of Kevin O'Higgins, expressed his desire 'to limit this Bill as much as possible'. Although he camouflaged his rebellion with attacks on the opposition and the importation of immoral publications, it was clear that he opposed the proposal. Hogan was an intelligent, skilled politician who represented a real threat to the bill. Law was a frequent contributor to the *Irish Statesman* and Allen has argued that Russell was effectively co-ordinating the opposition to the bill; Hogan was a confidante of Horace Plunkett, another ally of Russell's.[18] The evidence for this is largely circumstantial and seems to mistake Russell's influence for leadership. There is little doubt, however, that the bill's critics were all from literary or academic backgrounds and shared Russell's views on the matter.

Other TDs defended the censorship of books vigorously. Dublin deputy J.J. Byrne, himself a Protestant, particularly condemned *The Well of Loneliness* and *Lady Chatterley's Lover*. Domhnall Ua Buachalla, a Fianna Fáil TD from Kildare, argued that the object of the bill was to ban cheap novels, which were just as harmful as newspapers and were 'bought principally by young girls'. Somewhat begging the question he declared the classics to be safe from the censor as 'we all know that the amount of harm that is done by these books is infinitesimal'. The Minister declared that books should only be condemned if they were 'systematically indecent', though that phrase did not appear in the bill. He was not clear about what this meant. He seemed reluctant to concede any protection to artistic value, commenting 'I cannot understand the class of book which would excite some person just to proper love and might not excite others towards unlawful lust'.[19]

Fianna Fáil's policy on the bill was of immense importance and was heavily influenced by Seán Lemass and P.J. Little. When the party's justice committee was slow to produce amendments to the bill, Lemass had the issue moved to the general committee where he could be more closely involved. That body decided that the party would seek to amend the bill's provisions relating to the definition of 'public morality' and the size of the censorship board.[20] In the Dáil, P.J. Ruttledge offered moderates no support; 'we cannot see, on this side of the house, at any rate, how in any way whatever, literature or art can suffer in the slightest degree from the passing of this bill'.[21] At this time Fianna Fáil had no interest in gaining the gratitude of intellectuals. It was building a formidable party organization among the small farmers of the west and the urban working classes but it needed to win the acceptance of the Roman Catholic Church. After all, many of its members had been denied the sacraments during the Civil War and some priests and bishops still distrusted de Valera. By supporting measures such as censorship, the party made it harder for Cosgrave to pose as the champion of the Catholic nation.

Those looking for special provisions for literature were hampered by the fact that they were, quite openly, campaigning for the rights of an elite. Patrick Hogan, admitted that 'Thomas or Pat Murphy, who lives anywhere between Donegal and Cork, is not likely to read either Balzac or Aristophanes even in translation'. Indeed this was presented as positive reason to exempt the classics; they were unlikely to be read by the uneducated anyway. In the Senate, Sir John Keane believed that 'the mass of people' – who comprised two-thirds of the population – read too little to be concerned with banned literature.[22] Tierney admitted that Gibbon's *Decline and Fall of the Roman Empire* and Burton's *Arabian Nights* were obscene in parts but defended them as not only great works of literature, but also expensive and hard to get. His amendment to prevent a ban unless the book was 'wholly indecent' failed.[23] Another amendment proposed that the publisher or editor be allowed representation before the censorship board. T.J. O'Connell, leader of the Labour Party and a former member of the Committee on Evil Literature, questioned the logic of this proposal. He argued that the board was not meant to rule on the intentions of author, editor or publisher but on the effect the book was likely to have. Fitzgerald-Kenney seemed to agree and the amendment was lost. The pressure from moderate forces, including a Cabinet Minister and several government TDs, had some effect and the Minister introduced a series of amendments to make the censors take account of the artistic value of a book, the class of its prospective readership and the language in which it was written.[24]

The debate over how to define indecency was complicated. The biggest problem was whether it was the objective content of a work or the intent of its author, editor or publisher that made a book indecent. The Minister was adamantly in the former camp. His initial definition of indecent as including 'calculated to excite sexual passion or to suggest or excite sexual immorality, or in any other way to corrupt or deprave' was widely condemned as too vague, and Seán Lemass pointed out that there was nothing intrinsically wrong with 'sexual passion'. At the committee stage, a series of amendments were proposed. William Thrift, TD for Dublin University, wanted to ban only material that 'in its purpose' incited to sexual immorality. P.J. Little of Fianna Fáil countered that the law should follow the practice in libel cases where intention was not important but rather the effect on public opinion. Fitzgerald-Kenney was firmly of the same view, 'you are not dealing with intention. You are dealing with books objectively. You are considering what the effect of the book is going to be.'[25] This was the interpretation which was reflected in the eventual act.

The second controversy concerned whether censorship should be restricted to matters of sexual morality. Fianna Fáil, the experience of Civil War censorship still fresh in their minds, were afraid that political writing would be restricted. They were especially concerned by the use of the phrase 'public morality' in the bill. T.J. O'Connell agreed, pointing out that the committee had been unanimous that 'the type of immorality it sought to prevent was sexual immorality'. Patrick Hogan, unusually, agreed with Lemass but he commented acidly that more harm was done to public morality by 'pushing Bibles away and affirming oaths' than by indecent literature – a reference to the legal and philosophical hair-splitting employed by the Fianna Fáil party to allow its members to take the oath and enter the Dáil after years of abstention. By contrast, Tierney and Law argued that the bill's remit should be extended to include the reporting of violent crime. The Minister accepted both points, deleting the phrase 'public morality' and, reluctantly, including a clause allowing the board to ban reports of sordid trials. That he did the first despite the opposition of the Catholic Truth Society illustrates the limits of its power.[26]

The origins of Tierney and Law's amendment were curious. Tierney's stance on the bill was an embarrassment to the CTSI as he had sat on the committee which had decided its position on obscenity. After he made public his criticisms of the bill, the CTSI leaders met Tierney privately and agreed to accept some amendments to the bill on the subject of literary and artistic merit. In return, Tierney promised to introduce the amendment on the reporting of crime. This is not to suggest that he did not support such a measure anyway. Both men accepted the principle of censorship; indeed Law was scathing in his criticism of the newspapers. Tierney was likewise unequivocal in advocating the censorship of the press while protecting the rights of serious authors. Neither man was making a liberal case for freedom of speech, rather both were making a more sophisticated form of the conservative argument, which had underpinned the censorship campaign from the start. Despite this they faced ferocious criticism from the pro-censorship side. The CTSI publicly criticized these moderates and opposed allowing the importation of books for private use, limiting the censorship only to cheaper books and prohibiting only books that were intentionally obscene.[27] The amendment also gives us an insight into the how social class influenced the debate on censorship. Lurid reporting of crime was the province of popular newspapers, mostly imported from Britain. People like Tierney, Law and Hogan did not read such papers anyway and saw no reason why anyone else should do so. On the other hand, it was intolerable to them that the state should dictate their own reading. It also illustrates how a measure first proposed to deal with the foreign press was being debated in terms of its effects on books.

The bill proposed to ban all birth control literature without requiring a decision from the censorship board. The only dissenters to this provision were Tierney, Thrift and Craig in the Dáil, and Keane in the Senate. It is important to note that none of these was directly elected by the public. The silence of TDs from ordinary constituencies suggests that the public supported this part of the bill at least. An amendment from Tierney to have the censorship board deal with such cases failed. Fitzgerald-Kenney refused to accept it on the grounds that it was essential that birth control books be banned even if the censorship broke down. It was up to retailers to check their own stock and remove offending publications. Craig was the only member to actually speak out in favour of birth control. Keane was one of the few speakers in either house to frame the question in religious terms. He contrasted the Roman Catholic policy of 'prohibition and control' with Protestant respect for 'liberty of thought and freedom of conscience'; he argued that the former should be left to control its members without state help. Inevitably, given the tone of his remarks and the weakness of the Senate, he was ignored. The only limitation to the bill's provisions on the subject was an amendment in the Senate, accepted by Fitzgerald-Kenney, to exempt publications from prosecution if they merely advertised other publications about contraception but did not comment on it. The censors would still be free to ban these, however.[28] This was to prove an important modification in later years.

The actual mechanics of censorship received much discussion. The Minister was challenged on two important points. The first was the size of the censorship board; the second, and most embarrassing, was the idea of recognized associations. Given the small population of available and qualified persons in the country, it was obvious, though not mentioned, that a large board would be more likely to contain a mixture of conservative and liberal members and therefore would be prone to controversy. The Minister had advocated a five-person board to prevent the formation of factions and to promote consistency. Bryan Cooper, a former military censor, supported this argument, but Fianna Fáil opposed it and on a division a nine-person board was accepted by one vote. The Minister was able to reverse the change by amendment in the Senate but a proviso was included that two members of the board could always prevent a ban.[29]

The recognized associations were the Minister's most significant addition to the report of the Committee on Evil Literature. His argument for them was that they would keep the censorship process in touch with reality and would prevent it from falling into disuse through public apathy. They would not have any judicial power but would act as gatherers of complaints. He strongly resisted pressure to ensure that they would have to read a book in its entirety before referring it.[30] Earlier, Devane had complained that it was hard to 'maintain public interest' and that he did not think 'that the censorship committee will have many matters brought to their notice or be inundated with demands for censorship'.[31] The Minister's opponents were scathing, however: Ruttledge wanted to know if the associations recognized would include the CID, and Law remarked that he was more afraid of 'busybodies' than bishops.[32] As we have seen they also concerned Russell and his allies. Fitzgerald-Kenney watched as the Dáil unceremoniously dumped his proposal by a twenty-vote majority. Nor did the Senate agree to give it a second chance. The decision to drop the recognized associations was welcomed by the *Church of Ireland Gazette*, which observed that 'they would have been largely composed of cranks and the kind of people who try to see evil everywhere'. The Censorship of Publications Bill represented something of a disaster for Fitzgerald-Kenney. He had been forced to accept Fianna Fáil amendments, to broaden the scope of his bill and to face down a rebellion that included his Cabinet colleague Hogan. He had clearly lost control of the house. Things could have been worse, as O'Halpin has shown. Lemass had wanted to put down more amendments and had criticized his party's justice committee for failing to do so.[33] The removal of the recognized associations had been the main objective of Russell's circle but it was a Pyrrhic victory; although the legislation no longer gave the vigilantes any official role in the censorship process, there was nothing to stop them from organizing private submissions of books to the board from their members.

Implementing the Censorship of Publications Act

The day-to-day organization and interpretation of the act was now up to the Civil Service. The first test occurred in August 1929 long before the appointment of the first Censorship of Publications Board. A letter from the Department of Justice warned newsagents that the magazine *Health & Strength* was now banned as it contained articles advocating birth control. The police were not sent in immediately 'in view of the fact that the act is a recent one'. Eason and George Croker Ltd replied that they had already stopped selling the magazine. The department made it clear to the sellers that even after the board was appointed they would have 'a responsibility' under section 16 of the act to remove birth control literature from their stock.[34]

The Catholic Truth Society was eager to test the new law. The removal of the provisions for 'recognised associations' had deprived it of status but not of power and the Society simply instructed its members to submit books on their own account. It issued printed instructions on how to examine and submit publications and encouraged them to organize groups to deal with papers and magazines. They were instructed to look out for denials of the divinity of Christ, blasphemy, spiritualist practices, attacks on Roman Catholicism and violations of the Censorship of Publications Act.[35] The fact that these instructions included religious objections not specifically covered by the act suggests either that the CTSI was hoping to extend the censorship through test cases or that it had not ruled out a return to its earlier vigilante tactics. The CTSI's executive secretary, Frank O'Reilly submitted a novel, *Roper's Row*, to the Minister for Justice that, he claimed, advocated birth control. The complaint was rejected as 'on one page out of 400 there are a certain number of rhetorical questions regarding doubts on the question of contraception', though even this was deemed to tread on delicate ground. A week later, the editor of *The Standard*, Rev. Joseph Deeny, submitted an issue of *Passing Show* and complained that it advertised books on birth control. His complaint was rejected, as the advertisements themselves did not advocate contraception and 'advertisement *simpliciter* of such works in other publications' was not illegal; however, the Minister decided it would be submitted to the Censorship Board when it was established as it was 'sailing so close to the wind'.[36] By contrast, Protestants were not impressed by the new legislation. As Fitzgerald-Kenney later admitted to the Bishop of Ossory, 'much Protestant support was lost to the government over the Immoral Literature Bill [sic]' and, as a result, he refused to press ahead with a ban on the importation of contraceptives.[37]

The early days of the Censorship of Publications Board

The Censorship of Publications Act was a poorly drafted piece of legislation; substantially amended and stricken by compromises, it was certainly not as draconian an instrument of Catholic Action as advocates of censorship hoped. The Censorship of Publications Board, which was appointed to implement the act, was not very promising. It was chaired by Canon Patrick Boylan, the Professor of Eastern Languages at UCD and a scriptural scholar. He was joined by Professor W.E. Thrift of TCD and W.B. Joyce of the Dublin branch of the INTO who had testified in favour of censorship to the Committee on Evil Literature. W.J. O'Reilly and Patrick J. Keawell completed the board. As Æ was quick to point out, in the *Irish Statesman*, none of these was a literary expert. The board's immediate problem was not choosing what to ban but finding anything to examine. At its first meeting, it banned a small number of books but was afraid that if it published a very short list, people would be encouraged to seek the books out. It asked the government if it could purchase a selection of books 'which are likely to be the subject of an adverse report' and hoped that 'the public, having got a lead in the publication of the early lists could be trusted to do the rest'. The CPB initially wanted to buy *Elmer Gantry* by Sinclair Lewis, *Stories of Strange Happenings* by Dolf Wyllarde, *Portrait in a Mirror* by Charles Morgan, *Jew Süss* by Lion Feuchtwanger, and *Marriage and Morals* by Bertrand Russell. It was given ten pounds but warned that the system laid down in the legislation had intended that the public should pay for the work of the board. Within a few months the board again looked for ways to get the censorship process moving. As it was receiving so few books from the public it spent five pounds to join the *Times* book club, borrowed the titles it wanted, banned them and returned them. The officials in the Department of Finance were intrigued by this 'bright idea' as 'the subscription would obviate the need for the purchase of any books'. They were so pleased with the idea that they decided not to ask for the return of the remaining money.[38]

After four months of work, the board reported to the Minister for

Justice that there had been very few complaints from the public. It suggested that the regulations regarding the submission of books and periodicals be relaxed to require the submission of fewer copies of a publication. By July, Stephen Roche, Assistant Secretary of the Department of Justice, informed the Department of Finance that 'very few complaints are received'. This was disappointing as 'it was hoped at the time [that the legislation was passed] that the public would display a greater interest in the work of the board'. The CPB wanted to renew their subscriptions to the *Times* book club so that it could immediately ban objectionable books when it heard about them. The request was approved as 'the committee have a thankless task to perform and the Department of Justice is anxious to meet them in every way possible'. The subscription to the *Times* and later *Switzer's* circulating libraries was maintained throughout this period. When the library did not carry a book it was bought by the secretary to the board or through the Stationery Office – which got a discount.[39]

Complaints to the CPB

Had the job of submitting publications been left to the ordinary public, the censorship might have simply drifted into obscurity within a few years. There can be no doubt that the burden of supplying multiple copies of every book deterred potential complainants. Some of those who did complain were cranks. One sent in newspaper clippings showing photographs of swimmers whose groins he had circled in pencil. Another protested at the display of a photo of nude sculpture in the *Radio Times*. A third was offended by a picture in the *Daily Mail* of a female figure skater whose knickers could be seen. Another complainant refused 'to supply you with free copies of books'.[40]

The censorship was preserved by the determination of the Catholic Truth Society of Ireland, still under the leadership of Frank O'Reilly. At the end of its first year, the CPB reported that the CTSI 'has furnished the majority of the complaints received'. The Society itself claimed to have five hundred activists at work locating objectionable publications. Adams claims that this level of activity did not continue because Frank O'Reilly felt that the Society should promote good literature rather than spending its money locating bad books. He supplies no evidence for this claim and it is not supported by the Department of Justice files up to 1934. If the CTSI did diminish its activities after that date it would seem unlikely that it was due to any change of heart by O'Reilly given his fervent opposition to evil literature for the preceding decade. The board noted that few other social organizations had helped at all, despite the fact that their efforts were essential to the success of the censorship.[41]

In the early months of the censorship's existence, the CTSI tested the limits of the new law. O'Reilly submitted a complaint against a novel in April 1930, claiming that it contained a chapter advocating birth control, but it was rejected by the CPB. In May, he complained that English papers had carried a speech that included comments on birth control. This was dismissed by O'Friel, the Secretary of the Department of Justice, as not 'a serious contribution to the working of the act'. Other questionable complaints concerning birth control literature were submitted referring to such titles as *Caged Birds,* the *Leader* (an English racing paper), *Reynold's Illustrated News* and *Poultry World,* which all carried advertisements for books on the subject. There was also a complaint against the *Spectator* for publishing a review of a book on birth control.[42] Such complaints exposed the limitations of the Censorship of Publications Act. Although advocacy of birth control was forbidden, advertisement of publications which advocated it was not. This distinction escaped many complainants.

In August 1930 O'Reilly complained about an issue of *John Bull* which contained an article by Evelyn Waugh which, he held, advocated birth control. It was a somewhat more subtle piece than he claimed. Waugh argued for the division of sex-education between the Church and the state, with the former teaching sacramental values and the latter teaching birth control and sexual health. The Minister for Justice made it clear that he would not order the prosecution of distributors of the paper. The CPB did not recommend a ban either. Instead, Charles Eason asked the publishers to ensure that such material was omitted from their Irish editions in future.[43] As is discussed below, this was to become a common practice. In November 1930 O'Reilly submitted several copies of *Locomotive Journal* alleging that it was indecent, obscene and advocated birth control. This worried Fitzgerald-Kenney; noting that the magazine had such a small circulation that Eason didn't even stock it, he feared banning it would make the censorship board and his department look ridiculous. Instead, the department asked the publishers of the periodical to stop including advertisements relating to birth control.[44] O'Reilly's bizarre complaints were not the work of crank. He had carefully tested the limits of the act and had succeeded in getting the government to act unofficially even when it could not ban a publication. He had also exposed a serious weakness in the act: the inability of the CPB to ban publications which advertised publications about birth control but which did not themselves advocate it.

The northern experience

Having decided against introducing new laws to regulate publications, Northern Ireland had to implement the existing ones in a new context.

In this respect the region did not operate independently but as part of the UK. Customs were a reserved function and decisions reached in Britain had effects on what could be sold in Northern Ireland. This seemed to suit the northern authorities as the issue was not even discussed until 1927. At that time, the UK authorities reacted to a few, unnamed, instances of 'indecent wares' being sent from France to the province and decided that it was necessary to come to an arrangement with their counterparts in Belfast as to how such cases should be handled. If a letter were sent from England or Scotland ordering indecent material, it was forwarded to the Home Office, which would then decide whether to take action against the prospective purchaser or to simply confiscate it. When material from abroad, usually France, destined for England or Scotland was intercepted, the Home Office again decided whether to allow delivery of it, detain it or hand it over to the Director of Public Prosecutions.

The question was whether the Home Office should be allowed to make such decisions for Northern Ireland or whether the Ministry of Home Affairs in Belfast should take charge. Although prosecutions were to be dealt with by the Belfast authorities, the Home Office favoured handling other matters itself as it would be quicker, and concluded that 'it is desirable that the Home Office should act in regard to Northern Ireland in the first instance'. The Northern Ireland Ministries of Commerce and Home Affairs both agreed to this on the ground of convenience.[45] Effectively, the northern government handed over most of its powers to deal with obscene or indecent publications to the Imperial government.

The British government dealt with obscene matter in a somewhat ad hoc way. When the secretary of the Associated Booksellers of Great Britain and Ireland asked the Home Office for a copy of its list of banned books he was told that there was none. Officially speaking, there was no censorship of books in Britain. Instead the Ministry confidentially informed booksellers of any title about which it had received a valid complaint. The Home Office also liked to exert unofficial influence. For example, in 1928 the Home Secretary Sir William Joynson-Hicks wrote to a director of Mudie's circulating library about the scandal caused by the publication of Isadora Duncan's autobiography, asking them not to circulate it.[46] He probably wanted to return to the pre-war days when the circulating libraries could effectively ban a book. By the 1920s, times had changed and such measures were less successful.

In 1929 there were warrants in force to allow the search of post from 115 addresses to the UK. The vast majority of these were in France. The Post Office regularly seized only ten books. The most commonly found were *The Well of Loneliness* by Radclyffe Hall, *My Secret Life* by Frank Harris and *Lady Chatterly's Lover* by D.H. Lawrence. Between 1923 and

TABLE 3.1:
POSTAL PACKETS STOPPED IN THE UK 1926–28

	Home Office				Post Office				
	Books	Periodicals	Photos	Total	Books	Periodicals	Photos	Total	Grand Total
1926	149	2189	49	2387	160	13	28	201	2588
1927	100	1355	17	1472	12	13	19	44	1516
1928	125	329	7	461	21	11	16	48	509

1929 there were seventy-three prosecutions, usually as a result of the interception of indecent wares in the post. In 271 cases, a warning was given instead. Many of those warned were university and public school students.

Table 3.1 gives the numbers of postal packets stopped in the UK under Home Office and Post Office warrants. According to the Home Office, the decline in the number of seizures was due to the increasing strictness of the French authorities. 'The majority of the books which are now intercepted are flagellation works and cheap borderline books either in English or French.'[47]

The London Public Morality Council wanted stricter obscenity laws. According to one Home Office memorandum, they were 'flirting with the idea of censorship (influenced no doubt by what has been proposed in Ireland)'. Their campaign was also similar to that in the Irish Free State in that it emphasized the effects of cheap books more than outright pornography. In 1928 the Home Office had examined the Free State's Censorship of Publications Bill and concluded that it was 'a bold proposal' containing 'drastic and courageous provisions'. Not surprisingly the Ministry concluded that 'the proposals of the Free State government would not be acceptable to the general public in this country'.[48]

There were some demands in Northern Ireland for a censorship of publications. The *Derry People* was to the fore in seeking similar laws in both jurisdictions. The Unionist press also printed criticism of modern writing without always calling explicitly for censorship. An example was the speech by the Liverpool novelist Dr R.W. MacKenna to the Association of Booksellers of Great Britain and Ireland that was quoted at length by the *Ulster Gazette*. The modern novel 'was acclaimed as the voice of genius but it was only the gruntlings of a pig wallowing in its own mire', he claimed. Presbyterian writers published several articles which argued that bad books could do serious and lasting harm to the reader. These articles did not argue for censorship but instead recommended that the reader stick to wholesome literature.[49] The northern Roman Catholic bishops also campaigned on the issue. Bishop McHugh of Derry condemned 'infidel, irreligious and filthy literature' from 'across the channel' in his Lenten pastoral of 1925. Archbishop O'Donnell of Armagh also condemned imported indecent literature and called on people to support the CTSI. Bishop O'Kane of Derry took the opportunity in 1927 to emphasize the differences between the Churches on this issue. He argued that the policy of allowing unrestricted reading had devastated other Churches. 'Evil literature' was the subject of sermons during the mission of June 1928 in St Patrick's Cathedral, Armagh.[50]

The *Derry People* was enthusiastic about the Free State's censorship act. The bill would 'be welcomed by the vast majority of the people of Ireland', it said. It particularly hoped that something would be done about the 'cheap novels with which our bookstalls are flooded' and which were 'morally harmful to a class of people who would never dream of purchasing one of the more infamous Sunday newspapers'. It also called for action against Irish writers who 'produce novels that no self-respecting person would read ... under the guise of realism'. Lastly the paper argued that 'the northern government, in this as in other matters, would do well to follow the example of the Saorstát'.[51] There was little response to the legislation in the Unionist press. Lynn Doyle, who would later serve on and resign from the Censorship of Publications Board, expressed his reservations in the *Ulster Gazette*. His argument, echoing Russell, was that morality was only of value if freely arrived at. He asked if the Free State would be truly moral if it eliminated all vestiges of indecent literature. 'Obviously not,' he concluded, 'since the nation would be no more truly moral than the man deprived of alcohol is truly temperate.' He also feared that the censorship of literature would herald a return to Victorian standards of taste and dress. This would be counterproductive because 'the best way to promote vice is to make virtue ridiculous'.[52]

Not all censorship in Northern Ireland concerned obscenity or sedition. Along with the rest of the UK, the northern government tried to control advertisements for the southern-based sweepstakes from advertising in its region. In 1922 the *Belfast Telegraph* and the *Irish News* were taken to task for publicizing sweeps and were threatened with prosecution. In 1923 both the *Belfast Telegraph* and the *Derry Standard* took the precaution of sending advertisements to the Ministry of Home Affairs for clearance. Both were refused permission to publish. All the principal northern papers were warned in 1923 not to publish notices of sweepstakes or lotteries.[53] In 1924 a sweep planned by the Royal Naval Branch of the British Legion was prevented by the Ministry of Home Affairs, acting at the request of the Home Office.[54] A suggestion in the *Irish Churchman* that the government ban the publication of betting odds was not acted on, however. Other forms of publication were controversial. A reporter for the *Irish News* recalled that he was taught that 'the seamy side of life' was sometimes 'so shocking that it could not be reported'.[55] The fact that campaigners against Sunday newspapers did not target the domestic press suggests that such self-censorship was normal.

Censorship and self-determination

Censorship of publications was an attractive policy for Irish social reformers for many reasons. It served to correct what they saw as the decline in morality that had taken hold since the war. It also acted as a defence against dangerous ideas such as birth control. It allowed the Irish Free State to define itself culturally in a way that took control of the cultural revival out of the hands of the artists and writers whom the reformers regarded with suspicion. In their ideal world, Irish culture would be cleansed of modernism, realism, socialism and other imported evils. Censorship would also shut out foreign, especially British, newspapers and magazines with their reports of crime and divorce and their discussions of birth control. The campaigners were remarkably successful in presenting censorship simultaneously as a defence against the outside world and as an essential part of the apparatus of a modern state. By constantly referring to Canada, Australia and the United States, they were able to portray themselves as progressives. Their campaign was effectively organized through a variety of Roman Catholic lay organizations and supported by the hierarchy. By contrast, the artists who opposed censorship failed to create an organization to defend their interests or to mobilize popular support. This was partly caused by their contempt for conservative Catholicism, which is clear from the letters of O'Flaherty, Yeats, Hackett and Pound. As a result, they were ignored by the political parties. Their greatest achievement was the removal of the provisions for recognized associations but they had again underestimated the resourcefulness of their opponents who had campaigned for years without official recognition and were quite capable of continuing in that manner.

Northern Ireland experienced many of the same religious and social pressures as the Irish Free State. It had no interest, however, in establishing its independence, cultural or otherwise, from the UK or in following the example of foreign countries. Given the ambivalence of the Protestant Churches with regard to contraception, it would have been impossible for a northern government to legislate on the subject without offending one of the denominations. The Roman Catholic Church lacked the influence with the northern government that it enjoyed in the south and it also was less prepared to deal directly with Craig's administration. In the absence of significant campaigns from the Protestant Churches or the loyal institutions, it was in the government's interest to follow British practice. While the British state did intercept a certain amount of material in the post or through the customs, the total quantity was small in the context of the population of the United Kingdom. It is therefore likely that obscene publications, as defined by the Home Office, were rare in Northern Ireland and the government had no pressing need to introduce special provisions for them.

Book censorship around the world

To the opponents of Irish censorship, the very idea of banning books seemed provincial and small minded. Yeats, Russell, Shaw and the other major Irish writers lived in a cosmopolitan world, unimaginable to the average person. They read or corresponded with some of the brightest talents in literature and contributed to important journals. Censorship seemed to them to be a Cnut-like attempt to hold back the tides of modernity and international culture. To a great extent they were right but the international situation was somewhat more complicated and the view of the moral reformers was less distinctively Irish than is sometimes supposed.

Ireland's nearest neighbour, Britain, had a long history of banning literature as we have seen, but after the Great War the Home Office and the customs began to play an increasing role. The latter had the power to seize indecent publications and looked to the Home Office for guidance on the use of this power. The case of *Ulysses* gives an idea of how the system worked: seized in December 1922, it was passed on to the Home Office who gave it to the DPP, Sir Archibold Bodkin. Like many readers he did not make it all the way through but concentrated on the dirty bits, deeming it 'a filthy book' after reading pages 690 to 732. Both customs and the Post Office were asked to seize all future copies.[56] Interestingly, *Ulysses* was not banned in Ireland. From 1924 to 1929, the Home Secretary, Sir William Joynson-Hicks, pursued a personal campaign against what he considered immoral literature. Like the Irish censors he was derided by his opponents, who nicknamed him 'Jix', but his singleminded crusade led to the banning of several books, most notably Radclyffe Hall's *The Well of Loneliness*, despite the opposition of the Treasury.[57]

The United States may have possessed one of the most powerful constitutional defences of free speech in the world but that did little to inhibit the censors. The early 1920s saw a 'clean books crusade' in New York by the Society for the Suppression of Vice. In the nineteenth century, under the leadership of Anthony Comstock, the Society had been a powerful force but the post-war period saw several court decisions loosen the definition of obscenity in the state. The 'crusade' was an attempt to return to the supposedly better days of the past. Unlike their Irish equivalents, the crusaders failed and their defeat was confirmed when the New York courts cleared *The Well of Loneliness* in 1929 amid much publicity that probably gained the book more readers than it would otherwise have had. The real centre of censorship in 1920s America was Boston, where the Watch and Ward Society had collaborated with booksellers for decades to enforce a stringent censorship. Again, court decisions took their toll, but this time Roman Catholic campaigners took up the cause, and between 1927 and 1929 the clergy, police and laity were all involved in attempts to maintain Boston's notoriety.[58]

Australia brought in one of the strictest censorships in the world in the late 1920s. Due to the country's federal constitution it was impossible to introduce a national censorship system. Instead, the commonwealth government used the customs law to scrutinize all books imported into the country. The result put the Irish efforts to shame, and between 1929 and 1936 some 5,000 works were banned. Books were judged according to 'what is usually considered unobjectionable in the household of the ordinary self-respecting citizen'. This approach was supported by such groups as the Melbourne Women's Vigilance Association, the Victorian Housewives Progressive Association and the Sydney Cultural Defence Committee.[59]

What united all of these censorship campaigns and regimes was a nostalgia for the moral certainties of the nineteenth century, and also an element of that period's progressivism. Reformers of the late Victorian era had campaigned for better working conditions and more leisure time for ordinary people so that they could pursue moral and intellectual self-improvement. As they saw it, drink, cinema and immoral books threatened to corrupt leisure time and damage public morals. Therefore censorship and temperance campaigns were compatible with the same idealism that had motivated the fight against bad labour conditions or the exploitation of children. Irish republicanism had something of this moral fervour about it, particularly in its Gaelic revivalist incarnation, as did the evangelical Unionism of the loyal institutions.

Ireland's approach to censorship was unusual in its centralization, its national and Gaelic context, and in its severity. It was not unique, however, even in the English-speaking world. Vigilance associations existed in America and Australia. The same concern over sexual morality, modernism and popular culture motivated censors throughout the world. Irish Catholicism's fear of the corrupting force of immorality had an echo in Boston, and Ireland's sense of weakness facing the mass of imported culture from abroad was also felt in Australia. Ireland's experience of censorship was distinctive but it was not unique.

NOTES

1. Correspondence to *Irish Times*, 1–10 Sept. 1928.
2. *Church of Ireland Gazette*, 14 Sept., 5 Oct. 1928.
3. Ibid., 21 Sept. 1928.
4. B.C. Waller to Michael Tierney, 16 Oct. 1928, UCDA, Tierney papers, LA 30/334(6-8).
5. *Irish Times*, 26 Feb. 1929.
6. Devane, letter to TDs, no date [1928], UCDA, Tierney Papers, LA30/333; Catholic Truth Society to Michael Tierney, 21 Dec. 1928, ibid., LA30/334(13); Catholic Truth Society, Statement of 24 Nov. 1928, ibid., LA30/334(16).
7. *Derry People*, 23 Feb. 1929.
8. Hackett to FitzGerald, 2 July 1928, UCDA, FitzGerald papers, P80/1219(31); Pound to FitzGerald, 16 Aug., 6 Dec. 1928, ibid., P80/1207(10–12).
9. [Æ (George Russell)], 'The censorship bill', *Irish Statesman*, Vol.10, No.25 (25 Aug. 1928), pp.486–7; Nicholas Allen, *George Russell (Æ) and the new Ireland, 1905–1930* (Dublin: Four Courts Press, 2003), p.207.
10. G.B. Shaw, 'The Censorship', *Irish Statesman*, Vol.11, No.1 (17 Nov. 1928), pp.206–8.
11. W.B. Yeats, 'The censorship and St Thomas Aquinas', *Irish Statesman*, Vol.11, No.3 (22 Sept. 1928), pp.47–8; Yeats to Blythe, 14 Oct. 1928, UCDA, Blythe papers, P24/470; Blythe to Yeats, 15 Oct. 1928, ibid., P24/470(2).
12. Liam O'Flaherty to Jonathan Cape, 14 Dec. 1926, in A.A. Kelly (ed.), *The Letters of Liam O'Flaherty*, (Dublin: Wolfhound, 1996), p.170.
13. W.B. Yeats, 'The Irish Censorship' [Version A, 1928], NLI, Yeats papers, Ms. 30,105.
14. FitzGerald to Pound, 13 Dec 1928, UCDA, FitzGerald papers, P80/1207(13).
15. Jameson to Yeats, 2 Oct. 1928, in Richard J. Finneran, George Mills Harper and William M. Murphy (eds), *Letters to W.B. Yeats, Vol. 2* (London: Macmillan, 1977), p.485.
16. Gallagher to Rosamund Jacob, 5 Jan. 1928, NLI, Gallagher papers, Ms. 18,353 (9).
17. Dáil Debates, Vol.XXVI, 18 Oct. 1928, 625–8, 645, 657.
18. Ibid., 24 Oct. 1928, 829–31; Allen, *George Russell*, pp.211–13.
19. Byrne, Dáil Debates, Vol.XXVI, 18 Oct. 1928, 676–88; Ua Buachalla and Fitzgerald-Kenney, ibid., 690–1.
20. Minutes of the Fianna Fáil Parliamentary Party, 15 Nov. 1928, UCDA, FFA, P176/443; Minutes of the Fianna Fáil General Committee, 25 Sept. 1928, Ibid., P/176/452.
21. Dáil Debates, Vol.XXVI, 18 Oct. 1928, 615.
22. Hogan, Dáil Debates, 24 Oct. 1928, 829; Keane, Senate Debates, Vol.XII, 11 April 1929, 57.
23. Dáil Debates, Vol.XXVIII, 27 Feb. 1929, 268–484.
24. Ibid., 496–98, 509.
25. Ibid, Vol.XXVI, 18 Oct. 1928, 596, 639; Thrift, Vol.XXVIII, 20 Feb. 1929, 86; Little, ibid., 95.
26. Lemass, ibid., Vol.XXVI, 18 Oct. 1928, 638–40; O'Connell, ibid., 617; Hogan, ibid., 24 Oct. 1928, 830; Tierney, ibid., 625; Law, ibid., 642; Catholic Truth Society, Statement of 24 Nov. 1928, UCDA, Tierney papers, LA30/334(16).
27. Curtis, 'Catholic action as an organised campaign in Ireland, 1921–1947', pp.190–1; Dáil Debates, Vol.XXVI, 18 Oct. 1928, 623, 642.
28. Dáil Debates, Vol.XXVIII, 21 Feb. 1929, 271, 274; Craig, ibid., 28 Feb. 1929, 708; Keane, Senate Debates, Vol.XII, 11 April 1928, 67–71; Dáil Debates, Vol.XXXI 11 July 1929, 897.
29. Ibid., Vol.XXVIII, 20 Feb. 1929, 97–110; Vol.XXXI, 11 July 1929, 890–5.
30. Ibid., Vol.XXVI, 18 Oct. 1928, 601; 21 Feb. 1929, 226.
31. Evidence of R.S. Devane to CEL, 14 June 1926, NAI, Department of Justice DJUS, JUS7/2/9.
32. Ruttledge, Dáil Debates, Vol.XXVI, 18 Oct. 1928, 614; Law, ibid., 627.
33. *Church of Ireland Gazette*, 1 March 1929; Eunan O'Halpin, 'Fianna Fáil party discipline and tactics, 1926–32', *Irish Historical Studies*, Vol.XXX, No. 120 (Nov. 1997), p.587.
34. O'Friel to newsagents, 23 Aug. 1929; Eason Ltd to O'Friel, 28 Aug. 1929; George

Croker Ltd to O'Friel, 29 Aug. 1929; O'Friel to News Bros. Ltd, 6 Sept. 1929, NAI, DJUS, H305/14.

35. 'Examination of books, newspapers and periodicals in connection with the Censorship of Publications Act 1929', DDA, Byrne papers, Lay Organisations (5).

36. O'Reilly to Minister for Justice, 8 Oct. 1929, NAI, DJUS H305/14; O'Friel to O'Reilly, 19 Oct. 1929; O'Friel to Deeny, 4 Nov. 1929, NAI, DJUS, H305/14.

37. 'Report of Deputation to the Minister for Justice, 8 November 1929', DDA, Byrne Papers, Ossory Correspondence.

38. Michael Adams, *Censorship: the Irish Experience* (Dublin: Scepter, 1968), pp.64–5; S.A. Roche to Secretary, Dept Finance, 11 March 1930; J. Herlihy to Roche, 7 May 1930; Secretary Dept Justice to Secretary Dept of Finance, 22 May 1930; J.S. to Herlihy, 23 May 1930, NAI, DFIN, S/13/20/30.

39. B. McMahon, report, 28 June 1930, DJUS, H315/126; Roche to Secretary Dept. Finance, 1 July 1931; J.S. to Herlihy, 23 Oct. 1930; S.A. Roche to Secretary Dept. Finance, 22 Sept. 1938; S.A. Roche to Secretary Dept. Finance, 19 Jan. 1930, DFIN, S/13/20/30.

40. NAI, DJUS, H315/6; M.J. Garrett to H. O'Friel, 15 July 1930, ibid.

41. Curtis, 'Catholic action', p.193; Adams, *Censorship: the Irish experience*, p. 66; 'Report of the Censorship of Publications Board', 31 March 1931, NAI, DFIN, S/106/9/31.

42. O'Friel to O'Reilly, 19 April 1930, DJUS, H305/14; O'Reily to Minister for Justice, 20 May 1930, note by O'Friel, n. d., ibid, H315/6; ibid, H315/7.

43. *John Bull*, 28 Aug. 1930; Roche to O'Reilly, 6 Sept. 1930; J.S. Elias to S. A. Roche, 8 November 1930, ibid., H315/30.

44. Eason to Roche, 6 Dec. 1930; S.A. Roche to Secretary CPB, 10 Dec. 1930; Roche to Secretary, Associated Society of Locomotive Engineers and Firemen, 10 Dec. 1930, ibid., H315/40.

45. C.M. Martin-Jones to C.H. Blackmore, 22 Aug. 1927; W.D. Scott [NI Ministry of Commerce] to C.H. Blackmore, 27 Aug. 1927; Secretary, NIMHA to C.H. Blackmore, 19 Sept. 1927, PRONI, Cabinet Secretariat, CAB9B/102/1.

46. S.W. Harris, minute of meeting with W.J. Magennis, 12 Dec. 1928; Hicks to Sir Alan Burgoyne, 17 May 1928, NAGB, Home Office HO45/15139.

47. J.H., 'Obscene Publications', 5 March 1929, ibid.

48. Ryder, Memorandum for Home Secretary, 6 March 1929, ibid; A.H.S., 'The Irish Free State censorship of publications bill, 1928', 5 Sept. 1928; A.C., minute, 8 Sept. 1928, NAGB, HO45/20912.

49. *Ulster Gazette*, 30 May 1925; *Witness*, 27 Jan. 1922, 24 February 1922 and 12 Jan. 1923; Presbyterian Church in Ireland, *Annual Report of the General Assembly*, 1927, p. 33.

50. *Down Recorder*, 28 Feb. 1925; *Derry People*, 17 Dec. 1927; *Ulster Gazette*, 2 and 9 June 1928.

51. *Derry People*, 27 Oct. 1928.

52. *Ulster Gazette*, 2 Feb. 1929.

53. Chief Crown Solicitor to W.G. and Baird Ltd, 14 Nov. 1922; Chief Crown Solicitor to Irish News Ltd, 14 Nov. 1922; Chief Crown Solicitor to A. Stewart [*Belfast Telegraph*], 27 Feb. 1923; Chief Crown Solicitor to John C. Glendining [*Derry Standard*], 21 April 1923; Chief Crown Solicitor to the Manager, *Derry Journal*, 15 Feb. 1923, PRONI, Northern Ireland Ministry of Home Affairs NIMHA, HA/8/320.

54. Ernly Blackwell to Imperial Secretary to the Governor of Northern Ireland, 21 June 1924; W.A. Magill to Imperial Secretary to the Governor of Northern Ireland, 3 July 1924, NAGB, HO267/461.

55. James Kelly, 'Memories of the *Irish News*', in Eamonn Phoenix (ed.), *A century of Northern Life: the* Irish News *and 100 years of Ulster History (1890s–1990s)* (Belfast: Ulster Historical Foundation, 1995), p.43.

56. Alan Travis, *Bound and Gagged: a secret history of obscenity in Britain* (London: Profile, 2000), pp.22–5.

57. Ibid., pp.45–74.

58. Paul S. Boyer, *Purity in print: book censorship in America from the gilded age to the computer age* (Wisconsin: University of Wisconsin Press, 2002), pp.99–206.
59. Peter Coleman, *Obscenity, blasphemy, sedition: the rise and fall of literary censorship in Australia* (Potts Point NSW: Pan Macmillan, 2000).

CHAPTER FOUR

Censorship without censors: radio and theatre

Radio was the most modern medium of mass communication in this period, theatre one of the oldest. In Ireland, however, they had one thing in common: neither was subject to formal censorship. Their status seems, at first glance, to have been an anomaly; the power of radio was amply demonstrated by Roosevelt in the USA and by Hitler in Germany, while theatre in Ireland had been politically and socially controversial for several decades at least. In fact both were subject to interference from the state and other groups; however, power was exercised not through external regulation but through the ways in which theatre and radio were owned and funded.

I: BROADCASTING

The Irish Free State

Wireless broadcasting represented an early challenge to the Free State's policy makers. The Treaty gave the government control of radio but limited the state's right to set up a station capable of broadcasting to listeners outside Ireland.[1] In June 1922 the Marconi Company had asked the Postmaster General for permission to set up a Dublin broadcasting station but he preferred to wait and observe developments in Britain. The Civil War caused a further delay as private wireless sets were banned.[2] Despite this, the government commissioned a confidential report, by Professor W.B. Lyons of the Municipal Technical Institute in Kevin Street, Dublin, which recommended that the state establish and regulate an Irish broadcasting company and restrict the availability of amateur licences. In November 1923, the Post Office published a white paper with similar proposals.[3] The matter was referred to a committee of the Dáil.

Private wireless sets were officially prohibited in the state as the Postmaster General, J.J. Walsh, refused to issue licences. His justification for this policy was extremely complicated. He considered it unethical for people to receive the BBC without paying for it, describing it as 'pirating or stealing other people's property'. He feared that a foreign broadcaster might take legal action against the Free State for allowing its citizens to receive programmes for which they had not paid a license fee. Lastly, he was determined not to attend the coming League of Nations conference on the subject as a representative of a nation taking broadcasted 'product' but supplying none.[4] The effect was that only those applicants who genuinely sought experimental licences were allowed, officially at least, to own receiving sets. It is unknown how many people simply ignored the licence requirement but it is safe to assume that many did so.

The Dáil committee eventually decided against setting up a separate company and in favour of direct control of broadcasting by the Post Office. The director of the broadcasting station was to have a 'duty of preserving a proper standard of taste and morals'. The white paper and the committee hearings gave Walsh a platform to express his philosophy of how such a service should be controlled. He was opposed to allowing politics on the airwaves, especially from overseas. He described all government statements broadcast by the BBC as 'propaganda' and, when a government TD said that he had heard nothing wrong with a recent speech by Lloyd George, the Postmaster General replied that 'the sooner we take steps to see that you do not hear it again the better'.[5]

Walsh was unhappy at the idea of a state run service saying that the government was 'riding for a fall' if it followed this option. His objection was logical and prescient: 'we may conceivably find ourselves endeavouring to decide whether an Irish artist or an English artist should be employed, or whether an Irish say or an English song should be sung, or whether a particular speech, made in a particular way, was one which could be endorsed by a government department'. His white paper planned that only official government news would be broadcast before 7 p.m. This was to placate the newspaper industry which was unhappy with the idea of competition for advertising revenue and news services. The white paper also proposed that there be no broadcasts on Sundays but Walsh was open to the idea if the public wanted it. He was strongly opposed to carrying news from race meetings, describing them as the greatest scandal in the country.[6] The service was thus seen as a source of sober entertainment. Other witnesses called for 'very rigid' control of day-to-day programming or at least the use of 'official authority' in times of national stress.[7]

The Wireless Telegraphy Act 1926 put the broadcasting industry completely in the hands of the government. Section 10 gave the government the right, during an emergency, to control the possession of wirelesses, the sending of signals and virtually all other uses of such equipment. At any time, it was to be illegal to send messages that were obscene, indecent, offensive or subversive of public order. The Minister for Posts and Telegraphs, as the Postmaster General was by now known, was solely responsible for setting up radio stations, subject only to the approval of the Minister for Finance. An advisory committee was to help the Minister to run these stations. The station was eventually given the call sign 2RN, which was intended to resemble 'to Éireann'.

The problem of how to provide a news service was difficult to solve. The national press did not want to assist a potential competitor so the Department of Posts and Telegraphs approached local newspapers and British news agencies but was put off by the cost. Instead a journalist compiled broadcasts from an array of sources: the news services of foreign governments, Dáil reports, reports from local postmasters and gardaí, market reports from the Department of Lands and Agriculture, and Irish and British financial news courtesy of the Dublin Stock Exchange. The whole arrangement cost a third of what the news agencies would have charged but at the expense of quality and independence.[8] This system lasted until 1929 when the Department came to an agreement with the newspapers. The Dublin correspondent of the *Cork Examiner* provided two nightly bulletins. According to a J.B. Clark of the BBC, his editors conveniently ignored his double-jobbing so long as he did not broadcast any news concerning Cork.[9]

Government control of 2RN inevitably led to censorship. The biggest difficulties were with programmes relayed from the BBC. On one occasion, the relay was cut when the Irish realized that the night's entertainment included a sketch entitled 'Loyalty'. The same thing happened with the relay from Belfast when a song proposed the health of the King. There were also limits to the station's coverage of domestic politics. In 1926 a proposal that 2RN broadcast the budget debate to 'stimulate interest in the proceedings of the Oireachtas' was vetoed by the Executive Council who decided against any broadcasting of speeches in the Dáil. In 1928 Mrs Sidney Czira, who had broadcast under the name 'John Brennan', wrote to the *Irish Times* to protest against a speech in the Senate that had linked the 'Irish Volunteers' [IRA] with the murder of Kevin O'Higgins. Czira claimed that such speeches could prejudice the forthcoming trials of members of that organization. She was sacked from 2RN and told that her services would not be required again. She did not return to the airwaves until Fianna Fáil took power in 1932.[10]

The most blatant abuse of control of 2RN by the Minister for Posts and Telegraphs occurred during the 1927 election. Walsh had the station broadcast what he claimed was a party announcement that Cumann na nGaedheal would not enter coalition. In fact it came solely from Walsh himself. He tried to cover his mistake by approaching the other parties for announcements but it became obvious that he had misused his position. No repercussions resulted as he left the country in August 1927 and did not contest the October election. The incident led to a decision not to allow political broadcasts at all. It was also felt that if such broadcasts mentioned the Civil War or other controversial matters, they would cause offence but if they were censored, there would be allegations of political partiality.[11]

The opposition frequently criticized the government over broadcasting. An alternative philosophy of broadcasting was outlined in 1926 by the Labour Party. The party's Assistant Secretary argued that 'access must be given without distinction of persons or subjects'. The Minister for Posts and Telegraphs did set up a Broadcasting Advisory Board that involved members of the Oireachtas, the Gaelic League, the Wireless Society of Ireland, and the Royal Dublin Society, as well as artists and musicians.[12] Robert Briscoe, Fianna Fáil TD for Dublin South, attacked the use of BBC news programmes as 'propaganda' as they were controlled by 'British censorship'. Barry Egan, a government TD from Cork, also attacked the Minister for allowing foreign manufacturers of baking powder to advertise on the station. The Minister assured the Dáil that no foreign goods would be advertised if Irish products were in competition with them but pointed out that as yet there was no Irish maker of baking powder.[13]

The most difficult problem for 2RN was money. Even the paying of performers required government approval. Fees of over three guineas needed the permission of the Ministry for Posts and Telegraphs, while those over seven guineas necessitated a decision by the Department of Finance. A visitor from Britain noted that the station's newly refurbished control room still looked like 'a BBC provincial control room of at least six or seven years ago', and that 'government control of the service obviously makes for unimaginative rigidity'.[14] In short no formal censorship was needed as the service was run by Civil Servants on a tiny budget. 2RN did not become a purely propaganda station in part because the government recognized that such a development was not in its long-term interest, but also because its standard programming was music and gave little opportunity for partisanship.

Broadcasting in Northern Ireland

Unlike the Irish Free State, the Northern Ireland government had no power to control broadcasting as it was under the control of the Post Office, a reserved service run from London. Wireless licences were issued only with the permission of the Ministry for Home Affairs through a special arrangement with the Post Office in Britain. The CASPA did not apply. The Ministry of Commerce favoured liberalizing the regime and increasing the number of licences but the RUC opposed any change of policy.[15] The availability of the BBC in Northern Ireland made demand for licences too strong to allow such a restrictive policy to remain. The police were given the right to check Post Office records of who had been given licences. The government also claimed the right to stop transmission at any time.[16]

While the BBC favoured the broadcasting of at least some light entertainment, the transfer of such material from the music hall to the listeners'
living rooms was a difficult matter. Performers were warned, 'in as tactful
a manner as possible, that a wireless audience includes women and children
and others unaccustomed to broad humour. Nothing must be transmitted
by wireless that will offend sensitive folk'. Tragic material was preceded by
a warning to 'invalids and others' to lay down their headphones. Talks were
to be dealt with carefully to ensure that no advertising be broadcast. It was
also laid down that 'under no circumstances may they contain political
matter' and they were to be edited in advance by the Belfast Station
Director, Major Scott. The same rules applied to after-dinner speeches.
There was one nightly news bulletin and it was scrutinized in advance.
Unsuitable material was removed, as were party statements, except for
those by Cabinet ministers or leaders of parliamentary groups. The news
gave 'but the barest publicity to tragedies and other sordid happenings'. It
also avoided mentioning matters 'useful to gamblers'.[17] The news bulletin
was given by John Sayers of the *Belfast Telegraph* until 1930 when the BBC
appointed its own news editor for Northern Ireland. Sayers went on to edit
the *Telegraph* from 1937 until his death in 1939.[18]

In 1927, the then Station Director for Northern Ireland, Gerald
Beadle, advised John Reith, the Corporation's autocratic controller, that
'our position here will be strengthened immensely if we can persuade the
northern government to look upon us as their mouthpiece'. He went on
to ask, 'can I unreservedly place the station at the service of this government, to be made use of at this government's direction?' Reith replied
that as the Belfast station was responsible, through Head Office, to the
Postmaster General, he was willing 'to place our medium at the disposal
of the Government of Northern Ireland, but it must be clearly understood that this is a courtesy from the Corporation'.

Beadle wondered whether in the event of an emergency the government should be expected to ask for the BBC's assistance or to order it. If
the former was the case, should the request go to head office? If it were
the latter Beadle felt that the station 'must fall in with his [the Prime
Minister's] wishes, whatever they may be'. Reith considered this policy
'injudicious' and warned that while the government could ask for help it
could not require it. Beadle wondered what would happen if a minister
wanted to make a speech which would normally require Head Office
sanction. Reith reminded him that 'the decision rests with your headquarters, to whom you alone are responsible'. In a private note to his
secretary who was drafting his reply, Reith developed his position. 'We
cannot help the government in a *party* question. We can help them in
uncontroversial things', he explained. An emergency, declared 'by the
King in Parliament', was a different matter in which case 'they take us
over'.[19] The Northern government, like its southern counterpart, was

somewhat shy of using the radio; when Beadle offered it the chance to make a special broadcast on the Northern Ireland constitution, Craig demurred fearing that it might look like 'special pleading'.[20]

Some still saw the BBC as a tool of the government. John Nixon, the independent unionist MP, alleged that preference was given to 'official unionist' questions in parliament. He demanded that the BBC broadcast whatever was on the order paper. The BBC replied that it gave attention to what was newsworthy and that Nixon's questions about cabinet ministers' expenses, the cost of public service salaries and the pig marketing board had given way to a question on Northern Ireland's share of rearmament. Nixon responded that as the BBC was not a private company like a newspaper, 'it is no part of your duty to set yourself up as a judge of what political speech, question or matter is or is not important'.[21] The exchange illustrated both the BBC's determination to retain control over what it broadcast and the fact that by giving preference to party leaders and news of national importance, the corporation made it harder for independent voices to be heard. In particular, the BBC's sense of what constituted news fitted in poorly with the extremely parochial concerns of many northern politicians.

The BBC Charter also promoted a conservative ethos by forbidding controversial broadcasts. The special circumstances obtaining in Northern Ireland also had their effect; for example, the station decided not to include Irish history in the schools' broadcasts, as many schools did not teach it. The Education Officer for the North Western Area of the BBC concluded that 'even a superficial acquaintance with Irish affairs is sufficient to make one realise that there is wisdom in this and that any attempt of the BBC to provide Irish History broadcasts intended to "bring history to life by means of dramatic interludes" would be as unnecessary as they would be inadvisable'.[22] The problem with this, was that by excluding the extra material taught in nationalist schools, the BBC was effectively favouring the unionist side. Another proposed series of talks on 'How Ulster is Governed' was cancelled for reasons 'of a political nature'. The BBC even sought the permission of the Minister of Home Affairs for a series of talks on town planning; he was so enthusiastic that he introduced the series himself. Although the station took account of local feeling, this did not prevent a talk on the *Titanic* disaster being given despite fears that it would prove controversial in Belfast. The BBC was also very concerned not to be seen to endorse any group or product so, for example, the Belfast branch of the British Film Institute was not allowed to give a talk on its activities with the aim of boosting its membership. In 1936, Denis Johnston was warned 'to avoid any opinions or reminiscences of contemporary figures which might be calculated to give offence, however well meant'. The station advised him to write something 'quite rambling and inconsequential'.[23]

The BBC stepped gingerly around the national question. In 1937, a series of broadcasts, produced in England, on 'Northern Nationalities', began with 'The Irish' in which Irish listeners were invited to stand for the 'Soldier's Song'. This caused the Northern Irish director to rebuke his colleagues. 'There is no need to emphasise how disastrous it is for a region of the BBC to radiate a rebel song and to invite listeners to stand while it is played', he wrote, adding that 'it raises the acutest indignation in the six counties where the Irish have remained loyal'. The Regional Director responsible accepted that the broadcast had been 'perhaps unwise' but wondered facetiously why Ulster listeners were offended when they continually proclaimed that Erse [Irish] was a foreign language to them and both the announcement and anthem had been in that tongue.[24]

Religious programmes were also a source of controversy. A religious advisory committee was formed to organize such broadcasts but as the Roman Catholic Church refused to take part the membership was entirely Protestant. Catholic sermons were taken from other BBC stations instead. Successive Northern Ireland Regional Directors tried to entice the various Archbishops of Armagh to change their policy. Scott 'succeeded in getting into the Palace' but nothing 'transpired except a cup of tea'. His successor, Beadle, accompanied by the Moderator of the Presbyterian Church, visited Archbishop O'Donnell soon after his appointment but he had no interest in broadcasting. MacRory proved even less enthusiastic. The hierarchy in Ireland was unique in its attitude. In 1929, when the BBC began to broadcast distinctively Roman Catholic services, Reith commented that 'with the exception of Northern Ireland, there are now, I think, none of our important stations where there is any want of co-operation'.[25]

The refusal of the Roman Catholic Church to involve itself with the BBC had other effects. In 1932, special broadcasts for the 1,500th anniversary of St Patrick's arrival in Ireland were planned. There was, however, a fierce controversy over the saint, involving Protestants and Roman Catholics claiming possession of his legacy and this presented the BBC with a dilemma. If Irish Protestant celebrations were broadcast, 'no matter how uncontroversial the sermons may be, there is a danger of our [the BBC] appearing to support the Protestant claim', wrote Beadle. It was decided to use preachers from outside Ireland, so the Archbishop of Canterbury preached at Armagh while the Bishop of Birmingham gave the sermon in Belfast to honour the patron saint of Ireland. In general the Religious Advisory Committee was usually more concerned with the quality of the service or venue than questions of content. The only case in the BBC archives of a service being rejected because of its content was that of the Church of the Covenanters, an evangelical group.[26] The main Churches were free to give their services and, unusually for the BBC, even the Unitarians and other small denominations were represented on the Religious Affairs Committee and were allowed a broadcast every eighteen months or so.[27]

Some Catholics attacked the 'aerated form of Bible dumping' involved in broadcasting so many Protestant sermons. The experts of the *Irish Ecclesiastical Record* determined that while listening to such broadcasts was not technically *communicatio cum hereticis in divines* [consorting with heretics], it was a potential danger to one's faith.[28] There was also a controversy among Protestants in 1925 when the station began to broadcast religious services on Sunday afternoons. Those opposed based their case on the sanctity of the Sabbath while those in favour pointed out that one could always turn off the set and that continental broadcasts were already available.[29] In 1931, Cardinal MacRory criticized a broadcast on the reconciliation of faith with science given by a Roman Catholic priest, a scientist and the noted Anglican Dean Inge. He denounced it as 'anti-Christian propaganda' which should not be allowed in a country where Christianity was the state religion. As the broadcast originated with the BBC in Britain no notice was taken.[30] The BBC also limited its coverage of the loyal institutions. The director wrote that 'attempts are made to get us to broadcast a commentary on the 12th July processions' but they had not done so. He discussed the matter with Craigavon (James Craig) who promised not to interfere in the matter.[31]

Music and drama

Both 2RN and the BBC had to confront the hostility of some listeners to popular music. Although this music was labelled 'jazz' it was far from the sound of Louis Armstrong, Duke Ellington, Benny Goodman or Gene Krupa. From contemporary discussions, it appears that this was popular dance music that swung lightly if at all. Despite this, criticism of the music appeared in Irish papers on both sides of the border from the 1920s on. Opposition was strongest in the south during the mid 1930s and was led by the Gaelic League and the *Irish Radio News*. The latter mentioned in 1928 that the titles of 'jazz' tunes were so risqué that they could not even be announced. Its commentator, A.Z., declared that,

> 'Jazz' is essentially an American product or rather it is a nigger product taken up by the United States and popularised to such an extent that, like an infectious disease, it spreads throughout the world to the detriment of true music.[32]

He blamed the BBC in particular for this plague but also faulted 2RN. Later he called for censorship of the music. The fact that it was popular worldwide was 'not a very sound argument as to why we should not discard – if necessary by decrees – the music of the nigger in favour of products of our own artistic creation and the creation of a cultured people'.[33]

In 1934, the Gaelic League in Leitrim mounted a campaign against the new music. Though they 'excluded no dance that was in keeping with Christian decency', '"jazz" was something that should not so much as be mentioned among them, as it was borrowed from the language of the savages of Africa'.[34] The *Derry People* believed that it was 'undisguised barbarism and bound to have a degrading effect on public taste'. The worst culprits, as far as the campaigners were concerned, were the sponsored programmes on Radio Éireann. At a Gaelic League protest in Mohill, Co. Leitrim, a speaker attacked the Minister for Finance for 'selling the musical soul of the nation for the dividends of sponsored jazz programmes'. The Gaelic League also sought support from local authorities in its campaign to have 'jazz' removed from the airwaves.[35] In the campaign against popular music, the cultural protectionism that had given rise to censorship of films and publications was merged with blatant racism and artistic conservatism. This may explain why the campaign was unsuccessful. The music was popular and the campaign never attracted the sort of support from Catholic Action groups in the south or the loyal institutions in the north which would have strengthened its hand.

Radio plays were rarely controversial. The Theatrical Managers' Association in Northern Ireland initially refused to allow any to be broadcast – though for fear of competition, not because of content – but they relented in June 1925.[36] Plays intended for BBC Northern Ireland were screened by a reader appointed by the director. The reports of these readers for the period 1931 to 1936 show that a play was usually rejected for being of poor quality or because there were not enough qualified actors available to perform it. There were no cases of a play being rejected because of controversial content.[37]

II: THEATRE

In Britain, the Lord Chamberlain's office possessed a controversial control of public performances which included the power to read and censor plays in advance. The relevant legislation had never been applied to Ireland and its theatres functioned with little or no official restriction. When self-government came about in the two Irelands there was little immediate pressure for this situation to be altered. Plays were censored by unofficial, local action and protest rather than by the state. In 1924, Dublin Municipal Council appointed four members of the Irish Vigilance Association as inspectors of the city's theatres. It is not clear whether the council had any legal right to do this or what exactly the inspectors did. There are no reports of action having been taken by them or of prosecutions. It must therefore be supposed that they exercised at most an unofficial, restraining influence.

In Northern Ireland the question of licensing plays was briefly discussed. In 1922, the northern government asked its southern counterpart for a specimen of an occasional licence for dramatic performance. The Ministry for Home Affairs in Dublin could find no such licences for any county outside Dublin and there is no sign that the northern government took any action as a result.[38] The real censors were the audiences. In 1927, for example, the public in Limerick stopped *Biddy: an Irish Stew in Three Helpings* after twenty minutes. The offending scene involved a priest offering the village squire a dispensation in return for a contribution to the school building fund. The play had been performed in Belfast without controversy.[39]

The Abbey, the state and the nation

The Abbey held a unique position because it was funded by a government grant. This gave the state an uncertain influence over the theatre. It allowed Ernest Blythe to specify that the theatre should take on a Roman Catholic director to balance Lennox Robinson but it was not clear if he expected this director to act as a watchdog. The case of *The Plough and the Stars* highlighted the issue. There were concerns within the Abbey when the play was submitted about the suitability of its language. The normal practice at the theatre was to consult the actors about this as they knew 'the mind of the audience better' than the directors. This was complicated by O'Casey's resistance to changing his work and by the role of the director recommended by Blythe, George O'Brien.

As reported by Lady Gregory, O'Brien first objected to the text in late September 1925. She insisted that when Blythe had sought O'Brien's appointment, 'there was no word at all of his being a censor, but only to strengthen us on the financial side'. O'Brien was concerned about the love scene between Clitheroe and his wife in Act I and the introduction of a prostitute in Act II. Yeats's response was interesting. He agreed that the love scene was inappropriate because he felt that it was artistically false–'O'Casey is there writing about people he does not know, whom he has only read about' – but he defended the inclusion of the character of the prostitute, as 'to eliminate any parts of it on grounds that have nothing to do with dramatic literature would be to deny all our traditions'. On similar grounds he defended the use of the word 'bitch' in Act IV. O'Brien responded that he feared that the play as written might 'provoke an attack on the theatre of a kind that would seriously endanger the continuance of the subsidy'. This led to a confrontation at the directors' meeting where Lady Gregory forced O'Brien to admit that he 'had mistaken my position' and the play was accepted on a majority vote. Blythe's statements in the Dáil introducing the subsidy seem to support Gregory's views. He commented that 'we certainly are not too desirous to take responsibility for the working of such an institution [the Abbey]. Gregory and Yeats still intended that the play should be altered during the rehearsal process. Since the first night of the *Playboy of the Western World*, actors had been free 'to leave out anything they liked'. This produced confrontations between O'Casey, Eileen Crowe and F.J. McCormack who both refused to say some lines. O'Casey complained to Lennox Robinson that he was dealing with 'a Vigilance Committee of the Actors'.[40] The words themselves were quite trivial but the incident demonstrates that the play was controversial even within the artistic community.

The disruption of the play by outraged republicans is well documented. They objected to the portrayal of a prostitute, the presence of the tricolour and the starry plough in a public house and the generally irreverent approach to the revolution. Their position was put by Hanna Sheehy-Skeffington in a series of letters to the press and in a public debate with O'Casey. She insisted that the protest 'was on national grounds solely'. She attacked 'the Abbey, in short, that helped to make Easter Week, and that now in its subsidised, sleek old age jeers at its former enthusiasms'. She proclaimed that 'the only censorship that is justified is the free censorship of popular opinion'.[41]

O'Casey responded that his play was unpopular in some quarters because 'some of the tinsel of shame was shaken from the body of truth'. He defended the setting of a public house as 'some of the men of Easter Week liked a bottle of stout and I can see nothing derogatory in that'. He claimed the play reflected his own knowledge and experience. He dismissed her as hypocritical and nostalgic; 'the heavy hearted expression by Mrs Sheehy-Skeffington about "the Ireland that remembers with tear-dimmed eyes all that Easter Week stands for" makes me sick. Some of those men can't get a job.'[42]

Sheehy-Skeffington countered that O'Casey's supporters had no greater concern about poverty than had the republicans. She alleged that the play 'omits no detail of squalid slumdom ... yet omits any revelation of the glory and inspiration of Easter Week'. She also claimed that it represented the Irish Citizens Army as cowards.[43] Their public debate reiterated these points but was less illuminating as O'Casey was ill and spoke poorly. Sheehy-Skeffington used the occasion to raise an interesting view of the protests. To her the issue was not the right of self-expression of the playwright but of the audience. If a theatre was happy to accept applause, it should also accept boos, she claimed. She condemned the Abbey subsidy, alleging that the theatre had been reduced to a 'kept house'.[44]

There are a few points to be made about this. The play went ahead unhindered on its opening night. The protests against the play were countered by many in the audience with applause. It was never banned, the Abbey did not discontinue it and the incident allowed O'Casey, Yeats and the *Irish Times* to make strong statements defending artistic freedom. The latter pointed out that the opposition to the play was not merely political but was also inspired by the presence of a prostitute among its characters. As the paper pointed out, young people did not need the Abbey to meet prostitutes: 'they can rub shoulders with the real thing every night of the week in the central streets ... it is only when a prophet like Mr O'Casey takes the malady to its source ... that the name of decency is invoked'. In 1937, local Unionists demonstrated against a performance of *The Plough and the Stars* in Omagh by booing and throwing stink bombs; they thought it too republican.[45]

The subsidy was frequently used as a rod with which to beat the Abbey. In 1926, one TD declared that the theatre had produced a new form of the stage Irishman and demanded that 'if this be a national theatre and if the taxpayers are to support it by subsidy, then the board for selecting plays should be representative of the whole nation, and not any small clique or minority'. Blythe opposed such ideas, commenting that 'I think it would be impossible for the state to control the theatre', and claiming that 'we cannot act as censors and there is no use in blaming the playwright because he writes a particular sort of play'. In 1929, P.J. Little asked that 'the minister might exercise a certain influence in getting plays acted in the Abbey which are closer to real Irish culture'. Blythe's response distinguished between his personal views and political policy: 'I do not doubt that the particular type of play produced in the Abbey Theatre lately will go out of fashion in due course', but he refused to interfere.[46] This was in stark contrast to the government's policy on film or literature.

The Abbey may have been a home for artistic freedom but its directors were careful not to connect it to politics. In 1931, they refused to allow Saor Éire to use the theatre for its conference because, as Yeats explained, 'we are a state theatre and we cannot admit a meeting that wishes to destroy the state'. Peadar O'Donnell rejected this and wrote angrily that

> when Dublin workers protested against a play in the Abbey you stood up to the clamour and demanded a space for the dramatist and his audience but when a meaner censorship demanded that you shut your doors against the staging of a drama lit up with a greater mission and potency you collapsed. You stand exposed; your intellectual freedom wilts into the nothingness of a painted sham. I am ashamed for you.[47]

O'Donnell here confused freedom of expression with artistic freedom. As has already been seen, Yeats was unequivocally committed to the latter but was more ambivalent about the former and was politically astute enough to stay well clear of O'Donnell and his followers. By 1931 MacEntee presented the Fianna Fáil complaint about the Abbey grant in a slightly new way. He claimed that O'Casey's plays were 'a legitimate interpretation of one aspect of Irish life' but argued that the theatre put them on specifically when British tourists were in the city and this offended many Irish people who wanted visitors to be given a better impression. After Fianna Fáil came to power in 1932, the grant was cut to £750.[48]

A confrontation with the new government occurred soon enough. In 1933, when the company toured America, Roman Catholic groups complained that they were performing *The Playboy of the Western World* and *Juno and the Paycock*. The government told the theatre that 'if we [the Abbey] are to retain our grant we must leave out of our American repertory all plays that offend such persons or societies'. Yeats's answer was clear: 'we refuse such a demand; your minister may have it in his power to bring our theatre to an end, but as long as it exists it will retain its freedom'. The government also proposed to appoint the prominent conservative, Professor William Magennis, as its nominee to the board. Again, Yeats stood firm, 'we refuse to admit Professor Magennis to our board as we consider him entirely unfit to be a director of the Abbey theatre'. The board threatened to refuse the subsidy rather than accept him. The government consoled the Professor with a place on the Censorship of Publications Board. In 1934, the government tried a gentler approach and asked that no plays by O'Casey be performed in America or, failing that, that it be made clear that the Irish government was not responsible.[49]

Sean O'Casey's *The Silver Tassie* was controversial for two reasons. It was rejected by Yeats because he thought it a poor play, not because of objections to its content. The Lord Chamberlain did demand that the language be toned down before it could be performed in London and it was the play's success in England that led to its being performed at last in the Abbey. The protests that resulted sprang from a belief summed up by J. Murphy of University College Galway:

> When the Abbey Theatre Company accepted a grant from an Irish Government, it thereby created the taxpaying subjects of that government as its critics. Now I think that the Church of the majority of these critics and their National University may have at least a small claim to voice the opinion of the Abbey's legal governors – the people.[50]

Other correspondents saw the play as 'a statement, not a solution of suffering' and a work of 'Christian realism', although most considered it to be flawed.[51]

Aodh de Blacam had pre-empted the debate the previous March by attacking the Abbey for straying from what he considered the proper base of Irish culture: Roman Catholicism. He claimed that 'it is not the purpose of all imaginative writing to teach morality' but believed that a great writer 'must be sound in his morality'. Such a writer should deal with 'great, central, simple themes' in a manner 'consistent with our own [Roman Catholic] culture'. The critic James Devane defended those who protested at theatres: 'it seems a fine and healthy sign that the Irish should be interested enough in their own drama to raise a riot in the national theatre'. Another critic called O'Casey 'a terrible menace to the morale of Young Ireland'.[52] Again the important fact was that although the play did not run for long, the Abbey's grant was not withdrawn and no one was prosecuted. The incident divided the Abbey board and led to the resignation of Brinsley MacNamara. He alleged that parts of the play were altered at his demand after the second night. The board claimed that it had issued specific instructions 'to the company that no word of a play's text should be altered or omitted by a player', so it is unclear what really occurred.[53] The *Silver Tassie* affair showed the outer limit of what would be tolerated on an Irish stage. It also illustrated that theatres had more freedom than cinemas or publishers, as well as more allies to defend them if controversy erupted.

Theatre censorship and government policy

In 1927, the *Irish Catholic* called for a prior censorship of the theatre on the English model, particularly to deal with sketch and revue shows. The lack of action by the government in this regard was significant. It should be remembered that members of the Roman Catholic clergy could not attend theatres under normal circumstances. They were allowed to attend amateur dramatics in a school or temperance hall but these were not ideal places to educate them in the state of modern theatre.[54]

Opinion within the southern government on the censorship of theatre was made clear in 1930 when the Department of Finance considered the Censorship of Films (Amendment) Bill 1930. It was suggested that if sound films were to be censored, the same should apply to theatre. Against this it was argued that the two were different for five reasons: there were more cinemas in the country than theatres, far more films were produced than plays, more towns had a cinema than had a theatre, cinema was far more popular than theatre, and the number of performances of each film was greater than that of a play. The sanction of last resort was the cancellation of a theatre's charter but this had never been done. It was also felt that 'the audience can have a corrective influence on the live actor'.[55]

These discussions illustrate the fact that the theatre was seen as an entertainment for a comparatively small elite which was capable of protecting its own morals. This contrasted sharply with the belief that lower class and young audiences could not be trusted to decide what to read or watch. The Civil Servants involved offered no statistical evidence for their claims. Apparently they accepted it as a simple fact of life that cinemas attracted a different, larger audience than theatres. According to Morash there were seven main theatres in Dublin in 1930 – though there were several smaller ones. By 1935 there were 181 cinemas in the Free State. Of these sixty-one had a capacity of over 500 seats. An article by T.J. Beere in 1936 illustrated the fact that 30 per cent of cinema seats were in the greater Dublin area although it held only 15 per cent of the population. Furthermore she argued that a very large proportion of cinema seats were sold at the lowest possible price of 4d, which suggested that it was popular with working-class audiences.[56] These figures suggest that the bureaucrats were correct.

There were also obvious logistical problems with censoring plays. A government would have had to introduce a prior scrutiny of scripts, as existed in England, or a system of inspection by the police or other officials – possibly both practices would have been required. Prior censorship of plays was controversial in England and many plays banned there had already been performed in Ireland, from *The Shewing up of Blanco Posnet* by Shaw in the Abbey before independence, to Wilde's *Salome* in the Gate in 1928.[57] The inspection of theatres would have had echoes of the failed censorship of films by local authorities and would either have put extra demands on the resources of the police or given power to vigilante groups like the CTSI.

In Northern Ireland there were even fewer established theatres and both the Ulster Literary Theatre and the Belfast Repertory Theatre faced a constant struggle to find a home.[58] The province experienced few protests against plays. In 1930 at Newry Town Hall, a travelling company found the audience becoming restless when their play, entitled *Other Men's Wives*, was a quarter of the way through. Local politicians began to protest at the start of Act 2 and the actors stopped the play. They asked what parts gave offence and were told 'all of it'. The audience spurned an offer of a refund if they left. The cast tried to explain that the play had passed the Lord Chamberlain but were informed that 'it will not pass in Newry'. They then appealed to the audience to be broadminded but Mr Connellan, the local MP, responded that 'we know what that means' and eventually the actors were forced to perform another play instead.[59]

Popular theatre

In 1934 the Theatre and Cinema Association of Ireland met the Lord Mayor of Dublin to reassure him about the standards they applied to popular theatre. They promised him that all the shows they put on were in the form passed by the Lord Chamberlain in England but they accepted that British audiences were 'less sensitive than we are in this country'.

The Gaiety had a clause in its standard contract requiring touring managers to remove 'anything of an offensive nature', particularly 'suggestive and indecent jokes'. Artists were to be suitably clad and the theatre forbad costumes consisting only of brassiere and trunks. All shows were viewed by the resident manager and offensive material was cut. On one occasion, the managers boasted, they had incurred costs of £1,000 by cancelling a 'play they considered a reflection on the Irish character'. The Lord Mayor accepted their sincerity but pointed out that he still received a number of complaints from the clergy and the public.[60]

Smaller companies could not always survive attacks. In 1938, the Birr Little Theatre Company tried to put on *Shadows and Substance* by Paul Vincent Carroll. The play involved an educated parish priest who is forced by his curate into a confrontation with a local schoolmaster. The local vigilance association objected and the company lost both money and confidence. One actor claimed 'it was as if someone had died on us'.[61] This suggests that local theatres were more vulnerable to moral coercion and that such unofficial censorship, although there are few reported cases of it, may have affected their choice of material.

Censorship without censors

The histories of broadcasting and theatre in Ireland reveal two media that were regulated by very different mechanisms. Broadcasting was tightly controlled by the state in the south and, in the north, by a corporation that saw itself as having a heavy responsibility to avoid controversy. The BBC in Northern Ireland was not a neutral onlooker to the disputes between the two communities but saw itself as a natural, albeit independent, ally of the state. The southern broadcasting service was restrained by poverty, bureaucracy and conservatism. It was potentially vulnerable to political interference and the wonder must be that this did not happen more regularly. The dull, conformist nature of most of the programmes broadcast made it difficult to turn them to a political agenda.

Theatre successfully faced down all attempts by the state to control it. However, it faced public censors who saw it as their right to demand changes to plays in mid performance. The challenges to *The Plough and the Stars* and *The Silver Tassie* were an especially large and politically charged version of the sort of protests that could happen in any town in Ireland. Theatre did have a special status that allowed politicians like Blythe to assert confidently that it could not be censored. Books, magazines, newspapers and films did not receive such treatment. Although theatre was subject to many pressures it affected fewer people than cinema and was more restrained than the printed word. The theatre audience was educated, mostly urban and trusted by the religious and secular authorities; this gave actors and playwrights unusual freedom.

NOTES

1. John Horgan, *Irish media: a critical history since 1922* (London: Routledge, 2001), p.15.
2. Rex Cathcart, *The most contrary region: the BBC in Northern Ireland, 1924–1984* (Belfast: Blackstaff Press, 1984), pp.11–12.
3. W.B. Lyons, 'Report on wireless telegraphy and telephony in Ireland', UCDA, Mulcahy Papers, P/7/B/308; White Paper on Broadcasting, NAI, Department of the Taoiseach DT, S3532(A).
4. Dáil Éireann, *First, second, third interim reports and the final report of the special commission to consider the Wireless Broadcasting Report together with proceedings of the committees, minutes of evidence and appendices* (Dublin, 1924) [hereafter, *Committee on Broadcasting 1924*], pp.6–7, 196.
5. *Committee on Broadcasting 1924*, p.xi; Evidence of J.J. Walsh, 16 Jan. 1924, ibid., pp. 52, 63.
6. Ibid., p.63; 14 Jan. 1924, p.2, 25 Jan. 1924, p.192; White Paper on Broadcasting, NAI, DT, S3532(A); *Committee on Broadcasting 1924*, pp.308–9;
7. Evidence of Prof. F. Hackett, 26 Feb. 1924, ibid., p.293; Evidence of E.C. Handcock, ibid., p.127.
8. Secretary, Dept Posts and Telegraphs to Secretary, Dept Finance, 17 April 1926, 12 May 1926, NAI, DFIN, S104/5/27.
9. *Irish Independent*, 18 Feb. 1929, ibid.; Secretary, Dept Posts and Telegraphs so Secretary, Dept Finance, 13 Feb. 1930, NAI, DFIN S104/5/27; ibid.; J.B. Clark to Controller of Programming, BBC, 5 June 1935, BBC Written Archives Centre [hereafter BBC WAC], E1/947.
10. Maurice Gorham, *Forty years of Irish broadcasting* (Dublin: Talbot Press, 1976), pp.40, 59; Executive Council Minutes, 23 March 1926, NAI, DT, S7321.
11. Robert J. Savage, 'The Origins of Irish Radio' (MA thesis, UCD, 1982), pp.89–90.
12. *Irish Radio and Musical Review*, Sept. 1926.
13. Gorham, *Forty years of Irish broadcasting*, p.62; Egan, Dáil Debates, Vol.XXVII, 14 Nov. 1928, 5.
14. J.B. Clark to DEFS, 27 Oct. 1934, BBC WAC, E1/947.
15. M. Ward [GPO London] to Secretary NIMHA, 6 Feb. 1922, PRONI, Northern Ireland Ministry of Home Affairs NIMHA, HA/5/734; S. Watt to Secretary, Ministry of Commerce, 21 July 1922, ibid., HA/5/735; R.P. Pim, Minute, 27 April 1924; Wickham to Secretary NIMHA, 3 July 1923, ibid., HA/5/751.
16. W.A. Magill, to Inspector General, RUC, 17 April 1924; A.P. Magill to PMG, Belfast, 22 Nov. 1924, HA/5/735; W.P. Henry to Charles Blackwood, 24 April 1923, quoted in Gillian MacIntosh, *Force of culture: unionist identities in twentieth-century Ireland* (Cork: Cork University Press, 1999), p.74.
17. Director of Programmes to Station Director, 5 Sept. 1924, BBC WAC, R13/366/1.
18. Malcolm Brodie, *The Tele: a history of the Belfast Telegraph* (Belfast: Blackstaff Press, 1995), pp. 52, 62.
19. Beadle to Director General, 1 March 1927; J.C.W. Reith to Beadle, n. d., BBC WAC, R13/366/1.
20. NI Cabinet Conclusions, 25 April 1927, PRONI, CAB/4/192.
21. Nixon to Northern Ireland Region Director [NIRD], 26 March 1939; APD to NIRD, 27 March 1939; Nixon to G.L. Marshall, 29 March 1939, BBC WAC, NI/23/133/1.
22. MacIntosh, *Force of culture*, p.99fn; '"School Broadcasting in Northern Ireland", Report on the visit of the Education Officer for the North Western Area to Northern Ireland: 11–24 November 1938', BBC WAC, R16/129/2.
23. Programme Director to Director of Talks, 14 Oct. 1936; McMullan to Adams, 8 July 1936; Programme Director to D.R.R., 19 Aug. 1936; Director of Talks to Northern Ireland Regional Director [NIRD], 18 March 1935, ibid., R51/356/1; E.W.M. Richardson to Denis Johnston, 5 May 1936, Denis Johnston Papers, TCD, 10066/290/275.
24. NIRD to North Regional Director, 28 July 1937; Salt (for North Regional Director) to NIRD, 3 Aug. 1937, BBC WAC, E1/947.
25. Cathcart, *The most contrary region*, pp.29–30; J.C. Stobart to R.M.B., 15 May 1929; Beadle to Education Director, 15 March 1929; J.C.W. Reith to North Regional Director, 4 Feb. 1929, BBC WAC, R34/820.
26. Beadle to Religious Advisory Committee, 28 Jan. 1932; Minutes of the Religious Affairs Committee, 13 Feb. 1932, 24 March 1937, BBC WAC, R6/73/1.

27. Beadle to Religious Director, 12 March 1934, BBC WAC, R34/805/1.
28. *Irish Catholic*, 10 March 1928; *Irish Ecclesiastical Record*, Vol.XXIX (1927), p.411.
29. *Irish Churchman*, 22 Jan. 1925; *Irish Radio Journal*, 15 Jan. 1925.
30. *Down Recorder*, 24 Jan. 1931.
31. NIRD to Controller of Programmes, 23 June 1939, BBC WAC, R34/224.
32. *Irish Radio News*, 10, 24 March 1928.
33. Quoted in Robert Savage, 'The origins of Irish radio', p.88.
34. *Irish Times*, 9 Feb. 1934.
35. *Derry People*, 6, 13 Jan. 1934; Minutes of Dublin Municipal Council, 5 Feb. 1934 and 21 March 1935.
36. *Irish Radio News*, 1 Oct. 1924, p.479; 15 June 1925, p.910.
37. BBC WAC, R19/840/1.
38. Secretary, Ministry of Finance to Henry O'Friel, 9 Oct. 1922, O'Friel to Secretary to the Governor of Northern Ireland, 20 Oct. 1922, NAI, DJUS, H75/10.
39. *Down Recorder*, 10 Dec. 1927.
40. Lennox Robinson (ed.), *Lady Gregory's Journals* (London, 1946), pp.85–95; Dáil Debates, Vol.XI, 13 May 1925, 1480; O'Casey to Lennox Robinson, 10 Jan. 1926, David Krause, (ed.), *The letters of Sean O'Casey, Volume I: 1910–41* (London: Cassell, 1975), p.165.
41. Sheehy-Skeffington to *Irish Independent*, 15 Feb. 1926, in Krause (ed.), *The letters of Sean O'Casey* p.167.
42. *Irish Independent*, 20 Feb. 1926, in Krause, *The letters of Sean O'Casey*, p.170.
43. Ibid., 23 Feb. 1926, in Krause, *The letters of Sean O'Casey*, pp.171–2.
44. Ibid., 2 March 1926, in Krause, *The letters of Sean O'Casey*, pp.177–80.
45. *Galway Observer*, 13 Feb. 1926; *Irish Times*, 13 Feb. 1926, 6 Oct. 1937.
46. Dáil Debates, Vol.XVI, 22 June 1926, 1512–14, Vol.XXXI, 4 July 1929, 504.
47. W.B. Yeats, 'The Abbey Theatre and Saor Éire' [n. d.], NLI, Yeats Papers, Ms 30,159; O'Donnell to the Abbey Directors, 28 Sept. 1931, ibid., Ms 30,675.
48. Dáil Debates, Vol.XXXI, 9 July 1931, 1885; Christopher Morash, *A history of Irish theatre, 1601–2000*, (Cambridge: Cambridge University Press, 2002) p.188.
49. Yeats to de Valera, 1 March 1933, NLI, Yeats Papers, Ms 30,229; Secretary, to Lennox Robinson, 17 April 1934, ibid., Ms 31,067.
50. *Irish Times*, 3 Sept. 1935.
51. Ibid., 4 Sept. 1935.
52. Aodh de Blacam, 'What do we owe the Abbey?', *Irish Monthly*, Vol.LXIII, No.741 (March 1935), p.199; James Devane, 'Nationality and culture', *Ireland To-Day*, Vol.I, No.7, (Dec. 1936), pp.13–14; John Dowling, 'The Abbey Attacked - I', *Ireland To-Day*, Vol.2, No.1 (Jan. 1937), p.43.
53. *Irish Times*, 3, 7 Oct. 1935.
54. *Irish Catholic*, 2 April 1927; *Irish Ecclesiastical Record*, Vol.XXXIII (1929), pp.528–9.
55. Fagan to Lynd, 21 March 1930; J. Herlihy to Godling, 21 March 1930, NAI, DFIN, S/84/3/30.
56. Morash, *A history of Irish theatre, 1601–2000*, p.185; Deputy Commissioner Garda Siochána to Secretary, Department of Justice, 9 Jan. 1935, NAI, DJUS, H290/28; T.J. Beere, 'Cinema Statistics in Saorstát Éireann', *Journal of the Statistical and Social Inquiry Society of Ireland* (1936–37), pp.85 and 96.
57. Morash, *A history of Irish theatre*, p.183.
58. Ibid., p.196.
59. *Derry People*, 20 Dec. 1930.
60. *Irish Times*, 4 Dec. 1934.
61. Morash, *A history of Irish theatre*, pp.190–1.

CHAPTER FIVE

The security blanket: political censorship 1930–39

The opening years of the 1930s found the two Irish governments in very different positions. In Northern Ireland, Craig's government had defeated the military threat to the province's existence and, despite its failure to conciliate the nationalist population, enjoyed considerable security. The southern government under Cosgrave was under increasing political pressure and, especially given the recent assassination of O'Higgins, it was not certain that any transfer of power would be peaceful. Both governments had amassed an array of powers to suppress resistance but in each case it was questionable whether the circumstances warranted their retention. Despite this, the decade, although far more peaceful than its predecessor, saw each regime cling firmly to the comfort blanket of these security laws.

THE LEGISLATIVE BASIS

The Civil Authorities (Special Powers) Act 1933

The northern government remained committed to the maintenance of the Civil Authorities (Special Powers) Act. The annual renewal of this act had become a ritual which allowed the nationalist opposition, if they were attending the parliament that year, to criticize the government. In 1928, the Cabinet considered making the act permanent but decided instead to extend it for five years. In 1933,when the act came up for renewal, Dawson Bates presented a memorandum to the Cabinet proposing to extend it indefinitely. This developed the arguments put forward in 1928, namely that what had begun as an exceptional measure to deal with a state of civil war was still necessary to deter potential subversion. Dawson Bates attributed 'the immunity from organised disturbance' of recent years to the CASPA. He admitted that the act was still used to prevent 'meetings with the avowed object of spreading revolutionary propaganda', although officially meetings were usually suppressed on the ground that they could lead to a breach of the peace. The Minister was making explicit in private that the act was used to suppress republican political activity as well as violence. Despite this, he asserted that 'public opinion now recognises that there is no danger of these powers being arbitrarily employed'. He went further, arguing that 'even if it were never again necessary to utilise its special ability it would be most unfortunate from the point of view of the preservation of peace and order if this effective weapon were not available in reserve'.[1] The proposal put before the Northern Ireland House of Commons made two significant changes to the 1928 act: its duration was to be indefinite and the Minister was to have the ability to delegate his powers to a Parliamentary Secretary or senior RUC officer. Due to the absence of Nationalist MPs there was little debate on the measure with only John Beattie, the Labour MP for Belfast East, and John Nixon questioning it. Beattie asked why such powers were necessary in a time of peace, while Nixon demanded that the Minister not delegate his powers to anyone lacking a history of loyalty to Ulster.[2]

Report of the National Council for Civil Liberties

The decision to make indefinite the CASPA drew attention to the government's continued use of it. The National Union of Vehicle Builders described the act as a 'curtailment of any measure of freedom which the workers now have'. The Labour Party also protested, as did the National Union of Railwaymen[3] and the Irish Trade Union Congress.[4] The most substantial criticism came from the British National Council for Civil Liberties (NCCL). In 1934 it complained that a meeting called to protest against the Unemployment Insurance Act had been banned and its organizer arrested for trying to read a resolution. The NCCL decided to inquire into the workings of the CASPA and was 'determined to demonstrate the amazing degree to which the fundamental principles of British law have been abrogated under the Northern Parliament'. It was particularly concerned about the practice of making a person accused under the CASPA undertake to 'keep the peace', which 'would have prevented him from engaging in any political activity' due to the vagueness of the phrase.[5]

In April 1935, representatives of the Council met with northern contacts – mostly Labour party and trade union members – to decide on the composition of a committee.[6] It comprised: E. Alymer Digby, a KC, JP and retired Naval Commander; Margery Fry, a former secretary of the Howard League for Penal Reform and principal of Somerville College Oxford; William McKeavy, a Liberal MP and solicitor of the High Court, and Edward Mallalieu, also a Liberal MP and a former Parliamentary Secretary to the President of the Board of Education. The inquiry was to examine and report on the legislation itself, the manner in which regulations were made and powers delegated, and the act's effects on 'political life and on the liberty of the subject in Northern Ireland'.[7]

The northern government paid close attention to the Council's activities and its members were kept under observation by the RUC while they conducted their investigations. Although the committee used the premises of the National Union of Allied and Distributative Workers in Belfast, the police believed that 'the officials of the different trade unions were not at all keen on the inquiry and few, if any, attended the session'.[8] In May 1936 the report was finished and the government and the NCCL began a campaign of propaganda over the result.

On 20 May 1936, the editor of the *Northern Whig* wrote to Craigavon to tell him that the press had been warned that the report would be out the next week and that it would be 'violently hostile' to the CASPA. He recommended that the Prime Minister give the paper an official statement or a personal interview on the same day. The next day the paper attacked the Council for 'boostering' the report.[9] On 20 May, a representative of the NCCL travelled to Belfast and called at bookshops and newspaper offices to drum up interest.[10] The *Irish News* made much of the report in a leader headed 'Legal Dictatorship', while the *Belfast Newsletter* headed its leader 'An Impudent Report' and claimed it had been composed by little-known people, hostile to Ulster and influenced by anti-Unionist propaganda. Craigavon's own response went through several drafts that became steadily more *ad hominem* in their approach. It complained of the 'absence on it [the NCCL committee of inquiry] of any person of note' and claimed that only twenty-one people had come to its meeting. Neither charge was entirely true. The committee members might not have been well known but they were noteworthy, and the meeting referred to was an organizing committee to which only a small number were invited. The government pointed out a few errors of fact in the report and detailed the desperate state of the province in 1922 which led to the introduction of the CASPA. It concluded that 'the only thing the government requires from the citizens of Northern Ireland is loyalty to the Throne and Constitution and obedience to the rule of law'.[11] This analysis typified the government's approach to criticism of its security policy. By jumping forward a decade from the, indisputably dire, circumstances of 1922 without referring to the enormous improvement in conditions in that time, it was able to suggest that the CASPA was still essential to Northern Ireland's safety. It also begged the question with regard to the loyalty of its citizens; a crucial element of the province's problem was that the acceptance of the constitution and throne were the subject of political debate; indeed they were often the only such subject.

The NCCL report had several results. It was reported around the world, notably in Australia and South Africa, emphasizing Northern Ireland's image as a repressive, one-party state by providing a catalogue of facts and incidents.[12] It gave the nationalist community an external authority to bolster its belief that it was being persecuted while reinforcing Unionists' sense that they were the victims of republican propaganda. In the northern House of Commons, Sir Robert Lynn denounced the NCCL as 'the home of all the cranks in England' and condemned its committee as a group of atheists and anarchists.[13] Despite such vehement criticism, there was never any suggestion of acting to prohibit or restrict access to the report. Unionist papers reported its findings, albeit with caustic editorial commentaries, and nationalist papers published it in detail. Nor was the committee prevented from holding meetings or receiving evidence – though several witnesses decided not to send material through the post as they knew it would be opened.[14] When a letter reiterating many of the NCCL's charges was published in the *Boston Post* in 1937, Sir Charles Blackmore, the Northern Ireland Cabinet Secretary, asked whether 'we can do anything to prohibit the publication of such libellous articles'? He was told this was not possible because the letter 'is substantially accurate' but 'it is very easy to present facts in such a way as to convert the statement into what is practically a definite falsehood'.[15] The government's usual course when faced with such criticism was to claim that the CASPA was supported by most of the Northern Irish population – by which it meant Unionists – that law abiding citizens had nothing to fear and that the equivalent legislation in the south was even stronger.[16] The treatment of the NCCL shows that Northern Ireland occupied the middle ground between an open society and a police state. The report itself highlighted the many limitations on freedom of expression imposed by the state on its citizens but such criticism was permitted and publicized; a situation that would not have pertained in a fully totalitarian system.

Emergency law in the south

The northern government was right to point out that its southern counterpart was also infatuated with draconian security powers. In 1931 the Free State government introduced a powerful public safety act in the form of a new constitutional article – Article 2A, introduced by the Constitution (Amendment No. 17) Act 1931. It gave the government enormous powers but we shall only concern ourselves with how it affected freedom of expression. Section 23.1 of the article dealt with prohibited documents. It effectively banned all documents 'issued or published on behalf of an unlawful association'. Such associations were to be determined solely by order of the Executive Council. Any person found to have published, sold, distributed or offered for sale any banned document could be fined £100 or imprisoned for up to six months. Possession of such documents was also an offence. The new article also allowed the Executive Council to ban any meeting it felt could lead to 'a breach of the peace or to be prejudicial to the maintenance of law and order'. The Gardaí were given powers to stop and search anyone suspected of carrying seditious documents and to search premises believed to contain such documents. Reaction to the bill was mixed. The *Irish Independent* gave it enthusiastic support, emphasizing its role in combating communism. It portrayed the bill as regrettable but necessary. The *Irish Times* was also in favour of the measure although it admitted that it encroached on the liberties granted by the constitution. 'Nevertheless', it argued, 'the case for strong measures stands until Mr Cosgrave's essential statements are refuted and every reader of the newspapers knows that they cannot be refuted.' Predictably, papers supporting Fianna Fáil were less enthusiastic. The *Irish Press* called the amendment 'the most far-reaching measure of coercion since the Act of Union'. The *Derry People* felt that 'the law as it stands should be capable of dealing with the incidents which have occurred of late but on the other hand if these incidents are the work of an organisation bent on intimidation and terrorism to achieve their ends, then the act is quite justifiable as any reasonable person will agree'.[17]

Bunreacht na hÉireann

The 1937 constitution substantially changed the situation regarding freedom of expression. It marked the end of article 2A thus reversing the stringent powers discussed above but the rights granted were heavily qualified. Article 40.3.2 put the right to a good name on a par with that to life, person or property. Article 40.6 defined civil liberties but these were only to be guaranteed 'subject to public order and morality'. As if this was not sufficient qualification, the right to freedom of speech (article 40.6.1.i) was clarified as follows:

> The education of public opinion being, however, a matter of such grave import to the common good, the state shall endeavour to ensure that the organs of public opinion, such as the radio, the press, the cinema, while preserving their rightful liberty of expression, including criticism of Government policy, shall not be used to undermine public order or morality or the authority of the State.
>
> The publication or utterance of blasphemous, seditious, or indecent matter is an offence which shall be punishable with law.

The last phrase is unusual for a constitution in that it did not enable or even mandate the government of the day to ban the relevant forms of expression. Instead it placed the common law offence of blasphemy in the constitution and criminalized the publication and utterance of indecent matter – without defining indecency.[18]

Contemporary commentators understood that the rights given by this article were quite limited. Professor John Marcus O'Sullivan, the Fine Gael TD, described it as a set of 'splendid sentiments' but pointed out that Italy and Germany also claimed to safeguard 'the "proper" political

education of their people' through extensive censorship. His party colleague, Cecil Lavery, warned that a government could use the provisions
'to restrain a press which was critical of it'. De Valera himself had argued
that 'liberty is not inviolable. Liberty may mean licence, and licence has
to be checked and curbed in the common interest.'[19]

Some of the convoluted phrasing of this article had its origins in
Roman Catholic teaching. The wording suggested by the Irish Jesuits,
including the noted right-wing intellectual Fr Edward Cahill, in October
1936 was couched in similar terms: freedom of speech and of the press
would 'not extend to the utterance, publication or circulation of anything that is subversive of the Christian religion, or Christian morality or
of public order in the state'.[20] As he did throughout the constitution, de
Valera made significant changes: there was no reference to Christianity,
nor was the circulation of offensive matter made unconstitutional.
Nonetheless, the article gave Cahill and his allies at least some of the
support they sought in their fight against 'apostate and semi-apostate
writers who in varying degrees have used their undoubtedly high literary
gifts to excel in pornography and in bitter contempt for the Catholic
faith'.[21] John Charles McQuaid had also advised de Valera, quoting from
Leo XIII and anticipating the constitution's eventual ambivalence: 'If
unbridled license of speech and of writing be granted to all, nothing will
remain sacred and inviolate'; but 'in regard, however, to all matters of
opinion which God leaves to man's free discussion, full liberty of thought
and of speech is naturally within the rights of free speech'.[22]

Kelly has argued that de Valera saw these rights as 'primarily a set of
"headlines to the legislature"' and did not expect the 'legal shredding
machine, which a later generation of lawyers and judges would use with
devastating effect'.[23] His intention was to leave the question of freedom
of expression in the hands of the Oireachtas rather than, as in the United
States, opening the way for significant judicial review. Kelly has pointed
out that the article is at best vague and at worst self-contradictory. Is, for
example, the 'rightful liberty of expression' given to the radio, press and
cinema in paragraph 2 included in the 'right of citizens to express freely
their convictions and opinions', or is it an extension of it? Is the expression of factual information protected? It seems that de Valera expected
the Oireachtas to decide.[24] As such the constitution contained, at best, a
very weak freedom of speech principle.

Article 40.6.1.ii, regulating freedom of assembly, retained a vestige of
the old security legislation by allowing laws to control meetings 'calculated to cause a breach of the peace or to be a danger or a nuisance to the
general public and to prevent or control meetings in the vicinity of either
house of the Oireachtas'.[25] As mentioned earlier, it was accepted in Irish
law that the authorities had the right to disperse a lawful assembly to protect public order. Also, the rise of communist, fascist and Nazi forces in

Europe probably had an influence on these clauses. The report of the Constitution Committee in 1934 recommended allowing the state 'to control open-air meetings which might interfere with normal traffic or otherwise become a nuisance'. They also outlined the provisions for freedom of assembly in Belgium, Czechoslovakia, Denmark, Estonia, Germany, Spain and Jugo-Slavia. Several of these required prior notice before a meeting could be held and all allowed meetings to be controlled by law.[26]

The world's press paid little attention to the articles on freedom of expression and assembly, preferring to pursue the question – which today seems bizarre – of whether the President could become a dictator. The *Manchester Guardian* mentioned the issue, commenting that 'intellectual liberty is far from secure under an unintelligent censorship'. De Valera further elaborated on his own philosophy of press freedom in a speech to the Dublin and Irish District of the Institute of Journalists in January 1938. He defended the constitution as offering 'a reasonable meaning' of freedom of the press. He was concerned that without extensive qualifications the courts would overrule the state even when it acted 'as the supreme guardian of the common good'. Instead it was up to journalists to realize that,

> the press is a teacher that should realise the extent of its power for good or evil and the dignity of its function ... No reasonable man would blame the public authority for restraining newspapers that, by reason of its commercial interests had set out to foster a war fever, for example, or that callously pandered to unlawful passions or that really endeavoured to overthrow the lawful authority of the family or state.

The *Irish Times* detected 'a vaguely sinister ring' about the fact that he (and the constitution) left it to the government to judge whether the press had abused its rights. 'Does Mr de Valera seriously contemplate a time when he will deem it necessary, for the national security, to control the press?', it asked.[27] It would be answered in less than two years. The speech showed a view of the press formed in the heyday of yellow journalism and relating more perhaps to the activities of the great press barons such as Hearst, Rothermere or Beaverbrook than to the Irish situation.

The Offences Against the State Act 1939

The old emergency legislation enshrined in Article 2A of the Free State Constitution disappeared with its replacement so, when the government became concerned at the level of IRA activity in early 1939, they needed to reacquire those powers they had discarded in 1937. Although the Labour party disputed the necessity for such strong measures, P.J.

Ruttledge, the Minister for Justice, was inflexible, arguing that this time the IRA threat had gone beyond mere posturing.[28]

Fine Gael found itself in a quandary as to how it should oppose an act based so closely on its own legislation. It decided to debate the detail rather than the principle of the bill. No doubt remembering their own experience of emergency law during the Blueshirt period, its spokesmen also claimed that by incorporating such powers into the ordinary law the government had taken a more drastic step than had its predecessor. In particular they attacked the proposal to ban public meetings deemed likely to lead to a breach of the peace. Cosgrave correctly surmised that this would allow persons opposed to a meeting to have it banned by threatening violence themselves. 'Surely it is not the intention that ten persons who are going to obstruct or create disturbance at a public meeting have a right to stop it', he argued. James Fitzgerald-Kenney opposed the fact that the bill 'gives abnormal powers in normal times to guard or to soldier' by allowing a Garda Superintendent to order the suppression of a meeting. The party also questioned the sections of the bill that criminalized possession of incriminating documents and defined these as any document emanating from an illegal organization. Patrick McGilligan asked perceptively if the government would have been happy had Dawson Bates introduced similar legislation in Northern Ireland.[29] In fact the proposals in the Offences Against the State Bill were very similar to the provisions of the CASPA and its regulations as regards meetings and publications.

SECURITY AND FREEDOM OF EXPRESSION IN PRACTICE

Subversive publications

The two Irish jurisdictions had strict laws relating to the possession of documents related to illegal organizations. For example, in 1932 in the south, two women were prosecuted, not merely for possessing documents relating to Cumann na mBan, but for being at a residence where such material was found.[30] In Northern Ireland, arrests were made in Dungannon because of posters demanding the release of prisoners which the government claimed 'were of an openly seditious character, advocating armed revolution'.[31] The system allowed the police in both parts of the island a convenient method of prosecuting people they believed were subversives without having to prove that they were members of a particular organization. The northern government did consider trying to bring in a wider ban on subversive literature but the idea was abandoned because it would have given 'the impression that a general literary censorship was being established'.[32]

The suppression of newspapers remained a government tactic in both jurisdictions. The most blatant and controversial case of this in the Free State was the trial of Frank Gallagher, the editor of the *Irish Press* for seditious libel. Between December 1931 and February 1932, Gallagher published a series of statements by republican prisoners alleging that they had been physically abused while in military custody. He argued that there was 'reason to fear' that police violence was systematic. The paper called for Cosgrave to intervene and to end the practice of holding prisoners without access to their families. It also criticized the government for its inaction and demanded an end to emergency powers. The government charged Gallagher with intending to 'bring the administration of law into disrepute and to scandalise and vilify the government and the Garda Siochána'. Gallagher's defence was that, although he had in the past refused to publish allegations he considered exaggerated or that lacked authentication, he had 'a public duty' to act in this case because the charges were supported by Frank Fahy TD and he believed the men in question were in danger. He claimed that he did not approach the Minister for Justice because opposition complaints on the issue had already been ignored and Gallagher did not believe any action would have been taken. He had used the editorial column of the paper rather than the news pages 'in order not to agitate public opinion more than need be'.[33]

Stephen Roche of the Department of Justice was questioned on 2 February 1932. Gallagher's counsel asked why his client had been charged with seditious libel instead of criminal libel, and alleged that it was because the latter would have required the tribunal to investigate whether his allegations were true. Roche pointed out that only the seditious libel charge existed under the emergency legislation but this did not explain why the government took such extreme measures. Roche admitted that the issue of whether prisoners had been abused was in the public interest and that the *Irish Press* had no legal obligation to submit the reports to the state before publishing them, although 'prudent publications' did so. He asserted that sedition had occurred nonetheless because the paper had not ascertained the truth or falsehood of the reports before publishing. The tribunal found Gallagher guilty but the penalty was a mere £100 fine.[34] His supporters subscribed £500 in contributions and the *Irish Press* gained valuable publicity. The affair was damaging to Cumann na nGaedheal as the general election loomed and it may have been that the government's Pyrrhic victory served to deter future regimes from following their example.[35]

In the Free State, such blatant use of emergency powers against a major newspaper was rare. In another instance, the *Derry Journal* was removed from sale in some towns by the Gardaí amid rumours that the military tribunal was about to ban it for carrying reports of speeches made at a Fianna Fáil convention. The next day the incident was dis-

missed as a 'misapprehension' and the government assured the public
that the issue in question had been examined and found to be 'quite
innocuous'.[36] The situation arose because the suppressed paper
Republican File had carried reports from the *Derry Journal* and a solicitor acting for the military tribunal decided that it was necessary to
suppress the latter paper as well. What he failed to take into account was
the fact that the law only allowed an issue of a paper to be seized if that
issue was seditious. The Garda action in regard to the *Derry Journal* was
illegal and illustrated both the limitations of the southern emergency law
and how easy it was to abuse.[37] In 1933, a military tribunal imprisoned
Joseph Dennigan, of the *Irish Independent*, for refusing to reveal his
sources. While not strictly an issue of censorship, the case illustrated how
few rights the press had under emergency law.[38]

An *Phoblacht* was under constant scrutiny during this period. It was
suppressed in October 1931 which led to allegations from Fianna Fáil
that the government was censoring political material. The Department of
Justice evaded the question somewhat in its briefing for Cosgrave:

> there is no intention of establishing a 'censorship' in the full sense
> of 'issuing orders for the guidance of printers and publishers', but
> these businesses [the printers] were responsible for seeing to it that
> they did not produce seditious material and should know better
> than to publish a notorious journal like *An Phoblacht*.

The memorandum also recommended that the government indicate 'that
it will not encourage deputies to ask questions on behalf of seditious
persons and journals'.[39] Printers, publishers and newsagents were warned
that *An Phoblacht* was the organ of a proclaimed organization and this
deterred many shops from stocking it.[40]

Military tribunals banned several organs of radical groups such as *The
Irish World and American Industrial Liberator* and *Irish Freedom*.[41] In the
case of the *Irish World*, Eason & Son had contacted the Department of
Justice and asked for instructions before they distributed it. This meant that
the department had advance warning that the publication might be seditious and were saved the effort of seizing it from individual newsagents.[42]
After Fianna Fáil came to power and Section 2A was suspended, the republican press gained confidence. The Cosgrave government had withheld
government advertising from the *Derry Journal* and *Fáinne an Lae* but
Fianna Fáil reversed the policy. In October 1932, *An Phoblacht* published
an article attacking Cumann na nGaedheal headed 'No Free Speech for
Traitors', claiming that 'the only speech a traitor has a right to is an act of
contrition' and that its enemies had 'earned shooting or hanging'. The next
week's issue continued in similar vein.[43] The government came under pressure from the opposition to take action but Roche, then Deputy Secretary
in the Department of Justice, advised the Attorney General that the value

of suppressing such publications was questionable as it was hard to get convictions in the ordinary courts and the paper would get publicity during a trial.[44] As a result, no action was taken.

The government reintroduced emergency powers in August 1933 to deal with the perceived threat of the Blueshirts. Both *United Ireland* and *An Phoblacht* were seized under these laws in December 1933 and the former was again seized in February 1934.[45] It was later published with portions deleted by the police. This was the result of a voluntary agreement between the printers and the police that potentially seditious parts of the paper would be removed. Although the Attorney General denied that such a 'gentle hint' was censorship it is difficult to describe it as anything else.[46] In 1935, the Gardaí, using a similar tactic, warned several Dublin papers not to publish communications from 'unlawful associations' though they would not name the organizations concerned.[47]

The Fianna Fáil government also renewed the policy of suppressing *An Phoblacht*, but faced the problem that seizing individual issues of the paper was not effective. The police also had to decide whether each issue was sufficiently seditious to be referred to the military tribunal. In 1934, the government considered prosecuting the publishers. In contrast to his attitude in 1932, Stephen Roche, now the Secretary of the Department of Justice, advocated this approach strongly. By this time the suppression of the paper had evolved into a de facto censorship. Garda officers would seize an issue if they believed it was seditious, the printers would then edit it and bring out a new, less controversial edition.[48] Although the Gardaí were instructed not to tell the printers which passages of the paper were seditious, thus avoiding taking on an actual censorship role, this was ignored in several cases.[49] The Attorney General warned the Department of Justice to stop this practice as 'there is, I think, no legal justification for it'. Apart from the illegality of prior censorship it also made things too easy for the producers of the paper, in Roche's view: 'the object which the departmental instructions are intended to secure is to cause the printers and publishers of seditious issues of *An Phoblacht* the maximum of inconvenience and financial loss'.[50] This policy also drew protests from members of the old IRA and the National Union of Journalists.[51]

The Northern Ireland government also preferred to ban those publications espousing the views of a radical fringe. Such bans became more frequent in the 1930s than in the previous decade. Between 1924 and 1929 only eight orders were issued against five publications, but from 1930 to 1939 there were fifty-three orders against ten publications.[52] The government adopted a policy of annually renewing some bans, effectively making them permanent. The papers against which this system was used were: *An Phoblacht, The Irish World and American Industrial Liberator* and *Irish Freedom*. The left-wing paper the *Vanguard* was kept under close observation but ceased publication before it strayed over the line between what one Civil Servant called 'truculent' and seditious.[53] Surprisingly there does not seem to have been any proposal to allow for longer bans even after the CASPA was itself made indefinite nor did the government copy its southern counterpart and introduce a general ban on subversive publications. The Chief Crown Solicitor was advised that 'it would be difficult to frame a regulation on this subject which would not give the impression that a general literary censorship was being established'.[54]

Craigavon's government rarely used emergency legislation against popular papers. The *Irish News* was prosecuted in November 1932 for printing a letter referring to the visit of the Prince of Wales that described the proposed honour guard as 'liars and perjurers'. He was charged under the CASPA with spreading false reports that were prejudicial to public order, calculated to cause disaffection, likely to interfere with the work of the RUC and intended to hinder recruitment to the force. The paper's defence was that when it published reports of statements by loyalists that might be considered inflammatory or controversial no prosecutions resulted. It also contended, unconvincingly, that the letter referred to the unofficial 'guard of honour' arranged by the Orange Order, rather than the official RUC guard. The editor was found guilty of spreading reports likely to interfere with the work of the police and fined the maximum £100 and costs.[55] In 1938, the Ministry of Home Affairs threatened to ban the *Daily Mirror* after it erroneously reported that a riot had taken place in Belfast on 12 July. The government drew up a draft order to ban the paper before it emerged that the mistake had been caused by a misplaced full stop in a telegram and, after a long correspondence, the paper corrected its story.[56]

Flags and anthems

One of the most complicated problems confronting the Northern Ireland Ministry of Home Affairs was what to do about two symbols that republicanism shared with the southern state: the tricolour and the 'Soldier's Song'. A regulation made in 1933 prohibited the flying of the tricolour even if no breach of the peace was likely and the RUC were instructed to remove it unless it was clearly being flown as the flag of the Free State.[57] In 1934 they were further ordered to remove it when it was used as the emblem of the Republic at election meetings.[58] When a group of nationalists in Derry waved the flag as they returned from a meeting in Donegal, they were arrested and five of them were bound over.[59] Later that year, the Nationalist MP Joseph Stewart, protesting at the arrest of three men for flying the flag, produced a tricolour in the northern House of Commons and declared, 'This is the flag of the Irish Free State!' The speaker dismissed the protest, telling Stewart that he was 'entitled to bring any handkerchief he pleases into the House'.[60] The government were still not happy with the situation as it was incumbent on the prosecution to prove that the flag was being flown as an IRA emblem; Dawson Bates wanted to make it easier to secure convictions.[61] The problem with the regulation was obviously that it required police officers to make the metaphysical distinction between when the flag was flown as the emblem of a state, and when it represented the ideal of the Irish Republic.

Dawson Bates was also exercised over the 'Soldier's Song'. Although there were instances of individuals being convicted for singing the anthem, it was nearly impossible to enforce a ban during large meetings or other events. Unionist opinion as represented in the columns and letters page of the *Belfast Newsletter* was unhappy with this, seeing the song as an affront to their patriotic sensibilities.[62] The Minister decided to resolve the situation, conveniently in time for the 1935 elections, and commanded that the playing of the offending song 'should not in any circumstances be allowed to take place'. The RUC reported that the demand was impractical. As the actual playing or singing of the anthem was not an offence, it could only be prohibited if it was likely to cause a breach of the peace. Where the singing occurred in nationalist districts such as the Falls, South Down or South Armagh, they feared that they would face proceedings in the courts if they attempted to stop the singing and such an attempt would quite possibly cause disorder. The Ministry set to work drafting a specific order to ban the 'Soldier's Song'. By the end of November they had 'boiled down the suggested order … to the smallest possible compass'. Unfortunately, this involved leaving out any reference to the IRA, since it would be an 'offence to play this objectionable air even if played bona fide as the national anthem of the Irish Free State, and we may be accused of international discourtesy, but I think you [Dawson Bates] are not worrying about this aspect of the matter'. The idea of a general order allowing the Minister to prohibit songs, followed by an order against this specific one was rejected as 'the other side would immediately press for having orders made prohibiting "Dolly Brae" etc.' The Attorney General noted that 'I don't approve of the regulation itself' and warned that it should only be promulgated if necessary.[63]

Nothing more was done until 1938 when the idea was revived. This time the RUC Inspector General protested that 'the police already have ample powers to deal with any conduct likely to cause a breach of the peace and the proposed regulation would place them in no stronger position'. In fact, he felt that it would be impossible to enforce and would give nationalists an incentive to sing the song for the purpose of 'defying the police' while drawing complaints from Unionists if it was not enforced rigorously. The RUC would either have to attend nationalist events such as political meetings or GAA matches in overwhelming force or not at all 'to avoid being impotent in the face of a breach of the regulation'.[64] That stopped the proposal until November when, faced with a complaint from the chairman of the East Down Unionist Association about the singing of the offending song, Dawson Bates made a final attempt to ban it.[65] A new draft regulation was prepared forbidding the singing of the anthem 'in such a manner as is likely to cause a breach of the peace or to give offence to any of His Majesty's liege subjects'. The RUC Inspector General reiterated his force's objections and pointed out that the police already had powers to prevent a breach of the peace, and interpreted the causing of offence as likely to cause such a breach.[66] The proposal was finally abandoned. Overall it seems that this was a purely political issue which neither addressed a real policing concern nor offered the police any useful powers. Although it is clear from the Inspector General's comments that the RUC considered the singing of republican songs to be a more serious offence than singing loyalist ones, in at least one case a man was bound over for singing 'Dolly Brae' in 'a dangerous place'.[67]

Governments were not the only forces seeking to control the press. In 1935, the *Irish Times* was told by the Federation of Old IRA Associations not to publish photos of the Remembrance Day celebrations. Although no action was taken when the photos were published, it was an attempt to make the paper conform to the majority opinion. In 1937 persons claiming to be from the IRA visited the *Irish Times* offices in Cork and demanded that they remove photos of the British King and Queen, put there for the coronation, from their windows.[68] The government took no action in either case as neither act was strictly illegal.

The Blueshirts

The conflict between the de Valera government and the Blueshirts that occurred in the courts, the newspapers, the Dáil and on the streets from 1933 to 1934 raised several issues related to freedom of expression. As we have seen, the government revived emergency powers and used them to suppress newspapers. It also used them against Blueshirt members and their parades. After Eoin O'Duffy abandoned his intended parade of August 1933 after it was proclaimed, he attempted, unsuccessfully, to hold assemblies at local churches but was frustrated by the refusal of the hierarchy to co-operate.[69] His decision to proceed with parades in local districts led to the government banning his National Guard on 21 August 1933. The northern government had done the same a month earlier because of the organization's support for a united Ireland.[70] As an illegal organization, it effectively lost most of its freedom of expression rights under the constitution.

Even after Fine Gael replaced the Young Ireland Association with the League of Youth, the government continued to obstruct meetings and take action against its members. In December 1933, O'Duffy was arrested for trying to address a meeting at Westport, and his lieutenant, Ned Cronin, was charged with sedition after accusing police of planting evidence. Although Cronin was found not guilty on the sedition charge, O'Duffy was charged before a military tribunal with an array of offences including membership of illegal organizations, urging people to join illegal organizations, inciting his audience to murder de Valera and accusing members of the government of murdering Collins and O'Higgins.[71]

This resulted in a legal challenge by Fine Gael to the authority of the military tribunals. That it was the first such challenge of significance was due to the fact that, unlike the IRA, they were happy to use the courts and, unlike communist fringe groups, they had lawyers of the highest quality available to them. The tribunal postponed the O'Duffy trial to avoid a clash with the courts. The Attorney General argued that the powers of the military tribunal were not subject to the courts at all but to the Executive Council alone. The High Court ruled that although Section 2A was inconsistent with the rest of the constitution it was a valid amendment and could not be overturned. The military tribunals were therefore legal.[72] The court ruled that although O'Duffy could not be tried for sedition or incitement by a tribunal, he could be tried for membership of an illegal organization.[73]

The government's most drastic attempt to disrupt the public display which was central to the Blueshirts, the Wearing of Uniforms (Restriction) Bill, was defeated by the Senate in an act of self-immolation. Before the Blueshirts disintegrated amid the tension between Fine Gael and an increasingly fascistic O'Duffy, there were more convictions in the military tribunals; in 1934 there were 349 convictions involving the Blueshirts compared to 102 involving the IRA.[74] The government was under constant pressure from local Fianna Fáil organizations to act against the Blueshirts throughout the period.[75] None of this is to hold up O'Duffy or his movement as defenders of freedom of expression. What is significant is that the Blueshirts crisis marked a new phase in the use of emergency legislation and pushed Fianna Fáil into the enthusiastic use of such powers.

Processions and public meetings

Both governments faced the problem of policing large demonstrations and protests on a regular basis. In the south the IRA, reinvigorated by the Fianna Fáil government's decision to release republican prisoners, made several threatening statements against the former pro-Treaty side. There is less evidence that the IRA actually disrupted a large number of meetings or posed a real threat to Cumann na nGaedheal members but there were several individual instances of IRA activity against its perceived enemies.[76]

In Northern Ireland, religious events, which often aroused sectarian controversy, were treated differently to political meetings. Despite this, the government preferred that such events be organized according to the advice of the RUC and that priests not process publicly in their vestments. A group of Roman Catholic pilgrims who ignored this policy and were attacked on their way to the Eucharistic Congress of 1932 received no sympathy. The Ministry of Home Affairs told the Bishop of Down and Connor that, had the police known what was planned, the procession would have been banned as a danger to the peace.[77]

The northern government was placed in a delicate position when the Catholic Truth Society of Ireland, the vanguard of Catholic Action in the country, decided to hold its annual congress for 1934 in the Ulster Hall in Belfast, a sacred site of Protestant loyalism. Thousands attended a protest meeting in the hall.[78] The *Irish News* accused those present of committing acts of 'hooliganism' on their way home until they were stopped by police.[79] For a moment it seemed that sectarian tensions would spill out onto the streets once again. On this occasion, the Churches acted to quell the unrest. The protest was condemned by Cardinal MacRory and the Dean of Belfast, Rev. W.S. Kerr, while the Belfast Presbytery expressed its 'grave disappointment'. Dean Kerr pointed out that the Irish Church Congress had held exhibitions in the Mansion House, Dublin, in 1933 without any trouble.[80] The loyalist protesters were hard to calm, however; the *Ulster Protestant* urged its readers to 'Ban the Papal Tricolour' and warned that thousands of armed rebels would follow the CTSI into Northern Ireland. The Ulster Protestant League in Larne passed resolutions declaring that 'Ulster is a protestant territory'.[81] Eventually the CTSI agreed to use other halls and the Roman Catholic Bishop Magean asked his flock not to put up street decorations. Two protesters were charged in relation to their inflammatory speeches.[82]

Easter commemorations by nationalists and republicans were a different matter as far as the government was concerned, despite their religious dimension. From 1933 on, the RUC were told to stop all such meetings, even those not banned specifically by order, despite concerns that this meant stretching the concept of preventing a breach of the peace. In 1934 several hundred people were kept out of the Milltown cemetery by half as many police. Sinn Féin flags were torn down, Easter lilies were removed and men were arrested for putting up posters. In 1935, the *Northern Whig* justified the bans as it claimed 'that such assemblies would be calculated to provoke disorder or create disaffection is evident from their very nature'.[83]

In general between 1933 and 1939, the authorities allowed some purely religious acts such as the saying of prayers and the laying of wreaths but prohibited speeches, demonstrations, graveside orations, flags and posters. In 1932, Dawson Bates made it clear that the government objected to the political content of the speeches and commemorations:

> They are celebrating one of the most treacherous and bloody rebellions that ever took place in the history of the world and so long as I stand in this House I will not permit treasonable meetings of that kind to be held in Northern Ireland.

Against this, the nationalist leader Joseph Devlin argued that far more inflammatory speeches could be heard in Hyde Park and, more relevantly, that suppression caused 'subterranean dissatisfaction and resentment, which ultimately bursts forth'.[84] The RUC usually tolerated Easter lilies in nationalist areas – probably because any attempt to remove them would have itself caused disorder – but they had to be removed in mixed or Unionist areas or when the wearer was talking to the police. In Dungannon in 1930, for example, three men were arrested for wearing 'emblems indicating Republican sympathies [Easter lilies] under circumstances and conditions likely to lead to a breach of the peace' and were detained for several hours.[85]

In the first six years of the operation of the CASPA (1922–28), eight meetings were banned, but between 1929 and 1936, 47 such bans were imposed. The orders were overwhelmingly directed against nationalist, republican and left-wing gatherings. In 1932 an illegal meeting of outdoor relief workers in Belfast descended into a riot against the police and two workers were shot dead. The *Derry People* argued that 'the decision of the authorities in proclaiming a meeting called to voice a perfectly peaceful protest ... merely served to precipitate the crisis that led the workers to open defiance of law and order'.[86] A proposed series of marches from Dublin and Derry, converging on Belfast in October 1933 was banned by the northern authorities and the Dublin marchers found the journey to be beyond their strength and stopped at Dundalk. The Unionist press were supportive of the government's action.[87] In 1934 a procession was planned by the Irish Unemployed Workers Movement to commemorate the events of 1932 but was also banned and one of its organizers convicted under the CASPA.[88]

In contrast, no loyalist gathering was ever specifically banned under Section 4 of the CASPA in this period. The only case of a banned loyalist march occurred in 1935 when a general ban on parades in Belfast was issued and some Orange processions were caught in this. The ban was swiftly revoked and Dawson Bates considered issuing an apology.[89] The 1935 ban was the clearest example of a situation in which government action was required to control persistent rioting. By exposing the potential for sectarian violence underlying northern society, the riots in Belfast illustrated the difficulty in judging the validity of the government's policy on demonstrations. Even parades that might seem innocuous to modern eyes had the potential to precipitate trouble if they strayed into the wrong areas. Nonetheless, it is clear that the government took political considerations into account and was more lenient towards demonstrations of which it approved regardless of the issue of public order.

Connected with the issue of meetings and parades was that of the monuments, around which they often centred. In July 1931 there were complaints that an IRA monument in east Tyrone would serve as a republican rallying point. This led to the introduction of Regulation 8A of the CASPA permitting the state to prohibit the erection of monuments dedicated to proscribed organizations.[90] This was used in 1938 when the Newry Urban Council decided, by majority vote, to grant a site for a monument to the dead of 1916 to 1922 and Irish patriots through the ages. The application for the plan had come from the Newry branch of the Northern Old IRA Remembrance Association. Local Unionists protested that the monument was being erected by an illegal organization and would stand opposite a Protestant church. The monument was duly prohibited, to the disgust of the *Irish News*, which contrasted this with the fact that the British Legion had been allowed to erect a war memorial.[91]

In 1938 a large nationalist anti-partition meeting to be held in Newtownbutler was planned for 20 November. On 13 November the local Orangemen announced a meeting, generally understood to be a counter-demonstration, for the same date. The government responded with an order banning all meetings. The *Irish News* expressed nationalist fears that this would lead to loyalists effectively banning all nationalist meetings by threatening to hold their own demonstrations.[92] In the northern House of Commons, Dawson Bates made it clear that he had no interest in protecting nationalist gatherings. He claimed that the meetings 'have as their object the bringing about of the destruction of the constitution' and would not be tolerated.[93]

A nationalist meeting in Newtownbutler was set for 27 November but was postponed for a week after loyalist objections. A meeting in Dungannon was planned for 4 December but also faced threats of disruption. Although Craigavon preferred that 'nothing should be done to prevent hot air from escaping', the government again banned all meetings. The nationalists postponed their meetings for a week but these were again banned. The Ministry of Home Affairs considered issuing a general ban against all anti-partition meetings but found insuperable difficulties in framing one. The meeting was finally held in Donegal in March.[94]

The incidents did more than simply increase tension. It is hard to take seriously the argument that public order was the issue. Dawson Bates's House of Commons speech made his views clear and, as one nationalist put it, there was no doubt that an Orange procession would be less likely to be banned because of a nationalist counter-demonstration.[95] What is at issue was not whether the government's decision was correct but the fact that it showed what kinds of political demonstrations were considered legitimate expressions and what kinds were not.

In certain cases, loyalists were prevented from marching or flying flags. For example, in 1932, an RUC man was instructed not to fly Union Jacks from his house during July, and Coalisland Loyal Orange Lodge No. 93 had to take a new route after a period of trouble between the communities in the town.[96] In these cases, there was no government criticism of the nature of the displays or parades, just a pragmatic policing decision.

In southern Ireland, there were cases of loyalists being prevented from marching by republicans. In July 1931 the Royal Black Preceptories of Cavan and Monaghan were stopped from parading at Cootehill by hundreds of men with sticks and hurleys. Although gardaí were present, they were outnumbered. The authorities suggested that it might be necessary to restrict meetings 'which were, by their nature, likely to cause a breach of the peace'. By this they meant, not gatherings of armed republicans, but of recalcitrant Unionists.[97] Similar incidents occurred the next year in Monaghan.[98] The response of the authorities reflected the majoritarian culture in independent Ireland and the lack of sympathy with, if not outright hostility towards, expressions of loyalism. As Ewan Morris has pointed out, this hostility extended to the playing of 'God Save the King', though the southern government did not follow the example of its northern counterpart and consider banning the anthem.[99]

Postal censorship

The northern government used censorship of the posts to gather intelligence on nationalists and left-wing leaders. It was quite open about this when asked: Dawson Bates explained in 1930 that 'correspondence for delivery to, or emanating from, persons suspected of being engaged in seditious activities is still subjected to censorship in the interests of public safety'.[100] He declined to explain how the Northern Irish Ministry of Home Affairs could exercise the censorship when the Post Office was a reserved service or how it worked. He had good reason for being reticent for the whole process was an administrative mess of dubious legality. Until 1925, the UK Home Secretary had issued a general warrant allowing the northern authorities to censor the posts themselves but this was discontinued as it was manifestly unconstitutional. In theory the warrant should have been issued by the Governor of Northern Ireland but it was illegal for any northern minister to advise him to do so. It was therefore decided that the Government of Northern Ireland would send the details to the Home Office which would send draft warrants to the Governor. In practice the northern Ministry of Home Affairs submitted a list of persons whose post it wanted examined and 'it was understood that the Home Office would not be concerned to scrutinise the names'.[101] The files concerning individual cases of postal censorship in the British National Archives remain closed. The southern government had no such constitutional difficulties and its emergency powers gave it ample authority to censor post. Again there are no files available referring to individual cases.

Socialism and communism

Both jurisdictions expressed a common horror at communism and a suspicion of left-wing movements out of all proportion to their actual presence on the island. In part this was in keeping with what was happening in other countries such as the USA, Britain and Australia. It was also influenced by the rise to prominence of left-wing activists such as Peadar O'Donnell in the IRA, especially during the time when Saor Éire was active. As Mike Milotte has pointed out, communists were thin on the ground in Northern Ireland. Despite this, Saor Éire was added to the list of organizations banned under the CASPA in October 1931 and communist films were still subject to Home Office bans. In September 1930, a communist activist declared in a speech that 'it was only when you took the gun and threatened society that you ever got anything'; he was arrested and got six months.[102]

In the south, communism became a favoured target of Roman Catholic activists in the 1930s. In September 1931, Cosgrave, trying to rally support for his government's emergency legislation, wrote to Archbishop Byrne of Dublin to warn him of the rapid growth 'of subversive teachings and activities' which were a 'threat to the foundation of all authority'. He enclosed clippings from republican papers of a socialist and anti-clerical tone. The Minister for Justice also briefed the bishops in an effort to recruit them for the government's anti-communist crusade.[103]

After the passage of Article 2A to the Free State Constitution, the bishops issued a pastoral on 'the growing evidence of a campaign of revolution and communism'.[104] In Kilkenny, where a group of activists had set up the breakaway Irish Miners, Quarries and Allied Workers' Union, the Roman Catholic Bishop, Collier, told his people that they could not 'buy, sell, read, receive or support any communist literature, journal or paper such as the *Workers' Voice*'. He also called for vigilance committees against 'the Red Menace'. This call was echoed in the pastorals of the bishops of Kildare, Kilmore and Derry. The campaign culminated in violent attacks on communist offices and meeting places in Dublin following a service in the Pro-Cathedral. In August 1933, the communist leader Jim Gralton was deported. When Irish communists finally founded a party, they did so in rooms rented under the name of the 'Dublin Total Abstinence Society'.[105]

The new printers of the *Workers' Voice* wrote to the Department of Justice after the passage of the 17th Amendment. They wanted to know what their responsibilities were under the new law. They were told that it would be better if they stopped printing the paper altogether as 'it is probable that future issues will be of such a nature that it will be necessary to take action without notice against the proprietor, publishers and printers'. As this would have led to the printers losing money, they agreed instead to censor the paper themselves before printing it.[106] Through a vague threat that it was 'probable' that the paper would be banned at some time in the future, the government got a prior censorship of the paper without any action or expense on the part of the police or any judicial process whatever.

The northern government pursued the same policy as their southern counterparts, using exclusion orders as their weapons of choice. Harry Pollit, the General Secretary of the Communist Party of Great Britain, was deported before he could address a meeting, and the replacement speaker was served with an exclusion order. When he broke the order to speak in Belfast, he was jailed. Protestant and Roman Catholic leaders also warned the working-class members of their flocks to beware of communism.[107]

The outbreak of the Spanish Civil War intensified the pressure from religious leaders on both sides of the border. Bishop O'Kane of Derry condemned both Irish supporters of the republican cause and those who tried to 'combine profession of the Catholic faith with communism which Pius XI declares impossible'. Cardinal MacRory, in a detailed Lenten pastoral, carefully rebutted the idea that communism was compatible with the Catholic faith. The Bishop of Raphoe was more direct and condemned the 'Red Menace' as the 'most formidable that Christian Europe has to face at the moment' and one in which 'press, radio, cinema, novel, [and] drama are all used with an unholy zeal to spread the gospel of class warfare and militant atheism to the ends of the earth'.[108] In 1936, the board of Trinity College Dublin refused to recognize the Socialist club, and in 1937, in Queen's University Belfast, a meeting of the Literary and Scientific Society was banned by the Students' Representative Council and Students' Union because Peadar O'Donnell was due to speak on Spain. It was claimed to have been the first time in the society's history that a speaker was prohibited.[109] The *Catholic Truth Quarterly* described communism as a plague that 'is virulent, it is highly infectious'.[110] *Ireland To-day*, an intellectual journal with a small but influential readership, faced considerable pressure due to its support for the Republican cause in Spain. In the face of boycotts by shops and a decline in sales and advertising, the journal sacked its foreign affairs editor, Owen Sheehy Skeffington. He was asked to write a valedictory address but in the event this was not published. This did not save *Ireland To-day* which ceased publication soon afterwards.[111] Despite these campaigns, the southern government admitted that 'the communist organisation in Dublin is insignificant in numbers and influence'.[112]

Sedition and freedom of expression

The issue of parades and commemorations went to the heart of the northern government's attitude to freedom of expression. Only in countries with a very strong freedom of speech principle is it permitted to advocate the overthrow of the state by violence. It is more common to allow expressions of great dissatisfaction with the state as well as the government. In Northern Ireland, displays critical of the government were usually permitted, but those expressing allegiance to the south or attacking the institutions of the state were not. The northern government's actions can be seen as short-sighted. Devlin claimed that it was making a political mistake in treating Easter commemorations, the flying of the tricolour, the singing of 'the Soldier's Song' and anti-partition meetings as if they were as dangerous to the constitution as the intense IRA activity of the 1922–25 period. Arguably this fed the nationalist belief that their aspirations would never be considered legitimate, thus making constitutional progress more difficult. Against this must be put the fact that the government was under constant pressure from local Unionist Party organizations and loyalist bodies to take an even tougher approach. The size and visibility of nationalist and left-wing displays made the government more likely to act. By contrast the tiny number of fascists in Northern Ireland were not interfered with because the authorities did not want to draw attention to them.[113] The central problem was that loyalty to the state was the defining issue in Northern Irish politics; any statement of nationalist ideology was to some extent a challenge to the legitimacy of the state.

Comparing the northern government's attitude to that pertaining in the south is dangerous: the conflict there was within nationalism not between nationalism and Unionism. This led Cosgrave and de Valera to act in ways that can more clearly be seen to have been political, such as the trial of Frank Gallagher or the censorship of the *United Irishman*. Expressions of pro-British opinion, whether in singing 'God Save the King' or showing coronation films, were not prohibited by law – notwithstanding the actions of vigilantes – in the south as displays of Irish loyalty were in the north. Southern Unionists were too few and too cowed to pose a threat to the state. What north and south had in common was a very limited and carefully circumscribed view of freedom of expression. Neither the 1922 nor 1937 constitutions would have prevented most of the CASPA being incorporated into southern law; indeed the 1931 Article 2A and the 1939 Emergency Powers Act were remarkably similar to that northern legislation. Powers adopted in the worst years of civil war became the norm in what were, by the mid 1930s, fairly peaceful societies, and an opportunity to establish the authority of the state within the framework of normal law and a generous regime of freedom of expression was lost. This attitude was not unique to matters of security and it was on moral questions that the weakness of freedom of expression in southern Ireland in particular would be exposed.

NOTES

1. 'Memorandum by the Minister of Home Affairs in regard to the Civil Authorities (Special Powers) Act – extension of period of duration', 31 Jan. 1933, PRONI, Northern Ireland Cabinet Files CAB/9B/83/1.
2. NIHC debates, Vol.XV, 14 March 1933, 847–51.
3. William Boyd (Branch Secretary) to Craigavon, 11 April 1934; John Campbell to Craigavon, 25 Sept. 1934; W.J. Donaldson to Craigavon, 23 Feb. 1935, PRONI, CAB/9B/83/1.
4. Laura K. Donohue, *Counter-terrorist law and emergency powers in the United Kingdom, 1922–2000* (Dublin: Irish Academic Press, 2001), p.114.
5. *National Council for Civil Liberties: Annual Report 1934* (London, 1934), p.22, PRONI, Northern Ireland Ministry of Home Affairs files NIMHA, HA/32/1/619.
6. E. Gilfillan to Secretary Ministry of Home Affairs, 12 June 1935, ibid.
7. *Belfast Newsletter*, 10 June 1935.
8. E. Gilfillan to Secretary, Ministry of Home Affairs, 3 July 1935, PRONI, NIMHA, HA/32/1/619.
9. F.M. Adams to Craigavon, 20 May 1936, ibid.; *Northern Whig*, 21 May 1936.
10. E. Gilfillan to Secretary, Ministry of Home Affairs, 27 May 1936, PRONI, NIMHA HA/32/1/619.
11. *Irish News*, 23 May 1936, ibid.; *Belfast Newsletter*, 25 May 1936, ibid.; Statement by Dawson Bates, 26 May 1936, ibid.
12. *The Sydney Morning Herald*, 8 June 1936, ibid.; *The Star Johannesburg*, 25 June 1926, ibid.
13. NIHC debates, XVIII, 23 June 1936, 1966.
14. Gilfillan to Secretary, Ministry of Home Affairs, 12 June 1935, PRONI, NIMHA, HA/32/1/619.
15. Blackmore to W.A. Magill, 23 Aug. 1937; Magill to Blackmore, 25 Aug. 1937, PRONI, CAB/9B/83/1.
16. Blackmore to Miss Virginia Jones, 29 Sept. 1937, ibid.
17. *Irish Independent*, 15 Oct. 1931; *Irish Times*, 15 Oct. 1931; *Irish Press*, 15 Oct. 1931; *Derry People*, 17 Oct. 1931.
18. John M. Kelly, Gerard Hogan and Gerry Whyte, *The Irish Constitution*, 3rd Edition (Dublin: Butterworths, 1994), p.943.
19. O'Sullivan, Dáil Debates, Vol.LXVII, 12 May 1937, 225; Lavery, ibid., 11 May 1937, 128; de Valera, ibid., 62.
20. Irish Jesuit Archives, Cahill Papers J55/68.
21. Cahill to de Valera, 8 May 1937, quoted in Seán Faughnan, 'The Jesuits and the drafting of the Irish Constitution of 1937', *Irish Historical Studies*, Vol.XXVI, No.101 (May 1988), p.95.

22. UCDA, de Valera Papers, P150/1052/2.
23. John Kelly, 'Fundamental rights and the constitution', in Brian Farrell (ed.), *De Valera's constitution and ours* (Dublin: Gill & Macmillan, 1988), p.166.
24. Kelly et al., *The Irish Constitution*, pp.923–5.
25. Ibid., p.959.
26. Report of the Constitution Committee 1934, UCDA, de Valera Papers, P150/1047/1.
27. *Manchester Guardian*, 4 May 1937, ibid., P150/1036/2; *Irish Times*, 31 Jan. 1938.
28. Ruttledge, Dáil Debates, Vol.LXXIV, 2 March 1939, 1289.
29. Ibid., Vol.LXV, 19 April 1939, 614; Cosgrave, ibid., Vol.LXIV, 2 March 1939, 1295; Fitzgerald-Kenney, ibid., 1353; McGilligan, ibid., 1398.
30. *Irish Times*, 16 Jan. 1932.
31. NIHC debates, Vol.XII, 1 April 1930, 489–91.
32. E.W. Shewell to Chief Crown Solicitor, 17 March 1930, PRONI, NIMHA, HA/32/1/569.
33. Order of the Constitution (Special Powers) Tribunal, 17 Feb. 1932, Schedule, NLI, Gallagher Papers, Ms. 18365 (3); Mark O'Brien, *De Valera, Fianna Fáil and the Irish Press* (Dublin: Irish Academic Press, 2001), p.39; 'Editor's line of defence' Gallagher Papers, NLI, Ms. 18365(1).
34. *Irish Press*, 3 Feb. 1932; Order of the Constitution (Special Powers) Tribunal, 17 Feb. 1932, op. cit.
35. O'Brien, *De Valera, Fianna Fáil and the Irish Press*, p.40.
36. *Irish Times*, 5–6 January 1932.
37. Commissioner C.S. Branch to S.A. Roche, 5 Jan. 1932, NAI Department of Justice DJUS, JUS/8/696.
38. *Irish Times*, 16 Jan. 1934.
39. 'Note for the President' [Nov. 1931], NAI, DJUS, JUS8/696.
40. Commissioner Garda Siochána to Minister for Justice, 30 Oct. 1931, ibid.
41. *Irish Times*, 3 Jan. 1932.
42. Eason & Son Ltd to Department of Justice, 2 Nov. 1931, 5 Nov. 1931, NAI, DJUS, JUS/8/696.
43. Arthur Codling [Department of Finance] to Prof. J.W. Whelehan [Stationery Office], 22 March 1932; Codling to S. O'Neill [Department of Education], 26 March 1932, NAI, DFIN, S003/0011/34; *An Phoblacht*, 15, 22 Oct. 1932, NAI, DJUS, H305/31.
44. Roche to Attorney General, 31 Oct. 1932.
45. Maurice Manning, *The Blueshirts* (Dublin: Gill & Macmillan, 1970), pp.85, 114, 117.
46. *Irish Times*, 16–17 Feb. 1934.
47. Dáil debates, Vol.LV, 4 April 1935, 1896–98.
48. Roche to Attorney General, 19 Oct. 1934, 28 Nov., NAI, DJUS, JUS8/68.
49. Roche to Commissioner Garda Siochána, 25 March, 4 June 1935, ibid.
50. Attorney General to Roche, 28 May 1935; Roche to Commissioner Garda Siochána, 4 June 1935, ibid.
51. Seamas O'Brien to Minister for Justice, 26 June 1936; Sean Piondar to Minister for Justice, 29 June 1936, ibid.
52. Donohue, *Counter- terrorist law*, pp.89–90.
53. E.W. Shewell, note, 8 March 1930, NIMHA, PRONI, HA/5/79.
54. E.W. Shewell to Chief Crown Solicitor, 17 April 1930, PRONI, NIMHA, HA/32/1/569.
55. *Irish News*, 22, 29 Nov. 1932.
56. NIMHA, PRONI, HA/32/1/665.
57. NIHC debates, Vol.XV, 20 Dec. 1933, 137.
58. Donohue, *Counter-terrorist law*, p.95.
59. NIHC debates, Vol.XVI, 26 June 1934, 2248.
60. Ibid., Vol.4, Dec. 1934, 339.
61. Conclusions of Cabinet Meeting, 16 Jan. 1935, PRONI, CAB/4/333.
62. *Irish News*, 31 Oct. 1935, *Belfast Newsletter*, 1, 7 Nov. 1935, PRONI, NIMHA, HA/32/1/621.
63. W.A. Magill to Inspector General RUC, 8 Nov. 1935; Gilfillan to Secretary NIMHA, 9 Nov. 1935; W.A. Magill to Dawson Bates, 27 Nov. 1935; Note by Attorney General to Minute from W.A. Magill (29 Nov. 1935), 9 December 1935, ibid.
64. C. Wickham to Secretary NIMHA, 19 May 1938, ibid.
65. W.W. [Private Secretary] to Secretary NIMHA, 10 Nov. 1938, ibid.

66. Wickham to Secretary NIMHA, 3 Dec. 1938, ibid.
67. *Belfast Newsletter*, 21 Nov. 1935, ibid.
68. *Irish Times*, 14 Nov. 1935, 13 May 1937.
69. Manning, *The Blueshirts*, p.85.
70. Ibid., p.78.
71. Ibid., pp.114–16.
72. *Irish Times*, 21, 26 Jan. 1934.
73. Manning, *The Blueshirts*, p.117
74. Ibid., p.136.
75. NAI, DJUS, H306/31, H306/61.
76. Manning, *The Blueshirts*, p.35.
77. W.A. Magill to Bishop of Down and Connor, 1 July 1932, PRONI, CAB/9B/201.
78. *Belfast Newsletter*, 25 May 1934, NIMHA, PRONI, HA/32/1/609.
79. *Irish News*, 25 May 1934, ibid.
80. *Belfast Newsletter*, 30 May 1934; *Irish News*, 4 June 1934, ibid.
81. *Ulster Protestant*, May 1934, ibid.; Resolution, 14 May 1934, PRONI, CAB/9B/219.
82. *Belfast Newsletter*, 13 June 1934; *Irish News*, 18 June 1934, NIMHA, PRONI, HA/32/1/609.
83. Donohue, *Counter-terrorist law*, p. 83; *Irish News*, 4 April 1934; Gilfillan to Secretary NIMHA, 9 April 1934; *Northern Whig*, 19 April 1935, NIMHA, PRONI, HA/32/1/468.
84. NIHC debates, Vol.XIV, 22 March 1932, 541.
85. PRONI, NIMHA, HA/32/1/468; NIHC debates, Vol.XII, 7 May 1930, 1020.
86. Graham S. Walker, *The Politics of Frustration: Harry Midgley and the failure of Labour in Northern Ireland* (Manchester: Manchester University Press, 1985), pp.62–3; *Derry People*, 15 Oct. 1932.
87. *Belfast Newsletter*, 9 Oct. 1933.
88. PRONI, NIMHA, HA/32/1/469.
89. Donohue, *Counter-terrorist law*, p.77.
90. *Ulster Gazette*, 9 Aug. 1931; *Belfast Gazette*, 27 July 1931.
91. *Belfast Newsletter*, 11 Oct. 1938; Samuel J. Baird [Secretary Newry Unionist Association] to James Brown MP, 11 Oct. 1938, PRONI, NIMHA, HA/32/1/669; *Irish News*, 27 Oct. 1938.
92. Gilfillan to Secretary NIMHA, 25 Nov. 1938; *Irish News*, 18 Nov. 1938, PRONI, NIMHA, HA/32/1/473.
93. *Fermanagh Times*, 1 Dec. 1938.
94. Rowley Elliot to Dawson Bates, 14 Nov. 1938, PRONI, NIMHA, HA/32/1/473; C.H. Blackmore to W.A. Magill, 28 Nov. 1938; W.A. Magill to R. Gransden, 2 Dec. 1938; Gilfillan to Secretary NIMHA, 15 Dec. 1938; Magill to Gransden, 2 Dec. 1938, PRONI, CAB/9B/83/1; Donohue, *Counter-terrorist law*, p.82.
95. *Irish News*, 21 Nov. 1938, PRONI, NIMHA, HA/32/1/473.
96. NIHC debates, Vol.XIV, 29 Nov. 1932, 185, 189.
97. *Irish Times*, 13–14 Aug. 1931.
98. *Ulster Gazette*, 9 July 1932.
99. Ewan Morris, '"God save the King" versus "The Soldier's Song": the 1929 Trinity College national anthem dispute and the politics of the Irish Free State', *Irish Historical Studies*, Vol.XXXI, No.121 (May 1998), pp.72–90.
100. NIHC debates, Vol.XII, 13 May 1930, 1143.
101. 'Northern Ireland detention of correspondence of disloyal persons', NAGB, Home Office HO/45/24839.
102. Mike Milotte, *Communism in modern Ireland: the pursuit of the workers' republic since 1916* (Dublin: Gill & Macmillan, 1984), pp.122–6; *Belfast Gazette*, 30 Oct. 1931.
103. Cosgrave to Byrne, 17 Sept. 1931, DDA, Byrne Papers, Government and Politics 1922–39.
104. *Irish Ecclesiastical Record*, Vol.38 (1931), pp.540–3.
105. Milotte, *Communism in modern Ireland*, pp.116–20, 141.
106. Roche to Progressive Printing Works, 17 Oct. 1931; J.E. Duffy, minute, 26 Oct. 1931; Progressive Printing Works to Roche, 26 Oct. 1931, NAI, DJUS, JUS8/696.
107. Milotte, *Communism in modern Ireland*, pp.138, 147.
108. *Derry People*, 13 Feb. 1937.
109. *Irish Times*, 28 Nov. 1936; *Derry People*, 13 March 1937.

110. *Catholic Truth Quarterly*, Vol.1, No.2, Oct./Dec. 1937, p.1.
111. Donal O'Donovan, *Little old man cut short* (Bray: Kestrel Books, 1998), pp.14–16.
112. Dáil Debates, Vol.LXIV, 4 Nov. 1936, 10.
113. PRONI, HA/32/1/509.

CHAPTER SIX

See no evil, speak no evil: film censorship 1930–39

The Free State censorship and sound

Three years after the *Jazz Singer*, James Montgomery still watched films in silence and struggled to spot inappropriate dialogue with the help of a script.[1] After several years of investigation and discussion, the Oireachtas passed the Censorship of Films (Amendment) Act in June 1930, enabling him to censor sound pictures, and a statutory order requiring exhibitors to submit a script with the film was signed on 26 June 1930.[2] Even with new powers and equipment, the censor was not always able to deal adequately with 'talkies'. At the time, one of the competing forms of sound technology involved the use of a disc, similar to a record, which was synchronized with the picture. The disc was unalterable so it was almost impossible for the censor to cut such films. If the film proved at all undesirable he banned it. Fortunately for Irish audiences, the format was not common and did not survive.

Film renters and the film censorship in the Irish Free State

By September 1930, James Montgomery had been film censor for seven years and might have expected the system to run smoothly. Instead he faced another campaign against him by the film renters. The grandly titled Irish Advisory Committee of the Kinematograph Renters' Society of Great Britain and Ireland (hereafter KRSGBI) sent a statement to the government accusing Montgomery of being too harsh and ignoring their financial position. They wanted him to adopt 'a less rigid and narrow point of view' and be more responsive to the public taste. They claimed that he made unjustified inferences, labelling a flirtatious female character as a 'mistress', 'harlot' or 'prostitute', for example. Overall, 'the censor does not display a sufficiently broad mind on subjects of common occurrence in everyday life'. They were particularly upset over his opposition to images of women in scanty theatrical outfits, gym clothes or bathing costumes. He also inconvenienced them by insisting on having a script in front of him while he watched. They complained that the

Appeals Board met infrequently, rarely overturned the censor's verdict and that only the female and clerical members, who were particularly strict, attended regularly. The renters wanted these excluded in future and demanded that Montgomery be replaced by a three-man censorship board composed of businessmen under the age of 45.[3]

Although Montgomery was a strict censor, this was not an impartial assessment of his performance. The film industry was in the midst of a costly change from silent films to 'talkies', and, as Ruth Vasey has pointed out, 'sound movies were difficult and expensive to modify once they entered distribution'.[4] It was therefore in the financial interests of the renters, who had to cut the films, to minimize censorship of their product. There was also the fact, articulated by Montgomery, that,

> so far as Hollywood is concerned, the Free State does not exist, it is not even mentioned in their year book. So far as British production is concerned we are only a territory smaller than Manchester, consequently our influence on production is negligible.[5]

It could also be argued that Montgomery was not always wrong in his assessment of what the films were about but was instead correctly decoding the ambiguous characterizations and plots by which filmmakers concealed issues such as prostitution, abortion, suicide and pregnancy. Hollywood films of the period were frequently about sexual matters. As Vasey argues, they were socially conservative, frequently ignoring the corruption, poverty and labour radicalism that was part of American public life at the time. Instead their staple fare was illicit sex and pure romance.[6]

Montgomery denied that he was delaying the renters; it was they who were not sending films regularly enough. He accepted that there had been an increase in the number of rejections since 1929 but blamed this on three factors: a 'rising tide of unsuitable films', the fact that as he now had sound equipment he was rejecting films with unsuitable dialogue or songs, and the fact that the disc sound system on some films was impossible to cut, necessitating their rejection even if only a small part was unsuitable. He pointed out that the censors of Montreal and Quebec were also under attack from the renters and that 'there is a growing demand for a state censorship in Great Britain and in Northern Ireland'. In the eighteen months when he had been unable to censor sound because of lack of legislation, there had been numerous complaints about the films he permitted and many exhibitors had refused to show them. In the cases of girls in bathing costumes he claimed this referred only to beauty contests at which men were seen 'pawing girls' or 'vetting them' or to '"close ups" which are obviously pandering to exhibitionism'. The script was required by law and was essential in case his attention should wander for a moment and he should miss 'an undesirable gesture or action'. He tried to facilitate the renters by allowing them to defend a film – unlike the BBFC, he noted – but he complained that they sent 'young girls to witness many filthy stories'. He viewed the call for an age limit as being merely an attempt to get a more agreeable censor and defended his use of 'police court names': 'A rape will not be called "an erotic impulse", a paramour will not hide behind the euphemism of "lover" or "sugar daddy", and I will certainly not wrap a piece of tawdry tinsel around a prostitute or mistress by calling her a "Gold Digger".'[7]

The Appeals Board also rejected the renters' complaints that they did not meet regularly and always approved the censor's decisions. We have already seen that the number of appeals had increased in the late 1920s and that these had been increasingly successful. As the censorship was supposed to be about moral values, they found the idea of taking financial interests into account unacceptable but they already consulted renters about proposed cuts to minimize the expense. They were astonished at the idea of excluding clergy and suggested that it showed that the renters really wanted lower standards. This view was endorsed by the Roman Catholic *Standard* that saw a plan 'to force the censor to pass films that Christian morality and feminine modesty abhor'.[8] The renters' complaint on this matter was ill judged as an Irish government facing a strong Fianna Fáil opposition was unlikely to ban priests from a state board (although, based on its past record, it might well have banned women). They received no public support, although their statement was published in the press, and, despite the popularity of cinema in Ireland, they were not a powerful political force compared to the vigilance activists who wanted a stricter, not a laxer, censorship.

A somewhat chastened delegation of renters met the Minister for Justice in October. They denied being opposed to the censorship, claiming that, on the contrary, they favoured it. They also denied organizing propaganda against the censor. All they wanted was a censorship based on 'modern public opinion and standards'.[9] Having alienated the censor, the Appeals Board and, most importantly, the Roman Catholic Church, they had little prospect of achieving their aims and no reforms were instituted.

Film censorship and public opinion in the Irish Free State

In 1934, James Montgomery ruefully noted that while 'there are at least one million censors in Ireland, I am only the official censor'. Cinema was certainly growing steadily in popularity. Eighteen million tickets were sold in southern Ireland's 190 cinemas. The people of Dublin averaged twenty-three visits apiece.[10] In 1935, the Department of Justice counted 181 cinemas in the Free State, 160 of them equipped for sound. The vast majority (120) had fewer than 500 seats, fifty-one had between 500 and 1,000 seats while there were ten with capacities of over 1,000 seats.[11]

Cinema's very popularity, especially among the young, disturbed many people. The specific debate on children and cinema will be dealt with later but first it is important to examine the broader debate on film censorship.

During the Dáil debate on the Censorship of Films (Amendment) Bill 1930, one deputy called for 'positive' censorship; that is the power to 'reject not merely immoral and debasing pictures, but pictures that are entirely worthless'. An Ríoghacht, a conservative, Roman Catholic group founded by Edward Cahill SJ, made a similar call at its annual meeting the same year and focused its attention on soviet films[12] although these were rarely seen in Ireland – a fact lamented by cinema aficionados.[13] In 1931, Donegal County Council declared that many films passed by the censor were 'unsuitable and harmful' and called for a ban on all films 'dealing with matters of a sensual or criminal nature'.[14]

There were few constructive suggestions but a group calling itself the Friends of Film wrote to the Minister for Justice asking him to counteract the 'one sided portrayal of American manners and morals in our cinemas' by following a scheme recommended by Fr Richard Devane. They wanted an interdepartmental committee on the effects of cinema, cinema and education, domestic film production and the rental system. They also sought a reduction in tax for films of educational or artistic value. No action was taken at that time because the scheme was deemed impractical and because some of Devane's other ideas were considered undesirable, such as restoring the powers of local authorities to attach conditions to licences while maintaining a central censorship.[15]

Conservatives made a pastime of attacking cinema. The headmaster of Blackrock College and later Archbishop of Dublin, Fr John Charles McQuaid, condemned Hollywood's portrayal of religion as designed 'to show Christ only as a great man and a member of the Jewish race, and alleged that 'the powerful Masonic and Jewish group, the Benai Berith compelled the Jewish film producers even to alter the sacred history of the Gospel!'[16] The Lord Mayor of Dublin, Alfred Byrne, wanted changes to the law to make it more difficult for the Appeals Board to overturn the censor's decision.[17]

By the middle of the decade, as the effects of the stricter censorship in Hollywood began to be felt, the campaigners' tone moderated somewhat. An Ríoghacht considered setting up a special organization to improve cinema and turn it to 'the work of restoring Catholic ideals'. The organization still felt that although a film could be cut to remove obscenity, it could remain a menace if its essential character was immoral.[18] Similarly, Fr Owen Dudley, superior of the Catholic Missionary Society, admitted to the audience packing the Gaiety Theatre that there had been a marked improvement after mid 1934. The Roman Catholic Church was not opposed to cinema, he argued, only to those films 'tending definitely to evil'. These included films dealing with free love, promiscuity, near nudity, dirty speech and wisecracks as well as 'crime films into which ugliness, brutality, vileness, murder and suicide are packed'. He claimed that research in the USA showed that audiences saw nudity and sex appeal as pornographic even if it was portrayed artistically, and interviews with criminals showed that they were influenced by crime in films.[19] This seems to be a reference to the Payne Foundation studies which purported to give scientific evidence of the malevolent effects of cinema on the young. Fr Richard Devane expressed his willingness to see cinema positively in a radio broadcast in June 1935 in which he called for the setting up of a National Film Institute. The *Irish Times* commented that 'everyone seems to be agreed that the cinema has an enormous power for good and for evil but very few are inclined to do anything about it except in a purely negative way'.[20] It was not always easy to be constructive, however. The official journal of the CTSI, *Up and Doing*, printed a film guide provided by the League of Decency in the USA. Unfortunately it had to stop this as too many of the films had been cut or banned by the Free State censor and 'quite obviously the American standards of decency do not harmonise with ours'. This, it felt, was a good thing, as 'first of all our Film Censor is doing his work well; secondly, Ireland in its standards of propriety is still pronouncedly Catholic'.[21] The implication that an American Roman Catholic organization was recommending obscene films seemed to have escaped the editors. Despite this new approach to cinema from the advocates of Catholic Action, there was still only a small audience for artistic films. The *Irish Times* lamented the fact that G.W. Pabst's *Kameradschaft* was withdrawn after only six days while similar fare played to packed houses in the Abbey and the Gate. It took private clubs like the Dublin Little Theatre Guild to show films such as *Battleship Potemkin*.[22]

The publication of the papal encyclical *Vigilante Cura* in June 1936 stimulated the debate on cinema still further. It argued that the motion picture industry had reformed itself only after pressure from the Roman Catholic Church. The *Irish Times* responded that films were responsible for a subtle 'twisting of the normal values' of truth. In historical films, for example, facts were often ignored to promote drama while many American films carried real but unacknowledged political morals.[23] At the 1936 CTSI conference in Tuam, the critic Aodh de Blacam condemned films in strong terms. The *Irish Times* film correspondent responded that, while there were criticisms to be made, he was more surprised at how clean most films were. The studios, he argued, were too afraid of audiences to incorporate the worst features of modern novels into their offerings. He suggested that the critics attend the cinema for a few months before speaking out.[24] Unfortunately, such informed contributions were rare.

Fr Richard Devane continued his campaign to reform the censorship in a more positive way through a National Film Institute. It is worth looking at how his campaign operated. In 1937 Devane asked De Valera to receive a delegation seeking a government enquiry on cinema. The proposed delegation included members of trade unions, the GAA, the Gaelic League, academics, magistrates, a member of Dublin Corporation and the Dean of Christ Church. The comparison with the tactics used by pro-censorship campaigners in 1923 and 1926 is striking. de Valera did not meet them but did set up an interdepartmental committee on cinema. Devane had a low opinion of this committee as it did not meet in public. Regarding censorship, he wanted 'an adequate censorship code of a detailed character' to reflect the standards 'of the normal Irish Christian family', to guard the Christian faith, marriage and the family and to punish breaches of the moral law.[25]

In 1939, the Catholic hierarchy decided to prepare a report on film censorship and approached Devane to write a summary of his ideas that they could present 'as our own requests'.[26] The report, which the hierarchy presented to the Minister for Justice and the Interdepartmental Committee on the Cinema Industry, was effectively written by Devane. It advocated a detailed code, in plain language, which could be amended by the censor with the approval of the Minister. It also sought that a woman be appointed to work alongside the censor, as 'a man is quite unable to appreciate the moral and mental reactions of a child in the way a woman can'. The standard was to be 'that of the traditional Christianity of our people' and the 'angle of evaluation' to be that of 'a normal Irish Christian family'. The portrayal of divorce or infidelity were to be prohibited unless these were clearly portrayed as evil. There was to be no 'excessive and lustful kissing, lustful embraces or indecent postures and gestures'. 'Wild life' and suggestive dancing were to be forbidden, as were suggestive bedroom scenes, bathing scenes, vulgarity, drunkenness – particularly drunken women – pregnancy, maternity wards, childbirth and the ridiculing of any religious faith. Heroic criminals and instructive details of crime and cruelty were not to be passed. The wording for these sections derived from the Quebec code and the US Production Code both of which had been researched by Devane.[27] The interdepartmental committee dragged on and war broke out before the government had to make a decision about whether to alter the film censorship.

The hierarchy's proposals were not substantially different to what the film censor was already doing and were typical of a view among Roman Catholic activists that the censorship was much laxer than was really the case. This view was shared by the CTSI's journal, the *Catholic Truth Quarterly*, that claimed that 'a film censor, manacled by the liberalistic principles imposed by law, can do only his poor bit to protect us in our cinemas'.[28] It seems that these commentators started from the principle that what they saw in the cinema, assuming they ever went, was unsuitable and that such films were not shown in other countries. This suggests that they accepted at face value the propaganda of the American film industry which promoted and somewhat exaggerated the extent to which its morals had been reformed.

Concerns over whether films were harmful to children existed in both parts of Ireland but were especially prominent in the south. This stemmed from Montgomery's refusal to issue 'adults only' certificates. In 1930 he explained that he had offered to issue such certificates if the cinemas in question would exclude children at all times, but 'the offer was not availed of'. If he did issue 'adults only' certificates, there would have to be precautions taken to prevent children seeing the films and it 'would stimulate morbid curiosity and possibly excite the precocious to evade the law'. Instead he endeavoured 'to pass films suitable for family entertainment'.[29] Given the popularity of cinema among children it was unrealistic of him to expect any cinema owner to exclude children completely from his cinema.

The demand for change was not expressed in a well co-ordinated campaign but in sporadic statements from a variety of sources. In 1930, Archbishop Harty of Cashel warned the people of his diocese that the young should only go to the cinema if the films were of educational or religious advantage or at least entirely innocuous.[30] The same year, the Protestant *Irish Churchman* printed an article arguing that children under twelve should not see any films at all. It also quoted research from Switzerland that purported to show that the films seen by children usually contained scenes of rape, adultery, murder, robbery, arson, and often suicide. Limerick County Borough Council circulated a letter to other local authorities requesting that the government legislate to exclude persons under 16 from films 'dealing with matters of a sensual or criminal nature'. The *Irish Times* reported the views of several school principals – most of whom had rarely or never attended the cinema. They were perturbed by the increase in American slang among children. One commented that 'the standard they [the censor] have set is mostly an adult or at least, an adolescent one', while another felt that while girls were less influenced by immoral films than boys, they learned slang from the talkies.[31]

Although the *Irish Times* usually took a positive approach to cinema, it was in favour of special arrangements for children. It compared the fact that theatres offered pantomimes for children to the lack of special arrangements in cinemas. This it blamed on the censor as 'the official view of what is likely to pervert our minds is hardly complimentary. On the other hand its attitude towards the child's mind is all too flattering.' It favoured strictly enforced adult and child classifications. According to the paper, foreigners were often shocked at the films considered acceptable for children in Ireland. It compared the Irish situation to Holland,

Denmark and Belgium where 25–30 per cent of films were declared unsuitable for children.[32]

At the same time, Roman Catholic groups were renewing their campaigns for changes to the film censorship. The CTSI did not favour the prohibition of all children from cinemas, although some of its members did. It was concerned that declaring films to be unsuitable for children would only increase their attractiveness.[33] Fr Dudley, in his aforementioned speech in 1935, claimed that studies in the USA had shown that films increased sleeplessness in children and damaged their performances at school. He was supported by Terence de Vere White.[34] The INTO also called for 'legislation to regulate the admission of children to cinemas'.[35] The difference between the Catholic Action campaigners' demands and those of the *Irish Times* was that the latter wanted less strict censorship of films for adults while the former wanted stricter regulation all round.[36] Despite the pressure applied by these powerful organizations, the government refused to bring in new regulations. Montgomery's refusal to issue different certificates was part of the problem. There was also the question of enforcement and how to stop an 'A' certificate becoming a lure for children.[37] It was a problem that the government preferred to leave alone.

Film censorship campaigns in Northern Ireland

Film was a source of concern in the highly religious society of Northern Ireland. Like its southern counterpart, northern opinion on film censorship was affected by events in Britain, Rome and the USA. For reasons that are not entirely clear the members of the Protestant and Roman Catholic Churches began to seek reform of the film censorship system with greater enthusiasm in this decade. Inevitably given its size, Belfast was the most important site for this campaign, but it also affected other urban areas culminating in an experiment in strict censorship in Armagh in 1935.

In 1930, there were signs that the Protestant Churches were becoming concerned about films when the American evangelical Dr John Mott visited Belfast and warned his audience that films were undermining the work of church missions in the East by showing westerners in a bad light.[38] That year, the United Council of Christian Churches (UCCC) set up a committee composed of Anglicans, Presbyterians, Methodists, Unitarians, Roman Catholics and Jews to examine the film question. It expressed its dissatisfaction with the BBFC, as it had been established by the film trade, and recommended that towns make their own censorship arrangements.[39] Canon Thomas Brown, a member of the committee, wrote to the Ministry of Home Affairs. He was concerned at 'the kind of pictures displayed in our local cinemas and the language used' and wanted 'to redeem such a potent and popular engine of good from impure and dangerous use'.[40] Some campaigners suggested that exhibitors should only show films passed by the Free State censor but this idea was dismissed both because his decisions had no authority in Northern Ireland and because, as one exhibitor put it 'it's not censorship, it's a butchery'.[41]

In September 1930, the UCCC film committee sent a letter to the distributors explaining that it wanted to change the censorship rules in order to raise standards. The distributors responded that they had not received complaints from the public previously, that the government and the local authorities already had ample powers and that films passed by local censors in England and Scotland were turned down by the Northern Irish distributors because the people there would not tolerate bad films.[42] A member of the committee also wrote to William Joynson-Hicks, by then Viscount Brentford, asking for his support but he declined to give it, possibly because his health was failing. Joseph Connellan, MP for South Armagh, demanded 'the enforcement of a more stringent censorship' of films and advertisements. Dawson Bates replied that the BBFC was 'in every way adequate', that local authorities had the power to act if need be and that there was no need for new legislation.[43] Although some, such as Harry Midgley, protested against censorship particularly by religious groups, others echoed the sentiments of the Presbyterian minister who warned that Ulster faced 'a moral abyss' produced by 'Hollywood's most fleshy productions' and would suffer the same fate as Pompeii if it did not reform.[44]

At the 1930 Down Synod of the Church of Ireland, Bishop Grierson congratulated the UCCC committee and said that, 'the extreme puritanical kind of censorship we do not want, but we do want blatant impurities kept out'. A motion was passed supporting the committee's efforts 'to keep the cinema pure for the children in the diocese'. The bishop wrote to Dawson Bates in January 1931 asking him to issue new model conditions for the local authority film licences. The UCCC film committee was not, he claimed, a 'narrow or over puritanical' body and 'there is no doubt, I think, that at times pictures of a very objectionable nature, suggestive of much that is indecent are shown in some of the cinemas'. In common with other censorship advocates on both sides of the border, he was concerned that as the BBFC was appointed by the film trade, 'some of the worst [films] *are* passed by that board'.[45]

Governments may ignore the advice of a bishop but they usually respond to him and a minute was prepared assessing the state of film censorship in the province. It concluded that a great deal of the problem was the public image of the BBFC which the campaigners saw as a 'smoke-screen' for the film trade, whereas 'if these people appreciated the fact that the British Board of Film Censors is a *bona fide* concern they would probably be more or less satisfied'. There were obstacles to reforming film censorship in the province: exhibitors had spent heavily to upgrade their cinemas for sound films, the sound films themselves were hard to cut, and strict censorship required a long period of notice so that the film could be screened, altered and still released on time. The minute concluded dryly that censorship by local authorities was appropriate 'if it is thought that urban councils are fit persons [sic] to judge matters of morals and taste'.[46] The Permanent Secretary of the Ministry of Home Affairs wrote to the bishop to defend the government's policy. He claimed that although the BBFC was appointed by the film trade, it was independent in the exercise of its functions. He also claimed that 'it would be folly for us to contemplate the appointment of a special Board of Censors for such a small community as Northern Ireland'. Instead he proposed to issue new model conditions.[47] As this was what the bishop had asked for, he was doubtless satisfied.

The BBFC seemed to confirm the campaigners' sense that films were becoming increasingly immoral. In January 1931, the board issued a circular to local authorities in which it commented that there was a 'tendency to produce incidents of prolonged and gross brutality and sordid themes'. In such cases, 'no modifications, however drastic, can render such films suitable for public exhibition' so the board promised that it would not pass films 'in which the theme, without any redeeming characteristic, depends upon the intense brutality or unrelieved sordidness of the scenes depicted'.[48] A deputation from the UCCC film committee met the Belfast Police Committee in March 1931. Their demands were simple: no films or advertisements should be screened that were immoral or incited people to commit crimes; only films passed by the BBFC should be allowed; no children under the age of 16 should attend an adult ('A') film; no additions should be made to any film after it was passed by the BBFC; and cinemas should send a list of forthcoming performances to the local authority every week for scrutiny. The film trade dismissed these demands, arguing that it was impractical to allow advance scrutiny of films as they were booked a year in advance, no film was ever added to after being passed by the BBFC and the remaining demands were already being fulfilled. They objected to a complete ban on children attending 'A' pictures, claiming that they did not want to be held responsible for children slipping in.[49]

Against this background the Ministry of Home Affairs struggled to draft new model conditions that would satisfy all sides. Taking the English regulations as a starting point, the official responsible, Robert Pim, argued against placing 'on the cinema managers the responsibility that properly belongs to parents'. He suggested that the usual phrase prohibiting films 'injurious to public morality or that encourage or incite to crime' be replaced as the BBFC already dealt with these. Instead he recommended the words 'likely to be offensive to public feeling' or 'likely to lead to disorder' which 'gives licensing authorities quite as much power as the English regulation … but it does not sound so silly'. Regulation No. 7 in the English list, commanding that the cinema remain well lit at all times, seemed to Pim to have been 'composed by someone during a nerve storm' and was not retained in the Northern Ireland regulations.[50]

The new model conditions for the province had five clauses: no films, except current affairs and news films, were to be allowed unless they had been passed by the BBFC; the BBFC certificate and category were to be displayed on screen; licensing authorities were allowed to prohibit films likely to offend public feeling or to lead to disorder; no objectionable advertisements for films were to be displayed; and a notice giving the BBFC categories for each film on show was to be displayed outside the cinema. The Ministry informed local authorities that the purpose of the new conditions was to resolve the present anomaly whereby 'A' and 'U' films were shown 'indiscriminately in Northern Ireland'. They would also allow the authorities to ban films that 'while unobjectionable generally, might cause offence in some areas'. It was also made clear that 'in practice very little supervision will be necessary in rural areas' as all films on show there would have been censored in urban areas already.[51]

The conditions were adopted in Armagh and Derry but Belfast Corporation only included some of them because of its doubts about restricting the entry of children to 'A' films. Despite pressure from the Churches, the Belfast Corporation Police Committee did not prohibit children from attending 'A' films, if they considered them not unsuitable, but merely intellectually advanced.[52] They allowed a film committee run by the Churches to advise the Police Committee of any 'A' films that were unsuitable and these were rare. They also felt that to put up large signs in these circumstances would only have enticed children into the cinemas. The film exhibitors in the city agreed as they did not want to be held responsible if they mistakenly believed a child was over 16.[53] The Churches wanted stricter rules, prohibiting children from attending 'A' films even when accompanied by their parents and called for the appointment of a special censorship for children's films. The *Belfast Newsletter* supported the Churches' campaign. While the paper did not believe that immoral films were common, it did accept that they were shown in Belfast and that 'strong meat has no place in a diet for babies'.[54] The representatives of the Belfast film trade, the Amusement Caterers' Association, agreed to give two members of the Churches' film committee free admission to afternoon screenings, except on Wednesdays and Saturdays, so that they could advise the Police Committee.[55]

The government's new conditions did not meet the approval of the film trade or the UCCC film committee. The trade demanded that all films booked by them should be allowed, whereas the Churches wanted stricter regulation. In Londonderry, the corporation debated creating its own film censorship committee but decided not to because many of its members, including the Mayor, believed that it was not appropriate to take on the functions of the 'British censor [sic]'.[56] This reflected a common misconception among people debating film censorship: that the UK had an official censor. In June, the Presbyterian General Assembly adopted a resolution demanding 'a rigid censorship of films, books, and literature calculated to have an evil effect on the morals of the rising generation'.[57] This was no surprise as criticism of the cinema was a common occurrence at the General Assembly.

The Churches' organization (now called the United Council of Christian and Religious Communions in Ireland) debated the issue in November 1931. They recognized that cinema was an integral part of modern life but remained convinced that 'the amount of control of pictures exhibited is inadequate and unsatisfactory'. They believed that the BBFC allowed films portraying cases 'of marital infidelity and of a fast life as normal features of society and actual pictures of morally risky situations, bedroom scenes, etc.' They wanted it replaced with a censorship 'representing the most responsible elements in Northern Ireland'.[58] In St Anne's Cathedral Belfast, Rev. W. Popham Hosford preached a sermon arguing that bad films were symptomatic of a wider moral decline comparable to those of classical Greece and Rome before their civilizations fell. In the past twenty years, he said, standards in the UK had declined so that 'as a national consequence – perhaps I should say a divine punishment – our country is suffering from commercial disaster and the collapse of credit'.[59] In Derry, the Roman Catholic Bishop Bernard O'Kane discussed the cinema in his Lenten pastoral for 1932. He warned that

> our children's morals are being slowly sapped by the licentious picture house. In the Free State there is at least an effort at censorship; here it is nominal and a farce ... the best of modern pictures are dangerous; the worst abominable, rivalling the indecency of the paintings in the baths of Pagan Rome.[60]

It is interesting how these churchmen used allusions to pagan Rome, and to Pompeii in particular, to illustrate their point. The discovery, in the ruins of Pompeii, of many erotic works of art had shocked Victorians who had believed the Roman Empire in that period to be a high point of human virtue. That a city full of pornography was buried by the eruption of Mount Vesuvius was clearly too good a coincidence to ignore.[61]

Londonderry Corporation decided to use its Law Committee to scrutinize films and asked the cinemas to give its members free admission.[62] The *Irish News* also supported stricter censorship, arguing that Roman Catholics wanted 'a remedy' to bad films. It refused to blame the cinema owners who, it claimed, had 'very little room to exercise their own preferences' so that 'they deserve pity rather than blame'. It traced the problem back to its source: 'censorship when films reach the distribution and display stage is never likely to be either successful or fair. This work must be done at Hollywood and Elstree during production.'[63] The Churches' film committee reiterated their demand for radical reform. Although they co-operated with the exhibitors in Belfast, they continued to campaign.[64]

Some Protestant churchmen found themselves casting envious glances south. The Methodist Rev. Richard Waugh, in Newry, claimed that the 'chief of the Irish Board of Censors [sic] in Dublin was leading the world in fighting evil films. There was a fine censorship there.'[65] The Armagh diocesan synod of the Church of Ireland heard the report of the Diocesan Board of Temperance and Social Welfare, introduced by the Rector of Lisnadill, Rev. Henry Lamb, who claimed that films held up 'the sayings and doings of crooks, brigands, and immoral characters and undesirables' in a positive light. The board considered the censorship in Belfast successful but concluded that

> although good work may be done by local authorities in setting up committees of censorship, we believe that action should be taken by the government of Northern Ireland to appoint a board of censors similar to that in existence in the Irish Free State.

According to Lamb, judges and magistrates blamed films for an increase in crime by young people. He was opposed by the Rev. Canon Robert Ford who suggested that they 'content themselves with the evils they knew, and not fly to the evils – of censorship – they knew not'. In the Free State, he claimed, cinemas could not show films about the royal family or play 'God save the King'. Instead the Church should work against bad films in the parishes.[66] The *Derry People* praised the example of Quebec in banning children under 16 from all cinemas. 'On the whole, the cinema is a curse to the growing generation. There is no such thing as a good moving picture for children', it said.[67] This seems to have been one of the few complaints in the year 1933. Why the campaigners quietened down is not clear. The new model conditions may have pacified them, or perhaps they were waiting to see the effects of the reform movement in the USA. For whatever reason, the campaign did not re-emerge until late 1934 in Armagh.

At the Armagh diocesan synod of the Church of Ireland in October 1934, Lamb reiterated his committee's call for a film censorship modelled on that of the Irish Free State. He commented that a friend of his had seen a film in both Belfast and Dublin and 'he wouldn't have recognised the picture as being the same'.[68] Apparently concluding that this was a recommendation for the censorship, a deputation of clergy from the Church of Ireland, Methodists and Presbyterians met the City

Commissioner, George Hanna, who was running Armagh while the borough council was suspended. The deputation demanded that cinemas close on Sunday as they considered them to be a great temptation to young churchgoers, felt that it was unfair to make employees work that day and claimed that only Londonderry, Newry and Armagh allowed Sunday opening. They also wanted a strict censorship as many films 'were calculated to have an evil effect on the minds of young people'. Hanna responded that, as a Presbyterian, he was very sympathetic to their demands on the Sunday opening of cinemas but that as commissioner 'he was bound to appreciate that the majority of the citizens did not belong to the same faith as himself ... unless the ministers of the other churches urged him to close them [the cinemas] he could not accept responsibility'. In other words he needed to know if the Roman Catholic Church would support such steps. He was unwilling to act as censor but if the Churches set up a committee he would delegate 'such portion of his powers as he could do to it' while reserving the power to review their decisions.[69]

Hanna sought and received the approval of a representative of Cardinal MacRory. He also told the managers of the town's two cinemas of his decision. He then formally set up a six-man film committee made up of one priest and two laymen from each of the Church of Ireland and the Roman Catholic Church. Each of the clergy was allowed to appoint one of these lay members. They would inspect posters and synopses for films 'a reasonable time' before they were shown. The titles of films prohibited by the committee would not be made public. If the cinema managers were unhappy they could appeal to the commissioner. In addition to this he ordered all cinemas to close on Sundays from 31 March 1935 and to stop holding children's matinees on a Saturday. The latter ruling was made on the suggestion of MacRory's representative.[70]

It promised to be the most radical experiment in film censorship yet seen in Northern Ireland and the first to be run by the Churches. The cinema owners were concerned that their competitors in nearby towns would advertise that they showed films 'banned in Armagh'.[71] They met the commissioner and asked him to lift his ban on Saturday matinees and Sunday performances. Other exhibitors worried that their towns would follow Armagh's example.[72] The *Ulster Gazette* opposed the ending of Saturday matinees as these alleviated the Saturday evening crowds and spared adult audiences the chatter of children, but it supported the ending of Sunday shows. It was not happy with the censorship committee as it wanted this role to be taken by the central government.[73]

The cinema owners were particularly unhappy with the closure of their businesses on Sundays and decided to hold a plebiscite on the subject. Hanna allowed them to use the city hall for the purpose while, at the same time, he temporarily rescinded his ban on Saturday matinees and added two representatives of the cinema owners to the censorship committee.[74] The plebiscite divided the Churches as the Church of Ireland clergy saw it being mostly a problem for the Roman Catholics. The First Armagh Presbyterian Church called for the ban on Sunday opening to be kept.[75] The vote descended into farce because of a dispute over a children's film. When the censorship committee reviewed *Tarzan and his Mate* it decided not to ban it but verbally informed the town clerk that the cinema owner should not show it. He refused to obey as he was contracted to show the film unless it was officially prohibited. The Roman Catholic representatives on the committee promptly resigned and sermons were preached criticizing the cinemas and ordering a boycott of the plebiscite.[76] Only 527 out of an electorate of 2,600 voted. Even for these, it was unclear whether the 'for' and 'against' marked on the ballot papers referred to 'for opening' or 'for closing' on Sundays. With whatever intention, 'for' won by 302 votes to 219 with six votes spoilt.[77] At this point, Hanna gave up trying to reconcile the factions. He disbanded the film censorship committee and appointed the town clerk as sole film censor. He would read synopses of films in advance and view them if necessary. The prohibition on Sunday opening was retained.[78] The debate drew the attention of the cinema press in Britain and was reported in *Today's Cinema*. It was also watched closely by Fr Edward Cahill, the southern Irish Jesuit who was engaged in his own campaign for reform of the Free State film censorship.[79]

Sunday opening was not only a concern in Armagh. Though banning Sunday shows was not strictly speaking a matter of censorship as no distinction was made as to the content of the films prohibited, it did restrict access to the cinemas. Some felt that it was unreasonable for staff who were already working a six-day week to come in on Sundays.[80] When the proposed Sunday Performances Bill in the UK Parliament raised the possibility that local authorities would lose their power to regulate such events, Newtownards UDC circulated a resolution opposing it. Enniskillen narrowly decided not to endorse the motion but the local McKinley Loyal Orange Lodge No. 1539 supported it.[81] The urban council occasionally allowed films to be shown on Sundays for fundraising purposes but it refused a request from the local cinema to allow it to open every Sunday, by a narrow margin.[82] Another issue of concern was that crowds would distract worshippers at nearby churches. This led the Independent Loyal Orange Institution in Belfast to complain about the proximity of cinemas to places of worship.[83]

Derry and Omagh did not allow Sunday opening of cinemas despite challenges in the county courts, and Downpatrick only decided not to ban Sunday opening when it became clear that such a rule would force the town's only cinema to close.[84] Strabane decided to allow Sunday performances despite the opposition of several religious figures. The fact that no churches were actually open on Sunday nights in the town helped the case for relaxing the rules.[85] Belfast enforced its own prohibition so strictly that even the Belfast Zionist Representative Council was not permitted to show *Modern Palestine* on the Christian Sabbath.[86] Despite the experience of Sunday closing in Armagh in 1935, a correspondence on the subject broke out in the local press in 1939. Those advocating Sunday opening saw cinema as a relatively harmless recreation compared to simply loitering about the streets; they also complained that people simply went to Dungannon. The majority of correspondents favoured the ban; one writer suggested that people should be at home reading their Bibles after church on a Sunday night. The *Ulster Gazette* pointed out that Protestant Churches were opposed to all Sunday entertainments and the paper agreed with them.[87]

While Armagh tried its own experiment in film censorship, other campaigns continued apace. The nationalist *Derry People* compared 'the Catholic spirit of traditional Irish decency' which motivated the Free State censorship with the objectionable displays on view in the 'partitioned six counties'. Bishop O'Kane of Derry, in his Lenten pastoral of 1935, praised the tactics of US reformers in boycotting objectionable films which made cinemagoers 'ashamed to be seen frequenting such shows'. Cinema, he claimed, was 'seldom elevating, sometimes positively indecent [and] nearly always suggestive of indecency'.[88] Rev. Henry Lamb of Lisnadill renewed his efforts by leading a deputation of clergy to meet the Minister of Home Affairs.[89]

Events in the USA seem to have overtaken the Northern Irish campaigners at this time. In April 1935, the *Irish News* praised the success of Will Hays and 'the great Catholic campaign for the elimination of improper films'.[90] In June the General Assembly of the Presbyterian Church in Ireland did not hear a bad word about cinema, much to the shock of *Today's Cinema*.[91] Even Lamb and his Board of Temperance and Social Welfare reported that 'a marked improvement in the type of film had taken place during the past year [1935–1936]'.[92] The Roman Catholic Bishop of Down and Connor, Daniel Mageean, was less critical of cinema than usual but pointed out that while 'the pictures are not so grossly immoral and suggestive yet they often represent an outlook that either ignores religion or is openly anti-Catholic'.[93]

In this climate, supporters of cinema were able to be more open. In 1935, George Bernard Shaw, in a widely quoted BBC talk, argued that 'there are no "undesirable films". No film studio would spend £50,000 in making a film unless it was a very desirable film indeed, possibly not desirable by an archbishop, but certainly desirable by that very large section of the human race that are not archbishops.'[94] Harry Midgely questioned the censorship system in the House of Commons, and the Socialist Party of Northern Ireland complained to Belfast Corporation about the banning of several films. The Belfast Film Society was given permission to submit films not passed by the BBFC to the Police Committee for a special viewing.[95]

II: FILM CENSORSHIP IN ACTION

The film censor and the film trade

As we have seen, Montgomery was the subject of a series of complaints from the film trade who were unhappy with the way he did his job. He was hardly less complimentary about them. One of his most frequent complaints was that companies were cutting films before submitting them to him. His attitude to this practice has been criticized by O'Connor as 'hypocritical thinking'[96] as he would then order even stricter cuts, so it is worth examining Montgomery's own explanations:

> I must place on record the danger of passing films which are cut before presentation for censorship. This was brought home to me to-day when I had to deal with the import of a second copy of a film 'Hard to Handle'. This film was cut [on 22 September 1933], and the deleted parts were impounded – when a second copy is imported, the renter sends a notice to me – (I have no power to enforce this). I check-in by projecting the impounded parts, and comparing it by vision and measurement with the import. To-day there was a big shortage – in fact a most important scene was left in the film and omitted from the cut. If this can happen with impounded cuts, what about cuts we haven't seen?[97]

He feared 'some incident we have not seen being slipped into the film after the certificate is issued'.[98]

Montgomery was also frustrated that he was receiving 'many justified complaints by the public' about 'film butchery' for which he was not responsible.[99] By the 1930s, prior cutting was 'a growing practice, which is subjecting the censorship to ridicule'.[100] On this basis it seems unfair to accuse Montgomery of hypocrisy. He was certainly hostile to the film renters many of whom were doubtless simply removing material they knew would be cut. He was also being somewhat petulant about the fact that the public blamed him when they saw a film that had been crudely edited. The fact remains, however, that his motives were sincere and based on his distrust of the film renters who, he feared, would circumvent his decrees if given an opportunity. He certainly had an uneasy relationship with them. For example, when deciding on cuts to *Sign of the Cross* he commented that 'the renter contends that Poppeas's "dress" is *"period"* [his emphasis]. I question this – anyhow if he is correct what are we to do if a Garden of Eden film is presented?'[101] On another occasion, when censoring Colleen Moore's attire, he commented that 'it may be contended that she wears a flesh coloured bodice but it suggests semi-nudity'.[102] These comments suggest that there was a good deal of dialogue between the censor and the renter even if it did not always produce much understanding.

The Free State censor and outside influences

Although the law did not prohibit the film censor from taking advice, he was supposed to act independently. Montgomery sought guidance on occasion from the Roman Catholic Church and the Gardaí. In the 1930s, he became more open about the extent to which he took advice from the clergy. When he viewed Chaplin's *City Lights* he noted that 'Monsignor Cronin and Fr Dempsey saw this and said pass without a cut'. They encouraged Montgomery to cut less of the film than he had intended. Monsignor Cronin was also present when *Alexander Hamilton* was screened.[103] Montgomery also rejected or cut a variety of films as 'his Grace the Archbishop [of Dublin] will not allow the Canon of the Mass or the Monstrance in procession or Benediction to be shown in Dublin cinemas'. In the case of *Cloistered*, a documentary about monastic life, he commented that 'it is fine photography but some Catholics and high ecclesiastics to whom I showed the film were pained and indignant. If the renter insists, I'll issue a Limited Certificate for exhibition in such places as the "Father Mathew Hall" under the auspices of the "Fathers" … If the renter will withdraw the film I'll return the censorship fee.'[104] This is an extraordinary statement for several reasons. Montgomery gave no grounds for prohibiting the film – indeed his offer to refund the fee indicated that he had none. He also admitted showing the film to a variety of people who had no official role in the film censorship and sought to have the film withdrawn on the basis that they were 'pained'. Lastly there was his offer to grant a 'Limited Certificate' for a controlled screening. Given his continuing opposition to granting 'Adults Only' certificates, this was a departure from his normal practice.

He was also more subtly influenced by his own faith and the religious climate around him. His opposition to beauty shows was partly motivated by the fact that they had been 'condemned by the clergy and all decent minded people in Ireland'. In the case of *Green Pastures*, which portrayed God as a black man, he commented

> the naivety of a nigger's idea of Deity may be entertainment for people who understand the negro mind, but in Ireland such materialisation – however noble and dignified – may appear as blasphemous. Consider the effect on the visual memory of a child.

It would appear that two concepts were intertwined here. One was

Montgomery's long-standing objection to the portrayal of the material-ization of Christ – a view he shared with the BBFC. He reiterated this view strongly in the 1930s and rejected *From the Manger to the Cross*, as 'I consider that the exhibition of the materialisation of the figure of Christ for commercial profit in an ordinary picture theatre to a general audience amounts to blasphemy'. There was also a specific problem of the effect that he believed the image of a black God would have on the faith of children. A similar problem had occurred in 1933 with *Father Noah's Ark* which showed 'the singing of the negro spiritual by Noah and his family. Fancy the effect on the "Child Mind"'.[105]

He was similarly protective of the image of members of religious orders. He rejected one film, as 'caricatures of the clergy are not passed here'. Rejecting another, he complained that 'the heroine – a war moth-er – enters a convent under false pretences in order to secure custody of her illegitimate son. She is shown in the habit of a Dominican nun and there are many people who may not consider that mother love would jus-tify such an act.'[106] Perhaps because of his strong respect for the Church, he agreed to prepare a report for Monsignor Curran of the Irish College in Rome for a congress called in 1936 to celebrate the promulgation of *Vigilante Cura*, the papal encyclical on cinema. James P. O'Connor's com-parison of the censor's report with that of Frank O'Reilly raises interest-ing issues. O'Reilly argued that the country needed a specifically Roman Catholic body, with episcopal authority to deal with film. He accepted that the censor stopped films that were 'definitely dangerous to faith and morals' but claimed that the increase in juvenile crime was due to the influence of gangster films. Montgomery denied that there was a need for any body working parallel to the censor. He also claimed that 'the influ-ence of films in juvenile crime is debatable'.[107] As it is clear from Montgomery's notes that he did worry about the effect of films on chil-dren, it seems that he was trying to prevent any outside body interfering with his work.

Montgomery was also respectful of advice from the police and other legal authorities. In 1934 he remarked that 'suicide by gas is becoming quite common owing to its ease – and I have been repeatedly recom-mended by the coroner and the police to delete it from all films. Its appeal to a morbid and precocious child in this instance is dangerous.'[108] He also noted that

> at the request of the Chief of Police – which completely endorses my own attitude – I have never allowed scenes of all-in wrestling on the newsreels – it is the most brutalizing form of 'sport' since the days of the gladiators.[109]

This practice of banning wrestling scenes was not appealed until 1936. In his notes to the Appeals Board Montgomery included 'correspondence with the British Board of Film Censors – and the Assistant Commissioner of the Gardaí, also Australian censor's findings'.[110] Nevertheless, the board passed the film. This may have had something to do with the fact that, as 'interest' (non-fiction) films, newsreels were understood to be subject to different standards than drama.

Was Montgomery behaving properly in taking such advice from clergymen and the Gardaí? The Censorship of Films Act 1923 did not prevent him from doing so. It merely required that the censor 'be of the opinion' that a film was unsuitable (Section 7). How he came to form that opinion was not regulated by law and it may be seen as laudable that he sought expert help, especially where the police were concerned. The question is not whether Montgomery was autonomous but whether he was unfairly biased due to his personal religious beliefs. Here there is no doubt that he was. In common with many of his contemporaries, he considered Roman Catholicism as normative when dealing with religious and moral issues. Therefore, concerns that were exclusive to Roman Catholics, such as the showing of the Canon of the Mass, were incorporated into the censor's standards for all Irish cinemagoers. Given the failure of the legislature to define the terms 'obscene', 'blasphemous' or 'public morality', it is not surprising that the censor's religious views would be involved. There was also no rule preventing Montgomery writing a report for the benefit of any group in Rome.

The Free State film censor's decisions

Montgomery's standards remained identical to those he had been applying since 1923. A film involving divorce was still 'unfit for exhibition in countries where matrimony is a sacred contract. It might pass where the difference between marriage and a day licence is merely the cost.'[111] Nudity was strictly forbidden. This caused him to complain about beauty shows and dances. Montgomery described the former as 'indecent … girls paraded and pawed like cattle'.[112] The censor was so strict about dance scenes that in one case he favoured a cut because 'it [the body] is covered but it suggests nudity'.[113] He also ruled that 'I never have and never shall pass a nude waisted picture of a woman (except in travel films showing natives)'.[114] He maintained this rule although 'people say you can see it on the stage of the Royal – maybe they're right but I certainly will not accept the Royal as a criterion for decency'.[115]

He believed that films were changing for the worse in the early 1930s. The coming of sound had led to a plethora of musical comedies. One successful example was *Gold Diggers of 1933*, part of a popular series of *Gold Diggers* films. The first two reels contained 'so much semi-nudity, indecency and double meaning gags that I don't see how to deal with them'. He cut two bath scenes, two songs with double meanings and pronounced that '"girls who walk home" has only one meaning'. He also deleted several 'cheap and vulgar kisses'. What the audience made of the result can only be guessed. These changes were consistent with Montgomery's policy since his appointment and he was proud of his record. In 1933 he noted that

> this censorship is now ten years at work and it is a strange reflection on the mentality of the film trade that notwithstanding the inevitable rejection of divorce and bigamy stories by censor and Appeals Board, such films as this [*Second Hand Wife*], with its monkey-house morality and nauseating sentimentality are still imported.[116]

Some new problems did present themselves. Increasingly the censor referred to films as 'sophisticated'. This meant a film that was not immoral but dealt with inappropriate subjects for children. As Montgomery refused to issue 'Adults Only' certificates, he rejected these films regardless of artistic merit. In the case of *Sylvia Scarlett*, he said, 'this well acted picture might be described as a sophisticated and cynical idyll – cutting it would be a venial sin but passing it for general exhibition would be mortal so I reject it'. Similarly King Vidor's film of the Pulitzer Prize winning play *Street Scene* was dismissed as 'an ugly cross section of tenement life in New York. The murder of "a woman caught in adultery" by her husband is the crisis of the story. It is far too sophisticated and realistic for general exhibition.' In some cases the Appeals Board passed such films; for example, *Man About Town*, which Montgomery praised as 'a very fine film – if I were a drama critic I should pass it'.[117]

The consequence of the censor's policy was that films of genuine artistic value were heavily cut or not shown at all in Ireland. This may partly explain the low esteem in which cinema was held among the arts. As Montgomery only passed films suitable for children, it was easy for audiences to conclude that films were not of interest to adults. His cuts often rewrote important parts of a story such as the ending of *Dodsworth* where he directed that the renter 'end film *on deck of steamer – thus deleting his return to Edith* [his emphasis]'. A similar fate befell *Camille*, starring Greta Garbo, which he described as 'not only highly immoral but decidedly unhygienic – of course it may be advanced that "Traviata" is the same theme, however the censorship is dealing only with morality irrespective of art'.[118]

The most pressing new development for the censor was the popularity of violent films, particularly those about gangsters. The 1931 version of *The Maltese Falcon* (starring Ricardo Cortez as Sam Spade) proved 'extremely difficult to cut' as 'the whole atmosphere is amoral'. *Public Enemy* was allowed through with cuts, partly because it had been substantially edited before submission and also because it concluded 'with victory for law, dramatic justice'. This made it 'very rough stuff but a lesson'. Montgomery also took this approach with the prison drama *20,000 Years in Sing Sing* which he allowed as 'it isn't sexy, and as it contains a fair moral bias'.[119] By 1934, however, he was becoming frustrated, especially with the films of James Cagney. On viewing *The Lady Killer* he commented,

> Cagney is the most dangerous model to offer to our unemployed young men. His treatment of his women is always brutal. It is about time to stop the gilding of the crook he-man, and the showing of crime and criminals as if they were subjects for comedy. Adolescents are the greatest patrons of the cinema and this class of entertainment is poison for them.

The G-Men, although it featured Cagney as a reformed gangster who joins the FBI, contained 'all the ingredients that make the gangster film such a menace', he claimed. He ordered the distributor to cut scenes of a scantily dressed actress, the details of a bank robbery, a shooting and the rescue of a criminal. He also demanded the removal of the gangster's defence. He was particularly concerned about the climactic shooting, remarking that 'Greek tragedy was greater than Hollywood horror yet it did all its murders "off stage"', and so he told the renter to deal with it 'with great restraint remembering the outcry in the IFS about these scenes'.[120]

He was also becoming less convinced that a moral ending could justify violent content. In 1935 he declared that 'making the law triumphant is merely Hollywood's trick to fool the censors'.[121] This approach led him to alter *Angels with Dirty Faces* in a particularly strange manner. The film concludes with the gangster (James Cagney) repenting and, as he is being dragged to the electric chair, feigning terror so that the children who idolize him will think him a coward and will not follow his example. His childhood friend, a priest (Pat O'Brien), tells the children that his cowardice was genuine. Montgomery, in a fit of myopia, resolved that '"no motive, however good, can excuse a lie", so the priest's lie must come out. Delete the shot showing Cagney being dragged to "the chair", his screams are more than enough.' He ordered the renter to delete the words, 'it's true, boys,every word of it. He died like they said' and thereby considerably lessened the moral power of the film's ending.[122]

The censor's concern for impressionable children was not confined to gangster films. The word 'lousy' was always removed, along with other, harder terms.[123] He also cut 'the raspberry', in response to 'a well merited public protest'.[124] In 1934 he was confronted with a film in which 'an intestinal dyspeptic sound [belch] is emphasised and projected. It is a new development in screen vulgarity and makes us wonder how much lower Hollywood will travel on this sound track.' He was also disturbed that "gee" has come closer to the sacred name and it is now "jeeze" – we must stop this'.[125] Comedy did not escape censure: *Way Out West* was broadcast in Ireland without a dancing scene, an attempted hanging, jokes about sex appeal and 'the entire dialogue about pants'. The Marx Brothers' *Animal Crackers* fared even worse. Jokes about bigamy, double entendres and vulgar antics were omitted, leaving, one suspects, very little for the audience. Realizing this Montgomery rejected it instead.[126]

Audiences in the Free State were also not allowed to hear Popeye remark, 'I must be losing my sex appeal',[127] or see an 'obscene cow with apron' meet Tom and Jerry.[128] *Tarzan the Ape Man* received careful attention. Although Montgomery admitted that 'this film is so removed from probability that one cannot take it seriously', he was unable to tolerate the ending in which 'Jane elects to remain in the jungle with Tarzan. There is no suggestion of even a Hollywood marriage but it is evident that his he-manity is the lure.' The Appeals Board passed the film but ordered cuts. Montgomery returned to the theme for the sequel *Tarzan and his Mate*: 'it shows a "civilized" girl co-habiting with a "wild man" ... Both Tarzan and "his mate" are practically nude – the woman's nudity is the most daring and indecent exposure I've seen.' The Appeals Board again allowed an edited version of the film to pass. In a strange way, Montgomery had a point. *Tarzan and his Mate* was the last of the series to show Jane (played by the Irish actress Maureen O'Sullivan) dressed in a halter-top and tiny skirt. In later films she would wear knee-length dresses and the couple would adopt a son. Montgomery was also unhappy with the serial *Flash Gordon*. 'This plot is absurdly unsophisticated and could only be accepted by the young and adolescent, for that reason the persistence of the indecent dress of all the women in the cast is most demoralising.'[129]

It could be argued that Montgomery had a point in refusing to accept happy or moral endings as justifications for violent or immoral films. As Vasey has pointed out, Hollywood in this period developed a variety of strategies to cope with the diverse moral climates to which it exported. Moral endings, the changing of a character's role from that in the original novel, and other tricks were employed to allow films to deal with violence, divorce, abortion, rape and other issues without saying so. As Vasey puts it,

> subjects vulnerable to objection, while occasionally abandoned were more often rendered sufficiently cryptic to defray hostile analysis or displaced into forms that roundly declared their own fictional status, such as screwball comedies or 'fantasies' set in mythical kingdoms.[130]

Montgomery's powers of analysis may have owed more to the catechism than to a deep understanding of film studies but he frequently was successful in decoding these meanings. The problem was that the standards he applied were so strict. He commented that an adulterer's 'death satisfies the Hollywood code of honour' but it did not satisfy him.[131] He also complained, with some justification, that 'any dirt can be projected provided the last reel is devoted to sentimentality'.[132] His analysis of *Scarface* was coherent, if conservative:

> this is undoubtedly anti-gangster propaganda, and law is triumphant; but I consider that such films pander to sensationalism. What is to be gained morally by the exhibition of brutes with their mistresses and the horrors of gun bullies at their butchery? If this propaganda is justifiable where will it stop? Similar realism might be offered for say – the white slave traffic – or other social evils – apart from every other consideration is it desirable that our young should become familiar with such savage gunnery?[133]

In common with other censors, Montgomery was concerned about horror films and he dealt with them through substantial cutting. *Dracula* was passed after the renter deleted 'some of the horrors'. *King Kong* was 'not a "horror" to the sophisticated but it is too much for children' and was permitted only after substantial cuts. *Frankenstein* he considered 'horrid' and rejected. His main reason was that 'the child murder incident is the central theme and outrages on children have become very common'. The Appeals Board passed it despite Montgomery's protest that it was 'unfit for exhibition even to an adult audience'. *Dr Jekyll and Mr Hyde* was rejected because 'although very heavily cut before presentation to me the lengthy summary of this film (whose title is taken from RLS [Robert Louis Stevenson]) is unfit for General Exhibition'. On appeal, however, the film was passed.[134]

Table 6.1 shows a considerable decline in the number of objections by the censor after 1934. The percentage of drama films passed intact rose

TABLE 6.1:
IRISH FREE STATE - FILMS CENSORED 1930–39[135]

Year	Drama Films Presented	Passed Intact	%	Cut	%	Rejected	%
1930	1321	934	70.7	202	15.3	185	14.0
1931	1369	831	60.7	309	22.6	229	16.7
1932	1251	710	56.8	345	27.6	196	15.7
1933	1232	743	60.3	340	27.6	149	12.1
1934	1504	930	61.2	409	27.2	165	11.0
1935	1587	1260	79.4	239	15.1	88	5.9
1936	1683	1499	89.1	151	9.0	33	2.0
1937	1463	1315	89.9	124	8.5	24	1.6
1938	1506	1335	88.6	142	9.4	29	1.9
1939	1325	1187	89.6	109	8.2	29[136]	2.2

TABLE 6.2:
DECISIONS OF THE FILM CENSORSHIP APPEALS BOARD[137]

Year	Total Appeals	Censor's Decision Upheld	%	Passed by Appeals Board	%	Passed with Cuts by Appeals Board	%
1930	64	36	56.3	13	20.3	15	23.4
1931	61	40	65.6	9	14.8	12	19.7
*1932				16		21	
1933	102	53	52.0	16	15.7	33	32.4
1934	93	46	49.5	15	16.1	32	34.4
1935	60	30	50.0	11	18.3	19	31.7
1936	31	18	58.1	5	16.1	8	25.8
1937	19	9	47.4	4	21.1	6	31.6
1938	23	12	52.2	6	26.1	5	21.7
1939	13	9	69.2	1	7.7	3	23.1

*The total number of appeals for 1932 was not published in the press.

from 61.2 per cent in that year to 79.4 per cent in 1935, and reached 89.1 per cent in 1936; it stayed at around that figure for the rest of the decade. Furthermore, while the percentage of films cut fell from 27.2 per cent in 1934 to 9 per cent in 1936, the percentage of films rejected fell even more sharply from 11 per cent to 2 per cent. This reflected the effects of the system of self-regulation established by Hollywood in the form of the Production Code. The relatively larger fall in the proportion of films rejected demonstrates that they were also becoming easier to 'save' through editing. The overall themes of films were becoming more acceptable to the censor and the problems that did arise had to do with individual incidents.

The Film Censorship Appeals Board

Table 6.2 shows the decisions of the Film Censorship Appeals Board. It should be noted that the success rate of appeals was quite high. Normally over 40 per cent of appeals resulted in either the overturning of the censor's decision or the passing of an edited version of the film. Renters had become aware of what sort of films could be put before the board with a good chance of success and also that the board was more liberal than the censor. In the absence of the board's records for this period, it is hard to draw any conclusions about how exactly its views differed from those of Montgomery. Based on his own comments it seems to have been a more pragmatic body. When he rejected *Morning Glory* because 'I don't see how it can be cut, every film fan I've met knows the plot', the board simply cut it and let the fans see for themselves.[138] He may have been referring to this approach when he complained, 'Is this censorship being forced to alter its standard of decency in order to conform to Hollywood and British ideals?' when rejecting a film for displaying indecent costumes. If there was a difference of standard, it was not made public.

Neither the censor nor the members of the board gave much information to the press. Senator O'Farrell, the chairman of the Appeals Board, suggested one possible difference of opinion between himself and the censor when he argued that 'this board has nothing to say to education or vulgarity', when, as we have seen, Montgomery frequently took exception to vulgar language or jokes. However, O'Farrell agreed with the censor that 'We are not concerned with whether a film is artistic or not; but we cannot pass one because it is artistic if it be immoral.'[139]

In a later interview he claimed that the board took 'adult mentality as the basis of its decisions. It would be futile to try to scale down pictures to the child standard.' Despite this, he defended the censor's policy of only issuing certificates for 'General Exhibition' on the grounds that 'Adult Only' films would 'arouse a morbid and unhealthy interest in the picture' while special children's cinemas would not have been commercially viable.[140] Normally the censor did not attend meetings of the Appeals Board but instead sent a written report that was read by the members prior to their deliberations. On very rare occasions, more informal methods were adopted. In 1936, Montgomery rejected an interest film featuring all-in wrestling and as 'the Appeals Board was on vacation, I asked the chairman to see the all-in wrestling with me'. The board later confirmed this decision.[141] On another occasion, a quorum could not be found and the renter was convinced to accept 'arbitration' by two members of the board and Montgomery.[142]

Film censorship in Northern Ireland

As film censorship in Northern Ireland was less active and less centralized than its southern counterpart, there were fewer films censored and fewer records kept on the subject. Before 1930, the RUC had seized subversive films under warrant from the Home Secretary in London. This action was directed against communist films, but there were questions about its constitutionality, so in 1930 the Northern Irish government introduced a regulation under the Civil Authorities (Special Powers) Acts allowing it to prohibit films or gramophone records. The British Home Office promptly withdrew all outstanding warrants and left matters to the Belfast authorities. The *Irish News*, predictably, opposed the new regulation as it covered private screenings and, the paper argued, subverted the role of the BBFC. The *Northern Whig* called the decision 'a mild sensation' and expressed more surprise at the fact that soviet films were seen as a problem in the province than at the regulation to control them.[143] In fact it seems that the Ministry of Home Affairs considered the regulation to be just a precautionary measure. It applied only to films or records against which a specific order had been made and it was not expected to affect the cinemas, as they did not show soviet films. The police were told not to seize films or records on their own initiative.[144]

Local authorities, on which the burden of film censorship largely lay, approached their task with varying degrees of diligence. The most important centre remained Belfast and the Police Committee there showed considerable independence of mind. *Scarface* was passed although banned by the BBFC. *Outward Bound* received the same treatment. In the case of *Mother*, the committee watched the film before upholding the BBFC's decision. *Grand Hotel*, a star-laden production of the novel by Vicki Baum, produced complaints from the religiously run Film Committee but the Police Committee did not act, as several members who had seen the film assured the others that it was unobjectionable.[145] In the Free State, the film was heavily cut and the book was banned.[146] In the case of *Damaged Lives*, which was promoted by the British Social Hygiene Council, the committee gave its permission after viewing the film but set certain conditions: no one under 16 was to be admitted, all publicity material was to be approved by the committe, and only travel, interest, topical or educational films could play on the same bill with it. Despite the protests of several religious organizations, the committee allowed *Green Pastures*, black God and all, to be shown.[147]

One of the most controversial decisions of the films censors in Northern Ireland, and Belfast in particular, concerned *Frankenstein*. In April 1932, Rev. W. Popham Hosford, the joint honorary secretary of the Belfast Film Committee, wrote to the Police Committee to complain about the horror film. The members viewed it and ordered it to be withdrawn, offering no explanation. The proprietors of the cinema were shocked, as the film had been passed by the BBFC and even in the Free State (albeit in a heavily edited form). Their offer to cut the film was refused. The cinema owners' association, the White Cinema Club, met and its members described the censorship as 'a menace' and 'high handed'. They threatened to take legal action and the letters published in the press were overwhelmingly opposed to the decision. Of the members of the Police Committee, only John Nixon MP was prepared to defend the ban. He claimed that 'in our opinion this particular picture was clearly blasphemous' and also mentioned the child murder and the subsequent scene of the body being carried through the streets. A special screening of the film was arranged for the corporation, the members of the Northern Irish parliament, the newspapers and the cinema owners. This failed to change the decision. Harry Midgley tried to have the ban lifted but the committee refused to discuss it.[148]

Frankenstein highlighted the strengths and weaknesses of the UK's film censorship system. Despite the decision in Belfast, cinemas around the province were able to show the film as their local authorities either allowed it or had no working censorship system.[149] Londonderry Corporation's Law Committee acted as film censor for the first time and decided to pass the film.[150] Ballyclare UDC was unable to prohibit the film, as it did not know its own legal powers in the matter.[151] Debates in Portrush, Newry and Warrenpoint UDCs revealed the chaotic nature of the process outside Belfast. In Newry a censorship committee had been appointed some years previously but had been inactive until a cinema owner asked for a ruling on an unnamed film. The committee was swiftly reconvened and banned the film. Similarly in Warrenpoint, when considering a motion to establish a film censorship committee, the council discovered that they had passed such a motion several years earlier and decided to appoint five laymen and two clergymen.[152] In Portrush, the council had to ask the Ministry of Home Affairs for advice on how to set up a film censorship.[153]

One of the reasons for this lack of rigour in the region's local censorship was the fact that the cinema exhibitors practised extensive self-censorship. A northern official had commented a few months earlier that the 'purity enthusiasts' were

> making a great fuss about nothing ... the Belfast Exhibitors are extraordinarily careful not to offend anyone, and as a matter of fact, I could mention films which are generally regarded by critics as having been the best films of the past year, which have not been shown in Belfast simply because the exhibitors thought they might give offence.[154]

The government's opinion of the situation was that 'interference with business is unwelcome in Northern Ireland as it is in Great Britain'.[155] When the Armagh City Commissioner, George Hanna, banned the Mae West film *I'm No Angel* in 1934, the cinema managers were unhappy. It was the first film Hanna had prohibited and he came to the decision only because he had happened to see it when in Belfast and felt that it would offend religious sensibilities. The proprietor of the City Cinema, which had booked it, argued, somewhat bizarrely, that a film should not be banned for dialogue but only for what was seen. His rival at the Russell Street Cinema, not surprisingly, dismissed the banned work, which was not showing at his establishment anyway, as lacking merit, and emphasized that he always gave the commissioner a synopsis of forthcoming films three months in advance and had, on Hanna's suggestion, forbidden children from seeing a recent horror film. Many people simply travelled to Portadown to see West's film as the council there, after initially prohibiting it, decided to allow it. Mae West fared so badly at the hands of the Free State film censor that when one of her films was finally passed on appeal the news merited a special mention in the *Irish Times*. In Newry the council banned *I'm No Angel* but the cinema showed it anyway. The owner was required to promise to abide by the conditions of his licence in future and to contribute £10 to charity.[156]

Film censorship and national feeling

Both jurisdictions were faced with a small number of films that either roused or offended national feeling. Alfred Hitchcock's adaptation of *Juno and the Paycock* was seized and publicly burned in Limerick when it was screened in 1930. A group of National University of Ireland students, including Cearbhall Ó Dálaigh, Liam O'Leary and Cyril Cusack, stormed a cinema to stop the screening of *Smiling Irish Eyes,* starring Colleen Moore, on the ground that it was insulting to the Irish.[157]

Republican vigilantes, many of whom were acting on behalf of the IRA, frequently attacked films they deemed tainted by loyalism. In 1933, six Galway men were convicted of stealing the film *Gallipoli* from a local travelling show. They were also found guilty of being members of an illegal organization and claimed to be 'soldiers of the Irish Republic'. In 1934, several hundred men forced their way into the Savoy cinema in Dublin and stopped the showing of a film of the Duke of Kent's wedding. Similar scenes took place in Kilkenny and a Waterford cinema cancelled its planned showing of the film.[158] The incidents were very embarrassing for the Gardaí and the officer reporting made what excuses he could. To have prevented the vandalism in Dublin would have required 'a force out of all proportion to that which would be justified', he claimed. He also showed little sympathy for the cinemas or their patrons:

> Cinema mangers in this country who book this film must be prepared to suffer some consequences ... Advantage is being taken of these newsreel films to further political propaganda and I think that some steps should be taken to subject such films to some form of censorship before they are released in this country.

The Civil Servant reading this considered it 'astonishing that the police should be so out of touch with what is going on in the city underground that a raid of this kind could be carried out'. He also pointed out that the majority of the audience had wanted to see the film.[159]

The next year cinemas decided not to show newsreels of the King's jubilee because they feared republican attacks.[160] In 1937 a group calling itself the Association of Republican and Labour Organisations attempted to ban the showing of films about the coronation. Cinemas received threatening letters claiming that the films were part of 'the influence of British imperialistic propaganda that is flooding the country'. The film renters met the campaigners in a conference. Fox, Pathé, and General Film Distributors represented the trade, while the objecting organizations included Cumann Phoblachta na hÉireann, the Dublin Constituents Committee, the Labour Party, the Republican Congress, the National Association of Old IRA Men, the Irish Citizen Army and Cumann na mBan. Eventually it was agreed that no full length film of the coronation would be shown, that the event could not occupy more than half of any newsreel and that there would be no colour footage or close-ups used.[161] The next year a group of republicans were allowed to see and comment on *Victoria the Great* before it went on show at the Astor in Dublin. Despite this precaution, three men held up the cinema and stole the film anyway.[162]

James Montgomery had his own political and national objections to some films. *Black Fury* was rejected because its hero engaged in sabotage and 'the imitation of this method of a strike would be most mischievous in the event of labour trouble in Ireland'. He also tried to ban *Two Against the World* for being favourable to socialism but his decision was overturned on appeal. He wanted to prohibit John Ford's *The Informer* as it was

> based on a nest fouling novel purporting to depict the 'Black and Tan' period in Dublin ... It is a sordid and brutal libel and the issue of a certificate by the censorship could be used as an advertisement of the Free State's approval of the truth of the picture.

However, it was passed by the Appeals Board.[163] He also lamented the fact that the 'barefaced historical travesty (in more than a facial sense)' of Clark Gable playing a clean-shaven Parnell could not be rejected for 'insults to the feelings and intelligence of the Irish people'. He tried instead to ban it for 'dealing with divorce and justifying the consequent bigamy', but the Appeals Board saw things differently and passed an amended version of the film.[164] *Lives of a Bengal Lancer* was altered for Irish audiences by the removal of the poem 'England, my England' and the replacement of 'God Save the King' with 'Land of Hope and Glory' at the end.[165]

Roman Catholic groups also wanted films to be brought into line with national feeling. Fr Richard Devane, in a broadcast in 1935, called for the establishment of a National Film Institute to counter Ireland's 'cultural dependence on Great Britain'. His proposed body would take over the role of the censor and also control educational films, train teachers and produce documentaries and propaganda films. He even gave credit to the Soviet Union for its 'use of the cinema in the rebuilding of a nation', and Japan for producing films of 'a patriotic character'.[166] Aodh de Blacam, always more suspicious of cinema, was more concerned about who controlled the studios:

> If our schools were handed over to Jews there would be an immediate outcry. No clerical managers would allow a Jew, a non-Christian, even if he were a good man, as many of them are, to control a Catholic school, but this [film] trade is controlled by the very worst of them, and cinema has more to say in the moulding of the

imagination and the ideals of the race than the schools have. Interestingly part of his remedy was to abolish censorship so that people would be forced to use their 'Catholic consciences'.[167] In 1939, the Irish Roman Catholic bishops, in their report on film censorship argued that the Irish state should allow nothing derogatory to the Irish race, no 'stage Irish' production, no film calculated to offend friendly nations or stir up feelings against other races, no promotion of political ideologies, and no films about class struggle.[168]

In Northern Ireland films dealing with the Irish revolution were especially controversial. The region was partly protected by the BBFC. In 1934 the board demanded the deletion of five pages of dialogue from *The Informer* when it was shown the script.[169] *Ourselves Alone* was more controversial. One Unionist condemned it as 'Sinn Féin propaganda' and feared that trouble would result if it were shown. Special showings of the film were held for the Belfast Corporation Police Committee, the Ministry of Home Affairs, the RUC and members of the press. The *Belfast Newsletter* predicted that the film would offend extremists on all sides by trying too hard to be balanced. The Police Committee decided to allow the film but an order was issued under the CASPA on 27 November 1936 prohibiting it. The *Irish News* blamed pressure from the Minister's Unionist party colleagues for the decision, claiming that by accusing the film of having republican tendencies, politicians had created a situation whereby showing it might have led to disorder and therefore justified a ban.[170] John Maxwell of the Associated British Picture Corporation wrote to Dawson Bates to ask him to reconsider. The film had been produced in good faith, he claimed, and to ban it now would cost the company £1,000. The film had not produced complaints in Britain, even in Liverpool or Glasgow. The Minister was advised that the company might be planning to claim compensation. His reply therefore emphasized the risk of social disorder should the film be shown. An offer by the renters to cut the film was turned down.[171]

In 1937 *The Dawn*, another film about the War of Independence, was not banned but there were threats that screenings of it would be disrupted. Screenings of it in Enniskillen and Omagh were guarded by the RUC.[172] *Parnell* was also allowed by the Belfast Corporation Police Committee despite its nationalist plot.[173]

III: THE INTERNATIONAL CONTEXT

Hollywood self-censorship

For many Irish people the international cultural centre to which they looked was not London or New York but Rome. For the Church, cinema was part of the encroaching tide of modernity which it spent most of the period before Vatican II alternately condemning and attempting to understand. Roman Catholicism spent the 1930s attempting to devise principles by which to judge cinema. In 1930 the International Catholic Cinema Conference was held and widely reported on in Ireland. Delegate countries included France, Germany, Holland and Spain. They proposed the establishment of Catholic cinemas, an idea that echoed that of the Catholic press.[174]

Such measures were never likely to achieve the Church's aim of reforming Hollywood and other large film producers. In 1930, Will Hays, the Presbyterian head of the MPPDA, and Martin Quigley, a Roman Catholic publisher with close ties to the film industry, drew up a code of practice for Hollywood. They enlisted the help of Fr Daniel Lord SJ, a professor of dramatics and an adviser on *King of Kings*. The code regulated how filmmakers dealt with sex, vulgarity, obscenity, profanity, costume, dance, religion, locations, national feeling, salacious titles and repellent subjects.[175] The studios resisted the code, setting up a 'Hollywood jury' made up of producers to arbitrate on its rulings.[176]

It took a combination of four factors to make the code enforceable. The reformers had an intellectual foundation in the form of studies carried out by the Payne Fund that were widely and sensationally publicized. The studies seemed to confirm that films had a significant influence on morality and behaviour.[177] These were especially influential in Protestant circles and by 1933 a large number of religious and educational bodies had passed resolutions calling for federal censorship.[178] The Roman Catholic Church provided the second source of pressure for censorship. In 1933, an apostolic delegation of the Roman Catholic Church denounced the influence of bad films, and the American bishops appointed a committee on motion pictures. In April 1934 the Legion of Decency was founded; although this was primarily a Roman Catholic group it had the support of Protestant and Jewish leaders. Its tactic was to organize boycotts of objectionable films.[179] Thirdly, the campaigners were fortunate that the studios were in serious financial trouble because of the Depression. This made them vulnerable to boycotts and desperate for anything that could make their products more popular.[180] Lastly, they had powerful allies within the studio system in the shape of Joseph Breen and Will Hays who took control of Hollywood's regulatory apparatus. Breen, a conservative Roman Catholic, was made head of the Production Code Administration (PCA) which had the power to enforce the code by barring the release of offending films in cinemas run by the studios. In 1934 this meant that 77 per cent of all cinemas were effectively under Breen's control.[181]

It is important not to overstate the extent of the PCA censorship. As Maltby has pointed out, the studios publicized the new regime 'to create a dividing line' between the periods before and after 1934.[182] As Jacobs describes it, the reality was that 'industry censors negotiated with producers throughout the pre-production process. Self-regulation was above all a way of figuring out how stories deemed potentially offensive could be rewritten to make them acceptable.'[183]

British film censorship

The emergence of the sound film affected the BBFC much as it did its Irish counterpart, although it acquired the necessary technology more swiftly. One effect of the practice of censoring talking pictures without sound was that the board became attached to the practice of viewing scripts before production. Most English films were checked in this way and Hollywood was sometimes happy to oblige given the huge market that Britain provided for its films. The growth of horror films led to the introduction of a 'H' certificate in 1932 at the request of local authorities. This was intended to guide parents in deciding whether to allow their children to see such films.[184]

The BBFC seemed to have a considerable degree of public support. Between 1928 and 1931, only 21 of 603 local authorities received complaints about films. Five hundred and eighty-six of the authorities (97 per cent) did not ban films if they had been passed by the board. In the early 1930s, sexy films staring actresses like Jean Harlow were strictly censored. Mae West's films were also heavily cut. The board tended to accept Hollywood films produced under the Production Code and British producers were sufficiently well aware of what would be rejected that they rarely produced such material.[185]

The question of whether to admit children to the cinemas was treated seriously in Britain where the Incorporated Association of Assistant Masters of Secondary Schools called for a government inquiry into the effects of films on children.[186] In 1930, an all-party deputation of MPs asked the Home Secretary, Clynes, to hold a public inquiry into film censorship but no action was taken.[187] Liverpool City Council tried to prohibit children completely from 'A' films but the resultant flood of applications for exemptions overwhelmed the city's censors and a deal was done privately with the cinemas that they would notify the authorities of any films from which children should be excluded. Similar arrangements were made in Sheffield.[188] Croydon banned 200 films between 1932 and 1934. In 1933 Beckenham set up its own board of censors that cut films to which it objected. The public responded by not going to the cinema and, when the cinema owners refused to pay their rates, the experiment was abandoned after only nine months.[189] In Scotland, there was concern that large numbers of children were attending 'A' pictures. The Home Office considered the matter but refrained from action as there was little public outcry and its policy was not to interfere publicly with the BBFC.[190]

Film censorship around the world

Since censorship represented an added cost, it was in the studios' interests to modify their films to avoid incurring a ban. However, a small market like Ireland had no real importance to Hollywood. The UK provided 30.5 per cent of the US film industry's income from abroad, Australasia 15.2 per cent, France 8.5 per cent, Argentina and Uruguay 7.5 per cent, Brazil 6.8 per cent and Germany 5.25 per cent. Ireland was not even considered a separate region. What the American studios called 'A' pictures were made on large budgets and designed to earn money worldwide. The 'B' pictures were intended for distribution in the USA, UK and Australia. Therefore, as part of the UK region, Ireland received more cheap films than a comparable country in mainland Europe or South America. If a country were considered important, changes would be made to a film to avoid giving offence there. For example, *The Boudoir Diplomat* was set in 'the kingdom of Luvaria' rather than France or Spain as originally intended. After protests about *Scarface*, Will Hays told the Italian ambassador that it was now his policy to 'eliminate any reference in crime pictures to individuals with names that could be connected with any foreign country'.[191]

In Britain, it was suggested that the BBFC should do something similar to ensure that British films were suitable for the entire Commonwealth. The Imperial Economic Conference at Ottawa in 1932 agreed that films should be 'of a character and format requiring the minimum of censorship'. The BBFC interpreted this as an invitation to act as censor for the whole empire with the member countries acting like British local authorities.[192] The proposal never acquired any real significance.

Table 6.3 gives the results of the film censorships in five European counties. In Denmark, all cinemas were licensed by the government and film censors appointed by the state examined all films. Children under 16 could only attend films passed for universal exhibition. Films were prohibited if they were deemed to have a 'brutalising or demoralising effect on the audience'. This meant films with scenes of sexual immorality, imitable crime or depictions of religion that were irreverent or lacking artistic value. In Germany the official board of film censors checked all

TABLE 6.3:
FILM CENSORSHIP IN EUROPE 1930[193]

Country	Submitted	Passed	%	Cut	%	Rejected	%
Italy	773	585	75.7	141	18.2	47	6.1
Holland	2354	2117	89.9	211	9.0	26	1.1
Great Britain	2287	2084	91.1	191	8.4	12	0.5
Denmark	1249	1183	94.1	61	4.9	5	0.4
Germany (Berlin)	3152	3113	98.8	25	0.8	14	0.4

films imported into the country. They banned all films likely to endanger public order, brutalize or demoralize the German people or endanger the country's relations with foreign powers. No children under 16 could attend the cinema and the films to which a person under eighteen could go were limited. In Holland there was a mixed system similar to that in Britain. Each film was examined by five members of an eighty-five-person central censorship committee. Films were classified for all ages ('A'), over 14s ('B') or over 18s ('C'). Films were not to endanger public order or Holland's relations with other countries, present immoral situations or imitable crimes. In addition, local burgomasters could attach conditions to cinema licences. Italy had a five-member board of examiners which object-ed to films containing obscenity, threats to national decorum or public order and insults to national institutions, the police, military, public author-ities or private citizens. Films that condoned crime, suicide, cruelty or class hatred were also prohibited. This may explain why so few films were submitted.[194]

In France, a board of censors that included dramatists, critics and Civil Servants scrutinized films. The film industry was allowed to send representatives when a film was being examined. Most of the censorship was political. Films criticizing the military were often cut.[195] In moral matters the system was quite lenient. After 1936 there was a largely unsuccessful campaign in France for a version of the US Production Code. The French film commission of control was overhauled: the film industry's representation was removed and the commission was placed in the hands of public servants.[196]

One of the censorship systems most comparable to that of the Irish Free State was in Australia. There a committee of three film censors examined films imported into the country. As Australia was a federation, they operated under the customs law which only gave them authority over foreign films, and some states also had their own censorships. Table 6.4 gives the results of the federal film censorship of drama films for this period.

These figures are not directly comparable with those for Ireland as the definitions of a drama film varied, but the trend was very similar. After 1934, and the reforms instigated by Hollywood, the percentages of films

TABLE 6.4:
DECISIONS OF THE AUSTRALIAN FILM CENSORSHIP 1930–35[197]

Year	Submitted	Passed uncut	%	Cut	%	Rejected	%
1930	580	307	52.9	205	35.3	68	11.7
1931	466	223	47.9	164	35.2	79	17.0
1932	463	212	45.8	207	44.7	44	9.5
1933	425	253	59.5	192	45.2	50	11.2
1934	476	257	54.0	183	38.4	36	7.6
1935	481	335	69.6	115	23.9	31	6.4

cut or rejected fell sharply. This demonstrates that Montgomery's opinion that films were improving echoed that of other censors. The Australian censors resembled Montgomery in their belief that British films were of an inferior moral standard to those of America after 1934. Indeed, they were in correspondence with the Irish censor throughout this period. The rates of rejection for UK films were consistently higher than for those from the USA between 1929 and 1931.[198] Following the BBFC report of 1931, which warned of declining standards, the rejection rate for UK films fell from 8.7 per cent to 4.0 per cent in 1932, and to 0.9% in 1933.[199] It rose to 3.1 per cent in 1934 because of 'cheap and nasty "quickies" made to comply with quota legislation'.[200] In 1935, 6.5 per cent of UK films were finally rejected.[201] By contrast, the censors concluded that the US campaigns had 'a marked influence upon film standards' in Hollywood.[202]

Like their Irish counterpart, the Australian censors lamented that 'Australia is too small a portion of the world's market to induce producers to pay too much attention to our censorship procedures'.[203] They were concerned about the effects of film on children and felt that 'a higher standard should be imposed than if only a literary or dramatic censorship were exercised', which meant that 'films are frequently banned which have appeared in literary form or on the stage'.[204]

In 1932, the British Commission on Educational and Cultural Films issued a report entitled 'Film and National Life'. It concluded that,

> From a social point of view it is unsound to think of the cinema in terms of the stage or of popular literature; it has an infinitely wider scope than either and a much greater influence on the mentality of those who do not normally analyse their emotions but absorb what they see and hear uncritically, provided it supplies cheerful entertainment.[205]

This report was quoted with approval by the Australian film censor. It also shared themes found in the notes of James Montgomery. Film censorship originated from the belief that the popularity of cinema among the mass of the population made it more dangerous than other art forms. In Ireland, Britain and Australia this view was still held at the end of the 1930s and the censors acted accordingly.

The success of film censorship

The systems of film censorship in use in the two Irelands each fulfilled the role intended for them. In the Free State, Montgomery was appointed to mark out the difference in standards between the Irish on the one hand and the British and Americans on the other. He did this successfully, establishing a strict but consistent censorship based on Roman

Catholic morality and middle-class Irish manners. It was only when Hollywood adopted its own set of guidelines – partly written by a Jesuit – that he began to allow more American films to pass. He was not an enlightened or imaginative censor. He was at least partly responsible for the poor reputation of film among Irish artists and intellectuals because by applying standards appropriate for children he infantilized much of what was shown on Irish screens. He did so, however, against a background of constant pressure for a stricter censorship from clerical and lay activists.

In Northern Ireland, censorship of films followed two principles: British practice and the least interference possible with private enterprise. These were adhered to in the face of sporadic campaigns to introduce a more restrictive system and controversy over the political content of some films. This campaign was at its height just as the American film industry began to reform itself and, in its demands and criticisms, it echoed much of what was being said across the Atlantic.

The island of Ireland was an insignificant entry in the accounts of the big Hollywood studios. Like Australia it could not expect the producers of films to make changes to plots, scripts or standards. Northern Ireland, by accepting British standards, at once asserted its British identity and became part of an economic unit that warranted the attention of the studios. The Irish Free State, by using its own standards, was able to assert its independence and ally itself with Roman Catholic teaching around the world, but the consequence was that it had no power over the film industry outside its own borders.

NOTES

1. See, for example, *Woman Trap*, 19 June 1930, NAI, Record of Films Censored, FCO2/98/27/6.
2. Censorship of Films (No.1) Order 1930.
3. Irish Advisory Committee, KRSGBI, Statement, 10 Sept. 1930, NAI, Department of Justice DJUS, H231/41.
4. Ruth Vasey, *The world according to Hollywood, 1918–1939* (Exeter: University of Exeter, 1977), p.63.
5. Montgomery to O'Friel, 23 Sept. 1930, NAI, DJUS, H231/41.
6. Vasey, *The world according to hollywood*, p.195.
7. Montgomery to O'Friel, 23 Sept. 1930, NAI, DJUS, H231/41.
8. J.O'Farrell to Minister for Justice, 1 Oct. 1930, ibid.; *The Standard*, 4 Oct. 1930, ibid.
9. Minute of meeting 9 Oct. 1930, ibid.
10. *Chin Chin Chow*, 3 Aug. 1934, NAI, Film Censor's reserve books, FCO3/98/28/10/1; *Irish Times*, 29 May 1936.
11. Deputy Commissioner Garda Siochána to Secretary, Department of Justice, 9 Jan. 1935, NAI, DJUS, H290/28.
12. Dáil debates, Vol.XXXIV, 11 April 1930, 988; *Irish Independent*, 3 Nov. 1930, NAI, DJUS, H315/28.
13. *Irish Times*, 26 Feb. 1935.
14. Secretary Donegal County Council to Minister for Justice, 26 May 1931, NAI, DJUS, H231/43.
15. 'Memorandum to the Minister for Education and the Minister for Justice on Cinema', 11 March 1932; Minute [unsigned] to S.A. Roche, 23 March 1932, NAI, DJUS, H231/43.

16. John Cooney, *John Charles McQuaid: ruler of Catholic Ireland* (Dublin: O'Brien Press, 1999), p.71.
17. *Irish Times*, 4 Dec. 1934.
18. *Waterford News*, 29 March 1935; *Mayo News*, 30 March 1935, Irish Jesuit Archives IJA, Cahill Papers, J/55/39.
19. *Irish Times*, 18 Feb. 1935.
20. Ibid., 11 June 1935.
21. *Up and Doing*, Vol.1, No.5 Sept. 1935, p.2; No.3, July 1935, p.2.
22. *Irish Times*, 29 Jan. 1935, 18 Feb. 1936.
23. Ibid., 26 June 1936.
24. Ibid., 30 June 1936.
25. Devane to de Valera, 22 April 1937, IJA, Devane Papers, J44/10; Devane to provincial, n. d. [1937], ibid., J/44/12; Devane, note 'In confidence', ibid., J44/13; 'My suggestions for terms of reference for proposed cinema enquiry', n. d. [1937], ibid., J44/14.
26. Archbishop of Cashel to Devane, 29 Jan. 1939, ibid., J44/15; Bishop of Ossory to Devane, 13 June 1939; Bishop of Waterford to Devane, 2 June 1939, ibid.
27. 'Memorandum on Film Censorship presented to the Minister for Justice, Éire and the inter-departmental committee on the cinema industry by Most Rev Bishop of Ardagh and Most Rev Bishop of Kilmore', 5 July 1939, Dublin Diocesan Archives DDA, Byrne Papers, Government and Politics 1922–39.
28. *Catholic Truth Quarterly*, Vol.1, No.7, Jan. – March 1939, p.1.
29. Montgomery to J.E. Duff, 5 May 1930, NAI, DJUS, H231/33.
30. *Irish Catholic Directory 1931*, p.590.
31. *Irish Churchman*, 10 April 1930, 26 June 1930; Dublin Municipal Council Minutes, 4 May 1931, Dublin City Council Archives; *Irish Times*, 15 Jan. 1932.
32. *Irish Times*, 11 Dec. 1934.
33. Maurice Curtis, 'Catholic action as an organised campaign in Ireland, 1921–1947', (Ph.D. thesis, University College Dublin, 2000, p. 200.
34. *Irish Times*, 18 Feb. 1935.
35. *Irish Independent*, 30 March 1935, IJA, Cahill Papers, J/55/39.
36. *Irish Times*, 23 April 1935.
37. Dáil debates, Vol.LVI, 2 May 1935, 169–70.
38. *Irish Churchman*, 24 April 1930.
39. *Belfast Newsletter*, 23 May 1930, PRONI, Northern Ireland Ministry of Home Affairs NIMHA, HA/8/639.
40. Canon Thomas Brown to Brentford, 30 May 1930, ibid.
41. *Northern Whig*, 18 Sept. 1930, ibid.
42. Ibid.
43. Mrs U.B. Kinahan to Brentford, 18 Oct. 1930, ibid.; Connellan, NIHC debates, Vol.XII, 29 Oct. 1930, 2192.
44. *Belfast Newsletter*, 4 Nov. 1930, *Northern Whig*, 17 Nov. 1930, PRONI, NIMHA, HA/8/639.
45. *Belfast Newsletter*, 30 Oct. 1930; Bishop Grierson to Dawson Bates, 17 Jan. 1931, ibid.
46. R.P. Pim, Minute, 21 Jan. 1931, ibid.
47. G.A. Harris to Grierson, 9 March 1931, ibid.
48. BBFC, circular to local authorities, 1 Jan. 1931, Minutes of Belfast Corporation Police Committee, 22 Jan. 1931, PRONI, LA/7/10AB/1/19.
49. *Northern Whig*, 12 March 1931; R.P. Pim, minute, 21 Jan. 1931, PRONI, NIMHA, HA/8/639.
50. R.P. Pim, minute, 16 March 1931, ibid.
51. 'Cinematograph licences: model conditions' [March 1931]; Circular letter to the town clerks of the county borough councils, the clerks of the UDCs and the Town Commissioners, 26 March 1931; A. Robinson to Secretary Down County Council, 4 June 1931, ibid.
52. Secretary Armagh County Council to Secretary NIMHA, 31 March 1931, ibid.; Londonderry County Council, minutes, 9 May 1931, ibid.; Sub-Committee of the Belfast Corporation Police Committee, minutes, 10 April 1931, PRONI, LA/7/10AB/1/19; Joint Honorary Secretaries of the Film Committee to Belfast Corporation Police Committee, 5 March 1931, ibid.

53. Minutes of Belfast Corporation Police Committee, 8 Dec. 1931, 16 April 1931, ibid.
54. *Belfast Newsletter*, 24 Nov. 1931, 1 Feb. 1932, PRONI, NIMHA, HA/8/639.
55. Belfast Corporation Police Committee, minutes of sub-committee, 11 Feb. 1932, PRONI, LA/7/10AB/1/19.
56. *Northern Whig*, 18 April 1931, 22 April 1931, PRONI, NIMHA, HA/8/639.
57. William Mitchell to Minister of Home Affairs, 8 June 1931, ibid.
58. Resolution of the United Council of Christian and Religious Communions in Ireland, 13 Nov. 1931, ibid.
59. *Belfast Newsletter*, 25 Jan. 1932, ibid.
60. *Derry People*, 13 Feb. 1932.
61. Walter Kendrick, *The Secret Museum: pornography in modern culture* (Berkeley: University of California Press, 1987), pp.6–11.
62. *Northern Whig*, 13 Feb. 1932; *Irish News*, 15 Feb. 1932, PRONI, NIMHA, HA/8/639.
63. *Irish News*, 19 Feb. 1932, ibid.
64. *Belfast Newsletter*, 27 Feb. 1932, ibid.
65. *Northern Whig*, 15 March 1932, ibid.
66. *Ulster Gazette*, 8 Oct.1932.
67. *Derry People*, 11 March 1933.
68. *Ulster Gazette*, 13 Oct. 1934.
69. Ibid, 8 Dec. 1934.
70. Armagh UDC, Minutes of the General Purposes Committee, 5, 18 December 1934, PRONI, LA/10/15AA/7; Armagh UDC, minutes, 18 Dec. 1934, PRONI, LA/10/2CA/6; Minutes of meeting with Canon Quin, 5 Dec. 1934, ibid.
71. *Ulster Gazette*, 12 Jan. 1935.
72. Ibid., 19 Jan. 1935.
73. Ibid.
74. Report of the General Purposes Committee, 4 Feb. 1935, Minutes of Armagh UDC, PRONI, LA/10/2CA/6.
75. *Ulster Gazette*, 2, 9 March 1935.
76. Armagh UDC, minutes, 1 April 1935, PRONI, LA/10/2CA/6; *Ulster Gazette*, 6 April 1935.
77. Armagh UDC, minutes, ibid.; *Ulster Gazette,* 23 March 1935.
78. *Ulster Gazette*, 6 April 1935.
79. *Today's Cinema*, 1, 5 April 1935, IJA, Cahill Papers, J55/39.
80. *Belfast Telegraph*, 26 Jan. 1932, PRONI, NIMHA, HA/8/639.
81. *Down Recorder*, 7 May 1932; *Fermanagh Times*, 5 May 1932.
82. *Fermanagh Times*, 7 Oct. 1937, 8 Sept. 1938.
83. *Irish Times*, 14 July 1936.
84. *Daily Film Renter*, 20 March 1935, IJA, Cahill Papers, J55/39.
85. *Down Recorder*, 10 Feb. 1934.
86. Belfast Corporation Police Committee, minutes, 31 Jan. 1935, PRONI, LA/7/10AB/1/20.
87. *Ulster Gazette*, 24 Feb., 10, 24 March 1939.
88. *Derry People*, 15 Dec. 1934, 9 March 1935.
89. *Today's Cinema*, 1 April 1935, Cahill Papers, J55/39.
90. *Irish News*, 10 April 1935, ibid.
91. *Today's Cinema*, 13 June 1935, ibid.
92. *Ulster Gazette*, 10 Oct. 1936.
93. *Down Recorder*, 13 Feb. 1937.
94. *Irish Times*, 21 Jan. 1935; *Ulster Gazette*, 29 January 1935.
95. Midgley, NIHC debates, Vol XLX, 27 April 1937, 1049–50; Belfast Corporation Police Committee, minutes, 22 April, 4 Nov. 1937, PRONI, LA/10AB/1/21.
96. James P. O'Connor, 'Censorship of films 1894–1970, Hollywood, London and Dublin' (Ph.D. thesis, University College Dublin, 1996), p.211.
97. *Hot to Handle*, 15 Feb. 1934, NAI, Film Censor's Reserve Book, FCO3/98/28/9.
98. *I Love that Man*, 17 Oct. 1933, Register of Films Rejected, FCO4/98/29/3.
99. *Smiling Lieutenant*, 5 Nov. 1931, ibid.
100. *Rockabye*, 23 May 1933, Record of Films Censored, FCO2/98/27/9.
101. *Sign of the Cross*, 8 April 1933, Reserve Book, FCO3/98/28/8.
102. *Footlights and Fools*, 8 April 1930, ibid., FCO3/98/28/3.

103. *City Lights*, 15 May 1931, Record of Films Censored, NAI, FCO2/98/27/7; *Alexander Hamilton*, 12 Jan. 1932, ibid., FCO2/98/27/8.
104. *The Holy Ghost Fathers*, 6 Nov. 1937, Reserve Book, FCO3/98/28/14; *Cloistered*, 21 June 1937, ibid., FCO3/98/28/13.
105. *Glamour Girl*, 9 August 1938; *Green Pastures*, 11 Feb. 1937; *From the Manger to the Cross*, 28 July 1938, Register of Films Rejected, FCO4/98/29/4; *Father Noah's Ark*, 13 Dec. 1933, ibid., FCO4/98/29/3.
106. *Strictly Legal*, 8 March 1935, ibid.; *Melody Lingers On*, 19 Feb. 1936, ibid., FCO4/98/29/4.
107. O'Connor, 'Censorship of films', pp.202–3.
108. *Little Friend*, 8 Aug. 1934, Reserve Books, FCO3/98/28/10/1.
109. *Pride of the Force*, 14 March 1935, Register of Films Rejected, FCO4/98/29/3.
110. *All-in Wrestling*, 20 March 1936, ibid., FCO4/98/29/4.
111. *The Keyhole*, 13 July 1933, ibid, FCO4/98/29/3.
112. *Movietone News*, 4 March 1930, ibid., Reserve Book, FCO3/98/28/3.
113. *Rio Rita*, 31 Jan. 1930, ibid.
114. *Sally*, 7 April 1930, ibid.
115. *Pictorial*, 22 June 1936, ibid., FCO3/98/28/13.
116. *Gold Diggers of 1933*, 4 Aug. 1933, ibid., FCO3/98/28/9; *Second Hand Wife*, 1 May 1933, Register of Films Rejected, FCO4/98/29/3.
117. *Sylvia Scarlett*, 28 Feb. 1936, ibid., FCO4/98/29/4; *Street Scene*, 22 Jan. 1932, Record of Films Censored, FCO2/98/27/7; *Man about Town*, 8 Sept. 1932, Register of Films Rejected, FCO4/98/29/3.
118. *Dodsworth*, 13 Jan. 1937; *Camille*, 10 April 1937, Reserve Book, FCO3/98/28/13.
119. *The Maltese Falcon*, Aug. 1931, ibid., FCO3/98/28/7; *Public Enemy*, 8 Dec. 1931, ibid., FCO3/98/28/7; Record of Films Censored, FCO2/98/27/8; *20,000 Years in Sing Sing*, 13 March 1933, Reserve Book, FCO3/98/28/8.
120. *Lady Killer*, 28 June 1934, Register of Films Rejected, FCO4/98/29/3. The film was passed by the Appeals Board. *The G-Men*, 24 July 1935, Reserve Book, FCO3/98/28/12.
121. *Men without names*, 27 Aug. 1935, Register of Films Rejected, FCO4/98/29/4.
122. *Angels with Dirty Faces*, 27 Jan. 1939, Reserve Books, FCO3/98/28/14.
123. See, for example, *Cotton and Silk*, 13 Nov. 1930, ibid., FCO3/98/28/4.
124. *Love Business*, 9 Nov. 1931, Register of Films Rejected, FCO4/98/29/3.
125. *Jimmy the Gent*, 8 Oct. 1934, ibid.
126. *Way Out West*, 10 Nov. 1930, Reserve Book, FCO3/98/28/4; *Animal Crackers*, 8 July 1931, ibid., FCO3/98/28/5.
127. *I yam sick*, 17 July 1934, ibid., FCO3/98/28/15.
128. *Barnyard Bunk*, 11 Oct. 1932, Record of Films Censored, FCO2/98/28/9.
129. *Tarzan the Ape Man*, 30 Aug. 1932, ibid., FCO2/98/17/8; 30 Aug. 1932, Register of Films Rejected, FCO4/98/29/3; *Tarzan and his Mate*, 5 Sept. 1934, ibid.; *Flash Gordon*, 17 July 1936, ibid, FCO4/98/29/4.
130. Vasey, *The world according to Hollywood*, p.226.
131. *Dangerous Ground*, 25 Aug. 1932, Register of Films Rejected, FCO4/98/19/3.
132. *Born to be bad*, 16 Oct. 1934, ibid.
133. *Scarface*, 19 Aug. 1932, Record of Films Censored, FCO2/98/27/8; Register of Films Rejected, FCO4/98/29/3.
134. *Dracula*, 8 May 1931, Reserve Book, FCO3/98/28/5; *King Kong*, 29 April 1933, ibid., FCO3/98/28/8; *Frankenstein*, 5 Feb. 1932, Record of Films Censored, FCO2/98/27/8, 5 Feb. 1932, Register of Films Rejected, FCO4/98/29/3; *Dr Jekyll and Mr Hyde*, 27 June 1932, ibid.
135. Compiled from report by James Montgomery to Centro Catolico Cinemategraphico, December 1936, reprinted in O'Connor, ' Censorship of films', p.386; also reports of film censor's report in *Irish Times*, 1930–40.
136. Includes three rejected under Emergency order during World War II.
137. Sources are the same as for Table 6.1.
138. *Morning Glory*, 2 Feb. 1934, Register of Films Rejected, FCO4/98/29/3.
139. *Irish Times*, 6 Jan. 1932.
140. Ibid., 14 July 1934.
141. *Danno O'Mahony*, 21 Aug. 1936, NAI, Register of Films Rejected, FCO4/98/29/4.

142. *Chance of a High Time*, 4 July 1931, 4 Aug. 1931, Record of Films Censored, FCO2/98/27/7.
143. George A. Harris to C.M. Martin Jones, 2 April 1930; Regulation 26A, 2 May 1930; Trevor Bingham to C.G. Wickham, 31 May 1930; *Irish News*, 27 May 1930; *Northern Whig*, 26 May 1930, PRONI, NIMHA, HA/32/1/569.
144. 'Notes regarding new regulation under the CA(SP) Act', n.d. [1930], ibid.; R.P. Pim to Wickham, 13 June 1930, HA/32/1/640.
145. *Scarface*, Minutes of the Belfast Corporation Police Committee, 9 Nov. 1932, PRONI, LA7/10AB/1/19; *Outward Bound*, 15 April 1931, ibid.; *Mother*, 13 Oct. 1930, ibid., *Grand Hotel*, 13 Feb. 1933, ibid.
146. *Grand Hotel*, 26 Nov. 1932, 7 Jan. 1933, 7 Feb. 1933, NAI, Reserve Book, FCO3/98/28/8.
147. *Damaged Lives*, 19 Feb. 1934, Minutes of Belfast Corporation Police Committee, PRONI, LA/7/10AB/1/20; *Green Pastures*, 19 March 1937, ibid.
148. *Frankenstein*, 20 April, 26 May 1932, ibid.; *Belfast Newsletter*, 21–22 April 1932; *Northern Whig*, 22, 28 April, 3 May 1932, PRONI, NIMHA, HA/8/639.
149. *Northern Whig*, 23 April 1932, PRONI, NIMHA, HA/8/639.
150. *Belfast Newsletter*, 1 June 1932, ibid.
151. Minutes of Ballyclare UDC [extract], 5 May 1932, ibid.
152. *Belfast Newsletter*, 9, 22 Aug. 1932.
153. W.I. Cuningham to Secretary NIMHA, 13 Oct. 1932, ibid.
154. R.P. Pim, Minute, 9 Jan. 1932, ibid.
155. M.H. Kirk, Minute, n.d., ibid.
156. *Ulster Gazette*, 25 August, 1 Sept. 1934; *Irish Times*, 18 November 1934; Minutes of Newry UDC, 11 June 1934, PRONI, LA/58/2CA/9.
157. Kevin Rockett, Luke Gibbons and John Hill, *Cinema and Ireland* (London: Croom Helm, 1987), pp.53–5. In fact they had a point. Unfortunately for them Hollywood only took protests against 'stage Irish' films seriously when they came from the larger Irish-American community.
158. *Irish Times*, 7 Nov. 1933; Report of Garda J. Dooly, 4 Dec. 1934, *Irish Press*, 6 Dec. 1934, NAI, DJUS, JUS8/72; Dáil Debates, Vol.LV, 13 March 1935, 670.
159. Report of Garda Thomas Clarke, 4 Dec 1934; J.P., note on the above, 7 Dec. 1934, NAI, DJUS, JUS8/72.
160. *Irish Times*, 7 May 1935, 14 May 1935.
161. Ibid., 11 May 1937; *Ulster Gazette*, 15 May 1937.
162. *Irish Times*, 13 March 1938.
163. *Black Fury*, 3 July 1935, NAI, Register of Films Rejected, FCO4/98/29/4; *Two Against the World*, 13 Dec. 1932, ibid., FCO4/98/29/3; *The Informer*, 28 June 1935, ibid., FCO4/98/29/4.
164. *Parnell*, 19 Aug. 1937, ibid.
165. *Irish Times*, 30 April 1935.
166. Ibid., 11 June 1935.
167. *Irish Times*, 18 April 1938.
168. Hierarchy Report on Film Censorship, 5 July 1939, DDA, Byrne Papers, Government & Politics 1922–39.
169. Louise Burns-Bisogno, *Censoring Irish Nationalism: the British, Irish and American suppression of republican images in film and television, 1909–95* (North Carolina: McFarland & Co., 1997), pp.68–71.
170. *Belfast Newsletter*, 26, 28 Nov. 1936; *Irish News*, 30 November 1936, PRONI, NIMHA, HA/32/1/640.
171. Maxwell to Dawson Bates, 9 Dec. 1936; W.A. Magill to Dawson Bates, 11 Dec. 1936; W. A. Magill to Maxwell, 15 Dec. 1936; W.A. Magill, note, 21 Dec. 1936, on Private Secretary to B. Hurst, 17 Dec. 1936, ibid.
172. NIHC debates, XIX, 27 April 1937, 1049; *Fermanagh Times*, 2 Sept. 1937.
173. Minutes of Belfast Corporation Police Committee, 24 Dec. 1937, PRONI, LA/7/10AB/1/21.
174. *Derry People*, 19 July 1930.
175. Gregory Black, *Hollywood censored: morality codes, Catholics and the movies*, (Cambridge: Cambridge University Press, 1994), pp.21–49.

176. Lea Jacobs, *The wages of sin: censorship and the fallen woman film, 1928–1942* (California: University of California Press, 2000), p.19.
177. Vasey, *The world according to Hollywood*, pp.125–6.
178. Richard Maltby, 'Censorship and self-regulation' in Geoffrey Nowell-Smith (ed), *The Oxford history of world cinema* (Oxford: Oxford University Press, 1996), pp.235–47.
179. Vasey, *The world according to Hollywood*, pp.130–1.
180. Maltby, 'Censorship and self-regulation', p.243.
181. Jacobs, *The wages of sin*, p.20.
182. Maltby, 'Censorship and self-regulation, p.243.
183. Jacobs, *The wages of sin*, p.x.
184. Guy Phelps, *Film censorship* (London: Gollancz, 1975), pp.35–6.
185. Tom Dewe Mathews, *Censored* (London: Chatto and Windus, 1994), pp.55–7, 74–7.
186. *Irish Times*, 4 Jan. 1930.
187. *Belfast Newsletter*, 4 July 1930.
188. NAGB, HO/45/15206.
189. Dewe Mathews, *Censored*, p.56.
190. S.W.H., minute, 6 Feb. 1935, NAGB, HO45/17073.
191. Vasey, *The world according to Hollywood*, p.85, 117–20, 159–60.
192. J.F. Henderson to Brooke Wilkinson, 6 Nov. 1933, NAGB, HO/45/15207.
193. NAGB, HO/45/1/5207.
194. Ibid.
195. *Manchester Guardian*, 9 May 1932, ibid.
196. Colin Crisp, *The classic French cinema, 1930–1960* (Indiana University Press, 1993), p.251.
197. Film Censorship Report, 1930–35, National Archives of Australia (NAA), A425/65939.
198. Film Censorship Report, 1932, NAA, A425/65939/61; Kevin Rockett, *Irish film censorship: a cultural journey from silent cinema to Internet pornography* (Dublin: Four Courts Press, 2004), p. 103.
199. Film Censorship Report, 1933, NAA, A425/65939/51.
200. Ibid., 1934, A425/65939/46.
201. Ibid., 1935, A425/65939/10.
202. Ibid., 1934, A425/65939/45.
203. Ibid., 1930, A425/65939/92
204. Ibid., 1929, A425/65939/106.
205. Ibid., 1932, A425/65939/64.

CHAPTER SEVEN

A laughing stock? Censorship of publications 1930–39

The first year of the Censorship of Publications Board's operation was a frustrating one for all concerned. The board felt unappreciated. It reported that, instead of sending it obscene books to scrutinize, the contribution of public and the library committees 'consists of misdirected criticism of the board'. The board suggested that the papers should not be allowed to print the names of banned books, thus sparing it controversy. The public did not know the scope of the act, it claimed, and failed to understand that the people were ultimately responsible for the success or failure of censorship.[1] The CTSI for its part declared that it had no objection to what the board had banned but was unhappy that books and periodicals which the Society believed advocated birth control were escaping prohibition.[2]

By the end of 1930, the CTSI and the Department of Justice had reached an impasse over the question of prosecuting newsagents for selling periodicals that contained articles about birth control. Fitzgerald-Kenney blamed the problems with the censorship on the 'onslaught' on his bill a year earlier by the *Irish Times* and *Irish Statesman* which had led to the removal of the provisions for recognized associations. Frank O'Reilly replied in a letter to the *Irish Independent*, claiming that the system for complaints was still too costly and complicated. He also demanded that sellers of publications advocating birth control or carrying advertisements relating to birth control be prosecuted. The Private Secretary to the Minister for Justice pointed out that advertisements about birth control were not prohibited unless they actually advocated it. It was permissible, therefore for a publication to advertise a book which contained birth control information as long as the text of the advertisement did not advocate birth control. He also claimed that prosecutions of sellers were more difficult than O'Reilly imagined because they could claim not to have known the contents of their wares.[3] The Attorney General advised the government that, under section 16(3) of the act, the seller could claim that 'by the exercise of reasonable care' he could not have known the contents of the publications he sold. 'This defence may be a general one', he warned.[4] In effect, the act was unworkable when faced with reality of the newsagents' business. In 1931, responding to a complaint about the *Sunday Times*, Roche explained to O'Reilly that 'it would be unduly harsh to instigate such proceedings, which in any case would probably fail on the grounds that the newsvendor was not aware of the fact that the periodical in question contained objectionable matter'. This infuriated O'Reilly, who pointed out that one such article had been advertised on the front page of the paper. 'The only possible interpretation of your letter is, I submit, that the Minister has decided that Section 16 of the Censorship of Publications Act 1929, is inoperative as far as newspapers are concerned.'[5] The overall impression is of a system that was failing and a series of attempts by those involved in it to blame each other. Censorship was proving to be far more limited than its supporters had hoped and the general public, outside the ranks of the CTSI, were showing little interest in the process.

Unofficial influence and the censorship process

The Censorship of Publications Act seemed to lay down strict procedures. The complainant was to submit several copies of the offending publication, the board would give a verdict and the Minister for Justice then decided whether to impose a ban. In practice, the system was more flexible, and unofficial contacts, in particular with Charles Eason, were used to avoid embarrassing decisions.

Several publishers attempted to get the advice of the Department of Justice about whether their products would face censorship. In March 1930, the Director and Manager of the *Irish Independent* asked if there would be problems with a set of illustrated advertisements for 'Twilfit Corsets'. He was reassured that 'the Minister would not consider it necessary to direct the institution of criminal proceedings'.[6] In 1932, the British Social Hygiene Council got a very different reception when it asked for an opinion about a set of newspaper advertisements it had commissioned and which might find their way into the Irish Free State. They were told that 'the Minister cannot undertake to anticipate any decision which the board might come to in such a case'.[7] In 1937, on the advice of J.C.M. Eason, the *News of the World* received unofficial permission from the Minister for Justice to sell a sanitized Irish edition.[8] This could be a dangerous strategy, as the publishers of *Medical Views on Birth Control* discovered when they sent an advance copy to the CPB to ask if it would be banned given that the majority of views expressed in it were opposed to birth control. The next they heard was when the Department of Justice wrote to tell them that the book had been banned in Ireland.[9] The next year, a book of poetry was sent to the CPB prior to its publication. In its draft reply the board stated that it had refused to consider the book because it did not want to 'imply an assumption of licensing powers'. The Assistant Secretary of the Department of Justice, Stephen Roche, intervened and suggested that 'we might leave the [publisher's] letter unanswered' to avoid creating a precedent.[10] In another case, the Department of Justice received a complaint from a Dublin priest about a book. Instead of having it formally examined, the secretary to the CPB 'sent it to the most extreme member of the Board who said it was not worth considering'.[11] In 1932, a Co. Wicklow curate read two books which he considered objectionable. He consulted the chairman of the board, Canon Boylan, who recommended that he submit a complaint. He did this by sending in the two books accompanied by a letter. Although his submission was not on the proper form or correctly worded, the CPB was advised that 'the books can, of course, be considered by the board and reports made if they so think fit on their own initiative'. One of the books, *The New Law* by Lillian Clifford, was subsequently banned by this method.[12] This sort of ad hoc decision-making showed no sign of being governed by any consistent philosophy; the identity of the publisher, the manner in which the material was submitted and the peculiar circumstances of the case all seem to have affected the decisions.

Charles and J.C.M. Eason were the most important figures in the unofficial censorship of publications. As their company had a near monopoly of the wholesale newsagent trade, they were uniquely placed to act as intermediaries and their cooperation was essential to the working of the censorship. After the banning of the *World's Pictorial News* in May 1930 for excessive reporting of crime, Eason informed the Department of Justice that the publishers had renamed the paper the *Competitors' Guide* and that this would not report crime. He promised to send a copy to the department and that his shops would abide by its decision. In the event, the department 'informed Mr. Eason that there was no objection to the circulation of this paper'.[13]

As O'Friel explained it in 1930, Eason had offered that if he 'were informed unofficially of the facts', he 'might be in a position to take the matter up with the publishers and secure the removal of the offending matter'. The Department of Justice asked for his help to avoid embarrassment. The periodicals, *Caged Birds* and *Boxing, Racing and Football* were both innocuous enough but carried advertisements for birth control products. The CPB had refrained from making a report, but if Eason could not convince the publishers to remove such material from future issues sold in Ireland, they would be banned. Obviously such a ban would have invited ridicule. Eason was able to get the necessary guarantees.[14] Charles acted in this way in the case of *John Bull* in August 1930 and when a complaint was made against *Chamber's Journal* for publishing advertisements relating to birth control.[15] This procedure was also useful when the CPB was powerless to act. In July 1932, a complainant submitted a free copy of the *Sunday Dispatch* which had been delivered to her, describing it as 'filth'. As the CPB needed three recent issues, there was no official action that could be taken. The department called on Eason instead, telling him that the Minister for Justice 'is disposed to think' that the CPB would ban the publication if future issues were of the same type. Eason procured a promise that 'the editor will give special attention to this matter as a result of the communications which the office received from me'.[16]

The serialization in newspapers of novels banned in Ireland was a special problem. When the *Sunday Chronicle* planned to serialize *Grand Hotel* in 1931 using expurgated extracts, it asked the Department of Justice if this would incur the wrath of the censors. The department refused to advise them but warned Eason that, although the prohibition order on the book did not apply to the serialization, if a complaint were made it would be considered by the CPB in the usual way.[17] The Eason family, and Charles in particular, served as an informal liaison between those English publishers who were ignorant of the laws and procedures of Irish censorship, and the Department of Justice, which while unable to show flexibility openly was willing to do so quietly.

Unofficial complaints

The CTSI also made private representations to force publications to make changes. In 1933, O'Reilly wrote to the *Nursing Mirror* as he believed it was publishing 'contraceptive propaganda'. When this failed he reported it to the CPB. It faced a dilemma: advertisements relating to birth control only appeared in one of the three issues submitted and they were also unsure (even after three years operating the act) if such advertisements were sufficient grounds for a ban. Reassured by the Department of Justice, they banned the periodical.[18] This decision shocked the management of the *Nursing Mirror* who protested to the Irish High Commissioner in London that they had no policy on birth control but merely reported papers read and reviewed books on the subject. Irish nurses who read the periodical to find job advertisements were also inconvenienced.[19] As the first banning of a periodical lasted only three months, the *Nursing Mirror* was soon available and the ban was not renewed.

The CTSI regularly bullied publishers and printers. As a producer of religious pamphlets, it controlled both substantial printing contracts and a great deal of advertising. For example in the year 1931–32, it distributed over one million magazines and half a million pamphlets.[20] The *Irish Times* did not get CTSI advertisements and *Dublin Opinion* was forced to withdraw advertisements for 'art pictures' after threats from the Society. When an Ennis newsagent resisted a CTSI campaign against the *Daily Express*, O'Reilly wrote to his parish priest. Hugh Allen, the Society's organizing secretary toured the country and reported the regular intimidation of newsagents by local CTSI branches.[21] O'Reilly met his match, however, when he complained to Eason over the stocking of a periodical called *Freethinker*. Although O'Reilly threatened to organize a Roman Catholic boycott of the shop, Eason replied that they only sold twelve copies a week to customers who requested it and refused to be bullied. At this O'Reilly left the issue alone.[22] The socialist paper, the *Workers' Voice* faced constant pressure from Roman Catholic activists. The *Irish Catholic* called for its suppression 'for the immediate and effective stamping out of the plague that threatens to affect Irish life'. In 1930, O'Reilly threatened to withdraw his organization's business from the paper's printers, the Longford Publishing Company, if it continued to produce it. The paper was forced to move to the smaller Progressive Printing Company.[23]

What the board banned

To properly understand the CPB, we need to examine what it banned in detail. This sheds light on the standards set by the board as well as the effects of censorship on Irish culture. The board banned 1,193 books and 111 periodicals in this period: a daunting body of work for any critic. While many of the books were famous, most are now obscure. There are also two problems with any such assessment. The first is that books now considered classics were often not well received in their own time, and books once celebrated are now forgotten or denigrated. Therefore, hindsight is a significant problem for the historian of literature. The second problem is the lack of scientific test of literary quality: not only do critics disagree on what constitutes a good book but there is no agreement on how to define a term such as 'pornography'.

Michael Adams's approach to this problem was to look at the titles of the banned books. In 1982 he argued that notwithstanding the prohibition of many works of literature, 'most of the 1,900 titles banned in the first seventeen years read as if they came out of sex-shop catalogues'. His 1968 work, *Censorship: the Irish Experience* gave a 'short list of titles' intended 'to indicate the nature of some other books banned'. The validity of this test is dubious: titles are misleading and such enticing examples as *Lady Chatterley's Lover*, *Pied Piper of Lovers* and *Delilah Upside Down* refer to legitimate novels.[24] A work entitled *The Pearl* could be the novel by Steinbeck or one of the most notorious pornographic periodicals of the nineteenth century. Adams also postulates too stark a dichotomy between good novelists and pornographers: the fact that a book may have been unworthy of a place in the canon of classics but may be of value as a piece of popular fiction is ignored by this approach.

It is possible to avoid hindsight by looking at what contemporary critics were saying about the books banned in Ireland. The *Times Literary Supplement* offers both a large body of comments and a reasonable guide

TABLE 7.1:
BOOKS BANNED 1930–39, REASONS FOR BAN AND NUMBER REVIEWED IN *TLS*[25]

Year	Books Banned	Obscene and Indecent	%	Birth Control	%	Reviewed in TLS	%
1930	46	29	63.0	17	37.0	26	56.5
1931	96	84	87.5	12	12.5	76	79.2
1932	115	108	93.9	7	6.1	73	63.5
1933	118	104	88.1	14	11.9	85	72.0
1934	119	108	90.8	11	9.2	83	69.7
1935	151	129	85.3	22	14.7	108	71.5
1936	167	155	92.8	12	7.2	128	76.6
1937	106	95	89.6	11	10.4	69	65.1
1938	133	118	88.7	15	11.3	85	63.9
1939	142	134	94.4	8	5.6	102	71.8
Total	1193	1064	89.2	129	10.8	835	70.0

to moderate British literary opinion. It tended not to deal with outright pornography, so where a book reviewed in the *TLS* was banned in Ireland it was a clear case of the Irish board asserting different standards to those in Britain. These figures draw into question both the proportion of books banned that were pornographic and the importance of the issue of birth control in the censorship process. The *TLS* reviewed 70 per cent of the books banned in Ireland; very few of these were on birth control. As works about contraception accounted for nearly 11 per cent of all books banned, it seems that very few – between 20 per cent and 30 per cent – of the books banned by the CPB would have been defined as pornography by contemporaries. That is not to say that they were not considered obscene in Ireland, but that issue will be dealt with later.

The figures put in doubt later claims that the censorship was intended primarily to deal with birth control propaganda and only encapsulated novels through the perversity of the board.[26] The list of books banned in 1930 included a large number of referrals by the CPB to itself and also contains the highest percentage of books banned on the ground that they endorsed contraception. Thereafter there was a sharp fall in the number of such prohibitions despite the fact that at this time the largest number of referrals came from the CTSI. The organization was passionately opposed to birth control so its members would certainly have submitted what they could find. Indeed, as we have seen, many of the books they did send in were not banned as they contained only slight references to birth control. This suggests that books and magazines which really advocated contraception were not as available in Ireland as proponents of censorship had claimed. Despite this the CTSI did submit large amounts of allegedly obscene material, so they were clearly interested in that as well.

Table 7.2 shows the equivalent figures for magazines prohibited in the

TABLE 7.2:
PERIODICALS BANNED 1930–39 AND REASONS FOR BAN[27]

Year	Periodicals Banned	% of All Publications Banned	Obscene and Indecent	%	Birth Control	%	Reporting Of Crime[28]	%
1930	16	25.8	3	18.8	4	25.0	9	56.3
1931	6	5.9	1	16.7	3	50.0	2	33.3
1932	2	1.7	2	100.0	0	0	0	0
1933	4	3.3	3	75.0	1	25.0	0	0
1934	3	2.5	3	100.0	0	0	0	0
1935	3.2	5	5	100.0	0	0	0	0
1936	2	1.1	2	100.0	0	0	0	0
1937	17	13.8	8	47.1	0	0	9	52.9
1938	24	15.2	18	75.0	1	4.2	5	20.8
1939	32	18.4	23	71.9	1	3.1	8	25.0
Total	111	8.5	68	61.3	10	9.0	33	29.7

same period. These statistics confirm Frank O'Reilly's complaint that the censorship of periodicals had virtually ceased by 1936. Despite promising beginnings when 25.8 per cent of all publications banned were periodicals, that proportion fell to single figures and stayed there until 1937. Thereafter there was a surge in the number of periodicals banned. It is also interesting that 61 per cent of the publications banned were those which were considered obscene. Prohibitions due to the advocacy of birth control were only a significant proportion of the total in 1930 and 1931. This suggests that unofficial interventions by Eason, the CPB's inability to ban periodicals merely for advertising birth control books and products and the CTSI's disillusionment combined to reduce the numbers of complaints on these issues after 1931. The numbers of periodicals banned for reporting crime grew from 1937 on and the periodicals banned were often published in the United States. As there are no government records available for these years, it is unclear whether the changes after 1937 reflected increased popularity of periodicals reporting crime or increased activism by pro-censorship campaigners.

A surprising element of the list of publications banned in Ireland is what it omits. It is well known that *Ulysses* was not banned, but examining the list we find no *Decameron* or *Fanny Hill* and nothing by Rabelais, Balzac, Zola or Apuleius. There is only one work by de Sade. Comparing it with the US Customs list of publications proceeded against for 1928, we find only five matches – three of them books about contraception.[29] The US list contains many books in foreign languages, the Irish list very few. This suggests that not only were the concerns of the guardians of public morality in the US and Ireland very different, but that there was not a lot of obscene matter for sale in Ireland. Given that the importers of pornography were unlikely to send it to the CPB and that Catholic Action activists were unlikely to find it on their local bookstalls, the only

TABLE 7.3:
AUTHORS WITH THE MOST BOOKS BANNED BY THE CPB, 1930–39

Author	Banned	TLS	Author	Banned	TLS
Anonymous/NA	15	7	Vicki Baum	5	5
George Ryley Scott	9	1	G. Courtenay Beale	5	0
Neil Bell	9	9	John Brophy	5	4
Maurice Dekobra	8	1	Erskine Caldwell	5	4
David H. Keller	8	0	Joan Conquest	5	2
Marie Stopes	8	3	Elliot Crawsley-Williams	5	2
Richard Aldington	7	7	Rupert Croft-Cooke	5	5
Colette	7	6	Aldous Huxley	5	5
Rhys Davies	6	6	Norah C. James	5	5
William Faulkner	6	6	Jack Lindsay	5	5
Vardis Fisher	6	5	Norman Lindsay	5	2
Philip Lindsay	6	6	Liam O'Flaherty	5	5
Margaret Sanger	6	1	Kitty Shannon	5	2

other sources were the Customs or Gardaí. It is interesting that the CPB report did not mention the Post Office. Nor do the Post Office files in the National Archives show any great concern with the censorship process.

Table 7.3 gives the most commonly banned authors; it shows that twenty-five authors, not counting the anonymous, were responsible for 151 of the books banned. Such authors were generally reviewed in the *TLS* or wrote on the subject of birth control. It is very likely that they would have gained a reputation among those making complaints and therefore had all of their books referred to the CPB. It also illustrates that a large variety of authors were banned. The fact that seven of the anonymous works were reviewed by the *TLS* shows that the term did not simply signify a pornographer.

Table 7.4 gives the publishers whose books were most often banned. These nineteen publishers were responsible for 738 banned books, 62 per cent of the total. The names should come as no surprise. Victor Gollancz, Jonathan Cape, Heinemann and Chatto & Windus, among others, were famous for making the work of modern writers available in Britain.

TABLE 7.4:
PUBLISHERS AND NUMBERS OF BOOKS BANNED, 1930–39

Publisher	Banned	Publisher	Banned
W. Heinemann	70	Collins	38
Jonathan Cape	68	Putnam	29
Victor Gollancz	66	Faber & Faber	27
T. Werner Laurie	59	Arthur Baker	23
Jarrolds	51	Martin Secker	21
John Long	46	Bodley Head	20
Chatto & Windus	42	Peter Davies	20
Hutchison	41	Methuen	19
Cassell	40	Grayson & Grayson	18
Constable	40	Other	455

TABLE 7.5:
GENRES OF BOOKS BANNED, 1930–39

Genre	No.	%	Genre	No.	%
Anthropology	3	0.3	Politics	3	0.3
Autobiography	21	2.5	Psychology	9	1.1
Biography	5	0.6	Sociology	21	2.5
Fiction	734	88.0	Travel	3	0.3
History	2	0.2	Other	31	3.7
Medical	3	0.3			

TABLE 7.6:
FICTION BOOKS BANNED, 1930–39[30]

Genre	No.	Genre	No.	Genre	No.
Drama	257	Melodrama	47	War	26
Realist	163	Satire	45	Crime	14
Historical	60	Short Stories	32	Adventure	8
Ideas	54	Science fiction	27		

Table 7.5 details the genres of the books reviewed by the *TLS* and banned by the CPB and Table 7.6 gives details of the fiction category. Even taking into account the fact that many books banned on grounds relating to birth control were not reviewed in the *TLS*, the proportion of fiction books is striking. Almost all of these novels cost between 7s and 8s 6d so they were not cheap and would have been available only to the well-off or through libraries. As works of fiction were the most popular type of book at public libraries, these may well have been the true targets of the CPB. The books banned by the CPB did almost certainly include some pornography but what the list really demonstrated was how wide the gap between British and Irish opinion was.

In an attempt to delineate the tenor of the reviews and the extent to which the reviewers considered the books to be controversial, I have broken each into five categories. For the purposes of measuring controversy, grade A refers to a book that excited no comment while grade E refers to a work that was considered very controversial. Table 7.7 gives the results for these and demonstrates that the majority of the books reviewed in the *TLS* and banned in southern Ireland were considered either of average or good quality. Very few were hailed as masterpieces but neither were they without lit-

TABLE 7.7:
QUALITY AND CHARACTER OF THE BOOKS REVIEWED IN THE *TLS*

Quality	Very Poor	%	Poor	%	Average	%	Good	%	Very Good	%
Books	18	2.3	107	13.4	406	50.8	272	34.0	7	0.9
Controversy	A	%	B	%	C	%	D	%	E	%
Books	218	26.6	290	35.4	214	26.1	93	11.5	4	0.9

erary value, according to the British reviewers. Nor were they considered especially controversial by the reviewers. They were, however, often of a realist or slightly left-wing character, illustrating life in rural or industrial communities. This is suspicious as it is entirely possible that books that were politically unacceptable were banned on the grounds of a few pages describing sex. As we shall see, there is evidence that this happened in the case of G. B. Shaw and it may have been true of other authors also.

The role of the Customs and Gardaí

It was not enough just to ban a book. It fell to the law enforcement authorities to prevent its importation and distribution. In September 1930, the Revenue Commissioners made an informal arrangement with the CPB that they would detain all books dealing with birth control and forward them to the board. Such actions were not allowed by the act 'strictly speaking' but as a prohibition order 'would inevitably be made ... the slight irregularity would be covered up'.[31]

To import a banned book, a permit from the Minister for Justice was required. The most common applicants under this system were university libraries. In September 1930, the librarian at Trinity College Dublin informed the Minister for Justice that a book on contraception had been seized by the Customs authorities. He wanted a general exemption for the library. Previously, he pointed out, books intended for copyright libraries had not been examined. If they were to be scrutinized, great delays would result. The books were not for sale or distribution and any banned books were placed 'in a special press in the librarian's room' and only issued with his permission. The Secretary of the Department of Justice, Henry O'Friel, told him instead that he should submit a list in advance and apply for permits. The Revenue Commissioners for their part agreed to this but warned that they retained the right to search consignments addressed to the library to safeguard revenue. They agreed to instruct their people to do so with the minimum of inconvenience.[32] This system seems to have worked adequately. The government did sometimes try to use its power over the university; in 1931, for example, the librarian was refused a permit for the *Daily Worker* but this was issued when he applied again four months later.[33] University College Cork library suffered a similar problem when it tried to collect a complete set of Liam O'Flaherty's writings in the hope that 'somebody such as Professor Corkery will write a slashing attack' on him. The Customs seized the books and the Minister for Justice had to issue permits for their release.[34]

Members of the general public were also inconvenienced by the Customs. The brother of a professor at TCD had his holiday reading confiscated in June 1931 until the Minister for Justice issued a permit for the offending books.[35] James H. Webb, the chairman of Standard Hotels Ltd, attempted to liberate his copy of *Grand Hotel* by Vicki Baum on the ground that 'all literature having reference to hotels is of special interest to me'. The request was initially denied but as he persisted the Minister reconsidered. Having decided that Webb was a 'respectable man not given to reading indecent literature' who was also making a fuss, he decided to 'let him have the book, if that can be arranged rather than prolong this foolish controversy'. The next month, the indomitable Mr Webb tried to import Bertrand Russell's *Marriage and Morals*. When asked for a reason why he should be allowed to do so he replied that he was a Quaker, an article in the *Friend* had referred to the book and he liked 'to keep in touch and up to date'. Furthermore, 'I am 58 years old and a grandfather, and I submit that it is not at all likely that my morals will be unduly interfered with.' He got his way.[36] Francis Toner, a doctor at the Central Hospital Galway, was not so lucky. He sought to import Havelock Ellis's *Psychology of Sex* and the novel *Stallion* as part of his research for 'a complete and exhaustive study of sexual abnormalities'. He was allowed to import the book by Ellis but not *Stallion*.[37]

In 1934, in the Senate, Sir John Keane attacked the way that the Customs dealt with books. He spoke on behalf of 'a substantial number of people with intellectual interests' and questioned how the authorities were co-ordinating the application of Section 42 of the Customs Consolidation Act 1876 and the Censorship of Publications Act 1929. He claimed that the Customs act was applied in an arbitrary fashion with a book passing easily through one port and being held up at another. He named three books, none of which had been banned by the CPB but which had been held up at the ports.[38]

Prior to the debate, Keane had consulted J.C.M. Eason who had denied that there was a serious problem. He had seen only eight cases of seizure; six led to the books being banned, one book was released and one case was a mistake. Other booksellers had similar views.[39] The Customs retained the power to seize any books they suspected of being obscene and could then send them to the CPB. According to the Department of Justice, 'In fact the Revenue Commissioners estimate that nearly half of the books which appear on these lists [of books prohibited by the CPB] were taken by their officers in the first instance'. In the event of a conflict of views between the Revenue Commissioners and the CPB, the former 'would be prepared to accept the considered view of the board'. The specific case Keane referred to was the confiscation of *Straphangers* by Norah James from his sister. The officer in charge decided that 'the general tenor of portions of the book was definitely indecent' and 'one of the principal Dublin booksellers' did not stock it because he considered James's works immoral.[40] The book was sent to the CPB and banned. It is interesting that in his speech, Senator Keane mentioned that the book had been well reviewed in the *Times Literary Supplement*.

The question of how the Minister for Justice decided who should be granted permits was raised in 1936 by J. Walter Beckett, the Fine Gael TD for Dublin South, who wondered why a person known to him was refused a permit in November 1935 when another person had been allowed to import six copies of the same book that year. This seems to refer to the case of Seán Ó Faoláin who was allowed to import copies of his own book, *Midsummer Night Madness,* and gave them to his friends as Christmas presents. The *Irish Times* criticized the Minister for giving such a vague reply and suggested that he was 'thoroughly ashamed' of the censorship. To the paper, the censorship of publications was a bad joke.[41] It had a point but it may have missed the real purpose of the system. All of the people discussed here who were allowed permits were academics, businessmen, doctors or writers. They were educated and in many cases financially comfortable. In short they were respectable and mature. The corollary of this was that young, uneducated, poor people would not be given permits. Indeed, the procedures required even to apply for one meant that the issue was unlikely to arise: a farm labourer, factory worker or shop girl was unlikely to be in a position to import a book from abroad, write to the Minister seeking permission in advance and have a professional reason for needing to read it. The permit system was only futile if one believes that the censorship was intended to prevent the educated middle and upper classes from reading what they wanted. On the contrary, it was ideally suited to allow them their freedom while limiting that of others.

The Gardaí served as both an enforcement and a reporting agency for the censorship. At first there was some confusion over the way they should operate the new act. In January 1930, a garda seized a copy of *Point Counter Point* by Aldous Huxley from a local circulating library. The Obscene Publications Act 1857 having been repealed, he was left in a quandary about what to do with it. In the meantime, the CPB banned it so it could not be returned to the library, much to the relief of the local clergy. He was instructed that unless the former owner wanted it back, 'the matter should be allowed to rest'.[42] Three years later, the procedures were still unclear. A Dundalk Garda sergeant was told by a priest that an obscene magazine had arrived in the local Woolworths. He promptly got a warrant under the – now defunct – Obscene Publications Act and seized the offending item: a copy of *Real Detective* that had been sent to the normally sedate retailer by mistake. His manner of operation rendered any attempt at prosecution futile and the matter ended there.[43]

The police were capable of helping the CPB. An example, which seems typical of how they operated, concerned the magazine *Women's Friend*. A garda saw a poster advertising the magazine that emphasized such articles as 'sex knowledge', expert advice for the 'girl in her teens' and 'the bride to be' on 'married happiness'. The sergeant swiftly decoded these phrases and recommended that it be banned as 'it is likely to have a bad and evil effect on the minds of young people'. Two copies of the magazine were procured at Eason. It was not a very spicy publication; the cover invited the reader to 'knit these cosy undies!' Inside there was an advice column by 'Dr. Mary' who responded to questions about contraception by asking the reader to write to her privately and told a childless couple to go to the doctor. The CPB did not ban it but they did recommend that it be kept under close observation.[44]

The Gardaí also acted as a buffer for frivolous complaints. In 1931, for example, the editor of the *Irish Catholic*, P.J. Fogarty, sent a book he had bought in a communist bookshop entitled *The Jesuits: Religious Rogues* to the Gardaí. The Department of Justice recognized instantly that no prosecution or prohibition order was possible as the book's offence was political and religious rather than moral. No further action was taken.[45] In another case, in 1932, a complaint was received that the magazine *Talkie Topics & Theatrical Review* was being sold with an objectionable photographic supplement enclosed with it. There was nothing the CPB could do unless the periodicals could be shown to be regularly objectionable, nor was a prosecution possible as the publishers of *Talkie Topics* had not produced the supplement but had enclosed it in an attempt to increase sales. The Gardaí were dispatched to talk to the proprietors of *Talkie Topics* and they received an undertaking that the supplement would not be included again. The Department of Justice admitted that in such cases there were real difficulties using the Censorship of Publications Act but that the influence of the Gardaí had solved the problem.[46]

Opposition to the censorship of publications

Censorship was a painful experience for a writer. Marie Stopes wrote to the CPB to protest at the decision to ban *Radiant Motherhood*. She denied that it was a book advocating birth control and indeed claimed that she had only written one such book in her career. She was also angry that she had been given no right to make representations to the board. Her letters received no reply.[47]

Writers of fiction also expressed their upset at the actions of the CPB. When the CPB banned George Viereck's *My First Two Thousand Years* and *Salome, the Wandering Jewess* the author complained and enclosed letters of support from nine fellow writers including Lennox Robinson, Havelock Ellis and Padraic Colum. Fitzgerald-Kenney told Cosgrave that he had trouble replying as it was impossible to be 'at once truthful and placating'. He considered the first work 'a thoroughly undesirable book depending almost entirely on obscenity for its market'. Cosgrave told Viereck that 'it is the right of any people ... to decide through their institutions what does and what does not conform to their standards'.[48] J. Cunliffe Owens commented that he was 'very surprised indeed to hear of it [the banning of his book *Bencomo*] especially as I am a Catholic'.[49] Padraic Colum also protested that 'the censorship will drive writers out of Ireland ... it will strengthen the feeling that a Catholic State is intolerant as regards the presentation of certain compelling ideas'.[50]

When *The Puritan* by Liam O'Flaherty was banned, W.B. Yeats wrote to the *Manchester Guardian* to protest. He defended it as a good novel and an important satire on the very people who had objected to it. Yeats claimed that this was his first criticism of the CPB because up to that point it had behaved 'as fairly as could be expected'. This is a somewhat strange view of a body that had already banned works by O'Flaherty, Sinclair Lewis, William Faulkner, Aldous Huxley and John Dos Passos. It shows that even Yeats set a somewhat eccentric standard of artistic merit. Conservative opinion of O'Flaherty was less sympathetic. *An Leabharlann*'s reviewer of the year's fiction dismissed him as 'not worth mentioning'.[51] The Department of Justice's policy in regard to correspondence from writers was simply to quote back to them the wording of the prohibition order that the book 'was in the opinion of the censorship of publications board, indecent in its general tendency' or advocated contraception.[52]

Under the leadership of W.B. Yeats, the Irish Academy of Letters (IAL) took up several controversial cases. The most famous was that of G.B. Shaw's *The Adventures of the Black Girl in her Search for God* which was banned in 1933. The Minister for Justice, P.J. Ruttledge, initially refused to meet the IAL delegation until he had consulted the board.[53] He eventually did meet a group including Yeats, Russell and Frank O'Connor on 12 June and they asked him to reconsider the ban. As a result of this meeting, the Minister asked the CPB for a new report. The board's reasoning was not published but it remains in the Department of Justice files. Its members considered Shaw's book 'a blasphemous composition, deliberately offensive to the cherished sentiments of the vast majority of the people irrespective of religious opinion'. They pointed out that it had been excluded from several libraries in Britain. They then admitted that 'considerations of this character' could not be entertained under the law. Even so they asserted that the book 'is objectionable in its references to sex, indecent in its general tendency and liable to corrupt in sexual matters'. They particularly criticized 'the coarseness and vulgarity of the illustrations'. A later note by MacMahon, the secretary to the CPB, undermined these pieties admitting that 'the illustrations are the only justification under the act'.[54]

Why then did the Minister stand over such a questionable decision? He was advised that 'it is unlikely that the Attorney General would direct a prosecution for blasphemous libel' and it was hard to justify the argument that the book was obscene and indecent. De Brún, the Secretary of the Department, counselled that 'it may be dangerous to over-rule the censorship board. The board is doing good work. They do not appear to be unreasonable and they are working voluntarily.' Clearly he felt that members of the CPB would become demoralized or even resign if their decision was reversed in the case of a book that was also controversial in Britain. The Attorney General agreed that there was 'ample evidence' of blasphemy. Shaw had written 'an extremely clever attack on the funda-mental basis of the Christian religion'. It was 'more difficult' to show that the book was 'in its general tendency indecent'. He refused to commit himself, writing simply that 'I am not prepared to say that they [the CPB] are not entitled to arrive at this conclusion'. He argued that to lift the ban would be 'a serious matter' as it 'would stimulate interest ... even though he [the Minister] may feel that if he were dealing with the question for the first time he would have taken a different view from theirs'. According to Yeats, Ruttledge told him,

> I have been trying to get round that book but I can't get round it. Nothing to be done. I take the ban off it, what happens? All the cen-sors resign. I am not a narrow man but what is to be done?[55]

The next big controversy concerned *Bird Alone* by Seán Ó Faoláin. The ban provoked outrage in the letters column of the *Irish Times*. W.F. Trench of Trinity College wrote that 'an offence of the utmost gravity has been com-mitted against the human spirit'. He believed that this was a case of 'powers given to officials for one purpose being utilised by them for another'. In other words, the book had not really been banned for indecency but because the narrator was a lapsed Catholic. Trench's contribution was significant because he supported the principle of censorship. An anonymous correspondent to the Department of Justice later asked how *Bird Alone* was worthy of a ban when *Vile Bodies* was not. It also claimed that there were rumours that Waugh's book was not banned because 'ecclesiastical influence' had been exercised 'to prevent the scandal of the banning of a convert's book'. There is no evidence to support this claim and rumours were and remain especially unreliable sources in Ireland, but it illustrates the sort of controversy which the censorship process was creating. The CPB refused to revise their estimate of Ó Faoláin's work: it was 'an immoral and dangerous book, the more so because there is some good writing in it'. It may have been harmless to 'age-hardened professors' but not to the 17 to 22 year olds who would form nine-tenths of its readers. Furthermore, 'the writer seems rather to gloat over the sexual incidents he presents', they concluded.[56] The board did not mention religion in its minutes but whether this was because they genuinely thought the book was obscene or had just learned their lesson from the Shaw episode is impossible to know.

In 1935, a Dublin centre of the PEN club, a world association of writ-ers, was established. At its inaugural meeting, Francis Hackett argued that the author needed to be free of communism, language movements, 'and one Action or another'. Leslie A. Montgomery, who wrote under the name Lynn Doyle, told the PEN meeting that they needed to 'at least mitigate [the censorship] in such a way that the writers should tell the truth as they genuinely felt it'. He felt that writers had partly brought about the censorship as 'in order to promote the sales of their works they stressed offensive problems unnecessarily'. Reporting the meeting, the *Irish Times* also criticized the 'official' school of Irish literature that excluded Protestants, any criticism of Irish characteristics or non-Irish subjects. It argued on the other hand that there was nothing wrong with the writer being engaged in society. [57]

In January 1937, Montgomery was appointed to the CPB to replace W.B. Joyce. There should be no doubt as to the significance of this decision. A writer who had been critical of censorship was replacing an INTO official who had testified in its favour to the Committee on Evil Literature. He lasted less than a month, resigning in February, and published his reasons in the press. His most important complaint was that passages in the books were marked by a Department of Justice official in accordance with the page numbers specified in the complaint. Montgomery complained that 'it is nearly impossible to report on the general tendency after reading a marked passage. Even when one reads the book through afterwards, one is under the influence of the markings.' He also complained that the system was arbitrary in that it required that an offensive book be spotted by a complainant before it could be examined. Montgomery's point about the marked passages was a valuable one. His verdict seems to be supported by an earlier comment from de Brún that 'several books have been prohibited by reason of offensive matter contained in a few pages well advanced in the book'. Every complaint form required the complainant to specify the pages on which he or she believed the indecent parts of the book existed. This was contrary to the spirit, if not the letter, of the law's requirement that the book be judged to be obscene in its general tendency. Part of the problem was that that phrase was itself never defined. Did it mean that a book which contained a few offensive passages should be let through? Or did it require an artistic judgement as to whether those passages were exceptions or an expression of the central themes of the book? Montgomery had not had an easy time on the board. Other members had refused to sit with him because of his earlier criticisms. This meant that he did not see the CPB at work in a normal fashion but it did not weaken his main criticisms. Montgomery ended on a cynical note:

> I admit that in practice the Irish censorship works wonderfully well. Between a book's issue and its banning the more cultivated and the more hardened readers have read it. The unsophisticated have not

in general got to know about it. But I do not think that it is worthy of our state to trade on an act whose excellence consists in its bad drafting.[58]

This was not out of keeping with the arguments of other writers. The IAL's defence of Shaw and Ó Faoláin was based on the principle that their works were not obscene because they were great art. This formed part of O'Casey's argument against the IAL itself. In refusing to join the academy, he complained that it would impose 'the censorship of dull authority' by creating a hierarchy among writers and deciding which ones were worth defending. Although he did not use the analogy, O'Casey seemed to want to transfer the trade union code by which a hurt to one is a hurt to all to the creative arts. Despite this he told Gabriel Fallon that, while he was passionately opposed to censorship, 'I don't see why dirty and smutty things shouldn't be given the go-by'.[59]

Seán Ó Faoláin also offered a rigorous critique of the censorship. At a meeting of the Irish PEN club he put down a motion 'that this meeting is of the opinion that the Censorship Board has exceeded its powers' by banning books that were not obscene or were of artistic value. The motion was opposed by Professor James Hogan of University College Cork who argued that 'no person who accepted the Catholic point of view would place the claims of art before those of morality, truth and goodness'. The meeting divided between those like Stephen Gwynn and Monk Gibbon who opposed the censorship and those who believed it was necessary. The meeting did not accept Ó Faoláin's motion but instead adopted an anodyne amendment from Trench.[60] In 1936, Ó Faoláin returned to the theme in an article in *Ireland To-Day*. He was provoked by the banning of Francis Hackett's *The Green Lion*, Austin Clarke's *The Singing Men of Cashel*, and his own *Bird Alone*. His criticisms fell into two parts: the system of censorship and the principles underlying it. In practice, he felt that the system was unfair and brought the law into disrepute because there was a long delay before books were banned. There had been numerous scandals where books were banned that should not have been. He also demanded that an appeal process be established.

As regards the principle of censorship he claimed, 'we are not asking for the free circulation of books, we ask merely that the circulation of books should be interfered with only with the utmost circumspection'. He attacked the advocates of censorship. They were an alliance of 'Gaelic revivalists' and 'Catholic Actionists' who were afraid of 'the influence of European, and especially English literature' for reasons of nationalism and piety. This suggested that they believed that the Irish were too morally weak to resist 'a flighty book by some English chit of a girl-journalist; ... a whiff from Mr. John Dos Passos, a touch of anti-clericalism from Mr.

Sinclair Lewis, a hearty laugh from Mr. Shaw'. Instead censorship had inculcated a double life among Irish people whereby they publicly avowed loyalty to Roman Catholic teaching but privately lived their own lives. Public opinion was being pre-empted by the banning of books before the general public could read them. 'By depriving morality of its freedom it reduces it to a machine without virtue' and reduced the community 'to a condition of moral slavery'. Irish intellectuals were made to earn their living abroad while residing in Ireland. This had the advantage of removing any ulterior motive from their commentaries but it made Ireland 'a country deliberately deprived of its own intellectuals'.

He sought the formation of a 'spearhead' of independent, Catholic thinkers made up of 'University professors, professional men, private students, journalists and so forth'. Intellectuals needed to act as 'the sole bulwark between the national character and the disintegrating influence of the Censorial mind'.[61] The article reads like a bridge between the ideas of George Russell and the sort of critical thinking that would characterize *The Bell* some years later. What Ó Faoláin did was to turn the arguments of the censorship advocates against them. Where they demanded restriction to prevent social collapse and moral decay, he identified censorship as a cause of these very problems. His argument was also significant in that he did not merely uphold the right of art to be free from restriction, as Yeats had done, but put the onus on the censors to ban only when they could show it was necessary. His article illustrates what Riordan has described as the division created by censorship between the liberal and Roman Catholic intelligentsias. Both sides agreed on the need for a national literature but they could not agree on the proper role of the author in society.[62]

Similar complaints were made by other writers and intellectuals. Oliver St John Gogarty complained that a bill intended to stop birth control propaganda was 'now directed at any form of literature which will criticise or explode the Stage-Irishman'. 'If this country had produced great sinners there might be something to censor but even the Carrigon report [sic] was not made public so we didn't know what is the enormity of our crimes.'[63] Some Protestant correspondents to the newspapers complained that the censorship of publications violated freedom of religion, was a usurping of the role of the Church by the state or would lead to Roman Catholic standards being adopted in Irish law.[64] The presence of a member of the Church of Ireland on the CPB may have assuaged some of these fears. It should also be noted that with the exception of the birth-control issue, there was little disagreement between the Churches about what constituted an obscene book. One man made his protest by referring the Censorship of Publications Act itself to the CPB. He complained that it violated St Paul's injunction to treat the body as a temple and that it was a 'suggestive and prurient work'.[65]

Intellectuals in favour of censorship

Although many writers and intellectuals protested against the censorship, there were many others who approved of it and wanted it strengthened. Their resolve was reinforced by the 1930 papal encyclical *Casti Conubii* which reiterated the Roman Catholic Church's opposition to contraception. It asserted that 'the conjugal act is destined primarily by nature for the begetting of children' and that to curtail this purpose 'is beyond the reach of any human law'.[66] The reference to nature is significant as it meant that the encyclical claimed not just to offer Roman Catholic teaching on the subject, as its teachings on the mass or the priesthood did, but to state the natural law which was to be obeyed by all people regardless of religion. It was this view that led the *Catholic Mind*, a small radical paper, to denounce pharmacists who sold contraceptives.[67] Bishop Browne of Galway claimed that birth control advocates 'regard motherhood exactly as a prostitute does, something to be avoided at all costs'.[68]

The supporters of censorship were not simply concerned with birth control. Their aversion to the modern novel was partly rooted in a deep suspicion of psychoanalysis evidenced by this answer to a question on the subject from the CTSI publication *Up and Doing*,

> Q: What is the Catholic attitude to psychoanalysis?
> A: Psychoanalysis destroys the unity of the human personality, and makes the continuity of consciousness impossible. Free will becomes a delusion, moral responsibility an impossibility, and sin non-existent ... such teaching is mere pagan parody of the Catholic doctrine of the Fall and Original Sin.[69]

Given such views, it was inevitable that the modern novel, partly a child of Freudian thinking, would also face their opposition. Aodh de Blacam claimed that seven-tenths of modern literature was anti-Christian and only one-tenth was free of immorality.[70] The noted critic, Fr Stephen J. Brown SJ argued that sex was not a proper subject for a novelist at all because, unlike science, literature was not merely an enquiry after truth but also possessed a power to harm. Vice could only be dealt with if it was treated as a sin. As Riordan has pointed out this power to harm was considered to extend even to accidental exposure to unclean literature; an innocent could be corrupted by reading the wrong things. Rev. Cornelius Lucey, later Bishop of Cork, put it as follows,

> There is something seductive about the written word. Those who read it come almost unconsciously to make its ideas and its outlook their own. Only if they find one writer contradicting another do they exercise anything like judgement on it. Hence whoever can control the reading matter in a community can control too the minds and emotions of the citizens.[71]

Brown put forward a detailed defence of censorship in 1936. The government existed for the temporal welfare of the people. This must include public morality. If certain behaviour was deemed detrimental to the general welfare of the people it could be prohibited. As the government was powerless to stop the actual use of contraceptives, it needed to control their availability and propaganda for them. In the case of immoral literature, he distinguished between pornography, which even those opposed to censorship abhorred, and 'the book that makes a fetish of sex'. Such over-emphasis on sex was wrong, he argued. Furthermore, it was a matter of public morality because writing was an outward act. He countered the argument that censorship curtailed liberty by pointing out that all laws did so. He also refused to accept that an artist could not take into account the possible effects of his work, as no one could evade his responsibility under the moral law. In the case of immoral books, censorship was the lesser of two evils. The fact that the ban often came late was not an argument against the system as most novels stayed in circulation for about ten years, so even if they were banned after one or two, some good was done. The law existed for the ordinary citizen who 'is not looking for obscenity' and 'above all, the law is intended to protect the adolescent'. There was no right for 'adults, any more than of the young and innocent, to arouse and indulge in sensual feelings or to fill their imaginations with foul images'. In conclusion he believed that 'the repression of evil literature ought to be regarded as a matter of sanitation'.[72]

This argument rested on three premises: firstly that immoral books were capable of doing harm, secondly that writers had to take responsibility for this because writing affects others, and thirdly that even adults had no right to indulge in immoral literature. These being conceded, his argument proceeded logically. As we have seen, Irish writers and opponents of censorship tended to attack the idea that works of art could do harm or to assert the rights of adults to read what they liked. In many ways this dispute still sums up the arguments over obscenity: can obscene material do harm? Does the artist have a responsibility to avoid creating obscenity? Does the consumer have a right to consume obscenity even if it does harm?

James Devane launched a scathing *ad hominem* attack on the modern Irish novelist. 'He has no reading public here. Nine out of ten of his sales are sales out of Ireland', he complained. 'He can reflect Irish life as seen by an Irishman through the eyes of a British publisher and a British public.' By a rhetorical stroke, Irish writers had become foreign in Devane's eyes. Aodh de Blacam came to a similar conclusion and he argued that Irish liberals were 'fifty years behind their intellectual capital, Chelsea'. They dodged between arguing that art had no moral obligations, and that the Church had no authority. De Blacam believed that artistic merit was no justification for a bad book; indeed it made it more dangerous because good writing made it more enticing. Patrick J. Gannon SJ admitted that the censorship 'complicates the author's task' but claimed that in many cases it was used by vain writers to excuse their own failings, for an offensive book was an artistic failure. 'One would imagine that the Inquisition existed here, and had hauled off author after author to its torture chamber', he remarked. Instead, all that was required by the censorship was that 'thou shalt not write pornography'. Writers might be the best judges of literary quality but not of morality and he did not believe in letting them control what was published. He believed that even in the cases of Aristophanes, Chaucer and Shakespeare, a censor could have 'cut out every unsavoury passage and their fame will not moult a feather of its plumage'. Works of literature were 'legitimate only in so far as they promote the higher good of man'.[73] This preparedness to sacrifice even great art to protect the innocent was crucial to the outlook of the pro-censorship intellectuals and was entirely consistent with the logic of their arguments. It also made accommodation with the anti-censorship writers, for whom art was intrinsically unable to do harm, impossible.

Organized advocacy of censorship

Pro-censorship intellectuals produced a variety of arguments, many of which were logical if one accepted their premises. It fell to other organizations to present popular forms of these to the people. Often these sacrificed logic to make the case as clearly and loudly as possible. As we have seen, in the early 1930s the strongest supporter of the censorship was the CTSI. This support was expressed in its publications and at its meetings. As well as objecting to obscenity and advocacy of birth control, the CTSI complained about risqué humour, homosexuality, prostitution, suicide, adultery and blasphemy.[74] The Society preached a simple faith requiring complete obedience to the Church's teachings. This was exemplified by its complaint against *Reubens, Prince of the Jews*, O'Reilly wrote that

> The second half of the book is historical, but refers very much to the duplicity and other defects of the Pope and Papal government that are better forgotten. Some of it may be true, most of it exaggerated and disrespectful and none of it edifying reading for Catholic youth or for Catholics who have only a superficial knowledge of Medieval Church history ... it is beautifully written and so enticing and extremely interesting as to draw the reader on to the end.[75]

An attack on Sigrid Undset, the Nobel Prize winner and Dominican tertiary who wrote long, intricate novels about medieval Christianity, took the same approach. 'The picture drawn by Madame Undset may be historically accurate, but there ought to be some indication that it is philosophically false ... realism is not only bad art it is bad morals too.' She was a Catholic who wrote novels, but not a Catholic novelist.[76]

The society and its publications constantly attacked modern literature. Modern writers were

> slavishly following conventions and forgetting (simply because their conventions are new) that there are realities and eternal realities, standards and eternal standards; foundation. The result in art and letters has been a growing decentralisation (or in the most exact sense of the word a growing 'eccentricity') which may be disastrous ... At the present moment the destructive mind in literature is popular, fashionable.[77]

Literary merit was distrusted by the CTSI. O'Reilly complained of one book: 'there is nothing vulgar or downright indecent, but this makes the subtle undercurrent all the more dangerous'. The book was banned.[78] The Roman Catholic Archbishop of Tuam told the CTSI Congress in 1936 that it was evil literature that had caused Spain to descend into anarchy – a fact which Irish Roman Catholicism blamed on the anti-clericalism of the Republicans.[79] In 1937 the Society set up a committee to review the censorship laws. It reported that the system was failing as it was too slow and did not deal adequately with periodicals. The Society proposed a better-funded censorship with ten boards of three censors each and changes to make it easier to ban periodicals. Despite the Society's pressure, the government decided not to amend the act.[80]

The CTSI was joined in its campaign against evil literature by An Ríoghacht, a small right-wing Catholic association which appealed mostly to educated, middle-class laymen. At its 1930 ard fheis it adopted a resolution characterizing the new censorship system as inadequate. It demanded the examination of all foreign publications and the prohibition of any that offended 'the traditional standards of the people' or carried soviet propaganda.[81] In 1931 and 1932 it circulated a similar resolution to the county councils and municipal corporations. It claimed to have the support of Cork, Limerick, Waterford and Clonmel corporations, Limerick, Offaly, Waterford, Dublin, Wexford, Tipperary North Riding and Tipperary South Riding county councils, as well as three boards of health and three public library committees.[82]

The Ríoghacht resolutions seem to have sparked an interest in censorship within the Fianna Fáil party. A motion was proposed at the party's 1932 ard fheis 'that steps be taken to prevent the spread of anti-Irish and anglicising propaganda through the medium of the foreign daily papers' and was adopted by the national executive. The Department of Justice resisted the idea and informed de Valera that it would require new legislation.[83] A second motion was passed at the 1933 ard fheis calling for the censorship of 'anti-national propaganda' during the Economic War. In May, de Valera received a delegation from An Ríoghacht which included Fr Edward Cahill, the intellectual leader of the organization. Cahill told him that the censorship was insufficient and stricter customs controls and the registration of books were required. De Valera questioned the practicality of the scheme and pointed out that it would require a huge staff to implement. He also noted that Roman Catholics were not united on the issue of censorship.[84] An Ríoghacht, perhaps responding to some of the controversy about the CPB, insisted that its scheme be classified as 'protection', not 'censorship'. In fact this meant that it used terms and structures from economics to conceal its proposals. There were to be three classes of imported publications. 'Class A' were to be positively useful publications which would be allowed in for free; 'Class B' would be harmless but serving no useful purpose and would carry a tariff; 'Class C' were to be 'degrading, immoral, irreligious or otherwise harmful' material and would be prohibited. There were to be exceptions for prose fiction of 'exceptionally high literary merit' if they were unobjectionable.[85]

The Department of Justice dismissed the proposals as being 'of the most drastic and revolutionary character'. Its secretary pointed out that the country imported a large amount of literature and that the public had very varied tastes. Furthermore, there was a problem with the logistics of the proposal. A large staff would be needed to license all imported publications and putting together a censorship board capable of making consistent decisions would be nearly impossible. Interestingly, de Brún also claimed that it was 'highly fallacious' to argue that a censor could decide the tendency of a work on the basis of a few pages or chapters, while his subordinates were busy marking offensive passages to aid the CPB. The campaign to license imported publications was supported by Fr Richard Devane in 1934 as a mechanism for 'shaking ourselves off from the intellectual dominance of the English press'. The government did impose tariffs on imported newspapers in 1932 which substantially reduced their sales in Ireland.[86] It did not, however, go so far as to tax papers according to their moral standards.

Other groups supported the censorship. Although the INTO was officially neutral on the subject, one of its members was on the CPB, and John D. Sheridan, the editor of *Irish Schools Monthly*, the union's magazine and himself a popular writer, was an enthusiastic supporter. He used its pages to endorse the actions of the CPB, to criticize writers who attacked it and to advocate the use of Roman Catholic standards in the selection of library books.[87] As well as endorsing the Ríoghacht campaign, several local authorities protested against the *Daily Mail* when it published a series of articles on the life of Christ in 1931.[88]

The Catholic Young Men's Society took an interest in censorship in the later years of the decade. Its objectives were the suppression of bad films, indecent dances, evil literature and communism.[89] At its conference in 1938, the Society called on the government to extend censorship to include publications that supported suicide, divorce, euthanasia or free love and to establish a prior censorship. Canon Boylan, the chairman of the CPB, reproved them for seeking new laws when 'not one of them would help the censors keep the filth of modern romance out of the country'.[90] The Society sought guarantees from election candidates that they would support a stronger censorship. They set up vigilance committees in the Archdioceses of Dublin and Tuam to find immoral books and submit them to the CPB. In the diocese of Ross, censorship was 'one of the main activities' of the Society and they were supported in this by the bishop. In Bray they forced sellers to remove undesirable magazines, in Clonakilty they had four books banned, and in Kilkenny four more books were taken off the shelves after the Society put pressure on the sellers.[91]

Book selection in libraries

The county library system grew rapidly in both northern and southern Ireland in this period. Although the regulation of the libraries was slightly different in each region and there were two different associations of librarians, the systems remained very similar. The librarians' dilemma was expressed in 1932 by the Cork county librarian, Donal Cronin. They were overwhelmed by the quantity of books needed. They had to cater for 'highbrow', 'middlebrow', 'lowbrow', and 'nobrow' readers. In the south, the 'cumbersome' censorship had produced a 'censorship-conscious' section of the public who constantly complained; about books. There were five ways to select a book, he claimed: shopping in a bookshop was the ideal solution but was too time consuming, dust jackets were not a reliable guide to a book's contents, book reviews and publishers' catalogues were also problematic due to the differences between Irish and British tastes, and readers who requested books were usually acting on sources of information available to the librarian. The usual complaints about a book, according to Cronin, were that it was anti-religious, or anti-Irish, silly, insincere, historically inaccurate, immoral, or that it advocated birth control, evolution or divorce. He wanted the Free State to set up a national panel of readers which would filter out such books for the librarians. Perhaps harking back to the days of the nineteenth century British circulating libraries he hoped such a body would also influence publishers and improve the standard of literature.[92]

James Barry, the Dublin municipal librarian and the editor of *An Leabharlann*, wrote on the same subject in 1934. He emphasized the power of the librarian: 'it is my experience that the majority of borrowers are prepared to accept without complaint the fiction we give them'. He received few demands for banned or otherwise objectionable literature. He recommended that his colleagues remember their responsibilities to the thousands of readers trained by the schools every year who drifted into 'the haphazard selection of reading matter solely for amusement' that was 'absolutely without value from an educational standpoint'. For that reason they should avoid ordering modern fiction until it had proved its worth. The paper was well received by other librarians. They complained that the libraries needed better classification for fiction and did not have the time to select it properly. Fr Stephen Brown SJ commented that libraries were much safer than some people thought but wanted better classification so that 'inferior publications' did not get confused with the classics.[93]

Galway county librarian Samuel Maguire, outlined the system of censorship applied in southern Irish libraries in 1933. He argued that the Roman Catholic Church had become more hostile to the library movement after the Lennox Robinson affair. To preserve the support of the clergy, many libraries allowed them to examine their catalogues and promised 'that every care would be taken to keep out all and any books dangerous to faith and morals'. Books contrary to Canon Law or appearing on the Index Librorum Prohibitorum were removed. He believed that it was still inexcusable for such books to find their way into a library. Fiction represented a real challenge because it was often propaganda 'subtly veneered in the guise of novels'. He rejected a wide range of books: 'the psychology-cum-biological efforts of the declared literary elite', romance, detective and adventure stories that contained blasphemy, pornography or 'attacks on the universally recognised standards of what is honourable and decent and the sanctioned, honoured forms of social conduct'. He also opposed books, modelled on those of D.H. Lawrence, that conjoined mysticism with sex. He admitted the standards applied by the library committees around the country differed; for example, du Maurier's *Trilby* was allowed in Dublin and Cork but not in rural libraries. He also conceded that some objected to these restrictions and felt that they should only be applied to Roman Catholics.[94]

At this time, the southern library system was growing rapidly despite paltry funding. In 1929, 110,000 people had used the southern Irish libraries, borrowing 2.5 million books. In Britain the recommended ratio of books to total population was 3 to 10. In the Irish Free State the real ratio was 2 to 25.[95] In 1933/4 that entire Free State public library system, serving a population of 2.8 million, received £54,427; by contrast the city of Liverpool (population 861,000) spent £64,930.[96] Readers showed a preference for fiction, a fact which excited some controversy. *An Leabharlann* recommended that libraries stock a good range of fiction to attract 'large numbers of readers who would not otherwise use the library'. The librarian could then reform these unfortunates, although

It is difficult to convert the fiction reader but his supply can be reduced, and so the troublesome section is cut down in numbers to a small percentage of the whole stock, and as far as possible none but books of some literary merit stocked in it.[97]

This was not always of much use to a librarian whose readers had abandoned westerns and were confronting him with 'urgent demands for thrillers'.[98]

The exact method of book selection was up to the county library committees. In Roscommon for example, the committee contained three priests, two women and two lay men, one of whom was a TD. The librarian submitted a list of books to them which they often passed without changes. As the county librarian expressed it, the library's mission statement was to provide 'good, sound healthy literature to counter-check indulgence in the reading of the indiscriminate publications with which every country town is provided in its book-shop and railway stalls without supervision'.[99] At the Cork conference of the Library Association, one old hand commented that while he was impressed with the eloquence of the younger librarians as they explained their problems with book selection, he remembered similar discussions in the 1900s but the profession had survived somehow.[100] In Donegal, the Library Committee ordered books on approval. In 1938, they rejected forty books sent to them as unsuitable. The chairman of the committee, rather than the librarian, seems to have been mostly responsible for reading the books.[101]

Like their southern counterparts, Northern Ireland's libraries were often poorly funded and had many readers who were not interested in literary greats. In Armagh, for example, 317 of the 478 registered readers were non-ratepayers and the most popular types of books were westerns and detective stories.[102] Fermanagh county library increased the number of books it issued in 1934 by 6 per cent due to the increasing levels of unemployment. Fiction usually made up the vast majority of what it issued. This led to controversy when the library's grant was cut from £200 to £150 in 1934. One councillor proposed cutting it by £100 as so many fiction books were issued and these were not 'of practical utility to the readers'. He deemed 'the reading of books of fiction to be a lunacy'.[103] In Armagh library, book selection was in the hands of the librarian. Despite this there were sometimes complaints about the books. In one case, Senator Thomas McLoughlin complained that the library stocked 'a class of literature … which was not for the good of the community' but would not specify any individual books.[104] Such self-appointed censors were a hazard facing librarians in both regions.

Censorship of publications in Northern Ireland

Northern Ireland adopted no legislation or special procedures for dealing with objectionable publications in this period. This did not mean that there were no distinctively Northern Irish views on the question. Bishop Mageean of Down and Connor used his 1930 Lenten pastoral to condemn contraception and evil literature.

> I trust it is not too much to hope that the Free State will be henceforward largely free from this direful pest. Unfortunately we have as yet no such protection in the six counties. But it is to be hoped that here also something will be done to guard at least innocent children against such dangers.[105]

In the Northern Irish House of Commons, Cahir Healy complained that 'this city is full of books of an immoral character', and asked, 'Do you [the government] intend doing anything with regard to the flood of immoral literature scattered throughout the city?' Comparing the government's decision to bring in an order under the CASPA allowing it to ban seditious films and gramophone records with its inaction over obscene publications, Healy accused it of 'shying at straws and jumping over camels and beginning at the wrong end'. He declared that the government was 'afraid of that subject'. One of his colleagues argued that there was a public demand for 'a much more rigorous censorship'; citing a recent resolution at the Church of Ireland diocesan synod in Armagh condemning bad books and films, he asked if the Minister believed that the system in place was adequate. Dawson Bates answered that he did consider that system sufficient and said that he had not received any resolution from the synod.[106] To a great extent he was avoiding the issue as such resolutions were common and it is not credible that he was unaware of them.

These views were supported by articles in the press. One writer complained that 'our country is once more being ravaged by invaders of a "cunning, skilful and unscrupulous" neighbouring race'.[107] The government's view in 1934 was that 'no cases have come under their [the police's] notice in recent times that appear to justify prosecution'.[108] The government thus stubbornly insisted on conducting the debate on legalistic grounds rather than discussing the question of whether Northern Ireland needed or wanted a different system from that of the rest of the UK.

The demand for stricter censorship came regularly from nationalist politicians and Church leaders. They may have been motivated in part by reports that books banned in the Free State were advertised as such and sold at a higher than usual price in some Belfast bookshops.[109] Cardinal MacRory used the occasion of confirmations in Cookstown in 1934 to warn against 'the reading matter imported from Russia'.[110] That year the fact that the CTSI held its conference in Belfast inspired the *Derry People* to complain that 'the majority of current literary publications is definitely evil'. These were made up of definite attacks on the faith and attacks on morals. Fiction was the main carrier of the problem and it affected the rich less than the poor because 'people of means can discriminate in their reading matter, and good books are often dearer proportionately than bad books'.[111] In 1935, one MP asked the Minister of Home Affairs to set up a censorship board 'so that immodest and undesirable pictures shall cease to be exhibited, unbecoming plays withdrawn and prurient books and papers in circulation banned'. Dawson Bates again flatly refused, claiming that the existing law was sufficient.[112]

There were calls for change from Protestant and Unionist sources but they were more scattered. The *Fermanagh Times* raised the issue of war novels that emphasized the sordid and disgusting elements of soldiering. At one Orange service in Armagh, a speaker asserted that 'many of the leading English newspapers were, strictly speaking, under Romish influence'. The Presbyterian Church in Armagh heard that bad literature was a problem in the presbytery area but confined itself to calling on religious leaders to send a clear message. Individual complaints, of which these are just a sample, never amounted to a concerted campaign by Protestant groups. It is also important to distinguish condemnations of obscene literature – which were common to all Churches – from demands for an official censorship. Unionist papers sometimes published articles opposing censorship. In 1932, the novelist L.A. Strong argued that 'you cannot prohibit one sort of free speech without endangering others', and claimed, 'it is better to have freedom and punish the abuse of it than to have no freedom in case abuse may come'.[113] This summed up the attraction of the British system to many Protestants. Northern Ireland's newspapers took little interest in the obscenity trials of the period. In particular, the trial of *The Well of Loneliness* drew no press coverage from the province's daily papers despite the fact that it was reported in the major British papers.

This period saw few practical changes in British government policy. The British Customs list of books to be seized was not revised between 1930 and the 1950s. This was not a comprehensive list and only detailed borderline cases, which were mostly of French origin. Customs officers were expected to seize obviously pornographic material whether or not it was on the list. A list of periodicals banned by the courts had a decidedly French flavour with titles like *Venus*, *Paris Plaisirs* and *Paris Sex Appeal*. There were also a large number of American magazines. These publications fell into a variety of categories: some were illustrated or contained advertisements for erotic photographs, others were made up of flagellation stories or material that was considered borderline, lastly there were sealed envelopes containing stories of sadomasochism or child pornography.[114]

The Northern Irish authorities were given copies of the British list but had little to add to it. Prosecutions for obscenity were rare in the province; there were none between July 1937 and June 1938. Later in 1938 two shops in Belfast were raided by the police and several magazines taken. The publications seized included a number of American titles with such enticing names as *College Humour*, *Film Fun* and *Stocking Parade*. There were also several titles which at least purported to bear a French influence: *Gay Parisienne*, *Paris Gayety* [*sic*]and *Allure*. Of fourteen titles found by the police, nine were not on the British list. This showed that some material, though probably not much, did escape the UK Customs and find its way into Northern Ireland. It also illustrated the randomness of the British system and the fact that it did not offer comprehensive protection against the importation of such material.[115] There is no evidence that the authorities were concerned about the possibility of obscene material being smuggled into southern Ireland. Constabulary patrols engaged in customs work on the border were told to look out for explosives, munitions and dangerous drugs but obscene articles were not mentioned.[116]

In 1933, the Ministry of Home Affairs considered introducing a bill to regulate printers. Based on the Newspaper, Printers and Reading Rooms Repeal Act of 1869, it would have required that 'all printed and duplicated documents shall bear the name and address of the printer'. This would act to deter them from producing 'objectionable matter'. It was not made clear whether the matter in question was objectionable from a moral or a security point of view – possibly it hoped to deal with both problems at once. The Cabinet gave its permission for a bill to be prepared but, several months later, Dawson Bates announced that he no longer wished to proceed with it.[117] No explanation was given for this decision. The incident suggests that the content of material printed in Northern Ireland had become a matter of concern to the government but that the matter was not sufficiently urgent to justify new legislation.

The biggest effort to control post and publications on moral grounds concerned the Irish Hospitals' Sweepstake. Dawson Bates consulted the Home Office as to whether they would allow the northern government to take a much tougher line on the advertising of sweep tickets. He proposed a ban on all advertisements and notices for the sweep in any paper circulated in Northern Ireland. He particularly felt 'that certain articles which are appearing in the Free State papers published in Northern Ireland dealing with the recent lottery ... constitute a far greater evil than "advertisements"'. He hoped that the UK government would also prosecute such papers. Sir John Anderson at the Home Office 'told him quite definitely that we would not do so'.[118] The British authorities told their Northern Irish counterparts that they did not object 'to articles or reports in newspapers relating to a lottery or to the publication of a proposal or list of drawings. Should however the article amount to a publicising of a proposal or scheme for the sale of tickets action should be taken.' They had legal advice that the 1823 Lotteries Act did not prevent favourable comment or the giving of information on a lottery. The Home Office recommended that the warrants issued to the Northern Irish Ministry for Home Affairs to search post in 1926 be applied to searches for sweep tickets also.[119]

The Northern Irish authorities were forced to rethink their strategy as a result of the opposition of the Home Office. The Northern Irish Attorney General advised in March 1931 that 'news items in relation to the sweep after the draw has taken place are not objectionable'. Newspapers were warned not to publish advertisements for any lottery. The English *Sunday News* took the plans badly. 'What is news in England is poison in Belfast', it complained. It also pointed out that the new rules had not applied in the days of the Calcutta Sweep and its ilk. This, the paper felt, showed that the Northern Irish policy was motivated by dislike of the Free State.[120]

In 1933 the Northern Irish Attorney General still complained that 'the activities of the Irish Hospitals' Sweepstakes Ltd are a source of constant irritation to us'. He again suggested to the British that all references to the sweeps in the press should be banned. In support of this he presented a variety of rumours that the organizers were highly paid and maintained an 'army of workers and helpers'. They gave lavish parties and spent huge amounts of money advertising the draws. 'On all grounds, moral and constitutional, the activities of this Trust, outside their own territory should be curtailed as far as possible'. The Northern Irish press supported the plans as they did not want 'to publish this class of news'. The idea intrigued the Home Office. The British Attorney General, Inskip, suggested that this was an ideal chance to tighten UK law on the sweeps. There were problems, however; the existing legislation had never been used so extensively before and the Royal Commission on Lotteries and Betting did not favour the idea. The Home Office told the Northern Irish government that the British government would not be embarrassed if they chose to legislate and felt that it would test public opinion.[121] No such legislation was introduced, perhaps because the northern government could see that it would be acting on its own. The treatment by the Northern Irish government of the sweepstakes demonstrated that it was possible for the province to have its own system of censorship. It also demonstrated that such a policy would have required new legislation, close co-operation with and support from the Home Office and the Customs, and a strong political will from the northern government.

Publications and free expression in the two Irelands

No one seemed satisfied with the Censorship of Publications Act. To writers and liberals it was an unfair imposition on the writers and readers alike. To those who had campaigned for censorship for much of the previous decade, it was a disappointment. The act failed to deal satisfactorily with periodicals, although these had been an important issue in the campaigns of the 1920s. It worked inefficiently and mostly banned works of fiction. It was easy for middle-class intellectuals to evade the censorship by buying books abroad or getting licences to import them. It was less easy for those without wealth or standing to do so, and we cannot tell how many rural youths were deprived of some of the best examples of modern literature because their local library or town bookshop could not stock it. Censorship of publications failed to do what its advocates had wanted it to, but that did not mean that it had no effects. It was part of the apparatus by which nineteenth-century moral values were preserved in Ireland for half a century after their demise in other countries.

Northern Ireland provides an interesting contrast to the south. The weakness of the Roman Catholic Church meant that it could preach against evil literature but not act against it. The northern government followed British procedures in attacking pornography but made little effort to fight a sustained campaign to clean up publications. It reserved its zeal for the far more Protestant pursuit of fighting the Irish Hospitals' Sweepstakes in the region. Even in this it was restrained by its relationship with the rest of the UK. As discussed throughout this work, while the south used censorship to express its desire for separation from Britain, the northern government wanted the exact opposite and did all it could to follow British practice.

Censorship can be said to affect not what authors write but what they might have written, and we can never know to what extent southern writers self-censored or, and here the case of Liam O'Flaherty springs to mind, became deliberately more outrageous. The true victims of censorship were, as its architects intended, people whose books came from a local library or newsstand. In 1933 in New York, Judge John M. Woolsey rejected the Cockburn judgment as a test of obscenity in the case of James Joyce's *Ulysses*. He decided that a work should not be banned because of its effects on the most susceptible members of society but should be tested against the instincts of an average person.[122] In both Irelands the earlier test remained for several decades to protect the innocent 'young person' of legend from the threat of modernity.

NOTES

1. 'Report of the Censorship of Publications Board', 1931, NAI, Department of Finance DFIN, S/106/9/31.
2. *Irish Times*, 15 Oct. 1931.
3. *Irish Independent*, 3–6 Nov. 1930.
4. S.A. Roche to O'Reilly, 5 Dec. 1930, NAI, Department of Justice DJUS, H315/42; Attorney General's Directions, 8 Dec. 1930, ibid., H315/34.

5. S.A. Roche to O'Reilly, 12 Dec. 1931; O'Reilly to Roche, 14 Dec. 1931, ibid., H315/7.
6. S.A. Roche to James Donohoe, 10 March 1930, ibid, H305/26.
7. Secretary General, BSHC, to Secretary, CPB, 28 Nov. 1932, S.A. Roche to Secretary General, BSHC, 7 Dec. 1932, ibid.
8. L.M. Cullen, *Eason & Son: a history* (Dublin: Eason & Son Ltd, 1989), p.274.
9. Thorsons Ltd. to 'The Official Censor', 20 Jan. 1931; S.A. Roche to Thorsons Ltd, 28 Jan. 1931, NAI, DJUS, H315/46.
10. B. MacMahon to Felix Barbier, 12 April 1932; Roche, note, 13 April 1932, ibid., H315/110.
11. Note by B. MacMahon, 19 Jan. 1934, to letter by Secretary Dept Justice to Rev. E. Gallen, 4 Nov. 1933, ibid., H315/6.
12. John Dillon CC to CPB, 13 Feb. 1932; S.A. Roche, memo to CPB, 23 Feb. 1932; O'Friel to Dillon, 22 March 1932, NAI, DJUS, H315/109.
13. C. Eason to H. O'Friel, 19 May 1930; H. O'Friel to Attorney General, 22 May 1930; C. Eason to O'Friel, 24 May 1930, note by O'Friel, n. d., ibid., H315/5.
14. H. O'Friel to C. Eason, 14 June 1930; C. Eason to O'Friel, 30 June 1930, ibid., H315/112.
15. J.C.M. Eason, to Fitzgerald-Kenney, 16 Oct. 1930, ibid., H315/32.
16. B. Bean Mic a Báired to Minister for Justice, 10 July 1932; Roche to B. Bean Mic a Báired, 13 July 1932; Roche to Eason, 14 July 1932; Eason to Roche, 19 July 1932, ibid, H315/127.
17. J. Drawbell to Minister for Justice, 13 March 1931; Roche to Robert Eason, 18 Nov. 1931, NAI, DJUS, H315/39.
18. O'Reilly, complaint, 6 May 1933; MacMahon to Secretary, Dept Justice, 24 May 1933; Prohibition Order, 12 June 1933, ibid., H315/145B.
19. Secretary Dept. External Affairs to Secretary Dept. Justice, 10 July 1933; S.B. Skeffington to Sydney Walton, 28 June 1933, ibid.
20. CTSI, *The First Fifty Years* (Dublin: CTSI, 1950), p. 109.
21. Maurice Curtis, 'Catholic action as an organised campaign in Ireland, 1921–1947' (Ph.D. thesis, University College Dublin, 2000), pp.172–5.
22. O'Reilly to Fr Dunne, 21 March 1934, Eason to O'Reilly 20 March 1934, DDA, Byrne Papers, Lay Organisations (5).
23. Curtis, 'Catholic action', pp.103–4; H. O'Friel, memorandum to Executive Council, 7 Aug. 1930, NAI, DJUS, JUS8/692.
24. Michael Adams, 'Censorship of publications', in Desmond M. Clarke (ed.), *Morality and the law* (Dublin: Mercier Press, 1982), p.75; Michael Adams, *Censorship: the Irish experience* (Dublin: Scepter, 1968), pp.241–43.
25. Sources: *Register of prohibited publications 1940*; *Iris Oifigiúil 1930–39*; *Times Literary Supplement 1919–39*.
26. See, for example, Oliver St John Gogarty, *Irish Times*, 6 Feb. 1935.
27. Source: *Iris Oifigiúil 1930–39*.
28. Books could not be banned for excessive reporting of crime so there was no equivalent figure in the sort of books banned.
29. Deputy Commissioner of Customs to Customs Officers, 27 Aug. 1928, NAGB, Home Office HO45/15139.
30. It is important to note that these categories are quite subjective and are based on my reading of the book reviews. The exact point at which a drama becomes identifiable as a realist novel or a melodrama is a problem. I am using the term 'ideas' novel to denote books directed more at making a political or social point than at telling a story but without the use of humour associated with satire. Science fiction should be considered to include fantasy.
31. Minute, 26 Sept. 1930, NAI, DJUS, H315/31.
32. J. Gilbert-Smylie to Minister for Justice, 18 Sept. 1930; O'Friel to Gilbert-Smylie, 6 Oct. 1930; A.J. Donnelly to Joseph Hanna, 16 Oct. 1930, ibid.
33. Gilbert-Smylie to Minister for Justice, 10 Aug. 1931; permit, 27 Aug. 1931; permit, 7 Jan. 1932, ibid.
34. Alfred O'Rahilly to Minister for Education, 22 Oct. 1932; James Geoghegan to O'Rahilly, 12 Nov. 1932, ibid.
35. James Johnson to Secretary, Dept of Justice, 4 June 1931; Secretary Dept of Justice to Johnson, 16 June 1931, ibid.
36. Webb to Minister for Justice, 21 Sept. 1932; Minute to Duff, 12 Oct. 1932; Webb to Minister for Justice, 15 Nov. 1932, 22 Nov. 1932, ibid.
37. Toner to Minister for Justice, 7 Aug. 1933; Domhnall de Brún to Toner, 18 Aug. 1933, ibid.

38. Senate Debates, Vol.XVIII, 20 June 1934, 1663–7.
39. Cullen, *Eason & Son*, p.270.
40. 'Note for the Minister', 21 July 1934, NAI, DFIN, S13/20/30.
41. *Irish Times*, 11 March 1936; M. Ó Cuinneáin to Ó Faoláin, 5 Dec. 1935, NAI, DJUS, H315/114.
42. S.A. Roche to Commissioner Garda Siochána, 19 Dec. 1930, NAI, DJUS, H305/24.
43. F.W. Woolworth to Chief Supt. Garda Siochána, Dundalk, 5 April 1933; Dept Commissioner Garda Siochána to Secretary Dept Justice, 3 May 1933; Domhnall de Brún to Commissioner Garda Siochána, 9 May 1933, NAI, DJUS, H305/18/1.
44. Report of Garda Thomas Bryan, 25 Jan. 1932, Report of Sgt Edward Ryan; *Women's Friend*, 23 Jan. 1932; B. MacMahon to Secretary, Dept Justice 7 March 1932, ibid., H315/105.
45. Deputy Commissioner, Garda Siochána to Secretary Dept Justice, 26 Feb. 1931; Duff to Commissioner Garda Siochána, 2 March 1932, ibid, H315/6.
46. F. O'Reilly to Minister for Justice, 12 March 1932; C.A. Maguire to Secretary Dept Justice, 23 April 1932; Report of Detective Sgt P. Cullinan, 6 May 1932; S.A. Roche to F. O'Reilly, 13 June 1932, ibid., H315/112.
47. Stopes to P.J. Keawell, 1 April 1931; S.A. Roche to Keawell, 21 April 1931, ibid., H315/43.
48. Viereck to Minister for Justice, 19 Dec. 1930; Fitzgerald-Kenney to Cosgrave, 11 Dec. 1930; Cosgrave to Viereck, 29 Jan. 1931, ibid., H315/43.
49. Owens to Minister for Justice, 6 Nov. 1933, ibid., H315/150.
50. Colum to G.S. Viereck, n.d. [1930], ibid, H315/43.
51. *Manchester Guardian*, 24 Feb. 1932, NLI, Yeats Papers, Ms. 30224; A.A. Kelly, *The Letters of Liam O'Flaherty* (Dublin: Wolfhound, 1996), p.252fn. Kelly is incorrect in stating that the resulting embarrassment for the government prevented *The Puritan* being listed in the *Register of Prohibited Publications*. Its prohibition was announced in *Iris Oifigiúil* of 19 Feb. 1932 and the book was listed in subsequent editions of the Register; *An Leabharlann*, Vol.2, No.2. March 1932.
52. S.A. Roche to J. Cunliffe Owens, 14 Nov. 1933, NAI, DJUS, H315/150.
53. Domhnall de Brún to George Russell, 24 June 1933, ibid., H315/43.
54. De Brún to B. MacMahon, 12 June 1933; MacMahon to de Brún, 3 July 1933; Note by MacMahon, 23 July [1933], ibid.
55. S.A. Roche, minute, note by de Brún, 4 July 1933; report of the Attorney General, 24 July 1933; W.B. Yeats to G.B. Shaw, 30 July 1933, NLI, Yeats papers, Ms. 31020.
56. *Irish Times*, 22 Oct. 1936; Anon., 23 Feb. 1937, Copy of censor's minute [copy dated 23 Feb. 1937], NAI, DJUS, H315/38.
57. *Irish Times*, 5 Feb. 1935.
58. Ibid., 13 Feb. 1937; De Brún to Secretary to the Dept of the President, 2 May 1933, NAI, DJUS, H315/131; Adams, *Censorship: the Irish experience*, p. 73.
59. *Irish Times*, 11 Oct. 1932; O'Casey to Fallon, 8 May 1939, in David Krause (ed.), *The Letters of Sean O'Casey, vol.1: 1910–41* (London: Cassell, 1975), p.796.
60. *Irish Times*, 14 Nov. 1935.
61. Seán Ó Faoláin, 'The dangers of censorship', *Ireland To-Day*, Vol.I, No.6, Nov. 1936, pp.57–63.
62. Susannah Riordan, 'The unpopular front: Catholic revival and Irish cultural identity, 1936–48', in Mike Cronin and John M. Regan (eds), *Ireland: the politics of independence, 1922–49* (London: Macmillan, 2000), p.107.
63. *Irish Times*, 6 Feb. 1935.
64. See, for example, *Irish Churchman*, 10 April 1930; *Irish Times*, 21 Oct. 1938.
65. Complaint by Hamilton Stuart Gould-Verschayle, 1 Dec. 1931, NAI, DJUS, H315/90.
66. Anne Fremantle, *The papal encyclicals in their historical context* (New York: New American Library, 1963), pp.235–9.
67. Dermot Keogh, *The Vatican, the bishops and Irish politics* (Cambridge: Cambridge University Press, 1986), p.269fn.
68. *Catholic Truth Quarterly*, Vol.1, No.5 (July–Sept. 1938), p.6.
69. *Up and Doing*, Vol.1, No.12, (Jan.–March 1937), p.16.
70. *Irish Times*, 29 Oct. 1936.
71. Stephen J. Brown, 'The Catholic novelist and his themes', *Irish Monthly*, Vol. LXIII, No.745 (June 1935), pp.436–8; Riordan, 'The unpopular front', p.109; Cornelius Lucey, 'The freedom of the press', *Irish Ecclesiastical Record*, 5th Series, Vol.50, July–Dec. 1937, pp.584.

72. Stephen J. Brown SJ, 'Concerning censorship', *Irish Monthly*, Vol.LXIV, No.751 (Jan. 1936), pp.26–35.
73. James Devane, 'Nationality and culture', *Ireland To-Day*, Vol.I, No.7 (Dec. 1936), pp.10–13; Aodh de Blacam, 'Catholic action and criticism', *Irish Monthly*, Vol.LXV, No.780 (Aug. 1937), pp.556–9; Patrick J. Gannon SJ, 'Literature and censorship', *Irish Monthly*, Vol.LXVII, No.793 (July 1939), pp.434–7.
74. Frank O'Reilly, Complaints to CPB, 8 April 1931, NAI, DJUS, H315/71, 11 Feb. 1932, H315/107, 15 Jan. 1932, H315/101, 6 May 1931, H315/66, 7 March 1931, H315/57, 9 Dec. 1931, H315/93.
75. Ibid., 11 Aug. 1933, H315/149.
76. *Up and Doing*, Vol.1, No.1 (May1935), p.21.
77. *Up and Doing*, Vol.1, No.1 (June 1935), p.15.
78. O'Reilly complaint to CPB, 19 Dec. 1933, NAI, DJUS, H315/98.
79. *Irish Times*, 29 June 1936.
80. Adams, *Censorship: the Irish experience*, p.77–9.
81. *Irish Catholic Directory*, 1931, pp.642–3.
82. Minutes of Dublin Municipal Council, 5 Jan. 1931, 7 March 1932; 'Reasons why the Government should enact measures of protection against the imported press', n. d. [1933], NAI, DJUS, H315/131.
83. Report of the Fianna Fáil ard fheis, 1932, UCDA, Fianna Fáil Party Archives FFA, P176/746; Duff to Private Secretary to the President, 7 Dec. 1932, NAI, DJUS, H315/131.
84. Report of the Fianna Fáil ard fheis,1933, UCDA, FFA, P176/747; Duff, minute of meeting, 1 May 1933, NAI, DJUS, H315/131.
85. 'Reasons why the Government should enact measures of protection against the imported press', op. cit.
86. De Brún to Secretary to the President, 2 May 1933; Devane to de Valera, 9 March 1934, NAI, DJUS, H315/131; John Horgan, *Irish media: a critical history since 1922* (London: Routledge, 2001), p. 35.
87. Noel Ward, 'The INTO and the Roman Catholic Church, 1930–1955', (MA thesis, University College Dublin, 1987), p.87.
88. NAI, DJUS, H315/6. The complainants were Kilkenny, Youghal and Tullamore UDCs, Tipperary South Riding County Council and the Kilkenny County Library Committee.
89. *Irish Independent*, 2 April 1935, IJA, Cahill Papers, J55/39.
90. *Irish Times*, 6 June 1938.
91. *CYMS Quarterly*, Christmas 1938, Vol.1, No.1, pp.10, 40, 43–9.
92. Donal Cronin, 'The problem of book selection in Irish libraries', *An Leabharlann*, Vol.3, No.4, Dec. 1932, pp.118–23.
93. James Barry, 'The place of fiction in the public library', *An Leabharlann*, Vol.4, No.2, Nov. 1934, pp.90–4.
94. Samuel J. Maguire, 'Censorship in Irish county libraries', *An Leabharlann*, Vol.3, No.4, Dec. 1933, pp.125–8.
95. Report of Monaghan Co. Library, *An Leabharlann*, Vol.1, No.1, June 1930, p.26.
96. Eugene Carbery, 'The state and public libraries in the Irish Free State', *An Leabharlann*, Vol.5, No.2, Dec. 1935, p.60.
97. Editorial, *An Leabharlann*, Vol.1, No.4, March–May 1931, p.85.
98. Meath County Library Report, *An Leabharlann*, Vol.2, No.2, March 1932, p.53.
99. Roscommon County Library Report, *An Leabharlann*, Vol.2, No.1, Oct. 1931, pp.17–18.
100. M.K. MacNevin, 'Impressions of the Cork Conference', An *Leabharlann*, Vol.3, No.3, Sept. 1933, p.69.
101. *Derry People*, 3 March 1934, 12 Nov. 1938.
102. *Ulster Gazette*, 5 Jan. 1935.
103. *Fermanagh Times*, 2 Aug. 1934, 28 July 1932, 20 Dec. 1934.
104. *Ulster Gazette*, 8 April 1938, 6 Jan. 1934.
105. *Derry People*, 8 March 1930.
106. NIHC debates, Vol.XII, 29 May 1930, 1630, 2192–93.
107. *Derry People*, 8 March 1930.
108. NIHC debates , Vol.XVII, 4 Dec. 1934, 338.
109. *Irish Press*, 19 Oct. 1931.
110. *Ulster Gazette*, 16 June 1934.

111. *Derry People*, 10 March 1934.
112. NIHC debates, Vol.XVII, 22 Oct. 1935, 2669.
113. *Fermanagh Times*, 8 May 1930; *Ulster Gazette*, 1 July 1933, 9 March 1935, 2 July 1932.
114. Alan Travis, *Bound and gagged: a secret history of obscenity in Britain* (London: Profile, 2000), p.118; 'Titles of Periodicals recently condemned by courts in the United Kingdom; Home Office circular letter 678,544/9, 8 April 1938, NAGB, Customs Department CUST 49/2334.
115. H.C. Montgomery to Secretary to the NI Cabinet, 12 Oct. 1938; Assistant Secretary NIMHA to Secretary to the NI Cabinet, 15 Nov. 1938, PRONI, CAB/9B/102/1.
116. 'Instructions for Constabulary Patrols employed on Customs work', [1923], NAGB, HO267/49.
117. Dawson Bates, memorandum for Cabinet, [Nov. 1933]; Cabinet conclusions, 6 Nov. 1933, 6 June 1934, PRONI, CAB/9B/222/1.
118. Dawson Bates to Anderson, 10 Jan. 1931; Anderson, note, NAGB, HO45/24839.
119. Ernly Blackwell to Dawson Bates, 14 Jan. 1931, PRONI, HA8/320.
120. George Harris to Blackwell, 16 Jan. 1931, NAGB, HO45/24859; W.A. Magill to Chief Crown Solicitor, 6 May 1936, PRONI, HA8/320; Harris to Blackwell, 28 Jan. 1931; *Sunday News*, 5 April 1931, NAGB, H045/24839.
121. A.B. Babington to Sir John Gilmour, 3 Nov. 1933; Inskip to Gilmour, 13 Nov. 1933; F.A. N., Minute, 18 Nov. 1933; Gilmour to Babington, 22 Nov. 1933, NAGB HO/4524839.
122. W.B. Lockhart and R.C. McClure, 'Why Obscene?', in John Chandos (ed.), *'To deprave and corrupt': original studies in the nature and definition of 'obscenity'* (London: Souvenir Press, 1962), p.55.

Conclusion

How seriously did the two Irelands take freedom of expression? At one level their record was a positive one: the press was relatively free and governments were criticized in print, in parliament and in public. Both states allowed opposition parties to stand for election and to take their seats, unlike many European states. Beyond this minimalist protection, however, the commitment of the two states to freedom of expression was grudging and limited.

Censorship and security

In both regions, the right of the state to security was considered much greater than that of its inhabitants to express ideas freely. Despite this, both governments were careful in the kinds of restrictions that they placed on political speech. The emergency legislation used for this kind of censorship had a common parentage in the Defence of the Realm Acts and the Restoration of Order in Ireland Act. Concepts such as special military tribunals, an all-powerful civil authority and proscribed organizations were familiar to Irish emergency law.

There were differences between the approaches of the northern and southern governments to sedition. Northern Ireland had, in the CASPA, a simple, powerful weapon to control seditious publications and the police had broad powers of search and seizure. The fact that the act became part of the state's law indefinitely showed that it was effective. The government's refusal to consider a prior censorship of the press showed both a commitment to following British conventions and the fact that it was too closely allied with the Unionist press to require a censor and too alienated from the nationalist press to be able to expect their co-operation.

The northern government was prepared to punish publications and organizations for any attempt to undermine the state but was in fact quite restrained when purely political issues were at stake. It was usually possible to criticize the government's policy and performance. Measures were taken when a publication was seen as threatening to public order or the existence of the state. The problem was that there was a large grey area between these two extremes: nationalist publications were, by definition, dedicated to the eventual ending of the northern state. The extent to which they could pursue this policy without incurring the wrath of the government was hard to judge at any time. The result was the prosecution or proscription of publications like the *Irish News* or the *Irish Catholic* for attacking the police or the courts in too robust a manner.

In the south, the fact that there were many more acts, each containing different provisions on the question of sedition showed a greater ambivalence about the issue. The prior censorship of the Civil War was designed to combat Republican propaganda and to control foreign coverage of the conflict. To this extent it showed the influence of British policy in the period 1914–21. The short life of this censorship also showed that the government understood its limitations. It should be seen as much as a part of the pro-Treaty propaganda campaign as an attempt to control the media.

Later southern security legislation would have less influence on the normal press and would instead concentrate on the publications of illegal organizations. Compared to the CASPA, the Treason Act, 1925 and Article 2A of the Free State constitution were clumsy instruments for censorship. The government did not have sufficient authority to ban publications as it wished and, as the attempts to control *An Phoblacht* showed, the southern government was not as decisive in this regard as its northern counterpart. When it did attempt to use security legislation to silence its critics, such as during the prosecution of the *Irish Press*, the government looked partisan and achieved only Pyrrhic victories.

The two regimes' responses to controversial assemblies had much in common. The issue was more pressing in Northern Ireland where the competing demands of nationalists and loyalists to express their opinions through public gatherings drew an inconsistent response from the government. The policy which evolved placed more emphasis on the political objective of an assembly than on its likely outcome and led to nationalists feeling that they were the victims of bias. At the same time the government was careful to distinguish between political assemblies, with speeches, marches and flags, and commemorations and religious occasions which were permitted as long as their political components were muted.

Southern Irish policy on assemblies was less clear cut. Rather than consistently prohibiting gatherings associated with subversive organizations, the state acted when there was an atmosphere of crisis or when it feared public disorder. In part this must be ascribed to the fact that the ideologies of the two sides in southern Ireland were much closer than those in the north. Republicans and Free-Staters were both competing for the same symbolic inheritance and so it was harder to be sure what should be considered a legitimate assembly. In Northern Ireland nationalist gatherings were presumed to be illegitimate unless the government could be certain that they would be peaceful. The Blueshirts offered the Irish Free State a similarly clear-cut division of ideologies and it responded in a manner which would have been very familiar to Dawson Bates.

In regard to minority political beliefs, such as socialism, neither state showed much interest in pluralism. Both sought to suppress organizations, publications and assemblies which challenged the legitimacy of the state, and even small communist parties were included in this category. The result was that left-wing organizations in both regions faced censorship by the state and were left undefended by it when opposed by private groups. The Unionist minority in the south was also treated with scant sympathy by the state when it was attacked by republicans. While the state did not prohibit loyalist marches or films of royal events, it offered little support when republican groups attempted to suppress these expressions of Unionism. The activities of private organizations like the CTSI, the IRA, the Churches and the loyal institutions showed that the governments saw the right to freedom of expression as being about freedom from government interference rather than obliging the government to help the citizen to express themselves. In other words it was a negative rather than a positive right.

Overall, both governments allowed free criticism of their policies and actions; opposition parties were not prevented from speaking at election time, newspapers hostile to the government were usually permitted. This freedom was conditional on the parties or newspapers doing nothing to attack the legitimacy of the state or its institutions. When nationalists in Northern Ireland tried to call for the integration of the region into southern Ireland, they did face censorship. Likewise when it appeared that the Blueshirts, republicans, or socialists were a threat to the survival of the Irish Free State, they were also suppressed.

Censorship on moral grounds

The differences between the practice of censorship in Northern Ireland and the south said less about the moral climate in the two regions than about the power and priorities of religious groups. There were specific differences in the moral teachings of the major Churches. These were clearest in regard to contraception: the Roman Catholic Church believed in the suppression of all discussion of the issue, whereas the Protestant Churches, and the Church of Ireland in particular, wanted it to be open to debate. The Churches agreed about the issue of obscenity, however. They combined in both regions to call for state censorship of films; in 1923 in the Irish Free State and in Armagh in Northern Ireland in the 1930s. There were many people in every Church who were disturbed by the popular press, modern novels and films. The difference between Northern Ireland and the Irish Free State was in the power of religious bodies.

Censorship offers a case study in the power of Roman Catholicism in the Irish Free State. The campaigns for the censorship of films and publications began with a group of Roman Catholic activists,men like Richard Devane SJ, Fr M.H. MacInerny, Brother Craven and Frank O'Reilly. It was heavily influenced by papal teaching on Catholic Action, cinema and public morality. Where these groups could acquire Protestant allies, as in the case of the censorship of films, they did so. When, as in the case of the censorship of publications, they found Protestant opinion divided, they pressed on regardless.

The state was not always enthusiastic about these campaigns. Although the government was eager to establish a film censorship, it was less happy about a censorship of publications. It agreed to do so only after several years of campaigning, pressure for action on the issue by the Roman Catholic bishops and the report of the Committee on Evil Literature. This was not a case of the state taking orders from the hierarchy. Indeed, little activity on the issue was initiated by bishops. Instead the censorships of films and publications were the results of well organized, well run campaigns by priests and members of the laity.

In Northern Ireland, the Churches were quite capable of involving themselves in politics. The issues of education and temperance united Protestant denominations and the loyal institutions around causes that were no less complicated or radical than that of censorship. Nor was there anything inherent in Protestantism as a religious belief that prevented its followers from advocating censorship: the main campaigners for censorship in America and Britain in the nineteenth and early twentieth century had been Protestant. Irish Protestants did condemn immoral publications but they were reluctant to call for a state censorship. Synods and meetings did hear about the problem of obscenity but they usually called for the reform of society rather than of the law. The loyal institutions remained unmoved by the issue and the absence of their voices from the calls for censorship must have been significant. The Roman Catholic Church in Northern Ireland was never in a position to campaign for censorship. Its refusal to engage with the government or institutions like the BBC for many years, even on issues like education, meant that it had little influence. Nor was it likely that a Unionist government could have done as the Church asked even had it agreed with it: to do so would have risked accusations of 'Rome Rule'.

While the southern government was reluctant to censor publications, the government of Northern Ireland was opposed to any censorship of immoral works. For the south, censorship was part of a series of measures which allowed the state to distinguish itself from Britain. The northern government had the opposite objective. In the cases of film censorship and the treatment of reports about the Irish Hospitals' Sweepstake, the government considered more radical policies but did not follow them because of a desire to keep its practice in step with that of Britain.

In the areas of broadcasting and theatre, neither government took special action to control moral content because there was no need to do so. Although theatre in southern Ireland was controversial, it was seen by the state as an elite pursuit which was unlikely to affect public morality. This did not prevent private groups in both regions from taking action when they disliked what was on stage. This action could be a spontaneous demand from an audience for changes in a play or a script or more persistent pressure of the sort which caused theatres like the Gaiety to make a feature of their codes of morality.

Broadcasting was always heavily controlled at source by the BBC and 2RN themselves. The results were schedules lacking in excitement and heavily emphasizing music. It is interesting that such self-regulation was more acceptable to moral campaigners than that of the film industry. The difference was that the radio stations were more conservative and more closely linked to the state; indeed, 2RN was an arm of the government. The work put into choosing plays, talks and even music ensured that actual censorship was almost never necessary. Instead an ethos emerged at each station whereby the avoidance of controversy was instinctive. Despite this, issues like the playing of 'jazz' or of national anthems could still cause controversy.

Censorship and self-determination

Ireland was an importer of culture: almost all the films shown were British or American, most books were published in Britain and many British newspapers and magazines were on sale. This was true of both Northern Ireland and the south. Both faced the problem of being peripheral cultures facing the encroachment of the global power of British and American culture. The northern government chose the path of assimilation with Britain despite complaints from both its supporters and the nationalist opposition. British and American cultural power presented a significant challenge to nationalist ideas of cultural revival and self-sufficiency. The Irish Free State was not unique in this regard. Fear of American film imports led to the British quota system and Australian censors complained of the morals they saw in imported film. The importance of censorship as an expression of self-determination must be remembered. This explains many of the excesses of the censors in the south. Had the film censor or the Censorship of Publications Board followed international example, there would have been no point in appointing them.

The urge to set unique standards for the south led to one of the most extensive censorships of films and publications of any liberal democratic state in this period. Despite this, censorship was often characterized as ineffective. It is hard to judge the success of southern Irish censorship unless its objectives are considered. By these standards, film censorship was effective. It strictly controlled portrayals of sex, nudity, crime and religious imagery. Although it was often accused of being too strict, opposition to it was not widespread. By contrast, the results of the censorship of publications were not what its advocates of the 1920s had envisaged. Whereas they had emphasized the danger of British popular newspapers, birth control literature and the commercial power of the British press combines, most of the publications banned were novels. This was partly due to the drafting of the act which made it difficult to ban periodicals. The failure of the campaigners for censorship to submit complaints was also a factor. The exception to this was the CTSI which was one of the most important influences on the whole issue of censorship in this period.

Freedom of expression in the two Irelands

Citizens of Northern Ireland and the Irish Free State, or Éire, enjoyed more freedom of speech than their counterparts in many countries in Europe in the 1930s. The years 1913–1923 had seen a huge amount of violence, sectarian conflict and rhetorical attacks on the authority of the state. This made the control of sedition a priority for the new governments. They were also confronted with a general sense that those years had brought about moral chaos. The southern government introduced censorship both to silence campaigners for moral retrenchment and to establish the distinctive cultural values of the new state. Northern Ireland faced a far weaker campaign for censorship: the energies of moral reformers were directed towards temperance campaigns and education reform instead. They kept closely to British policy on obscenity and film censorship thus avoiding having to deal with such difficult issues and breaking culturally with the UK. Both Irelands used censorship to reinforce their national identities as a part, or opposite, of Britain. The price of this policy was considerable: the stifling of political dissent in the north and the cheapening of cultural debate in the south.

Bibliography

MANUSCRIPT SOURCES

Republic of Ireland
Dublin
Dublin City Council Archives
Dublin Municipal Council minutes and reports

Dublin Diocesan Archives
Archbishop Byrne Papers

Irish Jesuit Archives
Edward Cahill papers (J55)
Richard Devane papers (J44)

Irish Labour History Society Museum and Archives
Cathal O'Shannon papers (COS)

National Archives of Ireland
Cabinet minutes
Committee on Evil Literature (JUS 7)
Dáil Éireann files (DE2, DE4)
Department of Finance (Supply files)
Department of Foreign Affairs
Department of Justice (H files: H5, H69, H75, H84, H215, H231, H235, H236, H266, H277, H280, H290, Security: JUS8)
Department of the Taoiseach (S files: S2010, S2321, S3026, S3919, S3530, S3532, S3669, S7480)
Department of Tourism, Transport and Communications (D7888, F3341)
Record of films censored (FCO2)
Film censor's register of films rejected (FCO4)
Film censor's reserve books (FCO3)

National Library of Ireland
Piaras Béaslaí papers (Mss. 33911–87)

Frank Gallagher papers (Ms. 18341, Ms. 18353, Ms. 18361, Ms. 18365)
W.B. Yeats papers (Ms. 30159, Ms. 30229, Ms. 31020, Ms. 31067)

Trinity College Dublin, Manuscripts Library
Frank Gallagher papers
Denis Johnston papers
Oliver St John Gogarty papers

University College Dublin, Archives Department
Ernest Blythe papers (P24)
Eamon de Valera papers (P150)
Fianna Fáil Party Archives (P176)
Desmond FitzGerald papers (P80)
Richard Mulcahy papers (P7)
Michael Tierney papers (LA30)

Northern Ireland

Armagh
Tomás Ó Fiach Library and Archive, Armagh
Michael Logue papers
Joseph MacRory papers
Patrick O'Donnell papers

Belfast
Public Record Office of Northern Ireland
Antrim County Council files (LA/1)
Armagh County Council records (LA/2)
Armagh Urban District Council records (LA/10)
Bangor Borough Council (LA/20)
Belfast Corporation, minutes (LA/7/10)
Belfast Corporation Police Committee minutes (LA/7/10AB)
Belfast Library, Museum and Arts Committee minutes (LA7/14/AA)
Eason & Son Northern Ireland papers (D3981)
Fermanagh County Council records (LA/4)
Larne Urban District Council files (LA/43)
Lurgan Urban District Council (LA/51)
Midland Cinema, Belfast, records 1920–30 (D3413)
Newcastle Urban District Council minute books
Newry Urban District Council minute books
Northern Ireland Cabinet files (CAB/4, CAB/8G, CAB/9B)
Northern Ireland Ministry of Home Affairs files (HA/5, HA/8, HA/32, HA/41)
Northern Ireland Prime Minister's Office files (PM/2, PM/4, PM/7)
Omagh Urban District Council minute books

Tyrone County Council records (LA/6)

Great Britain

London
National Archives, Kew
Cabinet Office (CAB/49)
Colonial Office (CO904)
Customs Department (CUST/2134, CUST/1638, CUST/630)
Home Office (HO45, HO144, HO267)
Ministry of Defence (DEFE files)

Reading
British Broadcasting Corporation Written Archives Centre
BBC Archives

Australia

Canberra
National Archives of Australia (via online digitization programme)
Film censorship files (A318/1/1, 1943/2570, 1943/1790, CP4614,
   1935/2117)
Literary censorship files (N318/1/1)

OFFICIAL PUBLICATIONS

Dublin
Dáil debates
Seanad debates
Dáil Éireann, *First, second and third interim reports and the final report
   of the special committee to consider the Wireless Broadcasting Report
   together with proceedings of the committees, minutes of evidence and
   appendices* (1924)
Iris Oifigiúil
Irish Statute Book on CD-ROM (Dublin, 1999)
Report of the Committee on Evil Literature (Dublin, 1926)
Horgan, Michael and Patrick Carroll, *The Garda Síochána guide* (Dublin,
   1934)
Register of Prohibited Publications (Dublin, 1940)

Belfast
Belfast Gazette
Parliamentary debates: Northern Ireland House of Commons and Senate

NEWSPAPERS AND PERIODICALS

Belfast Newsletter
Belfast Telegraph
Catholic Bulletin
Catholic Truth Quarterly (1937–40)
Church of Ireland Gazette
Cork Examiner
Cork Weekly Examiner
CYMS Quarterly Review (1938–39)
Derry People
Down Recorder
Evening Herald
Fermanagh Times
Gaelic Churchman
Galway Observer
Ireland To-day
Irish Catholic
Irish Churchman
Irish Independent
Irish News
Irish Press
Irish Radio and Musical Review
Irish Radio Journal
Irish Radio News
Irish Rosary
Irish Statesman
Irish Times
Journal of Proceedings of the General Synod of the Church of Ireland
Kilkenny People
An Leabharlann
Limerick & Clare Advocate
Munster News
Northern Whig
Sacred Heart Messenger
Times Literary Supplement
Tyrone Constitution
Ulster Gazette
Up and Doing
Witness

BOOKS AND ARTICLES

'A German law against immoral publications', *Irish Monthly*, Vol.LV, No.648 (June 1927), pp.331–3

Adams, Michael, *Censorship: the Irish experience* (Dublin: Scepter, 1968)

Adams, Michael, 'Censorship of publications', in Desmond M. Clarke (ed.) *Morality and the law* (Dublin: Mercier Press, 1982), pp.71–9

[Æ (George Russell)], 'The censorship bill', *Irish Statesman*, Vol.10, No.25 (25 Aug.1928), pp.486–7

Allen, Nicholas, *George Russell (Æ) and the new Ireland, 1905–30* (Dublin: Four Courts Press, 2003)

Alomes, Stephen, *A nation at last? The changing character of Australian nationalism, 1880–1988* (North Ryde, NSW: Angus & Robertson, 1988)

Atkinson, Sir Edward Tindal, *Obscene literature in law and practice* (London: Christophers, 1937)

Attwater, Donald, 'Books and the child', *Irish Monthly*, Vol.LV, No.647 (May 1927), pp.270–7

Barry, Rev. David, 'The ethics of journalism', in *Irish Ecclesiastical Review*, 5th series, Vol.XIX (Jan.–June 1922), pp.514–26

Barry, Denis, 'The month in retrospect', *Ireland To-day*, Vol.2, No.2 (Feb. 1937), p.84

Barry, James, 'The place of fiction in the public library', *An Leabharlann*, Vol.4, No.2 (Nov. 1934), pp.87–93

Beere, T.J., 'Cinema Statistics in Saorstát Éireann', *Journal of the Statistical and Social Inquiry Society of Ireland* (1936–37), pp.83–110

Bell, Sam Hanna, *The theatre in Ulster* (Dublin: Gill & Macmillan, 1972)

Ben-Ami, Shlomo, *Fascism from above: the dictatorship of Primo de Rivera in Spain, 1923–1930* (Oxford: Oxford University Press, 1983)

Bertrand, Ira, *Film censorship in Australia* (Queensland: University of Queensland Press, 1978)

Bessel, Richard, *Germany after the First World War* (Oxford: Clarendon Press, 1993)

'Bibliophile', 'Modern fiction', *Irish Monthly*, Vol.LII, No.617 (Nov. 1924), pp.610–12

Black, Gregory, *Hollywood censored: morality codes, Catholics and the movies* (Cambridge: Cambridge University Press, 1994)

Black, Gregory, *The Catholic crusade against the movies, 1940–1975* (Cambridge: Cambridge University Press, 1997)

Blanshard, Paul, *The Irish and Catholic power: an American interpretation* (London: Verschoyle, 1954)

Bolster, Evelyn, *The Knights of Saint Columbanus* (Dublin: Gill & Macmillan, 1979)

Bonner, David, *Emergency powers in peacetime* (London: Sweet & Maxwell, 1985)

Bowen, Desmond, *History and the shaping of Irish Protestantism* (New York: Peter Lang Publishing, 1995)

Boyer, Paul S., *Purity in print: book censorship in America from the gilded age to the computer age* (Wisconsin: University of Wisconsin Press, 2002)

Boyer, Paul S., 'Boston book censorship in the twenties', *American Quarterly*, Vol. 15, No.1 (Spring 1963), pp.3–24

Broche, Peter, *Ulster Presbyterianism: the historical perspective, 1610–1970* (Dublin: Gill & Macmillan, 1987)

Brodie, Malcolm, *The Tele: a history of the Belfast Telegraph* (Belfast: Blackstaff Press, 1995)

Brown, Alec, 'The good censor', *Dublin Magazine*, 4 (April–June 1929), pp.21–30

Brown, Alec, 'Some observations on the decay of literature', *Dublin Magazine*, 7 (Oct.–Dec. 1932), pp.12–20

Brown, Stephen J., 'On book selection', *An Leabharlann*, Vol.1, No.1 (June 1930), pp.5–8, and Vol.1, No.2 (Sept. 1930), pp.33–7

Brown, Stephen J., 'The Catholic novelist and his themes', *Irish Monthly*, Vol.LXIII, No.745 (June 1935), pp.433–44

Brown, Stephen J.,'Concerning censorship', *Irish Monthly*, Vol.LXIV, No.751 (Jan. 1936), pp.25–35

Brown, Terence, *Ireland: a social and cultural history, 1922–1985* (London: Fontana Press, 1985)

Bryan, Dominic, *Orange parades: the politics of ritual tradition and control* (London: Pluto Press, 2000)

Bryson, Mary E., 'Dublin letters: John Eglinton and *The Dial*, 1921–1929', *Éire-Ireland*, Vol.29, No.4 (Winter 1994), pp.132–48

Buckland, Patrick, *The factory of grievances: devolved government in Northern Ireland, 1921–39* (Dublin: Gill & Macmillan, 1979)

Burns-Bisogno, Louise, *Censoring Irish nationalism: the British, Irish and American suppression of republican images in film and television, 1909–95* (North Carolina: McFarland & Co., 1997)

Cahill, E., SJ, 'Notes on Christian sociology – liberalism (continued)', *Irish Monthly*, Vol.LV, No.647 (May 1927), pp.265–9

Campbell, Colm, *Emergency law in Ireland, 1918–1925* (Oxford: Clarendon Press, 1994)

Campbell, James J., 'Catholics and the press', *Irish Monthly*, Vol.LXIV, No.761 (Nov. 1936), pp.715–21

Carbery, Eugene, 'The state and public libraries in the Irish Free State', *An Leabharlann*, Vol.5, No.2 (Dec. 1935), pp.58–64

Carlson, Julia, *Banned in Ireland* (London: Routledge, 1990)

Cathcart, Rex, *The most contrary region: the BBC in Northern Ireland, 1924–1984* (Belfast: Blackstaff Press, 1984)

Chandos, John, (ed.), *'To deprave and corrupt': original studies in the nature and definition of obscenity* (London: Souvenir Press, 1962)

Clarke, Desmond M., (ed.), *Morality and the law* (Dublin: Mercier Press, 1982)

Clarke, Paddy, *'Dublin calling': 2RN and the birth of Irish radio* (Dublin: RTE, 1986)

Clery, Arthur E., 'Truth adulteration', *Studies*, XIII (Dec. 1924), pp.590–6

Clyde, Tom, *Irish Literary Magazines, an outline history and descriptive bibliography* (Dublin: Irish Academic Press, 2003)

Coleman, Peter, *Obscenity, blasphemy, sedition – the rise and fall of literary censorship in Australia* (Potts Point NSW: Pan Macmillan, 2000)

Cooney, John, *John Charles McQuaid: ruler of Catholic Ireland* (Dublin: O'Brien Press, 1999)

Corish, P.J., 'The first fifty years', in *The Catholic Truth Society of Ireland: the first fifty years* (Dublin: CTSI, 1950)

Couvares, Francis G., 'Introduction: Hollywood, censorship and American culture', *American Quarterly*, Vol.44, No.4 (Dec. 1992), pp.509–24

Couvares, Francis G., 'Hollywood, Main Street and the Church: trying to censor the movies before the Production Code', *American Quarterly*, Vol.44, No.4 (Dec. 1992), pp.584–616

Crisp, Colin, *The classic French cinema, 1930–1960* (Indiana: Indiana University Press, 1993)

Cronin, Donal J., 'The problem of book selection in Irish libraries', *An Leabharlann*, Vol.3, No.4 (Dec. 1932), pp.118–24

Cronin, Mike and Regan, John M., (eds), *Ireland: the politics of independence, 1922–49* (London: Macmillan, 2000)

Cullen, L. M., *Eason & Son: a history* (Dublin: Eason & Son Ltd., 1989)

Czitrom, Daniel, 'The politics of performance: from theatre licensing to movie censorship in turn-of-the-century New York', *American Quarterly*, Vol.44, No.4 (Dec. 1992), pp.525–53

De Blacam, Aodh, 'What do we owe the Abbey', *Irish Monthly*, Vol.LXIII, No.741 (March 1935), pp.191–200

De Blacam, Aodh, 'Catholic action and criticism', *Irish Monthly*, Vol.LXV, No.780 (Aug. 1937), pp. 556–67

De Grazia, Edward, *Girls lean back everywhere: the law of obscenity and the assault on genius* (London: Constable, 1992)

Dean, Joan FitzPatrick, *Riot and great anger: stage censorship in twentieth-century Ireland* (Wisconsin: University of Wisconsin Press, 2004)

Devane, James, 'Nationality and culture', *Ireland To-Day*, Vol.1, No.7 (Dec. 1936), pp.9–17

Devane, R.S., 'Indecent literature – some legal remedies', *Irish Ecclesiastical Record*, 5th series, Vol.XXV (Jan.–June 1925), pp.182–204

Devane, R.S., 'The Committee on Printed Matter – some notes of evidence', *Irish Ecclesiastical Record*, 5th Series, Vol.XXVII (July–Dec. 1926), pp.357–77 and 449–66

Devane, R.S., 'Suggested tariff on imported newspapers and magazines', *Studies*, XVI (Dec. 1927), pp.545–54; 'Comments on the foregoing article' by Rev. M. H. MacInerny (pp.554–6), Michael Tierney (pp.556–8), P.J. Hooper (pp.558–60) and Thomas F. O'Rahilly (pp. 561–3)

Devane, R.S.,'The menace of the British combines', *Studies*, XIX (Mar. 1930), pp.55–69

Donohue, Laura K., *Counter-terrorist law and emergency powers in the United Kingdom, 1922–2000* (Dublin: Irish Academic Press, 2001)

Donohue, Laura K., 'Regulating Northern Ireland: the Special Powers Acts, 1922–72', *Historical Journal*, Vol.41, No.4 (Dec. 1998), pp.1089–120

Dowling, John, 'The Abbey attacked – I', *Ireland Today*, Vol.2, No.1 (Jan. 1937), pp.35–42

Dowling, John,'The National Gallery again', *Ireland Today*, Vol.2, No.1 (Jan. 1937), pp.62–4

Dowling, John, 'Bigger and better censors', *Ireland Today*, Vol.3, No.3 (Mar. 1938), pp.221–5

Elliott, Marianne, *The Catholics of Ulster* (London: Allen Lane, the Penguin Press, 2000)

Fallon, Brian, *An age of innocence: Irish culture, 1930–1960* (Dublin: Gill & Macmillan, 1998)

Farrell, Brian, (ed.), *De Valera's constitution and ours* (Dublin: Gill & Macmillan, 1988)

Farrell, Brian, (ed.), *Communications and community in Ireland* (Cork: Mercier Press, 1984)

Faughnan, Seán, 'The Jesuits and the drafting of the Irish constitution of 1937', *Irish Historical Studies*, Vol.XXVI, No.101 (May 1988), pp.79–102

Finneran, Richard J., George Mills Harper and William M. Murphy, (eds.), *Letters to W.B. Yeats, Vol.2* (London: Macmillan, 1977)

Fitzpatrick, David, 'Divorce and Separation in modern Irish history', *Past and Present*, 114 (Feb. 1987), pp.172–96

Fitzpatrick, David, *The two Irelands, 1912–1939* (Oxford: Oxford University Press, 1998)

Follis, Bryan A., *A state under siege: the establishment of Northern Ireland, 1920–25* (Oxford: Clarendon Press, 1995)

Frazier, Adrian, *George Moore, 1852–1933* (London: Yale University Press, 2000)

Fremantle, Anne, *The papal encyclicals in their historical context* (New York: New American Library, 1963)

French, Thomas M., 'Is personal freedom a western value?', *American Journal of International Law*, Vol.91, No.4 (Oct. 1997), pp.593–627

Gannon, Patrick J., 'Literature and censorship', *Irish Monthly*, Vol.LXVII, No.793 (July 1939), pp.434–47

Gannon, Patrick J., 'Art, morality and censorship', *Studies*, XXXI (Dec. 1942), pp.409–19

Glandon, Virginia, *Arthur Griffith and the advanced nationalist press in Ireland, 1900–1922* (New York: P Lang, 1985)

Gorham, Maurice, *Forty years of Irish broadcasting* (Dublin: Talbot Press, 1967)

Graham, Mark, *British censorship of civil mails in World War I, 1914–19* (Bristol: Stuart Rossiter Trust Fund, 2000)

Gwynn, Denis, 'The modern newspaper', *Studies*, XV (Sept. 1926), pp.368–80

Haight, Anne Lyon, *Banned books* (London: George Allen & Unwin, 1955)

Hanley, Brian, *The IRA, 1926–1936* (Dublin: Four Courts Press, 2002)

Harkness, David, *Northern Ireland since 1920* (Dublin: Helicon, 1983)

Harmon, Maurice, *Seán Ó Faoláin: a critical introduction* (London: Notre Dame Press, 1966)

Harrison, Nicholas, *Circles of censorship: censorship and its metaphors in French history, literature and theory* (Oxford: Clarendon Press, 1995)

Haste, Cate, *Keep the home fires burning : propaganda in the First World War* (London: Allen Lane, 1977)

Hébert, Pierre, *Censure et littérature au Québec: le livre crucifié (1625–1919)* (Saint-Laurent, Quebec: Fides, 1997)

Hegarty, Peter, *Peadar O'Donnell* (Dublin: Mercier Press, 1999)

Hill, John, '"Purely Sinn Féin propaganda": the banning of *Ourselves Alone* (1936)', *Historical Journal of Film, Radio & Television*, Vol.20, No.3 (2000), pp.317–33

Holguín, Sandie, 'Taming the seventh art: the battle for cultural unity on the cinematographic front during Spain's second republic, 1931–1936', *Journal of Modern History*, Vol.71, No.4 (Dec. 1999), pp.852–81

Holroyd, Michael, *Bernard Shaw, Vol. III: 1918–1950 – the lure of fantasy* (London: Chatto & Windus, 1991)

Hopkinson, Michael, *Green against green: the Irish Civil War* (Dublin: Gill & Macmillan, 1988)

Hopkinson, Michael, (ed.), *The last days of Dublin Castle: the Mark Sturgis diaries* (Dublin: Irish Academic Press, 1999)

Horgan, John, *Irish media: a critical history since 1922* (London: Routledge, 2001)

Horgan, John, 'Saving us from ourselves: contraception, censorship and the evil literature controversy of 1926', *Irish Communications Review*, Vol.5 (1995), pp.61–7

Ingram, P.J., *Censorship and free speech: some philosophical beginnings* (Aldershot: Ashgate Dartmouth Ltd, 2000)

Jacobs, Lea, *The wages of sin: censorship and the fallen woman film, 1928–1942* (California: University of California Press, 1995)

Jeffery, Keith, *Ireland and the great war* (Cambridge: Cambridge University Press, 2000)

Jones, Greta, 'Marie Stopes in Ireland – the Mothers Clinic in Belfast 1936–49', *Social History of Medicine*, Vol.5, No.2 (1992), pp.255–77

Jones, Greta, 'The Rockefeller Foundation and medical education in Ireland in the 1920s', *Irish Historical Studies*, Vol.XXX, No.120 (Nov. 1997), pp.564–80

Kelly, A. A., (ed.), *The letters of Liam O'Flaherty* (Dublin: Wolfhound, 1996)

Kelly, James and Dáire Keogh, (eds), *History of the Catholic diocese of Dublin* (Dublin: Four Courts, 2000)

Kelly, John M., *Fundamental rights in the Irish law and constitution*, 2nd edition (Dublin: Allen Figgis, 1967)

Kelly, John M., 'Fundamental rights and the constitution', in Brian Farrell (ed.), *De Valera's constitution and ours* (Dublin: Gill & Macmillan, 1988), pp.163–73

Kelly, John M., Gerard Hogan and Gerry Whyte, *The Irish constitution*, 3rd edition (Dublin: Butterworths, 1994)

Kendrick, Walter, *The Secret Museum: pornography in modern culture* (Berkeley: University of California Press, 1987)

Kennedy, Dennis, *The widening gulf: Northern attitudes to the independent Irish state, 1919–49* (Belfast: Blackstaff Press, 1988)

Kennedy, S. B., *Irish art and modernism* (Belfast: Institute of Irish Studies, 1991)

Kenny, Mary, *Goodbye to Catholic Ireland* (Dublin: New Island Books, 2000)

Keogh, Dermot, *The Vatican, the bishops and Irish politics, 1919–39* (Cambridge: Cambridge University Press, 1986)

Keogh, Dermot, *Jews in twentieth-century Ireland* (Cork: Cork University Press, 1998)

Keogh, Dermot, 'Ireland and "Emergency" culture between civil war and normalcy, 1922–61', *Ireland: a Journal of History and Society*, Vol.1, No.1 (1995), pp.4–43

Keshen, Jeff, 'All the news that was fit to print: Ernest J. Chambers and information control in Canada, 1914–19', *Canadian Historical Review*, Vol.LXXIII, No.3 (Sept. 1992), pp.315–43

Kiberd, Declan, *Inventing Ireland – the literature of the modern nation* (London: Vintage, 1996)

Kohn, Leo, *The constitution of the Irish Free State* (London: Allen & Unwin, 1932)

Krause, David, (ed.), *The letters of Seán O'Casey, Vol.1: 1910–41* (London: Cassell, 1975)

Leahy, Maurice, 'Some tendencies of present-day literature', *Irish Monthly*, Vol.LXI, No.722 (Aug. 1933), pp.492–8

Library Association of Ireland, *Report of the executive board, Oct. 1928 – April 1929* (Dublin: Library Association of Ireland, 1929)

Lin, Daniel and Neil Malamuth, *Pornography* (California: Sage, 1993)

Lockhart, W.B., and R.C. McClure, Why Obscene?', in John Chandos (ed.), *To deprave and corrupt': original Studies in the nature and definition of Obscenity* (London: Souvenir Press, 1962), pp.51–70

Lucey, Cornelius, 'The freedom of the press', *Irish Ecclesiastical Record*, 5th series, Vol.L (July–Dec. 1937), pp.584–99

Lyons, F.S.L., 'Yeats and the Anglo-Irish twilight', in Oliver MacDonagh, W.F. Mandle and Pauric Travers, (eds), *Irish culture and nationalism, 1750–1950* (Canberra: Macmillan, 1983), pp.212–38

McBrien, Peter, 'Art for art's sake', *Irish Ecclesiastical Record*, 5th series, XIX (Jan.–June 1922), pp.382–8

McDonald, Marc, *Irish law of defamation* (Dublin: Round Hall Press, 1987)

McGreevy, John T., 'Thinking on one's own: Catholicism in the American intellectual imagination, 1928–1960', *Journal of American History*, Vol.84, No.1 (June 1997), pp.97–131

MacInerny, Rev. M.H., 'Catholic lending libraries', *Irish Ecclesiastical Record*, 5th Series, XIX (Jan.–June 1922), pp.561–77

MacInerny, Rev. M.H., Michael Tierney, P.J. Hooper and Thomas F. O'Rahilly, 'Comments on the foregoing article', *Studies*, XVI (Dec. 1927), pp.554–63

McIntosh, Gillian, *Force of culture: unionist identities in twentieth-century Ireland* (Cork: Cork University Press, 1999)

MacIntyre, Stuart, *The Oxford history of Australia, Vol.4: 1901–1942 – the succeeding age* (Oxford/Melbourne: Oxford University Press, 1986)

MacMahon, Charles A., 'The American public and the motion picture', *Studies*, XV (Mar. 1926), pp.47–64

MacNeill, J.G., *Studies in the constitution of the Irish Free State* (Dublin: Talbot Press, 1925)

Maguire, Samuel J., 'Censorship in Irish county libraries', *An Leabharlann*, Vol.3, No.4 (Dec. 1933), pp.125–8

Maltby, Richard, 'Censorship and self-regulation' in Geoffrey Nowell-Smith (ed.), *The Oxford history of world cinema* (Oxford: Oxford University Press), 1996, pp.235–47

Maltby, Richard, '"To prevent the prevalent type of book": censorship and adaptation in Hollywood, 1924–1934', *American Quarterly*, Vol.44, No.4 (Dec.1992), pp.554–83

Manning, Maurice, *The Blueshirts* (Dublin: Gill & Macmillan, 1970)

Mathews, Tom Dewe, *Censored* (London: Chatto & Windus, 1994)

Maume, Patrick, *The Long Gestation: Irish Nationalist Life, 1891–1918* (Dublin: Gill & Macmillan, 1999)

Megahey, Alan, *The Irish Protestant Churches in the twentieth century* (London: Macmillan, 2000)

Miller, Frank, *Censored Hollywood: sex, sin and violence on screen* (Atlanta: Turner, 1994)

Milotte, Mike, *Communism in modern Ireland: the pursuit of the workers' republic since 1916* (Dublin: Gill & Macmillan, 1984)

Montgomery, James, 'The menace of Hollywood', *Studies*, Vol.31, Dec. 1942, pp.420–28

Montrose, J.L. and F.H. Newark, (eds), *The statutes relating to the constitution of Northern Ireland* (London: Butterworths, 1957)

Morash, Christopher, *A history of Irish theatre, 1601–2000* (Cambridge: Cambridge University Press, 2002)

Morris, Ewan, '"God save the King" versus "The Soldier's Song": the 1929 Trinity College national anthem dispute and the politics of the Irish Free State', *Irish Historical Studies*, Vol.XXXI, No.121 (May 1998), pp.72–91

Murphy, T.A., 'Evil literature in Ireland', *Irish Monthly*, Vol.LI, No.596 (Feb. 1923), pp.53–60

Murray, Patrick, *Oracles of God: the Roman Catholic Church and Irish politics, 1922–37* (Dublin: UCD Press, 2000)

National Council for Civil Liberties, *Annual report* (London: The Council, 1934)

National Council for Civil Liberties, *Report of a commission of inquiry appointed to examine the purpose and effect of the Civil Authorities (Special Powers) Acts (Northern Ireland), 1922 & 1923* (London: The Council, 1936)

Noble, William, *Book banning in America: who bans books – and why?* (Vermont: Paul S. Eriksson Ltd, 1990)

Nowell-Smith, Geoffrey, (ed.), *The Oxford history of world cinema* (Oxford: Oxford University Press, 1996)

Novick, Ben, *Conceiving revolution: Irish nationalist propaganda during the First World War* (Dublin: Four Courts Press, 2001)

Novick, Ben, 'Postal Censorship in Ireland, 1914–16', *Irish Historical Studies*, Vol.XXXI, No.123 (May, 1999), pp.343–56

O'Brien, Mark, *De Valera, Fianna Fáil and the* Irish Press (Dublin: Irish Academic Press, 2001)

Ó Broin, Léon, *Just like yesterday* (Dublin: Gill & Macmillan, 1986)

O'Callaghan, Margaret, 'Language, nationality and cultural identity in the Irish Free State, 1922–7: the *Irish Statesman* and the *Catholic Bulletin* reappraised' *Irish Historical Studies*, Vol.XXIV, No.94 (Nov. 1984), pp.226–45

Ó Cleirigh, Deasmumhan, 'Irish novelists in 1931', *An Leabharlann*, Vol.2, No.2 (Mar. 1932), pp.29–31

O'Connor, Emmet, *A labour history of Ireland* (Dublin: Gill & Macmillan, 1992)

O'Donovan, Donal, *Little old man cut short* (Bray: Kestrel Books, 1998)

Ó Faoláin, Seán, 'The dangers of censorship', *Ireland To-day*, Vol.1, No. 6 (Nov. 1936), pp.57–63

Ó Faracháin, Riobárd, 'Everyman talks to a cinema manager', *Irish Monthly*, Vol.LXIV, No.763 (Mar. 1936), pp.153–60

O'Halpin, Eunan, *Defending Ireland: the Irish state and its enemies since 1922* (Oxford: Oxford University Press, 1999)

O'Halpin, Eunan, 'Fianna Fáil party discipline and tactics, 1926–32', *Irish Historical Studies*, Vol.XXX, No.120 (Nov. 1997), pp.581–90

O'Higgins, Paul, *Censorship in Britain* (London: Thomas Nelson & Sons, 1972)

Paris, Barry, *Louise Brooks* (London: Mandarin, 1991)

Payne, Stanley G., *The Franco regime, 1936–1975* (Wisconsin: University of Wisconsin Press, 1987)

Phelps, Guy, *Film censorship* (London: Gollancz, 1975)

Phillips, John, *Forbidden fictions: pornography and censorship in twentieth-century French literature* (London: Pluto Press, 1999)

Phoenix, Eamon, (ed.), *A century of northern life: the* Irish News *and 100 years of Ulster history, 1890s–1990s* (Belfast: Ulster Historical Foundation, 1995)

Presbyterian Church in Ireland, *Annual reports of the general assembly*

Regan, John M., *The Irish counter-revolution, 1921–1936* (Dublin: Gill & Macmillan, 1999)

Rickard, John, *Australia: a cultural history*, 2nd edition (London: Longmans, 1996)

Riordan, Susannah, 'The unpopular front: Catholic revival and Irish cultural identity, 1932–48', in Mike Cronin and John M. Regan (eds.), *Ireland: the politics of independence, 1922–49* (Basingstoke: Macmillan, 2000), pp.98–120

Robertson, James C., *The British Board of Film Censors: film censorship in Britain, 1896–1950* (London: Croom Helm, 1985)

Robertson, James C., *Hidden Cinema: British film censorship in action, 1913–72* (London: Routledge, 1989)

Robinson, Lennox (ed.), *Lady Gregory's journals, 1916–1930* (London: Putnam, 1946)

Rockett, Kevin, *Irish Film Censorship: a cultural journey from silent cinema to Internet pornography* (Dublin: Four Courts Press, 2004)

Rockett, Kevin, 'Protecting the family and the nation: the official censorship of American films in Ireland, 1923–1954', *Historical Journal of Film, Radio & Television*, Vol.20, No.3 (2000), pp.283–300

Rockett, Kevin, 'From radicalism to conservatism: contradiction within Fianna Fáil film policy in the 1930s', *Irish Studies Review*, Vol.9, No.2 (2001), pp.155–65

Rockett, Kevin, Luke Gibbons and John Hill, *Cinema and Ireland* (London: Croom Helm, 1987)

Rose, Tania, *Aspects of political censorship, 1914–1918* (Hull: Hull University Press, 1995)

Savage, Gail, 'Erotic stories and public decency: newspaper reporting of divorce proceedings in England', *Historical Journal*, 41, 2 (1998), pp.511–28

Senex, 'The new girl', *Irish Monthly*, Vol.LIV, No.632 (Feb. 1926), pp.738–44

Shaw, G.B., 'The Censorship' *Irish Statesman*, Vol.11, No.11 (17 Nov. 1928), pp.206–8

St John Stevas, Norman, *Obscenity and the law* (London: Secker & Warburg, 1956)

Stanfield, Paul Scott, *Yeats and politics in the 1930s* (London: Macmillan, 1988)

Staunton, Enda, *The nationalists of Northern Ireland, 1918–1933* (Dublin: Columba Press, 2001)

Stewart, A.T.Q., 'The mind of Protestant Ulster', in Donald Watt (ed.), *The constitution of Northern Ireland: problems and prospects* (London: Heinemann, 1981), pp.31–51

Thompson, Anthony Hugh, *Censorship in public libraries in the United Kingdom during the twentieth century* (Epping: Bowker, 1975)

Townshend, Charles, *The British campaign in Ireland, 1919–1921: the development of political and military policies* (Oxford: Oxford University Press, 1975)

Travis, Alan, *Bound and gagged: a secret history of obscenity in Britain* (London: Profile, 2000)

Ua Mathghamhna, Eoin, 'Obscenity in modern Irish literature', *Irish Monthly*, Vol.LII, No.617 (Nov. 1924), pp.569–73

Vasey, Ruth, *The world according to Hollywood, 1918–1939* (Exeter: University of Exeter Press, 1997)

Vaughan, Stephen, 'Morality and entertainment: the origins of the Motion Picture Production Code', *Journal of American History*, Vol.77, No.1 (June 1990), pp.39–65

Walker, Dorothy, *Modern art in Ireland* (Dublin: Liliput Press, 1997)

Walker, Graham S., *The politics of frustration: Harry Midgley and the failure of Labour in Northern Ireland* (Manchester: Manchester University Press, 1985)

Walsh, Dermot P.J., *The use and abuse of emergency legislation in Northern Ireland* (Nottingham: The Cobden Trust, 1983)

White, Richard, *Inventing Australia* (St Leonards, NSW: Allen & Unwin, 1981)

Whyte, J.H., *Church and state in modern Ireland, 1923–79*, 2nd edition (Dublin: Gill & Macmillan, 1980)

Woodman, Kieran, *Media control in Ireland, 1923–1983* (Illinois: S. Illinois University Press, 1985)

Yeats, W.B., 'The censorship and St Thomas Aquinas' *Irish Statesman*, Vol.11, No.3 (22 Sept. 1928) pp.47–8

THESES AND DISSERTATIONS

Curtis, Maurice, 'Catholic action as an organised campaign in Ireland, 1921–1947' (Ph.D. thesis, University College Dublin, 2000)

Goldstone, Patricia, 'The Gate Theatre Dublin, 1928–1976' (M.Litt. thesis, University of Dublin, 1977)

Hall, Edward (Eamon) Gerard, 'The regulation of telecommunications including broadcasting in Ireland' (Ph.D. thesis, University of Dublin, 1992)

O'Connor, James P. 'Censorship of films 1894–1970, Hollywood, London and Dublin.' (Ph.D. thesis, University College Dublin, 1996)

Savage, Robert, 'The origins of Irish radio' (MA thesis, University College Dublin, 1982)

Walsh, Aisling, 'Michael Cardinal Logue, 1840–1924' (M.Litt. thesis, University of Dublin, 1996)

Ward, Noel, 'The INTO and the Roman Catholic Church, 1930–1955' (MA thesis, University College Dublin, 1987)

REFERENCE

Borgatta, Edgar F. and Rhonda J.V. Montgomery, *Encyclopaedia of Sociology*, 2nd ed. (New York: Macmillan, 2000)

Connolly, S.J. (ed.), *The Oxford companion to Irish history* (Oxford: Oxford University Press, 1998)

Fleming, Rev. W.E.C., *Armagh clergy, 1800–2000* (Dundalk: Dundalgan Press, 2001)

Fryde, E.B., D.E. Greenway, S. Porter, and I. Roy (eds.), *Handbook of British Chronology*, 3rd edition (London: Offices of the Royal Historical Society, University College, 1986)

Hastings, James (ed.), *Encyclopaedia of religion and ethics, Vol.III* (Edinburgh: T & T Clark, 1910)

Irish Catholic Directory (1911–39)

Oxford English Dictionary

Royal Irish Academy, *Dictionary of Irish Biography* (Cambridge, forthcoming)

Seligman, E.R.A. (ed.), *Encyclopaedia of the social sciences*, Vol.3 (New York: Macmillan, 1930)

ONLINE SOURCES

British Board of Film Censors, www.bbfc.co.uk

McCoy, Ralph, *Freedom of the Press*. www.lib.siu.edu/cni/alpha.html

FILMOGRAPHY

Angels with Dirty Faces (1938)
Animal Crackers (1930)
Battleship Potemkin (1925)
City Lights (1931)
Dodsworth (1936)
Dr Jekyll and Mr Hyde (1931)
Dracula (1931)
Faust (1927)
Flash Gordon (1936)
Frankenstein (1931)
G-Men (1935)
Grand Hotel (1932)
I'm No Angel (1933)
The Informer (1935)
It (1927)
King Kong (1933)
Lives of a Bengal Lancer (1935)
Private Life of Henry VIII (1933)
Public Enemy (1931)
Scarface (1932)
Sylvia Scarlett (1935)
Tarzan and his Mate (1934)
Tarzan the Ape Man (1932)
20,000 Years in Sing Sing (1932)
The Wedding March (1928)

Radio Telifís Éireann, 'The old hurdy gurdy', television documentary broadcast 17 September 2001

Index